Teaching and Learning in the Early Years

How can we help children to become independent learners?

The third edition of this invaluable companion for early years practitioners provides a broad-ranging and up-to-date review of current thinking and best practice within Foundation Stage and Key Stage 1 education.

An effective early years curriculum must start with the children, so this book focuses on their needs and their potential. The best teaching must have a strong element of fun, wonder and excitement; David Whitebread and Penny Coltman show how play is a crucial part of this.

Each chapter combines a review of important principles with practical and inspiring classroom examples. This third edition has been fully revised and updated in light of the introduction of the Early Years Foundation Stage, and includes completely new chapters concerned with classroom organisation to support independent learning, outdoor learning, speaking and listening and mathematics in the early years.

The authors review all major areas of the Foundation Stage and Key Stage 1 curriculum and a range of basic issues and principles, including:

- an analysis of current research into how children learn;
- discussions of general issues such as classroom organisation, curriculum management and assessment;
- a detailed section on play and language;
- chapters covering individual curriculum areas across all six Foundation Stage areas of learning and across the areas of the Key Stage 1 national curriculum.

The book is essential reading for all Foundation Stage and Key Stage 1 trainee teachers, their tutors and mentors, and serving teachers working with children in the 3–7 age range wishing to reflect upon and develop their practice.

David Whitebread is Senior Lecturer in Psychology and Early Years Education at the University of Cambridge Faculty of Education.

Penny Coltman is Lecturer in Early Mathematics and Science at the University of Cambridge Faculty of Education.

Teaching and Learning in the Early Years

Third edition

Edited by David Whitebread and Penny Coltman

Routledge
Taylor & Francis Group

LONDON AND NEW YORK

First published 1996
by Routledge
Reprinted 1997, 1998, 1999

Reprinted 2001, 2002 (three times) by RoutledgeFalmer

Second edition first published 2003
by RoutledgeFalmer
Reprinted 2003, 2004 (twice), 2005

This edition published 2008
by Routledge
2 Park Square, Milton Park, Abingdon, Oxon, OX14 4RN

Simultaneously published in the USA and Canada
by Routledge
270 Madison Avenue, New York NY 10016

Routledge is an imprint of the Taylor and Francis Group, an informa business

Typeset in Palatino by
RefineCatch Limited, Bungay, Suffolk
Printed and bound in Great Britain
by The Cromwell Press, Trowbridge, Wiltshire

British Library Cataloguing in Publication Data
A catalogue record for this book is available from the British Library

Library of Congress Cataloging in Publication Data
Teaching and learning in the early years / [edited by] David Whitebread and
Penny Coltman. – 3rd ed.
     p. cm.
   Includes bibliographical references and index.
ISBN 978–0–415–42479–0 (pbk. : alk. paper)   1. Early childhood education–Great
   Britain.   2. Early childhood education–Great Britain–Curricula.   3. Language arts
   (Early childhood)–Great Britain.   4. Learning.   I. Whitebread, David,
   1948–   II. Coltman, Penny.
   LB1139.3.G7T43 2008
   372.210941–dc22

                                                                          2007034553

ISBN10: 0–415–42479–8 (pbk)
ISBN10: 0–203–93082–7 (ebk)

ISBN13: 978–0–415–42479–0 (pbk)
ISBN13: 978–0–203–93082–3 (ebk)

DEDICATION

This book is dedicated to Dorothy Glynn (*née* Gardner), who was the professional tutor on David's PGCE course at Clifton College, Nottingham, during the academic year 1973–4. It was Dorothy who persuaded him to focus on the early years, and who, with her deep love and enthusiasm for young children, was an inspiration to all her students. She had been inspired, in her turn, by the work of Susan Isaacs. We thus like to think that we are continuing a long tradition of recognising that early years education must start with the needs and potentialities of the young child, and that this book will help to inspire others to continue it further.

CONTENTS

PART D   The way forward

FIGURES

TABLES

CONTRIBUTORS

Anthony Aguda has been teaching for eight years, but after experience as a Key Stage 2 teacher, he firmly focused his career in the Foundation Stage and has recently achieved recognition as an Advanced Skills Teacher in early years. With three young children of his own, Anthony feels he is living and breathing the early years, both at work and at home, but is also looking forward to seeing early education from a parent's point of view.

Sue Bingham ran a nursery school in Bedford for ten years, following her training as a Montessori early years teacher in California and London. During this time she became interested in young children's emotional and social development and in how teachers could support this within their classrooms. Recently she has worked as an early years adviser for Bedfordshire County Council, working in a variety of settings, advising and coaching practitioners in best practice, and currently as a professional studies tutor on the early years PGCE course within the University of Cambridge Faculty of Education. She is studying for a PhD concerned with children's emotional and social development in the early years.

Jane Bower has been a practising primary teacher since 1979, becoming coordinator of expressive arts for four primary schools in Cumbria in 1988, and later arts advisory teacher for Key Stages 1 and 2 in Cambridgeshire. Her published writing began with stories for BBC's *Playschool* in 1983. She now writes regularly on primary art for *Child Education*, *Child Education Topics* and other early years journals, and has produced teaching packs and books for a variety of publishers. Jane also works as an artist in residence, undertaking ceramic and mural commissions working alongside children in schools. For six years she worked part-time as an art teacher for reception and Key Stage 1 classes in a local school.

Helen Bradford is based at the University of Cambridge Faculty of Education where she teaches professional studies and English to early years and primary PGCE and GTP trainees. With a teaching background in early years, including working at Homerton Nursery School in Cambridge over a five-year period, her current research interests centre on young children's perceptions of themselves as writers.

Helen Bromley is a former infant teacher with 16 years' experience. She is now a freelance early years consultant delivering INSET throughout the country, most particularly on play, communication, language and literacy. She also works closely with schools wishing to introduce a Foundation Stage approach into Key Stage 1. She contributes regularly to *Nursery World* and *Early Years Educator* and has published widely in the field of early years. Her books include numerous contributions to the Lawrence Educational '50 Exciting Ideas' series, *Book Based Reading Games* for CLPE and most recently *'Making Your Own Mark': Writing through Play*, published by BAECE in July 2006.

Helen Broomby is currently working as a freelance consultant advising local authorities and early years, childcare and playwork providers. She works nationally with some of the key bodies commissioned by Department for Education and Science (DfES) to roll out training, consult with children and young people on issues such as inclusion and well-being. Helen has established a training centre providing CACHE qualifications as well as continual professional development. She was previously employed by Cambridgeshire County Council as the care and education training manager for the Cambridgeshire Care and Education Partnership. She has 37 years' experience of early years work in a range of diverse settings. She has undertaken research projects, training and consultancy for national bodies. Helen is committed to the promotion of a positive ethos for the personal, social, health and well-being of young children.

Penny Coltman gained extensive experience working in both pre-school and Key Stage 1 settings in Essex. She now lectures in early mathematics and science in the University of Cambridge Faculty of Education where she also co-manages the early years and primary PGCE course. Penny designed award-winning resources for mathematics teaching with Longman and

NES Arnold and has published an extensive range of curriculum materials, mostly working with BBC Education. Her research interests focus on aspects of children's early learning, especially those related to mathematics and science.

Dianne Conway studied geography as a special subject alongside her early years education course at Whitelands College, London. She taught for 22 years across Key Stage 1 and was geography coordinator at Stapleford Community Primary School, Cambridgeshire for 11 years. She taught geography for early years students in the University of Cambridge Faculty of Education for nine years. Currently she is giving special needs tuition and is involved in some Cambridgeshire schools on a voluntary basis.

Rebecca Dawkins has a BEd Hons in French and early childhood education (3–8 years). She has been teaching since 1989, primarily in the early years in Cambridgeshire. In her second year of teaching, she set up a new nursery unit and is now a nursery teacher, Foundation Stage coordinator and science coordinator in an infant school. Rebecca was involved in the early research in 2001 for the Cambridgeshire Independent Learning (CINDLE) project, and has helped to support members in the second and third cohort of training. This led to a 'Certificate in Educational Enquiry'. She has also taken part in lectures and made presentations of her CINDLE innovations, where her focus has been the importance of the learning environment and working closely as a team.

Mary-Jane Drummond was, until recently, a lecturer at the Faculty of Education at the University of Cambridge. She is a specialist in the field of early years care and education, and contributes to a variety of inter-disciplinary training programmes and development work. Her abiding interest is in children's learning, and a new edition of her book *Assessing Children's Learning* was published by David Fulton in 2003. Since her retirement, she continues to work closely with the Newcastle-based Sightlines Initiative, the centre of a national network of educators who are developing innovative and creative practice inspired by the pre-schools of Reggio Emilia, Northern Italy. Her most recent publication is the outcome of her research into the quality of the educational experiences offered to 4- and 5-year-old children in primary schools, which showed that there were few opportunities for authentic, engaging, first-hand experiences of the real world. This finding is the rationale for the widely acclaimed curriculum resource book *First-Hand Experience: What Matters to Children* (Rich Learning Opportunities, 2005).

Jane Edden is a retired senior lecturer in music education, previously at Homerton College. She has taught music to children in a variety of schools both in this country and in Trinidad. As primary music specialist for Cambridgeshire she was co-author of *Managing Music with Infants*, and she contributed a chapter to Eve Bearne's book *Use of Language Across the Primary Curriculum* (Routledge, 1998).

Sue Gifford is an experienced primary teacher who now lectures in mathematics education at Roehampton University. Her current interests are early years mathematics and preventing mathematics difficulties. She has recently published *Teaching Mathematics 3–5* (Open University Press) and reported on dyscalculia for QCA. She is a coordinator of the Early Childhood Mathematics Group.

Jayne Greenwood has been a practising teacher since 1977. She has taught in a variety of early years and Key Stage 1 settings and currently works part time as a teacher of Year 1 children at a primary school in the London Borough of Tower Hamlets. Jayne also teaches geography and design technology to early years trainees at the University of Cambridge Faculty of Education.

Kate Hemming graduated from Homerton College, Cambridge in 1998 with a BEd (Hons) specialising in early years education. She has nine years' experience teaching reception and Year 1 in London and Cambridge. Her involvement in the CINDLE (Cambridgeshire Independent Learning) project during 2003–4 gave Kate the opportunity to research the development of young children as self-regulated learners. Her particular interests through the project included peer tutoring and the importance of language acquisition in relation to independent learning. Kate is looking forward to continuing her research and intends to consider the importance of self-commentary as a means of children making sense of their educational experiences. Her classroom is a rich and vibrant environment where every child is given the opportunity to plan, evaluate and develop their unique learning experiences.

Lesley Hendy is a former senior lecturer in drama and education at Homerton College, and a senior research associate for the University of Cambridge Faculty of Education. Before retraining as a drama specialist, she worked as a nursery and infant teacher and was a headteacher of a first school. Over the past few years she has specialised in drama for the early years and is the author of *Supporting Drama and Imaginative Play in the Early Years* (Open University Press, 2001). Since leaving Homerton she has been an educational consultant and has recently been working with Creative Partnerships.

Patricia Maude has worked with children, trainees and teachers for many years in schools, in Homerton College and latterly in the University of Cambridge Faculty of Education. She is now more widely known as an author and as a consultant in the UK and abroad. Her specialist areas are in children's movement development and in enhancing the abilities of adults to ensure that children achieve their potential, confidence and enjoyment in all areas of their movement. In the New Year's Honours 2000, she received an MBE for services to physical education.

Christine Parker taught in primary, first and nursery schools in Sheffield, Leeds and Bradford for 20 years, before taking up the headship at Caverstede Early Years Centre, Peterborough in 2000. She had also worked in Karachi, Pakistan for two and half years as an advisory teacher, supporting teachers in a wide range of settings with pre-primary aged children. Christine's research interests have included children's mark-making, parents' involvement in curriculum matters and the needs of emergent bilingual children. Most recently, Christine has led projects that have explored the leadership role of early years practitioners.

Pam Pointon worked as a classroom teacher for 13 years and then as a research fellow at the Centre for Global Education, University of York. She is currently a lecturer in education at the University of Cambridge Faculty of Education. Her current research interests include work concerned with emotional literacy and outdoor education.

Sallie Purkis sadly died recently. She was formerly a senior lecturer in history at Homerton College and a consultant, reviewer and writer on *Primary History*. For many years she regularly contributed to *Junior Education*, the *TES* and *Teaching History*. She was the author of teachers' notes for the BBC (*Watch* and *Radio History*) and Thames TV (*Seeing and Doing*) and published, with Longmans, 'A Sense of History', a wide-ranging series of books and posters for pupils and teachers at Key Stages 1 and 2. More recently, a series for A. & C. Black, 'Real Lives', used original research to reconstruct biographies of individual children who, even though they lived at the same time in the past, had different experiences. She was also a Fellow of the Historical Association.

John Siraj-Blatchford is an independent educational researcher and consultant. He was previously employed at the University of Cambridge Faculty of Education and served as an associate director of the ESRC Teaching and Learning Research Programme. His previous publications include *A Curriculum Development Guide to ICT in Early Childhood Education* (with Iram Siraj-Blatchford, Trentham Books, 2006), *Supporting Information and Communications Technology in the Early Years* (with David Whitebread, Open University Press, 2003) and *Developing New Technologies for Young Children* (Trentham Books, 2004).

Rachel Sparks Linfield has worked in education for over 20 years, teaching throughout the Foundation Stage, Key Stages 1 and 2 and in higher education at both the University of Cambridge and Leeds Metropolitan University. She has written a wide range of books for early years practitioners, articles and non-fiction texts for children and was delighted when the 'Foundations' (London: A. & C. Black) series of books, of which she wrote three, won two national awards in 2004: the Educational Resources Primary Book Award and the National Literacy Association's WOW Award. Currently she is enjoying dividing her time between lecturing, working in nursery, writing and, most importantly being a mother to Connie (13), Rosie (10) and Leanne (3)!

Paul Warwick is currently a lecturer in primary science and professional studies at the University of Cambridge Faculty of Education. Before this he worked as deputy headteacher of a primary school and then as a primary science support teacher for Cambridgeshire Local Authority. Paul is engaged in a range of research and teaching activities in the Faculty that link directly with his interests in primary science education, the professional development of beginning teachers and new technologies in primary classrooms.

David Whitebread is a senior lecturer in psychology and early years education at the University of Cambridge Faculty of Education. Before coming to Cambridge he taught in several primary schools, mostly in Leicestershire, for about 12 years, predominantly with children in the 4–8 age range. His doctoral dissertation was concerned with the development of children's problem-solving abilities. Currently the main focus of his research is concerned with developing independent learning in the Foundation Stage. He has published extensively on psychological approaches to young children's learning in relation to a variety of areas. His other publications include *The Psychology of Teaching and Learning in the Primary School* (RoutledgeFalmer, 2000) and *Developmental Psychology and Early Childhood Education* (Sage, in press).

Sally Wilkinson taught in a primary school in Suffolk for eight years, teaching children aged 4 to 9. She now works as a primary curriculum adviser for Suffolk LEA. She is a member of the UKLA national committee and she has published articles in *Primary English, English in Education* and a teachers' resource book on using books by Michael Morpurgo in Key Stage 2. She is currently working on developing guided reading materials with leading teachers in Suffolk and UKLA.

Dominic Wyse is a senior lecturer in primary and early years education at the University of Cambridge and Fellow of Churchill College Cambridge. Dominic was a primary teacher for eight years, which included posts in London, Bradford and Huddersfield. Following his work as a teacher, he lectured at Liverpool John Moores University for eight years, latterly as a Reader in primary education. His main research interests are the teaching of English and creativity. His research articles have included analyses of the evidence base for English government policy on the teaching of reading, including phonics, and the teaching of writing, including grammar. Dominic's most recent book is *Help Your Child to Read and Write* (Pearson Education/Prentice Hall Life, 2007). Forthcoming books in 2007 include: the second edition of *The Good Writing Guide for Education Students* (2nd edn, SAGE); *Teaching English, Language and Literacy* (2nd edn, Routledge); and *Help Your Child Succeed at School* (Pearson Education/Prentice Hall Life). Dominic has appeared on television, radio and in print media in relation to his expertise on the teaching of literacy.

ACKNOWLEDGEMENTS

Vygotsky's model of the 'zone of proximal development', Figure 1.1, is reproduced with permission from *Understanding Children's Development 2nd edition* (p. 353) by Peter K. Smith and Helen Cowie, 1991, Oxford: Blackwell Publishers.

Bruner's nine glasses problem, Figure 1.2, from *Studies in Cognitive Growth* (p. 156) edited by J.S. Bruner *et al.*, 1966, New York: John Wiley & Sons Ltd is reproduced with permission from Jerome Bruner.

The growth of neural connections in the brain, Figure 1.4, from *Mapping the Mind* by R. Carter, 1998, London: Weidenfeld & Nicolson, is reproduced with permission from Malcolm Godwin.

Figures 4.2 to 4.8 are reproduced with grateful thanks to Kay Dimelow, Headteacher, Huntingdon Nursery School, Huntingdon.

The regular sequence of motor development in infants, Figure 11.1, from *Understanding Child Development 1st edition* (p.202) by Spencer A. Rathus, 1998, is reprinted with permission of Brooks/Cole, an imprint of the Wadsworth Group, a division of Thomson Learning.

A beginning thrower, Figure 11.2, and **A beginning and advanced runner**, Figure 11.3, from K.M. Haywood and N. Getchell, 2001, *Life Span Motor Development 3rd edition* (Champaign, IL: Human Kinetics) are reprinted with permission from Human Kinetics. The figures **A beginning thrower and a beginning runner** were originally redrawn from film tracing provided by the Motor Development and Child Study Laboratory, University of Wisconsin-Madison.

An advanced 6-year-old-kicker, Figure 11.4, and **The leap**, Figure 11.5, are reproduced by permission of PCET Wallcharts Ltd, 27 Kirchen Road, London W13 OUD. Photographs are by Jan Traylen, 1994, from wallcharts entitled *Games Skills* and *Gymnastic Skills*.

Snake paintings, Figure 13.1 and **Sewn pizzas**, Figure 13.2, are reproduced with grateful thanks to Anne Horler, principal, Horler's Preparatory School, Comberton. We would also like to thank Birmingham City Council, Curriculum Support Service for allowing us to use Figures 17.4 to 17.6. This material comes from *Harborne Infant School Local History Project*.

Goodey's (1973) model of geographical experiences, Figure 18.1, is reproduced by permission of the University of Birmingham Centre for Urban and Regional Studies. The diagram, originally titled **Child in information space**, is from *Perception in the Environment: An Introduction to the Literature*, occasional paper n.17 by B. Goodey, 1973 (p.7).

The extract on p.322 from *Geography in the National Curriculum: Non-statutory Guidance for Teachers*, 1991 is reproduced by permission of the copyright holder, the Curriculum Council for Wales, Cardiff.

The extract on p. 379 from *Geography for Ages 5–16*, DFES, London, 1990, extract from *Geography from 5–16*, DES, London, 1986, and p. 380 **Aims for geographical education**, from *Geography for ages 5–16*, DES, London, 1990 are all reproduced with permission. Crown copyright is reproduced with the permission of the controller of HMSO, Norwich.

Exploring the seaside: a geographical enquiry, Figure 18.2, from *Non-statutory Guidance for Geography*, 1991, is reproduced by permission of the Curriculum Council for Wales, Cardiff.

PREFACE

When the first edition of this book was originally published, eleven years ago, it was noted that we found ourselves publishing at a time of critical importance for early years education in the UK and maybe in other parts of the world as well. At long last the crucial importance of good quality early years education was being recognised. Research evidence that children's success in school and other aspects of their life can be significantly enhanced by quality educational experiences when they are very young was finally being taken seriously.

As a consequence, in 1996 a number of changes in the educational provision for young children were beginning to emerge and there have certainly been very significant developments in the UK which continue to the present day. Just since the second edition of the book came out in 2003, we have seen the transformation of educational administrative structures at national and local government levels (with a Minister for Children and Local Authority Children's Services Departments integrating aspects of previous Education and Social Services activities relating to children and families). The Every Child Matters initiative and the newly published Early Years Foundation Stage curriculum document (integrating previous documents relating to Birth to Three and the Foundation Stage) have also begun to have a significant impact. The continued emphases on play, on personal, social and health education, and on children's self-initiated activities, have been hard fought for and continue to serve our 0–5 year old children well.

However, it was noted in 2003 that the situation for 5–7-year-olds was not nearly so promising and, sadly, this continues to be the case. Despite developments in Wales to integrate the Foundation Stage and Key Stage 1 into a Foundation Phase, the situation in England remains as it was, with continuing concern about the effects of the introduction of the Literacy and Numeracy Strategies at Key Stage 1. While both these strategies are bristling with ideas for good practice, the overall effect of the introduction of literacy and numeracy 'hours' into many Key Stage 1 classrooms has resulted in an unrelieved diet of seat-based, teacher-directed tasks throughout the morning which does not meet the needs of many 5–7-year-olds. Imaginative play, for example, has more or less disappeared beyond the Reception year. Opportunities for these young children to develop independent learning skills also continue to be much more limited than we would hope.

The inevitable downward pressure continues on Reception class teachers to introduce elements of the literacy and numeracy hours with their children, to 'prepare' them for Key Stage 1. By contrast, many early years educators continue to argue that 5–7-year-old children would benefit from the extension of the principles of the Foundation Stage to cover all children aged 3–7 years. Happily, there are the beginnings of signs that this message is being taken on board by policy makers. The publication by the QCA Primary National Strategy and the Sure Start teams of the *Continuing the Learning Journey* training package is a very encouraging sign in this regard, intended as it is to build on the principles of the Foundation Stage and show how these can be translated into practice in Key Stage 1.

What is clearly the case, however, is that all these concerns and developments continue to enhance the status and numbers of well-qualified early years teachers working with our young children. Resources are now being made available by the UK government to ensure that our young children are being educated by teachers and other educators who are better trained and more professionally prepared than ever before. We continue to hope, of course, that this book will help to enhance the quality of their preparation for the endlessly fascinating and challenging task of educating 3–7-year-old children.

The original impetus to produce this book arose from a perceived absence of published material written in a way which would interest and serve the needs of our early years trainees. We wanted to produce a book which introduced and discussed general principles of early years education, but at the same time showed how these translated into practical activities in the classroom. The book is intended to convey the strong research base related to children's learning and development upon which all good early years teaching must be founded. It is also intended to demonstrate that the best teaching of young children must have a strong element of fun and wonder and excitement.

All sound teaching of young children is based upon understandings about how young children learn, and the book begins with an analysis of current research in this area. Principles that derive from this research inform the subsequent sections of the book concerned with different aspects of early years teaching and the early years curriculum.

There follows a section on basic principles and approaches, which discusses issues related to the management of the early years learning environment. This is followed by a series of chapters concerned with play and language, the basics of early years education. A further section examines the wider curriculum of the arts, maths, technology and science, the social sciences and physical development. Each chapter examines basic principles and illuminates them with inspiring, practical examples of classroom, outdoor and out-of-school activities.

In this third edition, of course, there has been yet again extensive revision and updating in many chapters. The chapter concerned with the organization of the early years classroom has been completely re-written, with four new contributions from Foundation Stage and Key Stage 1 teachers. Following the major research project that we have conducted since 2003, the Cambridgeshire Independent Learning in the Foundation Stage (CINDLE) project, this chapter now has a new focus on encouraging independent learning. The chapter on PSHE has also been revised to include a new section on encouraging young children to take responsibility for dealing with organisational and behavioural problems in the classroom. The chapter on mathematics has been completely re-written to include material related to children's learning about shape as well as number.

There are also two completely new chapters. The first is concerned with the outdoor learning environment, which has been a major area of development in provision in the last few years; and the second is concerned with speaking and listening, the importance of which for young children's learning in general, and for their early engagement with literacy in particular, continues to be recognised.

The book is principally directed at early years trainee teachers, but it is also hoped that it contains material which will be of interest to the whole range of teaching and non-teaching professionals and other adults concerned with the education of young children. The term 'educator' has been used throughout the book in preference to 'teacher' in an attempt to include and recognise this wider group of adults working in early years education.

British nursery and infant education has long enjoyed an international reputation for high quality. This book is most of all a re-affirmation of this tradition, and an attempt to help maintain and improve the quality of the education offered to our young children.

David Whitebread and Penny Coltman
June 2007

CHAPTER 1

Introduction

YOUNG CHILDREN LEARNING AND EARLY YEARS TEACHING

David Whitebread

There has traditionally been a strong association between understandings about child development and early years teaching. This book is written, however, at a particularly exciting time in this regard. The relationship between developmental research and the practices of teaching young children is currently a rich area of growth and development. This book is an attempt to distil the current state of knowledge about the ways in which young children (up to the age of 7) develop and learn, to show how educational principles derive from this, and to illustrate these principles with practical examples drawn from work in early years classrooms. In this introductory chapter I want to show how psychological research concerned with child development informs the principles of practice exemplified throughout the rest of the book.

There is a long tradition of ideas about children and their learning in early years education. In the nineteenth and early twentieth centuries these were largely developed by a number of outstanding and inspiring educators. Tina Bruce (1987) has provided an excellent review of the ideas of Froebel, Montessori, Steiner and others, derived Ten Common Principles of early years education and attempted to show how these relate to modern research. These principles emphasise the holistic nature of children's learning and development (as distinct from learning separated out into subjects), the importance of developing autonomy, intrinsic motivation and self-discipline through the encouragement of child-initiated, self-directed activity, the value of first-hand experiences and the crucial role in children's development of other children and adults.

As we shall see, many of these ideas have been reinforced by modern psychological research; they have also been extended and developed in interesting and important ways. Much of current thinking about children's learning has been influenced by the work and ideas of three outstanding developmental psychologists – Jean Piaget, Lev Vygotsky and Jerome Bruner – and so it is with their contributions that we begin.

Piaget

The first major developmental psychologist to influence classroom practice was, of course, Jean Piaget. His ideas were welcomed enthusiastically in the 1960s because they were a reaction to the 'behaviourist' view of learning current within psychology and education at the time, with which people were increasingly unhappy. The behaviourist view placed the child in a passive position, and viewed learning simply as a combination of imitation and conditioning by means of external rewards and reinforcements. This model works quite well as a way of explaining how you can teach parrots to roller-skate, but it is a woefully inadequate explanation of the range and flexibility of the achievements of the human child.

A huge amount has been written about Piaget's theory and its influence upon Primary education. Brainerd (in Meadows, 1983) and Davis (1991) provide good reviews of the impact on education. On the positive side, the most important contribution of Piaget's work was to alert educators to the child's active role in their learning, and the importance of mental activity (see Howe, 1999). Piaget showed how children actively attempt to make sense of their world and construct their own understandings.

On the negative side, Piaget's emphasis on stages of development appears to have been ill-founded and resulted in serious underestimation of the abilities of young children (see Wood, 1998). The work of Margaret Donaldson (1978) and many other developmental psychologists sub-sequently has demonstrated that Piaget's tasks (such as his famous conser-vation tasks) were difficult for young children for a whole range of extraneous reasons unconnected to the child's understanding of the under-lying concept. These tasks were too abstract and did not make sense to young children, they over-relied on rather sophisticated linguistic com-petence, and they were embedded in misleading social contexts. Interest-ingly, one of the major areas of discovery as regards young children's learning in recent years has related to their peculiar sensitivity to these kinds of contextual factors. This is an issue to which I want to return later in the chapter and, as we shall see, it has important implications for early years teaching.

More recent evidence has suggested that young children arrive at school with many more capabilities than was previously thought, and was suggested by Piaget. The pioneering work of Tizard and Hughes (1984) in the area of language, and of Gelman and Gallistel (1978) in relation to young children's understandings about number, are good examples. Both suggested that children's abilities were being systematically under-appreciated by teachers, for much the same reasons as they had been by Piaget. In school, children were being faced by ideas or tasks taken out of any meaningful context, and for no clear purposes, and they were finding them difficult. In the home environment, when the same ideas or tasks occurred naturally, embedded in real meaning and purposes, the same children understood and managed them with ease.

Vygotsky

Piaget has also been criticised for under-emphasising the role in children's learning of language and of social interaction with other children and with adults. The ideas of the Russian psychologist, Lev Vygotsky, have been an important influence in this area (see Smith *et al.*, 1998, for an introduction and Moll, 1990, for an extensive review of educational implications).

Piaget had emphasised the importance of the child interacting with the physical environment, and his followers in the educational sphere argued that the role of the teacher should be that of an observer and a facilitator. The general view of this approach was that attempting to directly teach or instruct young children was a mistake. It was claimed that whenever teachers attempted to teach children something, they simply deprived the children of the opportunity to discover it for themselves.

This view was partly a reaction against the simplistic 'behaviourist' model that children only learnt what they were taught. To some extent, however, it can be seen to have thrown the baby out with the bath water. More recent research inspired by the work of Vygotsky has argued that there is a much more central role for the adult, and, indeed, for other children, in the processes of learning. This role is not as an instructor delivering knowledge, however, but rather as a 'scaffolder' (a metaphor suggested by Jerome Bruner; see Smith *et al.*, 1998, pp. 437–41) supporting, encouraging and extending the child's own active search for understanding.

Perhaps the most significant idea within Vygotsky's model of human learning is that of the 'zone of proximal development', as illustrated in Figure 1.1. Faced with any particular task or problem, a child can operate at one level on their own, described as their 'level of actual development'. But they can perform at a higher level when supported or 'scaffolded' by an adult or more experienced peer, described as their 'level of potential

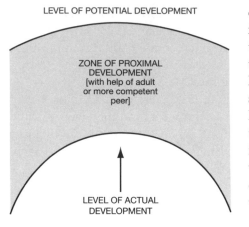

development'. The 'zone of proximal development' (or ZPD) is that area of learning described by the difference between these two levels of performance or understanding. Vygotsky and his followers have argued, therefore, that children learn most effectively through social interaction, when they are involved in jointly constructing new understandings within their ZPD.

Figure 1.1 *Vygotsky's model of the 'zone of proximal development'*

Bruner

This view has been supported by evidence of the significant role of language within learning. The work of Jerome Bruner has been influential in regard to this issue (see, for example, Wood, 1998, for a discussion of Bruner's ideas on language and thought). Bruner described language as a 'tool of thought', and demonstrated in a range of studies the ways in which language enables children to develop their thinking and perform tasks that would otherwise be impossible. In his famous 'Nine glasses problem' (see Figure 1.2), for example, he showed that children who could describe the patterns in a 3 × 3 matrix of glasses (which were taller or shorter one way and thinner or fatter the other) were also able to transform the matrix (i.e.

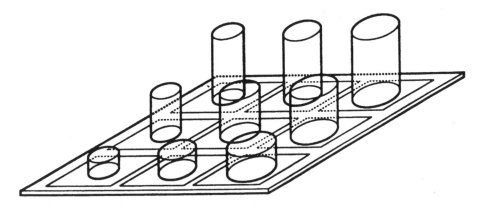

Figure 1.2 *Bruner's nine glasses problem*

arrange the glasses in a mirror image pattern). Children without the relevant language to call on, however, were only able to reproduce the pattern exactly as they had seen it.

It is now widely recognised that providing children with a relevant vocabulary and requiring them to formulate their ideas in discussion is a vital element in helping children to develop flexibility in thinking and construct their own understandings about the world. This has led to the recognition that a certain style of interaction between adults and children, and between pairs or small groups of children, can be enormously beneficial to learning. Paul Light (in Meadows, 1983) has provided a useful review of research indicating that this style involves dialogue between adults and children in which there is 'co-construction' of meanings. Forman and Cazden (1985) have reviewed work demonstrating the help to learning provided by collaboration and dialogue between children.

Jerome Bruner's other major contribution to our understandings about young children as learners is encapsulated in his phrase 'the spiral curriculum'. This is his view that, in principle, anything can be taught to children of any age, provided it is presented in a way that is accessible to them. Thus, having encountered a set of ideas at a practical level when they are young, they will use this knowledge to help them understand the same ideas at a more symbolic or abstract level when they are older. So learning is viewed as a spiral in which the same point is returned to and revisited, but each time at a higher or deeper level. He demonstrated this by, for example, successfully teaching 8-year-old children to understand quadratic equations. He achieved this by providing them with the practical example of working out the area of rectangles (see Wood, 1988, ch. 7, for a review of this work).

Bruner's view about the constraints upon children's learning is very much in line with a whole range of contemporary research. Piaget's earlier notion that children are limited in what they can understand by certain kinds of logical deficiencies in their reasoning powers has been largely dismissed. As Margaret Donaldson (1978) argued, research shows that adults make the same kinds of logical errors as children, and have difficulties with the same kinds of reasoning problems. Children's learning is now seen as being limited much more simply by their lack of experience and of accumulated knowledge. This makes it more difficult for them to see what is relevant in any new situation, and to see what is the best way to proceed. When this is made clear by the context in which a task is presented, however, children's potential for learning is phenomenal and often way beyond our normal expectations, as Bruner ably demonstrated.

The current view of the child as learner, therefore, is one that recognises their considerable appetite and aptitude for learning. However, it is also important to recognise the nature of children's limitations and their particular needs if they are to flourish. These needs are both emotional and intellectual. As we shall see, research evidence suggests that to become effective learners young children need love and security, and they need intellectual challenge. In the remainder of this chapter I want to examine these needs and their implications for educational environments. The chapter concludes with a brief look at emerging knowledge about the brain and some tentative thoughts about implications for early years education. Then finally, lest we forget the importance of the enterprise upon which we are embarked, there is a short discussion of the evidence concerning the impact of quality early years education on children's later development. This final section links with Chapter 2, where the emerging theme of the young child as an independent or 'self-regulating' learner is more fully explored.

The need for love and security

On the emotional side, in order to develop into effective learners within the school context it is clear that young children need love and security. An important element in the tradition of early years education has always been a recognition of the need to consider the whole child. Children's learning and intellectual development is inseparable from their emotional and social development. In their early years, as well as mastering fundamental skills and understandings, young children are also forming their basic attitudes to themselves as people and as learners. The basic attitudes they form at this stage have major implications for their future educational progress.

An enormous body of research evidence collected by developmental psychologists supports this view. High self-esteem and feelings of self-efficacy are strongly related to educational success, and low self-esteem and what has been termed 'learned helplessness' are equally related to educational difficulty. It is difficult to attribute cause and effect here, but there is clearly a positive cycle of mutual interaction between self-belief and achievement and, sadly, a negative downward spiral associated with self-doubt and failure. Rogers and Kutnick (1990) have provided a useful survey of work in this area and its important implications for teachers.

Essentially, there are three aspects to this. If they are to thrive emotionally and intellectually, young children need to feel *love and self-worth*, they need to feel *emotionally secure* and they need to feel *in control*.

Love and self-worth

Psychologists have investigated in considerable detail the ways in which the young child's sense of self develops in the first few years of life. From the earliest emergence within the first year of bodily awareness, and the recognition of the distinction between self and not-self, the young child's sense of self becomes rapidly differentiated. They develop a self-image of themselves as an individual, a self-identity of the sort of person they are and to which groups they belong (child, boy/girl, race, types of ability and so on), a distinction between their private and public selves (with an increasing number of roles within which they see themselves – son/daughter, sibling, friend, pupil), an ideal self to which they aspire, feelings of self-esteem and of self-worth.

In all this a crucial element is the ways in which they are viewed and treated by significant others in their lives. The metaphor has been developed by psychologists working in this area of the self as a mirror. Children's views about themselves develop as a reflection of the views transmitted to them by others in social interaction. This has also often been referred to as the Pygmalion effect, after the famous play by Shaw. In the play a flower girl is treated by everyone as a lady (after some grooming by Professor Higgins) and so she starts to view herself as a lady, and becomes one. All the evidence suggests that children who develop positive self-images and feelings of self-worth are those who have been surrounded in their earliest years by unconditional love and emotional warmth. Their parents or other carers have transmitted to them very powerfully that they are valued by others, and so they come to value themselves.

Emotional security

Alongside positive attitudes to themselves, young children need to develop feelings of trust in relation to their environment. The significance of feelings of emotional security was first highlighted by Harlow's famous experiments in the 1950s with baby monkeys. The initial experiments offered the babies a choice of two substitute but inanimate 'mothers', one which was soft and cuddly and another which was metal and hard but provided milk. The babies spent the vast majority of their time cuddling up to the soft model. Perhaps even more significantly, Harlow discovered that babies provided with a cuddly 'mother' of this kind became much more adventurous in exploring their environment than babies who were deprived this obvious source of comfort.

In the 1950s the view was advanced by Bowlby that the emotional security needed by young children should ideally be provided by the biological mother or, failing that, by one constant adult figure in the child's life. In his excellent review of this and subsequent research, however, Rudolph Schaffer (1977) demonstrated that care did not need to be provided by one particular adult continuously. Rather, the quality and consistency of care emerged from research to be the crucial factors. The quality of care appears to be mostly a matter of how responsive the adult is to the child. The consistency of care is vital in giving the child a sense that their world is predictable. This has two elements: first, that the same actions by the child produce the same responses by the adult and, second, that the transitions between adult carers are handled carefully so that the child understands the programme of events.

Young children's almost obsessive concern for fairness (with rules applied consistently) and their strong preference for routine can be seen as clear outcomes of their need for emotional security. Their love of hearing familiar stories endlessly repeated is possibly a manifestation of the same phenomenon. This need for their experience to be predictable and to follow clear rules is very much linked to their need intellectually to make sense of their world, to which we return later. Emotionally, it is also strongly linked to their need to feel in control, to which we turn now.

Feeling in control

We have probably all played that game with young children of a certain age where the child performs an action, we respond in some way, and the child laughs (the 'dropping things out of the pram' game is a good example). Immediately the child does it again, we repeat our response and there is more laughter. And so it goes on, and on, and on. The adult always tires of this game before the child does because the child is in the process of discovering something really wonderful. They are in control of their world, they can make things happen.

This feeling of empowerment is fundamental to children developing positive attitudes to themselves, and particularly to themselves as learners. Within modern developmental psychology there has been a huge amount of research about this aspect of emotional development and its relation to motivation. This research has been concerned with examining what is called 'attribution theory' because it is concerned with the causes to which children attribute their successes and failures. Where children feel that their performance is determined by factors within their control (for example, how much effort they put into a particular task), they will respond positively to failure and try harder next time, believing all the time in their own ability to be successful on the task. Where they feel that their performance is determined by factors outside of their control (for example, their level of ability, or luck), they will respond negatively to failure and give up, believing that they will not succeed, however much they try. It is clear that such 'learned helplessness' is extremely damaging to children's development as learners.

This model of 'attributions' explains well how poor self-esteem can result in lack of motivation, which in turn leads to lack of effort and consequent poor performance, confirming the child's view of themselves. The failing child thus becomes locked into a destructive self-fulfilling prophecy. In order to avoid this, it is clearly vital that adults working with young children do everything in their power to give them the feeling of being in control.

Research on parenting styles is quite helpful here. Broadly speaking, researchers have found that it is possible to categorise parenting styles into three broad types. First, there is the 'autocratic' style, where rules are entirely constructed by the parent and enforced arbitrarily and inconsistently without explanation. At the opposite extreme there is the 'laissez-faire' style where there are no rules to which the child is expected to conform. Both these styles communicate low expectations to the child, a lack of responsiveness and consistency, and children suffering under these kinds of regimes typically have low self-esteem and little emotional security.

The third style is what might be termed 'authoritative' or 'democratic'. Here there are rules to which the child is expected to conform, they are applied consistently and they are discussed and negotiated with the child. Under this kind of regime children typically have high self-esteem and feel in control.

Implications for the early years teacher

- Create an atmosphere of emotional warmth, within which each child feels individually valued.
- Communicate high expectations to all children.
- Praise and recognise children's achievements, particularly when they are the result of a special effort.
- Run an orderly classroom that has regular classroom routines.
- Always explain to the children the programme of events for the day and prepare them for transitions.
- Put children in control of their own learning; allow them to make choices.
- Exercise democratic control; involve children in decisions about classroom rules and procedures and enforce rules fairly.
- Criticise a child's actions, but never the child.

The need for intellectual challenge

While it is clear that there is an intimate link between emotional and intellectual development, love and security on their own are not enough. Young children also need intellectual challenge. As we have reviewed, Piaget first argued, and it is now widely accepted, that children learn by a process of actively constructing their own understandings. All the evidence suggests that a learning environment that helps children to do this will, not surprisingly, be one that challenges them intellectually and stimulates them to be mentally active. It also turns out to be crucial, once again, that the children are put in control. Such an environment will provide **new experiences**, embedded in **meaningful contexts**, opportunities for **active styles of learning**, involving children in **problem-solving**, **investigations** and opportunities for **self-expression**, and, perhaps most crucially of all, opportunities for learning through **play**.

Play

If we are to understand anything about the ways in which young children learn, we must understand first the central role of play. The distinction between work and play is entirely misleading in the context of young children's learning, for much of the evidence suggests that play is when children do their real learning (see Moyles, 1989). Children's language development, for example, is commonly associated with playful approaches and activities – making up nonsense words, verbal jokes and puns, silly rhymes and so forth are all much enjoyed and of great benefit.

It was Bruner (1972), in a famous article entitled 'The nature and uses of immaturity', who first pointed out the relationship across different animal species between the capacity for learning and the length of immaturity, or dependence upon adults. He also pointed out that as the period of immaturity lengthens, so does the extent to which the young are playful. He argued that play is one of the key experiences through which young animals learn, and also the means by which their intellectual abilities themselves are developed. The human being, of course, has a much greater length of immaturity than any other animal, plays more and for longer, and is supreme, of course, in our ability to learn.

The crucial aspect of human intellectual ability which enables us to learn so effectively, Bruner argues, is our flexibility of thought. Play, he suggests, is all about developing flexibility of thought. It provides opportunities to try out possibilities, to put different elements of a situation together in various ways, to look at problems from different viewpoints. He demonstrated this in a series of experiments (e.g. Sylva *et al.*, 1984) where children were asked to solve practical problems. Typically in these experiments, one group of children was given the opportunity to play with the objects involved, while the other group was 'taught' how to use the objects in ways that would help solve the problem. When they were then asked to tackle the problem, similar numbers of children in the two groups were completely successful. However, the 'taught' children who failed to solve the problem gave up very quickly. By contrast, the children who had the experience of playing with the materials persevered longer when their initial attempts did not work, were much more inventive in devising a range of strategies to solve the problem, and generally came much closer to a solution. Crucially, while the 'taught' children appeared to be just learning, or failing to learn, one specific 'menu' to solve one specific problem, the children who played were learning far more generalisable skills, and far more positive attitudes to problem-solving. They were, indeed learning how to learn.

Observation of children at play gives some indication of why it might be such a powerful learning medium. During play children are usually totally engrossed in what they are doing. It is quite often repetitive and contains a strong element of practice. During play children set their own level of challenge, and so what they are doing is always developmentally appropriate (to a degree to which tasks set by adults will never be). Play is spontaneous and initiated by the children themselves; in other words, during play children are in control of their own learning.

Mari Guha (1987) has argued that this last element is particularly significant. There are many examples in psychological research of tasks where being in control has turned out to be crucial for effective learning. Guha cites, for example, experiments concerned with visual learning in which subjects are required to wear 'goggles' that make everything look upside down. They are then required to sit in a wheelchair and learn to move safely through an environment. The results of such experiments show that subjects moving themselves around the environment (and having a lot of initial 'crashes') learn to do this much more quickly than those who are wheeled safely about by an adult helper.

The parallels here with Bruner's 'play' and 'taught' groups is striking. The implications for how we can most effectively help young children to learn are striking. A simple model which suggests that children learn what we teach them is clearly unsustainable. There is a role for the adult, however, in providing the right kind of learning environment, and this clearly needs to provide opportunities for play. Whenever a new material or process is introduced, for example, it is clear that children's learning will be enhanced if they are first allowed to play with them. When new information is being introduced, children need to be offered opportunities to incorporate this into their play also. As we discussed earlier, there is also a role for the adult in 'scaffolding' children's experiences within the learning environment, and various ways of participating and intervening in children's play can be enormously beneficial. Manning and Sharp (1977) have provided a very thorough and practical analysis of ways in which educators can, by these means, usefully structure and extend children's play in the classroom.

New experiences

Anyone who has spent any time at all with young children, and attempted to answer all the questions they keep asking, will be well aware of their apparently insatiable curiosity. I am reminded of the manic robot Johnny 5 in the film *Short Circuit* who continually and voraciously craves 'input'. Part of the notion of young children as active learners is a recognition of their compelling need for new experiences. Providing that they feel emotionally secure, as we have discussed, they will enthusiastically explore their environment and are highly motivated by novelty.

From the psychological perspective this is not surprising. It is one of the other distinguishing features of the human brain that it does, indeed, require a certain level of input. Unlike almost all other animals, we are very easily bored. If insufficient new information is being provided by the environment, furthermore, the human brain will provide its own amusement. Every day, we all daydream. In extreme circumstances (for example, in sensory deprivation experiments where the subject is kept motionless in a completely dark, soundproof booth) this can result in powerful hallucinations.

Within psychological research this kind of work has underpinned a well-established relationship, known as the Yerkes-Dodson law, linking an individual's state of arousal and their performance on a task. Too little stimulation produces boredom and too much stimulation produces anxiety. Both are dysfunctional in terms of performance on a task, and of learning.

Thus, while we need to ensure that children feel in control of their classroom environment, we also need to ensure that they find it a stimulating, exciting and motivating place to be. We must never underestimate young children's abilities to absorb new information and to cope with new ideas. Young children, for example, love being introduced to new vocabulary, especially if the words are long and/or difficult (e.g. tyrannosaurus, equilateral, strato-cumulus, etc.). Further, there is an age-related factor here, whereby typically our optimum level of stimulation decreases as we get older. The chances are, therefore, that if you as an adult are feeling really comfortable with the pace of events in a classroom, some of the children will be bored!

Meaningful contexts

The dominant model in contemporary psychological research concerned with human learning is that of the child as an active information processor. As such, the child attempts to make sense of, and derive meaning from, experience by means of classifying, categorising and ordering new infor- mation and relating it to what is already known. This inductive style of learning involving the identification of patterns and regularities from the variety of our experience is a very dominant aspect of human functioning. The astonishing facility with which children learn their first language, by working out the rules for themselves (aided by a little 'motherese') is a good example of the power of inductive processes.

This search for patterns and regularities within the variety of experience has important implications for the ways in which young children make sense of new experiences. They expect to find pattern and regularity, and they expect new experiences to fit together in some way with what they already know. This was beautifully illustrated by an experiment in which young children were asked 'bizarre' questions, such as 'Is milk bigger than water?' and 'Is red heavier than yellow?' (see Hughes and Grieve in Donaldson *et al.*, 1983). What happened was that the children answered the questions and did so in ways that illustrated their attempt to make sense of them in terms of the context in which they were asked and their own previous experience. Thus, they might reply that 'Milk is bigger than water because it's creamier' or 'Red is heavier than yellow because the yellow is a little plastic box and the red paint's got a big plastic box'.

As Hughes *et al.* point out, what the children were doing in response to these bizarre questions is what they do all the time when they are faced with new information or problems. It is for this reason that children's per- formance and understanding is always likely to be enhanced when tasks are presented in ways that help young children to make sense of them in the light of what they already know. In other words, tasks need to be placed in contexts that are meaningful to young children.

As we noted earlier, many of Piaget's tasks have been criticised precisely on the grounds that their meaning was not clear and children misinter- preted them in their attempts to make sense of them, based upon their previous experience. Donaldson (1978) reviewed a number of alternative versions of Piagetian tasks where an attempt had been made to place them in meaningful contexts and thus make their purpose more intelligible to young children.

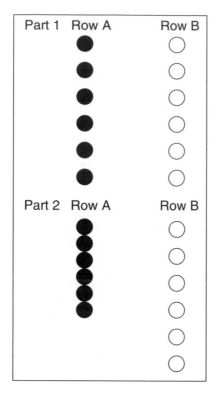

Figure 1.3 *Piaget's number conservation problem*

For example, Piaget's famous number conservation task consisted of showing the child two equal rows of buttons (as shown in Figure 1.3, Part 1) and asking the child whether there are more white buttons or black buttons, or whether they are the same. One of the rows was then transformed by the experimenter (as shown in Figure 1.3, Part 2) and the question was repeated. Piaget found that many young children could correctly recognise that the first two rows contained the same number, but said there were more white buttons in the second condition. He concluded that these young children were overwhelmed by their perceptions and that they lacked the logical understanding of the conservation of number.

When this task was repeated by a colleague of Margaret Donaldson's, however, the transformation of one of the rows of buttons was effected by a 'naughty teddy' glove puppet. In these circumstances many more young children were able to say that the two rows still contained the same number.

Donaldson concludes that the introduction of the naughty teddy changes the meaning for the child of the second question. This question is made sense of by the children in relation to the social situation and their own previous experience. When the adult transforms the pattern and repeats the question, this means to some children that their first answer was wrong and the adult is helping them to see the correct answer. In the amended version, the second question is a cue to check that the naughty teddy hasn't lost or added any buttons during his mischief.

The lessons for the early years teacher are clear. Young children do not passively receive the information we provide for them. They are engaged continually in a process of active interpretation and transformation of new information. If we want to help them to make sense of their educational experiences we must ensure that we place new tasks in contexts that will enhance their meaning for young children. This often means actively making links with what the children already know and presenting the activity in the context of a story or game. As a consequence of children's limited symbolic understandings, it also means that hands-on experiences, where the children are gaining information directly through their senses, is always likely to be more effective. It is also a rationale for organising activities within the meaningful context of children's interests or a cross-curricular topic.

If children are to use their powerful inductive processes to find patterns and regularities in their experience it is also important to present the same ideas, concepts or processes in a variety of such meaningful contexts. Only in this way can children begin to disentangle what is relevant and what is irrelevant in relation to any particular idea. Children who are taught one way of carrying out a particular process are often left confused about the essential nature of the task. I have been told by young children that you cannot add together two numbers written side by side, you have to put one of them underneath the other. I also remember one of my own young daughters, on returning from a visit to the Science Museum, telling me excitedly about this machine she had seen (which sounded like an internal combustion engine from her description). When asked what she thought it was for, she replied that there was a lot of gravel all around it, so she thought it might be making that. Now she has seen lots of machines in different contexts, she has induced that the gravel around museum exhibits is usually purely cosmetic.

Mental activity

An important feature of the human brain is that we all find enjoyment in mental activity. As we have discussed, it was Piaget who first drew attention to the fundamental relationship between mental activity and learning. The kind of mental activity we need for learning can be stimulated in two main ways, through problem-solving and self-expression. Both of these processes require us to restructure what we know and to make use of it in new ways. It is well established within modern developmental psychology that this kind of restructuring is required to integrate new information into our existing conceptual framework. In a very important sense, this is the essence of real learning.

Within a number of areas of research, the relationship between mental activity and learning has been clearly demonstrated. For example, within memory research, a range of research has confirmed what is known as the 'generation effect'. Information which has at least been partly generated or transformed in some way is always more memorable than that which has been simply received. It is for this reason that teaching spellings by providing anagrams from which the children have to generate the words is always more effective than simply giving a list of the words. Michael Howe (1999) usefully reviews a number of experiments that have demonstrated this point, and that suggest more active ways of presenting information to young children.

Problem-solving is fundamental to human intellectual functioning. It is part of our need to make sense of our experience and gain control over our environment. Robert Fisher (1987, 1990), among others, has argued that, as educators, we can most effectively harness the power of young children's abilities to learn by presenting new ideas and information as problems to be solved, or areas to be investigated, for purposes that are meaningful and real to the children. He has also produced excellent reviews of the justification and practice of this kind of approach within primary education.

Within the purely cognitive sphere, however, it is also important because of the processes of cognitive restructuring involved. There is good evidence to suggest that the process of self-expression is important in helping child-ren to understand and make sense of their experiences. The Vygotskian notion of learning through the co-construction of meanings in social situ-ations (as reviewed by Light, in Meadows, 1983) and Bruner's notion of language as a 'tool of thought' are important here. In their explorations of young children's use of language in the home and school, Tizard and Hughes (1984) have presented evidence of children engaging in processes of intellectual search through talk. The kinds of meaningful dialogues with adults that are likely to stimulate this kind of mental activity, however, they found to be much more common in the home environment than in the school. They argue that, as educators, we must find means of developing quality conversations between ourselves and the children in our classrooms.

One way into this kind of activity which would appear to be well worth pursuing is that offered by the 'philosophy for children' approach origin-ally developed by Matthew Lipman and reviewed by Costello (2000). In essence, this approach consists of posing moral or ethical problems to children through the contexts of stories and then engaging them in philo-sophical debate about the issues raised. Children are encouraged to clarify their meanings, make explicit their assumptions, expose ambiguities and inconsistencies and so on. Exciting work has been done by using picture books with very young children (see, for example, Murris, 1992). Young children reveal impressive abilities to reason, argue and use talk to com-municate meaning through this kind of activity, and develop a range of vital intellectual skills in the process.

One of the clear disadvantages of the classroom environment relative to the home is, of course, to do with the adult–child ratio. For this reason, it is also important to stimulate challenging talk between the children. As a consequence, a range of educators have urged the more extensive use of collaborative groupwork in primary classrooms (see, for example, Dunne and Bennett, 1990). As we reviewed earlier, research adopting a Vygotskian perspective (Forman and Cazden, 1985) has demonstrated the various ways in which peer interaction during collaborative groupwork can enhance performance and stimulate learning. Requiring children to work in groups to solve problems, carry out investigations, or produce an imaginative response in the form of writing, drama, dance or whatever is potentially of enormous benefit.

It is important to recognise that the value of self-expression is not limited to the medium of language. Requiring children to transform their experiences into various 'symbolic' modes of expression is likely to aid the processes of learning. When children draw, paint, dance, construct, model, make music and, indeed, play, they are engaged in the active process of making sense of their world in a way that is unique and individual to them, of which they are in control. The sheer vigour and enthusiasm with which young children engage in these kinds of activities is an important pointer to their significance.

Although I have attempted to separate out different elements in the psychological processes that relate to children's need for intellectual challenge, I must conclude by emphasising the powerful ways in which all these elements are of a piece. When children are playing, they are also nearly always problem-solving, or investigating, or engaging in various forms of self-expression. Play often helps children to place new information in meaningful contexts.

It is also important to recognise the ways in which intellectual challenge contributes to emotional or affective elements of children's development. It is no accident that humans find activities of the type we have discussed here immensely enjoyable. Adults at play, for example, are often enjoying the mental challenge of solving problems (crosswords, jigsaws, puzzles, games), or of expressing themselves (music, art, drama). With enjoyment comes concentration, mental effort, motivation and achievement. Self-expression is important in its own right because it builds upon and enhances children's sense of individuality and self-worth. A child who has experienced the excitement of finding things out for themselves or of solving problems is learning to take risks, to persevere and to become an independent learner.

Implications for the early years teacher

- Provide opportunities for play of all kinds.
- Provide vivid, first-hand, new experiences.
- Place tasks in meaningful contexts: help children to make sense of new experiences by relating them to what they already know.
- Introduce the same idea in a variety of meaningful contexts.
- Organise tasks to stimulate mental activity: adopt problem-solving and investigational approaches wherever possible.
- Provide opportunities for self-expression: when children have learnt something new, give them a chance to make something of their own from it.
- Provide opportunities for meaningful conversations between groups of the children, and between the children and adults.

The brain and early years education

I have referred here and there in this chapter to evidence about the ways in which the human brain learns and develops. Following the huge expansion of research in neuroscience during the 1990s – dubbed the 'Decade of the Brain' – we now know enormously more about brain functioning and development than we did even when the first edition of this book was published 12 years ago. Neuroscientists and educators are increasingly talking to one another and some commentators have rushed to justify particular educational arguments by reference to brain research.

At this stage, we need to approach neuroscientific evidence with a good deal of caution, however. Serious research into the brain is still very much in its infancy and the one finding about the human brain that is incontrovertible is that it is enormously complex. The possibilities for misinterpretation and oversimplification are legion. Talk of 'educating the left side of the brain' or the 'brain-friendly' classroom is dangerously premature.

However, a number of useful reviews have already been compiled of evidence that is of relevance to early education (Blakemore, 2000) and education generally (Byrnes, 2001). The evidence we have so far does, at least, seem to support a number of important, general positions in regards to early education:

- The brain develops and learns by forming vast numbers of connections between brain cells in 'neural networks'; this supports the inductive nature of human learning and its implications for experiential learning, play and meaningful contexts.
- The overwhelming majority of these connections are formed in the first few years of life (see Figure 1.4) causing the human brain, uniquely, to quadruple in size between birth and 6 years of age; babies literally build their own brains, and the environments in which they do so are clearly significant.
- Processing in the young brain is quite generalised; specifically adapted regions gradually form over the first few years; consequently, requiring young children to learn in ways which depend upon later emerging functions is futile and potentially counter-productive; there are important implications here for the introduction of formal, disconnected learning and of tasks involving the manipulation of symbolic representations such as letters and numerals.

As we learn more about the early development of the brain, it will clearly be of interest to early years educators. Those readers who wish to be better informed at this stage might like to look at Rita Carter's (1998) excellent and well-illustrated introduction.

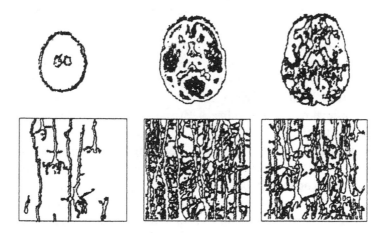

Neural connections are sparse at birth (left), but new connections are made at a terrific rate during infancy and by the age of six (middle) they are at maximum density. Thereafter they decrease again as unwanted connections die back. (right.) Adults can increase neural connections throughout their life by learning new things. But if the brain is not used the connections will become further depleted.

Figure 1.4 *The growth of neural connections in the human brain*

The impact of quality in early years education

It is now well established that a child's educational experience in the early years has both immediate effects upon their cognitive and social development and long-term effects upon their educational achievements and life prospects. Sylva and Wiltshire (1993) have reviewed a range of evidence that supports this position. This evidence includes studies of the Head Start programmes in the USA, the Child Health and Education Study (CHES) of a birth cohort in Britain and Swedish research on the effects of day care.

To begin with, these various studies appeared to produce inconsistent findings. Early studies of the Head Start programmes suggested immediate cognitive and social gains, but little lasting effect. The CHES study, on the other hand, found a clear association between pre-school attendance and educational achievements at age 10. Further analysis, however, reveals that lasting long-term effects are dependent upon the quality of the early educational experience. Sylva and Wiltshire note particularly the evidence of long-term impact achieved by High/Scope and other high-quality, cognitively orientated pre-school programmes. Findings from the more recent EPPE project (Sylva *et al.*, 2004) have further supported this position, finding clear links between the quality of early years educational provision and a range of intellectual and personal gains.

What emerges as significant about these particularly effective early educational environments is very much in line with the kinds of directions indicated in this chapter. These environments offered real intellectual challenge in the ways we have discussed, with the adult educators very much in the Vygotskian role of 'scaffolding' the child's experience. Sylva and colleagues (2004) particularly identified, within the highest-quality settings, the occurrence of episodes of 'sustained shared thinking' between adults and children. Within this kind of pedagogical approach, the child is put very much in control of their own learning. This theme of the central importance of encouraging young children to become independent, or 'self-regulated' learners, is one that we develop more fully in Chapter 2, when we look at the organisation of the classroom environment.

In the High/Scope regime, for example, the central model of learning is the 'plan, do and review' cycle. Each child plans their activities for the session or the day in a small group with an adult educator. They then move off to carry out the planned activities, and later return to review progress again with their small group and the adult educator. This pattern builds in purposeful adult–child and child–child conversations which seem to Sylva and Wiltshire to be 'an embodiment of Vygotsky's notion of effective instruction within the zone of proximal development' (1993, p. 36).

This way of working also places the responsibility very much on each child for their own learning. What all the high-quality early years regimes identified by Sylva and Wiltshire did was to help children develop what they term a 'mastery' orientation to learning and to themselves. This relates very closely to the emotional issues we discussed earlier in the chapter. Children in high-quality early years environments developed feelings of high self-esteem, with high aspirations and secure feelings of self-efficacy. Such children grew to believe that, through effort, they could solve problems, understand new ideas, develop skills and so on. They felt in control of their environments and confident in their abilities.

These are some of the themes that this chapter has attempted to illuminate, and that permeate all the other chapters of this book. If we wish to provide quality learning environments for our young children, these need to be informed by understandings about how young children learn and develop. The rest of the present volume is dedicated to indicating how these understandings can be translated, imaginatively and reflectively, into the everyday practice of the early years classroom.

References

Blakemore, S.J. (2000) *Early Years Learning, Report 140*, London: POST (Parliamentary Office of Science & Technology).

Bruce, T. (1987) *Early Childhood Education*, London: Hodder & Stoughton.

Bruner, J.S. (1972) 'The nature and uses of immaturity', *American Psychologist*, 27, 1–28.

Byrnes, J.P. (2001) *Minds, Brains, and Learning*, London: Guilford Press.

Carter, R. (1998) *Mapping the Mind*, London: Weidenfeld & Nicolson.

Costello, P.J.M. (2000) *Thinking Skills and Early Childhood Education*, London: David Fulton Publishers.

Davis, A. (1991) 'Piaget, teachers and education: Into the 1990s', in P. Light, S. Sheldon and M. Woodhead (eds) *Learning to Think*, London: Routledge, pp. 16–31.

Donaldson, M. (1978) *Children's Minds*, London: Fontana.

Donaldson, M., Grieve, R. and Pratt, C. (eds) (1983) *Early Childhood Development and Education*, Oxford: Basil Blackwell.

Dunne, E. and Bennett, N. (1990) *Talking and Learning in Groups*, London: Macmillan.

Fisher, R. (1987) *Problem-solving in Primary Schools*, Oxford: Basil Blackwell.

Fisher, R. (1990) *Teaching Children to Think*, Oxford: Basil Blackwell.

Forman, E.A. and Cazden, C.B. (1985) 'Exploring Vygotskian perspectives in education: the cognitive value of peer interaction', in J.V. Wertsch (ed.) *Culture, Communication and Cognition*, Cambridge: Cambridge University Press, pp. 323–47.

Gelman, R. and Gallistel, C.R. (1978) *The Child's Understanding of Number*, Cambridge, MA: Harvard University Press.

Guha, M. (1987) 'Play in school', in G.M. Blenkin and A.V. Kelly (eds) *Early Childhood Education*, London: Paul Chapman.

Howe, M.J.A. (1999) *A Teacher's Guide to the Psychology of Learning*, 2nd edn, Oxford: Basil Blackwell.

Manning, K. and Sharp, A. (1977) *Structuring Play in the Early Years at School*, Cardiff: Ward Lock Educational/Drake Educational Associates.

Meadows, S. (ed.) (1983) *Developing Thinking*, London: Methuen.

Moll, L.C. (ed.) (1990) *Vygotsky and Education*, Cambridge: Cambridge University Press.

Moyles, J.R. (1989) *Just Playing? The Role and Status of Play in Early Childhood Education*, Buckingham: Open University Press.

Murris, K. (1992) *Teaching Philosophy with Picture Books*, London: Infonet Publications Ltd.

Rogers, C. and Kutnick, P. (eds) (1990) *The Social Psychology of the Primary School*, London: Routledge.

Schaffer, R. (1977) *Mothering*, London: Fontana.

Smith, P.K., Cowie, H. and Blades M. (1998) *Understanding Children's Development*, 3rd edn, Oxford: Basil Blackwell.

Sylva, K. and Wiltshire, J.(1993) 'The impact of early learning on children's later development: a review prepared for the RSA inquiry "Start Right" ', *European Early Childhood Education Research Journal*, 1, 17–40.

Sylva, K., Bruner, J.S. and Genova, P. (1984) 'The role of play in the problem-solving of children 3–5 years old', in P. Barnes, J. Oates, J. Chapman, V. Lee and P. Czerniewska (eds) *Personality, Development and Learning*, Sevenoaks: Hodder & Stoughton, pp. 55–67.

Sylva, K., Melhuish, E.C., Sammons, P., Siraj-Blatchford, I. and Taggart, B. (2004) *The Effective Provision of Pre-School Education (EPPE) Project: Technical Paper 12 – The Final Report: Effective Pre-School Education*, London: DfES/Institute of Education, University of London.

Tizard, B. and Hughes, M. (1984) *Young Children Learning*, London: Fontana.

Wood, D. (1988, 1998) *How Children Think and Learn*, 1st/2nd edn, Oxford: Basil Blackwell.

Basic principles and approaches

CHAPTER 2

'Our classroom is like a little cosy house!'

ORGANISING THE EARLY YEARS CLASSROOM TO ENCOURAGE INDEPENDENT LEARNING

David Whitebread with Rebecca Dawkins, Sue Bingham,
Anthony Aguda and Kate Hemming

Among the many challenges and complexities involved in teaching young children is the recognition that, as truly 'active' learners, they do not just learn what they are taught; rather, they learn what they experience. The effective early years teacher, therefore, has to consider not only their own interpersonal style as a teacher, and not only the learning activities they will devise and provide for the children, but also the entire classroom environment and ethos within which they and the children will live and work.

It is always very sad to see the consequences of a poorly managed classroom: children standing around in queues waiting for a small amount of attention from the teacher; the children becoming over-dependent on adult support and unable to function without constant intervention; the teacher under constant pressure and frustrated that they never have time to do anything properly; equipment forever being lost in the general chaos; and so on. Lofty ideals about being child-centred, encouraging creativity and teaching the children to think for themselves all come to naught in such an environment.

This chapter contains outlines by four experienced and highly skilled early years teachers describing how they organize their classrooms. While a number of themes emerge from these descriptions, what is clear is that each of these teachers has thought very carefully and deeply about what they are trying to achieve for the children in their class, and how the environment they create supports this. A key theme guiding much of their thinking relates to supporting children in becoming 'independent' or 'self-regulated' learners. There are two very clear justifications for this approach. First, at the practical level, if the children are able to operate independently, taking initiatives, setting their own goals, accessing resources as they are required, supporting and helping one another, working together cooperatively and so on, then this can release the teacher from the roles of traffic policemen, fire-fighter and general troubleshooter, and allow them to spend more time in more educationally productive activities. Second, at a deeper educational level, there is now strong evidence to suggest that developing the skills of 'self-regulation', sometimes referred to in the psychological literature as 'metacognition', is crucial to becoming an effective learner. As we shall see, this development of young children as independent *learners* crucially depends on meeting the needs of young children discussed in Chapter 1 – the needs for emotional support and intellectual challenge.

There is currently widespread interest in fostering 'independent learning' among young children, as attested by a number of publications (Featherstone and Bayley, 2001; Williams, 2003) and by recent official government guidelines. Recent initiatives, circulars and curriculum documents from various government agencies have offered a range of suggestions as to what independent or self-regulated learning might involve. In the revised QTS Standards entitled *Qualifying to Teach* (TDA, 2006), for example, teacher trainees are required under Standard S3.3.3 to:

> . . . teach clearly structured lessons or sequences of work which interest and motivate pupils and which make learning objectives clear to pupils . . . [and] promote active and independent learning that enables pupils to think for themselves, and to plan and manage their own learning.

In the *Curriculum Guidance for the Foundation Stage* (DfEE/QCA, 2000), which established the new curriculum for children between 3 and 5 years of age, one of the stated 'Principles for early years education' (p. 3) is that there should be 'opportunities for children to engage in activities planned by adults and also those that they plan and initiate themselves'.

While a commitment to encouraging children to become self-regulating learners is very common among early years teachers, at the level of everyday classroom realities, however, there are a number of problematic issues. The need to maintain an orderly classroom, combined with the pressures of time and resources, and teachers' perceptions of external expectations from headteachers, parents and government agencies, can often militate against the support of children's independence. This is unfortunate and often counter-productive. The kind of overly teacher-directed style this tends to engender may create an impression of having 'covered' the curriculum, but is largely ineffective in promoting learning in young children, and does not help at all in the larger project of developing children's ability and confidence to become independent learners.

There is also often, unfortunately, a lack of clarity as to the nature of independent learning. Evidence from a study across the Foundation Stage and Key Stage 1 conducted by one of the present authors (Hendy and Whitebread, 2000) found that the early years teachers interviewed shared a commitment to encouraging greater independence in learning among young children, but held a wide spectrum of views about the essential key elements within it, and of their role in fostering the necessary skills and dispositions. There was a dominant concern, for example, with the purely *organisational* element of children's independence, at the expense of any concern with cognitive or emotional aspects of independence. Perhaps most worrying, however, was the finding that the children appeared to become more, rather than less, dependent on their teachers during their first few years in school.

Over the last few years, the present author has worked with 32 Cambridgeshire early years teachers (including two of the teachers describing their classes here) on the Cambridgeshire Independent Learning (CIndLe) Project (Whitebread and Coltman, 2007; Whitebread *et al.*, 2005). This research has established that young children in the 3–5 age range, given the opportunity, are capable of taking on considerable responsibility for their own learning and developing as self-regulated learners, and that their teachers, through high-quality pedagogical practices, can make a highly significant contribution in this area.

From this work emerged four underlying principles for a pedagogy of self-regulation, which clearly relate back to the issues highlighted in regard to young children's learning in Chapter 1. These principles were as follows.

Emotional warmth and security

Classrooms which support children's growing confidence as learners are first and foremost characterised by emotional warmth, mutual respect and trust between adults and children, and by structures which provide emotional support (for example, clear and consistently applied rules). This kind of emotional atmosphere gives young children the confidence to play creatively, to take risks emotionally and intellectually, and to persevere when they encounter difficulties. In the absence of this kind of support, many young children will remain timid and passive in their general demeanour in the classroom, will be unwilling to try out new or unfamiliar activities and will give up on tasks as soon as they encounter difficulties.

Among many other things, to provide emotional warmth and security in the classroom environment, teachers can:

- provide a model of emotional self-regulation, talking through their own difficulties with the children;
- show that they appreciate effort at least as much as products;
- show an interest in the children as people, and share aspects of their own personal lives;
- negotiate frameworks for behaviour with the children which are seen to be fair and supportive.

Feelings of control

Feeling in control of their environment and their learning is fundamental to children developing confidence in their abilities, and the ability to respond positively to set-backs and challenges. Human beings are quite literally control freaks. An early experiment carried out in California by Watson and Ramey (1972) involved the parents of 8-month-old babies being given special cots which came complete with attractive and colourful 'mobiles'. The parents were asked to put their babies in the cots for specified periods each day for a few weeks. In some of the cots the mobiles either did not move, or moved around on a timed schedule. But in other cots the mobile was wired up to a pillow, so that the mobile would move whenever the baby exerted pressure on the pillow. At the end of the experiment, the parents of the babies who had experienced these 'contingency mobiles' wanted to pay the research team large amounts of money to keep the cots because their babies had enjoyed these so much.

It is vitally important that teachers of young children allow sufficient flexibility in their classroom organization for children who have been inspired by a particular experience to pursue their interest. Allowing opportunities for child-initiated activities enhances children's sense of ownership and responsibility in relation to their own learning. Other practices that are helpful in giving children this feeling of control include:

- making sure that children have access to a range of materials for their own purposes;
- giving children the opportunity to make choices about activities;
- understanding that a beautiful teacher-made role-play area or display may not be as valuable for the children's learning as one to which children have contributed;
- adopting a flexible approach to timetabling which allows children

to pursue an activity to their satisfaction, avoiding unnecessary interruptions.

Cognitive challenge

The third underlying principle of good practice that encourages self-regulatory and independent learning is the presence of cognitive challenge. Children spontaneously set themselves challenges in their play and, given a choice, will often choose a task that is more challenging than the task which an adult might have thought was appropriate. Providing children with achievable challenges, and supporting them so they can meet them, is the most powerful way to encourage positive attitudes to learning, and the children's independent ability to take on challenging tasks.

More generally, to promote this kind of cognitive challenge in their classrooms, teachers can:

- Require children to plan activities.
- Consider whether activities planned to be carried out individually could be made more challenging as a collaborative group task.
- Ask more genuine, open-ended questions that require higher-order thinking, for example, 'Why?', 'What would happen if …?', 'What makes you say that?'
- Give children opportunities to organize activities themselves, avoiding too early adult intervention.

Articulation of learning

Finally, it is clear that if children are going to become increasingly aware of and in control of their own mental processing, the processes of thinking and learning need to be made explicit by adults, and the children themselves need to learn to talk about and to represent their learning and thinking.

Building in to the regular practice within a classroom opportunities for the children to reflect upon their thinking and decision-making during and after activities is enormously advantageous in this regard. Other strategies which are effective in stimulating children to talk about their learning include:

- peer tutoring, where one child teaches another;
- involving children in self-assessment;
- making learning intentions explicit when tasks are introduced, or

discussed either while the children are engaged in the task, or afterwards in a review session;
• modelling a self-commentary, which articulates thinking and strategies;
  for example when solving a mathematical problem.

In the following accounts by four experienced and skilful early years
teachers many of these themes and principles can be seen to be brought to
life through their classroom organizational practices.

A nursery class

The first account is from Rebecca Dawkins, who teaches the nursery class in
an infant school whose catchment area contains areas of reasonable afflu-
ence but also of relative economic deprivation. Perhaps partly in response
to the characteristics of the individual children she receives into her class,
what is noticeable in her account is the emphasis she places on the emotional climate of the classroom, and providing the children with a secure
and supportive emotional environment. For many of the children, of
course, who are only 3 years of age when they join the class, this is their first
significant experience that requires them to cope outside of the home.
Making very strong links between the environment of the home and that of
the classroom is a key and highly significant element of Rebecca's practice.
As she was involved as a teacher in the CIndLe project, the emphasis on
supporting children to develop as independent learners is also clear, and
she recognizes some ways in which this has influenced her practice.

Nursery ethos and classroom environment

For some of our children, nursery may be one of their first experiences they
have away from home and their parents. It is therefore vital that we make
the children's transition from home to school as smooth and enjoyable as
possible.

A child once said to me: 'Our classroom is like a little cosy house!' She
may have been referring to the classroom atmosphere or possibly the
layout of the room – an area we will visit later. Our priority is to provide a
homely, warm and calm learning environment.

Settling in . . . moving on

Our nursery is purpose built and is in the main building of the infant
school. We have two part-time classes of 26 children. There is a full-time
nursery teacher and nursery nurse.

The beginning of the session is the most important time for us. It is a time when the children are invited to join both myself, the teacher and nursery nurse in a short circle time. As the children come in with their parents they are greeted individually by name and encouraged to sit down facing into the circle. If a child is unsure or unsettled, the parents are invited to stay with their child for as long as they need. It is vital that the parent is involved in the settling-in process.

Circle time

The circle time becomes an intrinsic and valued part of the daily routine. The children gradually become more familiar with the pattern of the day and the circle time gives them the feeling of warmth and security and the opportunity to settle down.

Although it is brief, the staff have the opportunity to gauge how the children are feeling during the first few minutes of the session They may be happy or sad, angry or excited and we can respond immediately to their needs. Sometimes an upset child may need some quiet time away from the rest of the class on our comfortable armchair.

At the beginning of the year, when the children are new to the class, they say very little and lack confidence at speaking in front of a large group. Together, they are encouraged to say 'Good morning' to staff members and the class and to respond to the register being called – even if they wave instead of speaking when their name is called! The children take great delight in taking the completed register to the school office.

Circle time provides an excellent opportunity for the staff to model a conversation. The nursery nurse and I engage in simple dialogue such as talking about the weather or what we are planning to do in the nursery today. The children observe us taking turns to speak and responding to simple questions. As they become more confident, we begin to involve them in the conversation. Through circle time, we are able to seek the views of the child in a protected environment and consult the children regularly about their attitudes, skills and knowledge.

Circle time helps the class to focus on the structure of the session and we make use of the situation to give a brief run-down of the programme of events during that session. During the second term individual children are chosen to visit different areas of the room to describe what is available to the rest of the class.

Circle time may also take place later in the session. It provides an ideal opportunity to introduce an idea, concept or topical artifact. An object is sometimes placed on a small table in the middle of the circle to stimulate the children's curiosity and to encourage them to focus as they come in.

This gives them a taster of what is to follow and a stimulus for discussion. The children are also given the opportunity, if appropriate, to pass the artifact around the circle and explore it using their senses.

The making of class rules: why?

We have found that even the youngest children, who are just 3 years old, already have an awareness of what is right and wrong and the concept of fairness. The setting of class rules is a gradual but important process that evolves from one term to the next. During the first few weeks of term, we sit with the children and ask what is important to them and what we as a class need to remember. These thoughts are scribed by the teacher on a big sheet of paper and are revisited for the next few days. Once everyone is satisfied with these rules, they are displayed in the classroom with accompanying photographs of the class to illustrate positive behaviour. The rules are constantly reviewed and adapted to suit the changing needs of the class and to include the outdoor environment. By setting the rules together, the children have immediate ownership of them. The rules help the class to establish a busy, working atmosphere and self-discipline from an early stage. The children can also enjoy their rights within clear boundaries. The photographs that accompany the class rules provide the children with a visual reminder of what is expected of them.

The organisation of the classroom and its resources

In order to make decisions for themselves and informed choices, the children need to be able to develop a sense of trust with the adults and peers they work with. To develop this sense of trust, they need to be familiar and comfortable with their surroundings both indoors and outdoors. Our classroom is organised into separate bays or areas (see Figure 2.1) with clearly labelled resources giving pictorial clues to the contents.
There are the following areas:

- computer bay;
- office bay;
- interest tables;
- mini-world low tables;
- recycled materials bay;
- easel bay;
- construction area;
- comfortable area;
- story-time carpeted area;

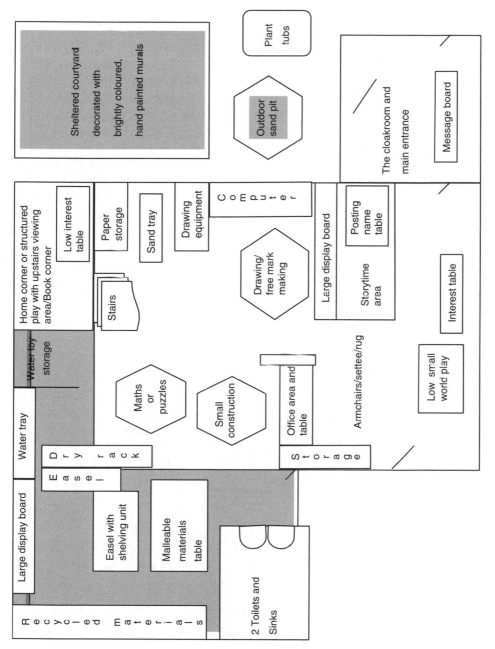

Figure 2.1 *Plan of Rebecca Dawkins' nursery classroom*

- structured play area;
- book corner.

Some areas are in a fixed position due to the need for power sockets, others, such as the structured play area, change each half term to suit the topic or by request from the children for more floor space. Many activities can be set up outside during dry weather. When the children are new to the class these areas are set up to invite them to explore freely. We have found that children enjoy revisiting activities, gradually in more depth. We are therefore not so hasty now to change resources. Sometimes the children request particular equipment for the sand and water tray and can access it for themselves. Over the past few years and since being involved with the CINDLE research we have taken away some of the larger furniture to provide more floor space for the children to expand their play. Rather than having either carpet activities or table activities, we have introduced lower surfaces which children can kneel at to play with small-world figures or topic resources (see Figure 2.2). We have found that they revisit these small, quiet areas time and time again, and seem to find them therapeutic. Perhaps their appeal comes from the fact that these areas are cosy, accessible and at child height.

Figure 2.2 *Exploratory play with topic resources*

The large floor-length display board near our carpeted area lends itself well to whole-group activities. The children have had the opportunity to fill a blank piece of backing paper with their mark-making or collage work. This two-week project gave the children (and staff!) the opportunity to choose a section of blank wall and fill it with their own creations. As the 'masterpiece' (named by the children) evolved, the children decided on a new rule – that people should not be allowed to cover someone's design but should work around it (see Figure 2.3). Not one child out of 52 disobeyed the rule! Even tidying up the activity became a popular social event, where the children learnt to collaborate as a team. Working on a grand scale encouraged the children to be imaginative and take safe risks with their learning. Many interesting observations could be made about each child's social, cognitive and physical abilities. Afterwards the display area became a viewing art gallery for the first half of the session, where children could come to admire and reflect. By providing resources and a simple structure, we could gradually see the children becoming more independent thinkers and learners.

We have concluded that it is important to give the children both time

Figure 2.3 *Having time to negotiate*

and space to reflect on their ideas and thoughts and make sense of their experiences. It is sometimes so easy for us to jump in – albeit with good intentions – and distract the child from what he or she is planning to do and change the outcome completely. The children need to absorb their experiences and tackle things at their own pace. Our miniature settees and armchairs have provided a comfortable, homely area where they can relax, rest, think . . . or even sleep! It is our role to nurture and encourage the children to take safe risks and to provide an appropriate environment for them.

As the year progresses, the children have more ownership of their learning and are capable of making good use of their time at nursery. They become more adventurous in their play, seeking out new experiences and making sense of the World around them. I feel very privileged to be a part of this.

Figure 2.4 *Having time to reflect*

Key points

So, Rebecca feels that it is important in her classroom to:

- Set clear rules and routines *with* the children and staff so everyone has ownership of them.
- Use circle time to bring everyone together as a 'family' group.
- Experiment with arrangement of the furniture; try some areas for kneeling, lying down standing and sitting.
- Give the children time and space to explore, reflect and relax.
- Have clearly designated bays with clearly labelled resources.

A Montessori nursery

Our second account is by Sue Bingham, who is a fully qualified Montessori teacher and runs a nursery within a private day school. What is interesting here is that while the Montessori philosophy is fully implemented in her classroom, including the use of the highly specialised equipment, and while the school serves a rather different clientele in terms of the children's home backgrounds, there are many clear commonalities between Sue's practice and that of Rebecca. Both have a strong commitment to the emotional and social well-being of the children, and to developing their independence. Both also make the purposes of different learning activities very explicit to the children, partly by organising the classroom into clearly identified learning areas (although the nature of the areas is in some cases quite different, as Sue makes clear in her account).

It is interesting to note that Piaget was himself a great admirer of Montessori's work and it is possibly partly from her that he developed his view (as we reviewed in Chapter 1) that teachers of young children should be mostly observers and facilitators, rather than attempting to directly teach or instruct. It is important to recognise, however, that this does not lead at all to a version of child-centredness that allows young children free rein to do whatever they like. On the contrary, both Rebecca and Sue place great emphasis on classrooms with rules, and both have a clear idea of what young children need to learn. In the Montessori setting there is also a clear attempt to provide a range of prescribed 'child-friendly' activities which are specifically designed to support particular aspects of learning.

Background

There is a strong emphasis within a Montessori setting upon providing appropriately for the child's emotional and social needs, as a basis for all their other learning. The physical layout of the rooms, the interaction with other children and adults, and the curriculum content itself all reflect this central tenet. Although some of the equipment and materials seen in a Montessori setting are specific to this method of early years education, a focus upon a child's emotional and social well-being and learning is not of course limited to just this type of setting. Many teachers, in all sorts of educational establishments, coming from a variety of backgrounds, with different training and experiences believe and recognise that children are biologically 'pre-programmed' to learn and that the best way they can support this learning is to provide a rich and appropriate environment and then to stimulate and encourage the children's natural appetite. In this section, we look specifically at how the physical environment, the quality and type of adult interaction and the content of one particular curriculum area come together within a Montessori setting to support a child's innate desire for independent learning and give them an emotional and social bedrock to underpin all other learning.

From the very first Casa dei Bambini (Children's House) set up by Maria Montesssori herself in the slums of Rome in the early 1900s, the central pivot around which the rest of the Montessori philosophy and practice revolves is that the learning environment belongs to the children, rather than the teacher. Within our nursery of 32 3–5-year-olds, we have tried to bear this 'ownership' principle in mind at every decision point and reflect it in our everyday practice. It is a starting point that has implications that are not only physical, in terms of the layout of the rooms or the size of the furniture, or the fact that there is no visible teacher's desk for example, but also shapes how we, as the teacher and staff, perceive our roles and how we interact with the children. We see ourselves as directing or facilitating the children's learning rather than 'teaching' them; we are part of the environment, rather than the centre of it.

It is sometimes difficult in today's society, which is frequently not just conscious of, but is actually restricted by health and safety legislation, for young children to enjoy as much 'freedom' as they perhaps need within a setting. We want to give the children boundaries within which to explore and experiment at length, but in physical safety. One way to do this is not simply to remove the opportunities for children to learn how to do challenging things – such as cutting up food with a real knife, or banging nails in with a real hammer, for example – but to provide appropriately sized tools so that the child can hold and wield them effectively and then to provide plenty of opportunities for practising the necessary skills, initially supported by an adult, so that the child gains in confidence and is safe to manage the 'risk' by himself.

A second issue related to promoting a culture of 'freedom' within a classroom, relates to behaviour. For most of the children in our nursery, this is their first experience of belonging to a group outside the family circle, their first opportunity to direct their own actions and behaviour without the constant presence of a parent. Clearly, different families have different ways and rules within their own homes, so an important part of what a child needs to learn as he comes into a new society such as a nursery class, is that the 'rules' may be different here and that sometimes compromise will be needed!

We have found that it helps the children to understand and remember the 'rules' for nursery if they are part of discussions early in the academic year, in which the children decide how they want their nursery to work. If children, even as young as the age of 3 have the opportunity to share ideas, air their own views and listen to those of others, they are more likely to see the sense in them and adhere to them. This needs to be gently but consistently maintained by all the adults. Of course, we try to frame the 'Ways We Do Things at Nursery' ideas as positively as possible, for example:

- We have gentle hands with our friends and with our things.
- We use walking feet inside.
- We use 'inside voices' in the classroom.

When the notion of 'compromise' is too abstract for our young ones, we also try to provide as many tangible reminders to the children that they can independently come to agreements with their friends about sharing and taking turns without recourse to an adult to sort out the problem. The trusty 'sand timer' is a very visible prop, encouraging children to sort out taking turns independently. In order to sort out turn-taking, two or more children agree to share the particular resource that they all want and then the sand-timer, which takes 3 minutes to empty, is turned over. While one child has a turn, the others wait for the sand to all trickle down, before swapping over to the next child and turning the sand-timer over again to start the next turn. Other physical supports in our setting to promote the children's independent resolution of sharing include bracelets at the sand-box and hats at the water-tray. A limited number – usually four – placed near the box and tray indicate that there is only room for that number of children to play there comfortably. As a child comes to play, he puts on a hat or bracelet. If there are none left, a child will need to come back later for a turn.

The physical environment

In originally setting up our classrooms, we had several key objectives, which are outlined below.

The basic layout of the classrooms needed to be stable and constant; we felt that the children would gain a degree of security from knowing how to navigate themselves around the different 'areas' of their environment. Within a traditional Montessori environment, these areas are the 'Practical Life' area, the 'Sensorial' area, the 'Language' area, the 'Maths' area, the 'Cultural' area and the 'Creative' area. In my classroom there is also an area for role-play (see Figure 2.5).

Montessori was a pioneer in terms of the physical layout and furniture of the Children's Houses and we have tried to adhere to her principles. She had to have special furniture and child-sized cutlery and tools made – thankfully our society has become much more child-centred and the catalogues are full of low-level chairs, tables and shelving, book storage units and trolleys, all at child height, enabling independent access to resources. This means that the children can select the resources they want without relying on an adult for direction or to physically reach or retrieve the materials. The child can place the resources where they want, using space at the tables or on the floor. A carpet tile is sometimes used by a child if he wants to define clearly the parameters of his workspace on the floor, indicating to others that they must not interfere with it while work is 'in progress'.

Children need the security of a regular routine as much as a constant environment, so we try to keep activities with the same overall pattern every day as far as possible. Knowing that 'circle time' comes first, followed by 'snack time' and so on helps a child to feel that time is ordered and predictable, which imparts a sense of stability and security to the child.

The contents of each classroom area, however, need to be dynamic and constantly providing a challenge and stimulus for every child. Within the nursery we are lucky enough to have good storage facilities, so that new or different resources can be introduced when we observe that a child is ready for them, but in the meantime, the shelves and floor spaces do not need to appear overly cluttered and unattractive. For aesthetic reasons we have tried to choose resources made of wood wherever possible and there is a schedule for their regular cleaning and maintenance. Resources are either placed directly on the shelves, which have little photographs of the materials pinned on them, indicating their normal position to the children as an aid at 'tidy up time', or they are placed in baskets or containers, again with small photographs attached to indicate the contents so that reliance on an adult is minimised.

The 'Practical Life' curriculum

Usually when a child comes into our nursery setting at the age of 3, they are somewhat 'overwhelmed' by the range of activities on offer to them – either through feeling bewildered at having so much choice, or daunted at the prospect that they need to share the resources with other children! Experience has shown us that the 'Practical Life' area is a good place for the adults to introduce a child to short, focused tasks with an obvious beginning and end, based on a skill and using equipment that is usually familiar in some way, similar to objects the child will have seen at home. The 'Practical Life' curriculum is central to all others within Montessori philosophy and practice, as it was designed to support the development of children's self-esteem and confidence first and foremost. Certainly, practical life skills are acquired by the child as they practise physical skills such as cutting (in cooking activities) or sawing (in woodwork activities), but it is the self-assurance and positive attitude to tackling new tasks, the ability to persevere through the 'tricky bits' and the sense of accomplishment in completing the activities which form the primary learning objectives in this curriculum.

Caring for the environment

Much of the Montessori Practical Life curriculum focuses on helping a child to take care not only of his own personal physical needs (dressing and eating skills, for example) and his social needs, but also his environment, because as a child learns to master skills in his environment, such as tidying up, sweeping the floor or pegging up his own painting to dry, for example, he gains a degree of control over his world and his routines that can greatly enhance his self esteem. We provide real tools, scaled down to fit a child's hand where necessary, not replicas made of plastic which cannot perform the required action. Over the years we have observed that the child more than rises to the trust and expectation shown by the adult in providing 'real' equipment for them to use in attempting a 'real' everyday task; rarely has a china plate or cup been broken as a child practises laying the table, and rarely has a child used the shoe polish inappropriately! Children within the nursery are encouraged to try a variety of everyday activities in caring for their environment, such as washing (dolls') clothes and pegging them out to dry on a line, sweeping the floor, polishing a mirror or some shoes, and washing up. In each activity the secondary objective is to learn a practical skill that will be useful in life, and the third objective is to strengthen and refine gross and fine muscles in preparation for pencil or paintbrush control, for example. The primary goal is to enable the child to master their surroundings and routines and thereby increase in self-worth.

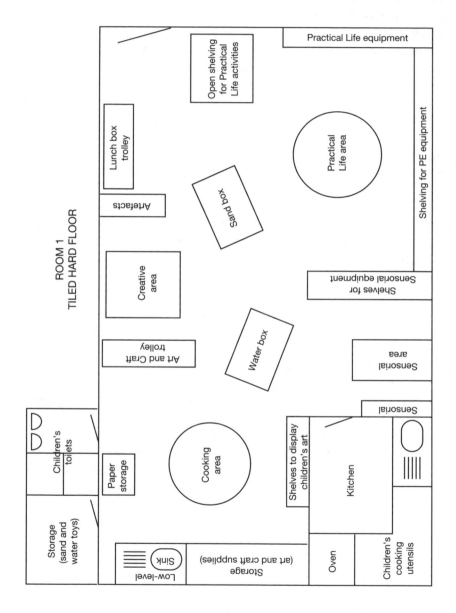

ROOM 1
TILED HARD FLOOR

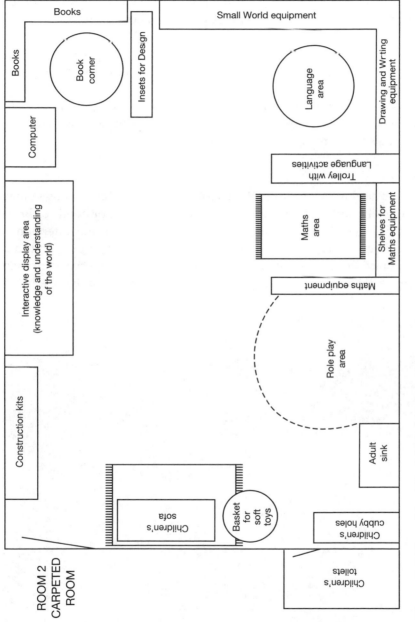

Figure 2.5 *Plan of Sue Bingham's Montessori nursery*

The sense of everyone in our little community contributing to a joint goal, namely that of looking after 'their' nursery, is also not to be underestimated.

Figure 2.6 shows a photograph of shelves containing some of the Practical Life resources available to the children. These include:

- table mats to enable the children to define their work-space;
- tasks to develop the pincer grip: a tweezers task, a spooning task, a lacing task;
- tasks to develop fine motor control and independence: pots and jars for screwing on lids, stacking cups, table laying, pouring tasks with dry materials (e.g. lentils) as well as liquids.

Care of the self

Mirrors placed at the appropriate height encourage a child to notice what they look like and whether they need to wash their face or hands or brush their hair – thereby developing a sense of self-respect and attention to detail. In our nursery, dressing skills such as buttoning, zipping and folding are practised when the child desires, using a range of special equipment to support their dexterity and self-confidence – there is nothing we like to

Figure 2.6 *'Practical Life' resources in the Montessori classroom*

hear more than someone saying 'No help thank you! I can do it myself' as we offer to do up a zip or shoe buckle! Opportunities for cooking are also important within our setting; we start with simple skills such as spreading – making sandwiches for our friends, for example – and go on to more complicated skills such as crumbling or creaming using appropriate tools. Again, the primary objective is not so much the physical dexterity that comes through practising such activities, as the self esteem and social prowess that a child experiences as they pass around the jam tarts which they themselves have made!

Grace and courtesy

Old-fashioned though this undoubtedly sounds, the principles behind the 'Grace and Courtesy' part of the Montessori 'Practical Life' curriculum are timeless and equally applicable in non-Montessori environments. In working with children living in deprived areas, whose parents had had little or no education, Montessori observed the self-confidence that developed as a result of children feeling secure in the knowledge that they were learning the 'right way' to behave in certain situations. For example, she taught the children how to welcome and greet people, how to hold their knife and fork properly and even how to blow their noses appropriately! She stressed that although each child had the right to control his environment, there was an associated responsibility attached to this freedom and any potential negative impact on others must be minimised – so, in moving around the room, opening or closing a door, moving a chair from one place to another, within the room, for example, the needs of others must be considered and the action must be performed gently and 'gracefully'. Nowadays, we probably take for granted the security that comes from knowing how to behave appropriately within a particular group of people, or in other words, having what we might call appropriate 'manners' – but in our nursery we believe that there is still merit in supporting children's learning in this area to give them a social confidence.

Key points

The key points that emerge from Sue's account are as follows:

- The teacher's role is one of facilitator, rather than 'instructor'; children are not empty vessels to be filled up with knowledge by teachers.
- Risk-taking is to be encouraged, not avoided. Life demands that

> we take risks – including emotional and social ones, so where better to learn how to do so, than in a safe, caring environment among people we can trust?
> • The attitudes and skills acquired through a 'Practical Life' curriculum enhance a child's self-esteem above everything else.

A reception classroom

Anthony Aguda teaches a reception class in a one-form entry primary school serving a busy part of a city with three other schools nearby. In his account of his work with these slightly older children there is perhaps less direct emphasis on emotional support, but still a very clear emphasis on making the classroom somewhere that the children feel is theirs, and is mostly designed to meet their needs rather than those of the adults. Once again the organisation of the classroom is designed to make the purposes of learning activities explicit, with clearly designated areas or 'corners'. There is also a continuing emphasis on making resources easily accessible. While there is order in Anthony's classroom, there is also flexibility and an openness to change where it serves a useful purpose. There is also a great sense of shared enjoyment of learning.

Anthony's classroom

We are not lucky enough to have a nursery class on site, so organisation for me begins with fostering and maintaining good links with the nearby nursery providers, making sure that I have had contact with the children that I will be receiving before they arrive on my doorstep in September. Once the children start at primary school, they come into the reception class for mornings only during the first two weeks. This means that they all begin to mix with one another from the start, but do not wear themselves out too quickly. The resulting afternoons are perfect for the preparation time that early years demands. It's also an ideal time to sit with my teaching assistant to talk about how we are planning to manage the class together. During these two weeks, we all get to know each other and begin to learn how 32 people are going to share a small space all day, every day!

Classroom layout

Teaching a reception class is a bit like being in the cub scouts – with the motto 'Be Prepared' being the most important thing to remember. This starts with the way that I lay out the classroom. However, two weeks into it I sometimes realise that I forgot to take the 32 people using it, and the space they take up, into consideration!

I love setting out a classroom, the more challenging the space, the better. I make a list of what I would like to have in it, and split the list into 'need' and 'would be nice' features. These lists will be the basis of how I zone the room. Reception classes need to be constructed out of corners. Recently, an extension to my room was built, and I was able to discuss the need for corners with the architect. In the design, bits of wall are left jutting out, creating extra corners.

The plan shows the layout of my teaching space (see Figure 2.7), unfortunately not including the outdoor space. (The outdoor space is just as important as the indoors, and includes outdoor storage, a climbing frame, white and blackboards and racks for wellies.) The most important decision I ever made was to take out half of the tables. The children shouldn't be sitting all day, so why have them? I used some of the redundant chairs in the role-play area and writing area and was left with two main teaching tables. Perfect.

Once I have the skeleton of the room, the next decision to make is where all of the extras go, such as stationery, toys, and of course the things that belong to me. I think it important to remember that this is a shared room and that everyone respects that. Children know not to touch my laptop, and special models and pictures, which mean the earth to their creators, are given a designated space. I have managed to have my room changed so that there are shelves high up and displays down low. This means that anything not used every day can go up in a clearly labelled box ready for next time, and displays are at the children's height and so are much more meaningful.

I never forget that wonderful space 'the ceiling', although there are curses daily from parents and the headteacher, who constantly knock into hanging displays. But kneeling down at child height gives me a fresh insight into the room and ducking and weaving between hanging items soon becomes second nature. An example of this kind of display was put together during our 'Minibeast' topic. The children made papier mâché creatures which were displayed on an old football net, bunched up onto the ceiling. I also like to use 'hanging things' to compartmentalise the room. Large sheets of clear polythene and strips of crepe paper both make effective but unobtrusive barriers.

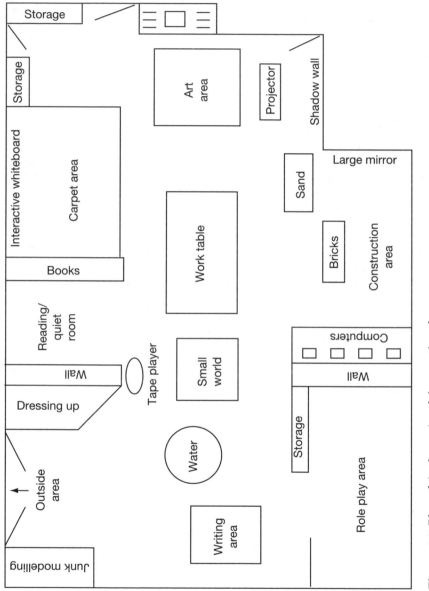

Figure 2.7 *Plan of Anthony Aguda's reception classroom*

The resources

In the first half term I spend a great deal of time explaining where resources belong in the classroom and why they are there. This not only ensures that the children 'own' the classroom, but it also frees me to concentrate on teaching and observing. I try to organise resources into boxes on the shelves. Two shelves are full of role-play boxes used throughout the year. Everything needed for each of a variety of themes is packed in a separate box. The same is done with small-world resources – Outer Space, The Jungle, African Savannah, etc. (see Figure 2.8). There are also boxes of natural things such as shells, bark, conkers, glass nuggets, etc., as I find them much nicer for counting than plastic cubes. Toys that the children use are in storage units that are labelled by the children with a transcription underneath if necessary.

In my view the way that the resources and furniture are managed can really develop and enhance the children's independent learning. For example, I make sure that the writing area has all of the needed resources: variety of paper (colours, shapes and sizes), envelopes, pens, pencils, stencils, alphabets strips. With the addition of a key word display and a whiteboard, the children can be autonomous in their exploration of writing.

I have great fun organising my classroom and resources, and am always prepared to do a little risk-taking. If you don't try something, you'll never

Figure 2.8 *Small-world resources in the reception classroom*

know how successful it might have been, but if you try and it doesn't work, you'll know for next time!

Key points

For Anthony, the key points to bear in mind when organising a reception classroom are as follows:

- The classroom is a workspace shared by adults and children.
- A creative use of corners generates valuable spaces for children.
- Accessible and well-ordered organisation of resources supports children's developing independence.

A Year 1 class

Our final account is from Kate Hemming, who teaches a Year 1 class in an independent school. She was also a teacher involved in the CIndLe project. While her school is independent, and the children in her class come from relatively affluent home backgrounds, she shares the common difficulties currently being experienced by all Year 1 teachers nationally, of managing the children's transition from the play-based curriculum of the Foundation Stage to the very much more directed approach required in Key Stage 1 of the national curriculum. Kate's account is particularly interesting in this respect, as she has taught reception classes for a number of years before her recent move to Year 1. What she has managed to achieve with great skill, as is clear in her account, is to bring the best of her early years practice and modify it advantageously to this slightly older age group (who, it must be remembered are still just 5 or 6 years of age and, in many European countries, would still be in kindergarten). She shows how the requirements of a more formally academic curriculum can be met, while still allowing the children a good deal of control over their learning. Like Anthony, she also emphasises flexibility, so that she is constantly monitoring provision in her classroom to ensure that her organisational arrangements are supporting the children's learning. Like the other contributors to this chapter, Kate also emphasises the value of consulting the children about classroom rules and organisational decisions; this not only involves the children and gives them a sense of ownership, it also often results in far better decisions.

Kate's classroom

I teach a Year 1 class in a large independent school. My teaching experience is based firmly within early years education. On moving from teaching reception to Year 1, the challenge was to bring all my philosophies and insight in the Foundation Stage into a more demanding and potentially more restrictive Key Stage 1 curriculum and timetable.

While teaching reception, my practice evolved as I experimented and researched different ways of organising my classroom to encourage independent learning. Now teaching Year 1, it is clear that the children, although more confident and capable of self-regulated learning, continue to crave a supportive yet challenging environment in which to practise and reinforce their independence.

The layout of the classroom

Planning the layout of the classroom is an important part of providing a supportive learning environment. The layout is changed as the needs of the children evolve.

I like to 'zone' the classroom into distinct areas (see Figure 2.9). This helps the children to feel secure with the expectations of their environment, for example, if they want a quiet time, they know that the reading corner is the place to go for relaxation. Of course, there is always scope to overlap, for example, when construction play is generated from enjoying a 'story sack' in the reading corner or when a role-play game inspires some writing in the 'office'. It is vitally important to value and encourage fluidity of learning from one 'zone' to another.

My classroom always has:

- a reading corner – with story sacks, non-fiction, fiction and poetry books;
- an 'office' to encourage independent writing or artwork with resources, such as different textured paper, pens, envelopes, telephones and diaries, and bluetac to display work on the wall;
- a numeracy corner with calculators, number lines, shapes and dominos;
- a role-play or 'small-world' area;
- space for construction activities – and a space to display the items made.

All other classroom resources are easily accessible and the children know that they are able to use them to support their learning. They include cubes, whiteboards, scissors, glue, magnetic letters and dictionaries (see Figure 2.10).

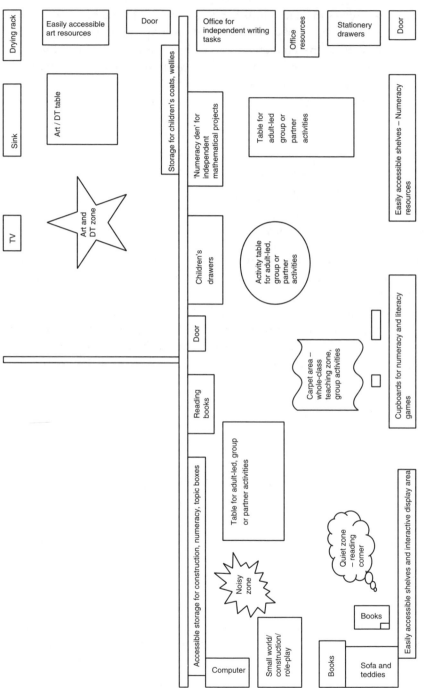

Figure 2.9 *Plan of Kate Hemming's Year 1 classroom*

Figure 2.10 *Independent use of the whiteboard by Year 1 children*

Planning for independence

In Year 1 it is essential to build upon the children's Foundation Stage experiences, where sustained periods of learning are encouraged. My time-table has been adapted to support the transition from reception to Year 1. Rather than diving straight into a distinct literacy and numeracy hour, during the autumn term, the timetable has been rewritten to allow whole mornings of either literacy or numeracy. This enables the children to enjoy extended learning opportunities within a familiar structure and time scale. For example, throughout the morning, there may be two adult-led activities, group problem-solving activity, construction, role-play, ICT, a creative activity, and sand or water play – all linked to the literacy or numeracy objective but with scope for independent exploration. The emphasis is on free flow within the classroom; the aim is that all the children will have experiences of all available activities throughout the day.

This way of working has been immensely rewarding for the children. I feel it enables them to have more control over their learning, knowing they can develop their activities with greater autonomy. It certainly helped the children to settle in their new environment and it has given me the opportunity to support children's initiative through spontaneity.

Issues that I consider while planning the environment for independent learning

Is each style of activity designed with a specific independent learning objective?

If so, make these explicit to the children so that they understand your expectations, for example, for a collaborative group work objective: '*I am really hoping to see you working as a group and listening to each other in the role-play corner.*'

Or, for a peer-tutoring objective: '*You played this game yesterday, can you teach it to two more children? You will need to make sure that they understand how to play.*'

Once the children are confident, they may be able to work out what the focus might be for the activity and could set the objective for the rest of the group.

Consider the space available

In order for the children to engage in a construction activity, is there enough carpet/table space for them to utilise?

I involve the children in the planning of the space. Discussions about why certain resources are placed in specific areas encourage the children to think about the way they play with them and the types of learning involved.

When setting up a classroom office or numeracy workshop, I ask the children which resources they would need and then ask them to arrange them in the designated area themselves. The children make a list, as a group, of required resources; for example, number lines, calculators, dice, counters, clocks.

Of course the planning of the space is a lesson in independent learning in itself: observe the children negotiating with each other, making decisions and problem-solving. Having ownership of their environment and knowing that they have control over their learning empowers children and results in meaningful learning experiences.

Think about the time constraints

Have all the children been given enough time to evolve their learning?

Balance the needs of the individuals

Think about how you group children – those who are more confident independent learners can support others. Children learn so well from observing others. Use the children to scaffold and guide their peers. This reinforces independent learning at all levels.

Consider appropriate adult intervention

Be confident enough to sit back and observe the children's learning, but know when to step in to move the activity along.

Above all: be flexible!

Working with young children requires immense flexibility. Flexibility is demanded from the environment as the curriculum changes and the children mature. In order to maintain a challenging yet supportive learning environment, we need to be flexible enough to recognise that changes need to take place. Knowing when to intervene and move the learning forward is vital.

Assessment and regulation within the learning environment

Discussing thinking and learning with young children is rewarding and is an essential part of developing independence. The environment needs to be supportive in order for the children to extend their higher-order thinking without fear of failure. It is important to model this type of thinking for young children and to engage them (either as a class or as individuals) in genuine conversations about their learning. Observe the children talking to each other about their learning, listen in to self-commentary and challenge the children to explain to you about what they have found out.

Key points

So, for Kate, the key points to consider when organising her Year 1 classroom are as follows:

- In Key Stage 1, build on the children's experiences from their Foundation Stage environment and aim to mirror some of the key features in terms of freedom of choice of activities, space and time.
- Involve the children in the planning of the environment,

therefore developing the children's sense of ownership of their learning. This includes devising and sharing explicit independent learning objectives.

- Encourage flexibility and freedom: consider the flexibility of the environment (allow the layout of your classroom to evolve throughout the year), the timetable, children and adults, and the impact this flexibility has on developing independent learners and practitioners.
- Provide a supportive and nurturing environment where discussions about learning are valued by adults and children.

Conclusions

Within cognitive developmental psychology over the last 30 years or so there has been a very considerable body of research evidence related to the development of children as independent learners. Within the psychological literature this has been variously characterised as 'learning how to learn', 'self-regulation' (Schunk and Zimmerman, 1994) and 'metacognition' (Metcalfe and Shimamura, 1994), all of which are concerned with children's developing self-awareness and control of their own mental processing. What has emerged is a body of research and theory which suggests that it is this aspect of development that is crucially responsible for individual differences in children's development as learners.

The term 'metacognition' was first coined by Flavell in the late 1970s (Flavell, 1979), arising from his studies of memory development. Since then, the crucial significance of an individual's ability to monitor and regulate their own cognitive activity has been demonstrated across a wide range of human development. Indeed, in a review of the extensive literature in just the first decade of research, Wang *et al.* (1990) concluded that metacognition was the most powerful single predictor of learning.

In its application to education, work in this area has been inspired by the sociocultural tradition founded on the work of the Russian psychologist, Lev Vygotsky (1978, 1986), some of whose key ideas were reviewed in Chapter 1. He lived in the first three decades of the last century and died tragically young. But he produced a set of ideas about children's learning which have inspired many developmental psychologists, particularly in the last 20–30 years, to explore the social and cultural origins of children's learning. For Vygotsky, the development of children's learning was a process of moving from other-regulation (or performing a task while supported by an adult or peer) to self-regulation (performing a task on one's own). Crucially, research stimulated by these ideas has shown that a key characteristic of a good supporter or 'scaffolder' (to use Bruner's metaphor) is the ability to sensitively withdraw support as the child becomes able to carry out the task more independently, or to take over more of the regulatory role for themselves (for an excellent review of work in this area, see Schaffer, 2004).

In recent research in this area there has been the recognition of metacognitive processes in very young children. In the early work on metacognition, some writers argued that it is a late-developing capability. However, this very quickly became an untenable position, as it became clear that early research methodologies were systematically under-estimating the abilities of young children. In a recent and very comprehensive overview, Bronson (2000) demonstrates that the development of metacognitive and self-regulatory processes is fundamental to the whole range of young children's psychological growth. She lists work with children concerned with the development of the regulation of arousal, of emotional responses, of adaptive control of behaviour in familiar settings, of problem-solving and of motivational patterns. She goes on to describe in detail extensive research that has explored the emotional, prosocial, cognitive and motivational developments in self-regulation throughout the different phases of early childhood.

Our experience in early years educational settings clearly accords with this body of research. Throughout all the fieldwork and subsequent training courses associated with the CIndLe project, whenever a teacher moved to give young children more responsibility for their own learning, or allowed them to be more involved in decisions regarding the running of the classroom or the organisation of the curriculum, these teachers have always been deeply impressed by the response from the children, and have seen the benefits for the children's motivation and learning very quickly.

When they enter school the vast majority of young children are voracious in their enthusiasm for life and for learning and, sadly, for many the experience of schooling diminishes rather than supports these appetites. Education has become, for too many of our children, something that is done to them, rather than with them. We hope that some of the ideas in this chapter will help readers to make the educational experience in their classrooms one that genuinely supports young children's development as confident and self-regulated learners.

Pointer for organising the early years classroom

Themes which emerge from all four accounts concerned with organisation of the early years classroom to support independent learning:

- Think carefully about the children's transition from their immediately previous environment into the world of your classroom.
- Involve the children in decisions about class rules and organisation.
- Make the resources the children will need accessible to them, so that they can make choices and decisions.
- Organise your class to provide a range of different spaces and learning environments (this may involve getting rid of some of the chairs and tables!) which have clear and explicit purposes.
- Be reflective about the organisation of your classroom and be prepared to be flexible and make changes in the interests of the children's learning.

If you would like to know more about the CIndLe project you can access further details, downloadable versions of publications and an order form for the CD-based training resource produced by the project team at: http://www.educ.cam.ac.uk/cindle/index.html

References

Bronson, M.B. (2000) *Self-Regulation in Early Childhood*, New York: The Guilford Press.

DfEE/QCA (2000) *Curriculum Guidance for the Foundation Stage*, London: DfEE.

Featherstone, S. and Bayley, R. (2001) *Foundations of Independence*, Lutterworth: Featherstone Education.

Flavell, J.H. (1979) 'Metacognition and cognitive monitoring: a new area of cognitive developmental inquiry', *American Psychologist*, 34, 906–11.

Hendy, L. and Whitebread, D. (2000) 'Interpretations of independent learning in the early years', *International Journal of Early Years Education*, 8, 3, 245–52.

Metcalfe, J. and Shimamura, A.P. (eds) (1994) *Metacognition: Knowing about Knowing*, Cambridge, MA: MIT Press.

Schaffer, H.R. (2004) 'The child as apprentice: Vygotsky's theory of socio-cognitive development', in *Introducing Child Psychology*, Oxford: Blackwell.

Schunk, D.H. and Zimmerman, B.J. (1994) *Self-regulation of Learning and Performance*, Hillsdale, NJ: Lawrence Erlbaum.

TDA (2006) *Qualifying to Teach*, London: TDA.

Vygotsky, L.S. (1978) *Mind in Society*, Cambridge, MA: Harvard University Press.

Vygotsky, L.S. (1986) *Thought and Language*, Cambridge, MA: MIT Press.

Wang, M.C., Haertel, G.D. and Walberg, H.J. (1990) 'What influences learning? A content analysis of review literature', *Journal of Educational Research*, 84, 30–43.

Watson, J.S. and Ramey, C.T. (1972) 'Reactions to response-contingent stimulation in early infancy', *Merrill-Palmer Quarterly*, 18, 219–27.

Williams, J. (2003) *Promoting Independent Learning in the Primary Classroom*, Buckingham: Open University Press.

Whitebread, D. and Coltman, P. (2007) 'Developing young children as self-regulating learners', in J. Moyles (ed.) *Beginning Teaching: Beginning Learning in Primary Education*, 3rd edn, Buckingham: Open University Press.

Whitebread, D., Anderson, H., Coltman, P., Page, C., Pino Pasternak, D. and Mehta, S. (2005) 'Developing independent learning in the early years', *Education 3–13*, 33, 40–50.

CHAPTER 3

'My mum would pay anything for chocolate cake!'

ORGANISING THE WHOLE CURRICULUM: ENTERPRISE PROJECTS IN THE EARLY YEARS

Penny Coltman and David Whitebread

In the last few years, with the introduction of a statutory national curriculum in maintained schools in England and Wales, there has inevitably been huge controversy about the curriculum. As regards its impact on the education of children in the 3–8 years age range, some commentators have taken the extreme view that the national curriculum is fundamentally at odds with early years education (e.g. Blenkin and Kelly, 1994). Others have argued, however, that while there are dangers and difficulties, with imagination early years educators can be true to their principles, stay within the law, and provide the young children in their care with an appropriate, rich and stimulating curriculum (see, for example, Early Years Curriculum Group, 1989). This is the position taken within the present chapter. We want to discuss what the principles for such an early years curriculum might be, and then to demonstrate how these might be brought to life through one particular approach involving the use of enterprise projects.

The national curriculum and the early years curriculum

This chapter is not intended as a critique of the national curriculum. However, its introduction in England and Wales has raised a number of issues which need to be addressed when we come to think about organising a curriculum for young children. These issues can be identified in terms of dangers or problems, on the one hand, and benefits, on the other, inherent in the national curriculum approach.

Dangers and problems of the national curriculum

There are a number of dangers in the approach to the curriculum under-lying the national curriculum. We want to just mention three.

The early years and Key Stage 1

There has been a lack of clarity, and some consequent debate about precisely when young children should begin the national curriculum. As a result, in some schools children have been introduced to elements of the national curriculum during their reception year (i.e. the year in which children become 5 years old), as they become 'ready', while in other schools the national curriculum has not been begun until Year 1 (i.e. the year which all children begin as 5-year-olds). Whichever date is taken, however, there is a very real danger of 'downward' pressure on the early years curriculum. Early years educators working with 3–5-year-olds may be encouraged to view their work as a 'preparation' for the national curriculum, and this can have a distorting influence. The more recent introduction of the Foundation Stage, covering the nursery and reception years, with its own curriculum guidance (QCA, 2000), might have helped here, but its beneficial effect has been badly damaged by the insistence that reception children should be introduced to the literacy and numeracy strategies (DfEE, 1998, 1999)

In particular, there is a danger that this kind of pressure can result in young children being hurried on to tasks for which they do not have the prerequisite skills and understandings. Particular concern has been expressed about the influence on 4-year-olds in reception classes (e.g. see Cleave and Brown, 1991, whose book provides an excellent outline of an appropriate curriculum for 4-year-olds). Here there is some evidence that children have been provided with a diet of seat-based, pencil-and-paper types of tasks at too early a stage. This kind of inappropriate provision can result in a loss of confidence among young children, and the development of entirely unhelpful anxieties about certain kinds of tasks (e.g. reading and writing, written numbers, etc.). In the home context, young children learn very effectively through various informal means when no-one is deliberately attempting to 'teach' them anything. Continuity in terms of the ways in which young children are expected to learn is just one of the features of good links between the worlds of home and school that need to be in place if young children are to thrive in their first years in school.

We know from a range of research (e.g. Bennett *et al.*, 1984) that it is enormously difficult to set tasks which are at precisely the appropriate level for each of the individual children in a primary school classroom. It is clearly vital that educators of young children make their judgements about appropriate tasks entirely on the basis of their understandings about young children's learning, and their knowledge of the particular children. Pressure to 'prepare' pre-school, nursery and reception children for Key Stage 1 can be entirely counter-productive. Indeed, the Early Years Curriculum Group (2002) has recently argued that our children would be better served if the principles of the Foundation Stage (including learning through play, supporting child-initiated activities, allowing children time to explore ideas in depth and adopting a more cross-curricular approach to learning) were translated upwards into Key Stage 1.

A curriculum of separate subjects

A number of features of the ways in which the national curriculum was established have been unhelpful in relation to the early years. From the outset the curriculum was conceived as consisting of a list of separate subjects. The curriculum for each of these subjects has been drawn up and revised by committees which have been dominated by subject specialists with higher education and secondary school backgrounds. It has been a major source of concern that separating out the curriculum into subjects in this way can lead to an 'artificiality' or lack of coherence in the educational experience offered to the young child. There is a strong tradition among early years educators that young children need an integrated curriculum, and this is a view supported by recent research (reviewed in Chapter 1) emphasising the significance of 'meaningful contexts' for young children's learning. While the national curriculum may have been presented as separate subjects, it is therefore vitally important that an integrated, topic-based approach is maintained within the early years. Palmer and Pettitt (1993), among others, have demonstrated very well how such an approach can be developed which is compatible with the national curriculum. The enterprise projects described within this chapter are a particular example of a method of providing young children with a powerful, holistic experience which nevertheless covers a wide range of curriculum areas.

The 'delivery' model

The language of the national curriculum documents has also reflected a bias towards an inappropriate model of teaching and learning in relation to the early years. These documents talk of the educator 'delivering' the curriculum to the children. Concerns about this model, and a perceived emphasis (particularly in earlier versions of the national curriculum) on subject knowledge, have led to worries about the young child being placed in an unhelpfully passive learning role. As has also been reviewed in Chapter 1, there is clear evidence from research that young children learn most effectively by means of 'active' styles of learning.

Allied to this concern has been the danger of a kind of 'tick list' approach to the curriculum. Once a particular aspect of the curriculum has been 'delivered' to the children, and some rudimentary assessment has been made that they have 'received' it, this aspect can be ticked off as having been covered, and we do not need to worry about it any more. In fact, of course, as anyone who has ever worked with young children is only too aware, the relationship between what we as educators attempt to 'teach' a child and what that child actually learns from the experience is often far more complex. Certainly, the development of skills and understandings by young children involves a highly active and complex set of processes which we are far from understanding. It is clear, also, that there are many and various ways and styles of learning, so that an activity or experience that might be highly effective for one child will be no help whatsoever to another. Effective teaching is, therefore, likely to involve constant revisiting of areas through a diversity of meaningful tasks which engage, in a variety of ways, the active involvement of young learners.

Benefits of the national curriculum

On the other hand, the introduction has brought a number of direct and indirect benefits to early years education. Once again, we want to mention three.

Skills and understandings in the Foundation Stage and Key Stage 1

The concerns about the overloading of the curriculum with subject content have not been nearly so great in the early years as they have been at later stages. On the whole, the curriculum at the Foundation Stage and Key Stage 1 has been a helpful description of the skills and understandings that might reasonably be expected of young children. If anything, the main criticism would be that in some areas the abilities of young children have been under-estimated. Nevertheless, the statement of the curriculum contained in the Foundation Stage and Key Stage 1 Statutory Orders has largely given official recognition to a process of change in the early years curriculum from 'product' and towards 'process' that has been proceeding and gathering pace throughout the second part of the last century. Fisher (1987) has neatly described this gradual but inexorable change in practice as one which:

> . . . moves from simply teaching the children the facts of language, mathematics, history, geography, science and other 'disciplines',

towards encouraging children to be scientists, historians, geographers, linguists and mathematicians, through the use of appropriate problem-solving skills and processes.

(Introduction)

A broad and balanced curriculum

As well as giving official backing to modern early years practice in terms of styles of teaching and learning, the curriculum guidance for the Foundation Stage and the Key Stage 1 national curriculum has confirmed the expansion of the curriculum for young children from the traditional 'Three Rs' to a broader and more balanced diet. This, once again, is the culmination of a process that has been developing officially and unofficially for many years. The areas of learning and experience identified by HMI (DES, 1985) in an earlier attempt to define the school curriculum (linguistic and literary, mathematical, aesthetic and creative, human and social, physical, scientific, technological, moral and spiritual) had already been widely accepted and used by early years educators (e.g. Drummond *et al.*, 1989; ILEA, 1987). To some extent, these have now been enshrined in the six areas of learning within the Foundation Stage. While there may be concerns about the separation of the curriculum into distinct subjects, the requirement to introduce young children to skills and understandings under such a wide range of subject headings does help to ensure, as Palmer and Pettitt (1993) have argued, that each child receives the broad and balanced curriculum to which they are entitled. Regrettably, the current pressure to introduce the literacy and numeracy 'hours' into reception classrooms can result in a backward-looking narrowing of the curriculum, but it is to be hoped that this will be resisted.

Re-evaluation of young children's learning

Some aspects of the introduction of the national curriculum have obliged early years educators to re-evaluate their understandings about children's learning. The concomitant new arrangements for assessment have obliged teachers to make assessments of children's skills and understandings in a much more analytical manner than hitherto. This has resulted in wide discussion among teachers and other early years educators concerning such matters as the validity and reliability of different kinds of evidence for children's learning, the sequence of children's learning in different areas, different levels of learning or understanding, and so on.

The arrangements for school inspections, organised by OFSTED (Office for Standards in Education), have obliged teachers to produce plans which, more explicitly than before, identify the intended 'learning outcomes' of the various activities and tasks for the children, and to think critically about the quality of learning taking place in their classrooms. As Anning (1991) has argued, there is a range of influences on early years educators' beliefs and understandings about young children's learning. They are influenced by the traditional beliefs and values of early years education as identified so helpfully, for example, by Bruce (1987). They are also influenced by their social and cultural surroundings, by the findings of developmental psychologists, by their own experiences as a learner, and by their experience of working on a daily basis with young children. What is clear, however, is that the quality of early years education can only be enhanced by these beliefs and understandings being made explicit, being articulated, and being constantly re-evaluated and examined in the light of new evidence.

There is no doubt that the last few years have been ones of considerable turmoil in education, and that teachers and other educators have been pulled in different directions, often as a consequence of muddle and lack of forethought among those in positions of power. However, now that the dust has settled to some extent, a clearer picture is emerging, and it is not one that is entirely incompatible, in the present authors' view, with early years principles. One example of this might be the role afforded to play as a learning medium in early years classrooms. The important role of 'active', self-directed modes of learning, often in the form of one or other kind of play, has long been recognised by early years educators. There appears to have been a decline in the provision for play within early years classrooms, however, possibly under the pressure referred to above to 'prepare' children for the national curriculum, and the literacy and numeracy strategies. It is significant, if perhaps a little ironic, that in an OFSTED report on teaching in reception classes (OFSTED, 1993), which was generally very complimentary, the one area of concern expressed related to the lack of opportunities for children to learn through appropriately structured play. It is to be hoped that the new emphasis on learning through play set out in the *Curriculum Guidance for the Foundation Stage* (QCA, 2000) will give reception and other early years educators the strength to provide appropriately in this regard for their young children.

Principles for an early years curriculum

Through all this debate, in the view of the present authors, there remain a number of important principles which should guide the content and organisation of the early years curriculum. These principles derive from the evidence about children's learning, and from the collective experiences and views of early years educators, as discussed in Chapter 1. Despite the dangers, the national curriculum is not necessarily incompatible with these principles, but they should guide the way it is taught and managed.

At this point it is worth reminding ourselves about the needs of young children identified in Chapter 1. For the curriculum to be effective and appropriate, it needs to take into account these needs. As was argued, to learn effectively young children need a curriculum and a style of teaching that provides them with emotional security and feelings of being in control. Young children need a curriculum which starts with what they understand and can do already, and that helps them make sense of their world by providing them with meaningful tasks, which require their active engagement, and which give them opportunities to express their understandings in a variety of media, principally through imaginative play and talk. Young children's natural curiosity can be stimulated to help them learn effectively by providing novel first-hand experiences and opportunities to explore, investigate and problem-solve.

From these understandings we have derived four principles that we believe should guide the organisation and management of the early years curriculum. These principles are as follows. Young children's learning will be enhanced when:

1 the content of the curriculum is **'meaningful'** to them and related to their existing knowledge and interests;
2 they are **active participants in their learning** rather than just passive recipients – they should have opportunities to make their own decisions about their learning;
3 they are encouraged to indulge their natural inclination to engage in **imaginative play** related to significant life experiences;
4 they are **emotionally secure** because there is continuity and good communication between the worlds of home and school.

Enterprise projects

These principles clearly support an integrated, topic-based approach, and this can be carried out in a whole variety of ways. In the remainder of this chapter, however, we want to demonstrate one kind of approach which seems to embody these principles in a particularly powerful way. This approach consists of what has been termed 'Enterprise' projects (see DES, 1990, for a general review of this kind of work in primary schools). In essence these consist of using some kind of adult 'enterprise' or place of work as a starting point, and enabling children to explore and investigate it, partly by carrying out a similar kind of enterprise themselves.

Over a period of five years the authors carried out an enterprise project each year with classes of young children ranging from reception to Year 2. These have been focused on a bakery, puppet theatres, a newspaper, a museum and a fashion show. The details of some of these projects have been reported elsewhere (Coltman and Whitebread, 1992; Whitebread *et al.*, 1993, 1994, 1995). What follows is a description of these projects and an analysis of the ways in which such projects provide a powerfully effective curriculum for children in the early years, particularly in relation to the four principles identified above.

All the projects involved the following basic elements:

- a visit to a local workplace to find out, by a variety of means, about the kinds of work carried out and the people who worked there;
- the children engaging in a related, small, real enterprise of their own, which involved research, planning, production, advertising, accounting, etc.;
- opportunities for the children to represent their experiences for themselves in a variety of ways, through talk, play, drawing, modelling and writing;
- a fixed 'end point' in the form of an event towards which children could work and to which friends and families could be invited.

Learning through 'meaningful' work

The first principle is concerned with the extent to which the content of the curriculum is 'meaningful' to young children and related to their existing knowledge and interests. This also relates to the links between home-based styles of learning, which are informal and for real purposes, and school-based styles of learning, which sometimes suffer by comparison by being formal and purposeless from the child's point of view. Research in relation to both language (Tizard and Hughes, 1984) and mathematics (Hughes, 1986) has demonstrated that most children find the informal, 'real' world of the home and the community a much more conducive environment for learning than the artificial and, from the child's point of view, 'meaningless' tasks of traditional schooling. This has led to a developing new pedagogy which emphasises the importance of children within school carrying out tasks for 'real' purposes within the context of real-world situations and problems (see, for example, Hall, 1989, in relation to language and Atkinson, 1992, in relation to maths).

This 'authenticity' was established within the enterprise projects we carried out in a number of ways:

- **The localness of the workplaces** visited gave them a meaningfulness to the children through familiarity. The local newspaper was taken by many of the children's families, many had already visited the local museum and some of the children's friends and relations worked at the local bakery;

- **Projects related to the children's interests** (e.g. the bakery mainly made Christmas puddings; the puppet show gave them an opportunity to re-enact one of their favourite stories (Cinderella and Snow White were chosen, somewhat adapted to give everyone a part!); the contents of the newspaper they produced contained items of interest to them: reviews of latest children's films, a fashion page complete with photographs of 6–7-year-old 'models' (an interest later developed in the fashion show project), Aunt Sherry's Problem Page (Dear Aunt Sherry, my brother is a pain in the neck!), and a page of Houses for Sale (the children's own houses, drawn and described by them – see Figure 3.1); the museum set up by the children exhibited artifacts provided by themselves, their families, village friends and the school, and focused on the history of the school and the village.

- **A wide range of opportunities for learning through 'real' work provided**:

  Writing for real purposes: the children wrote scripts, programmes, posters, price lists, guidebooks, official invitations to special guests, press releases, a whole newspaper, and, most excitingly as it turned out, a range of business letters. These included letters accompanying the donations to charities, but also letters to local businesses selling advertising space in the class newspaper, bids for an arts grant to support the puppet theatre companies, and for sponsorship for the class museums and the fashion show (see Figure 3.2). All these letters received formal and entirely business-like replies which were much treasured by the children.

  Real maths: a lot of book-keeping and accounting, of course (see Figure 3.3), but also measuring ingredients for refreshments when parents and friends were invited in for the grand launch or opening; handling real money when children sold tickets, postcards, programmes, etc.; setting out the seats in the 'auditorium' for the puppet shows, with tickets corresponding to numbered seats; measuring and making patterns and costumes for the fashion show; making decisions about what to charge for various items in all the projects.

  Genuine economic transactions: real money was used throughout; all costs

House for sale. 5 bedrooms.
Dining room. Conservatory.
2 toilets. Kitchens. Large
pond in garden. Quiet area.
Good Price.
£80,000.

A lovely house with a large garden.
Close to the shops. Near to a school.
It has 1 main bedroom and a lounge.
1 roof garden and your own little
parking space next to the house.
Price £40,000.

This house has 2 bedrooms.
1 pool. Room under stairs.
Double glazing. Double bed.
A vase of flowers. It's a
bargain.
Price 70,000.

1 bed. home. Ballet room.
Disco room. 1 big bathroom
and a nice size kitchen.
Swimming pool and stable.
Come soon.
Price £100,000.

Figure 3.1 *The children advertise their own houses for sale*

were charged, but all the projects managed to make a good profit! The children were confronted with the simple realities of costs, prices, consumer preferences, profits and losses throughout the projects. Our records are full of fascinating discussions we held with children, particularly when they had to make decisions about pricing, for example. How much profit was it fair to make? What price would people pay for a newspaper? Children had to use their real-world knowledge to help

Back to the Past Museum Company.
(a division of Class 4 enterprises).

27.1.94.

Dear Sir,

Please may you consider sponsoring our posters for our Back to the Past museum. We estimate the cost will be about 10 pounds. Your company logo will appear on all posters and we anticipate a large crowd of people attending.

Thankyou for your kind attention.

Yours Faithfully,

Matthew Paddick,

(Company Secretary.)

Figure 3.2 *Writing for real purposes: Matthew writes applying for sponsorship*

them solve these problems. On one occasion a child volunteered that his mum would pay anything for chocolate cake!

Work roles and processes emulated authentically: work roles were made explicit to the children. To help with this process, for example, badges for 'cook', 'market researcher', 'editor', 'museum guide', 'designer' and so on were often worn by the children when they carried out these roles. Processes seen by the children on visits were emulated in ways which made them as real as possible. Good examples of this would be the cataloguing procedures developed during the museums project, the computer booking system developed during the puppet theatre project, the operation of a real telephone by the children during the newspaper project on which they took calls to a 'tele-sales' service, and computer aided design for T-shirts in the fashion show (see Figure 3.4).

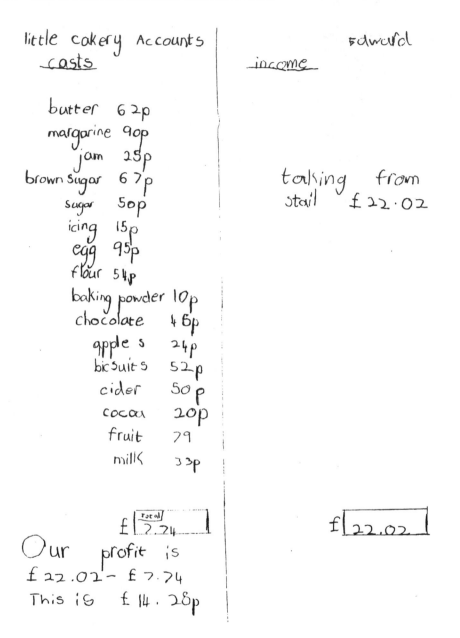

Figure 3.3 *Real maths: Edward's cake stall accounts*

Children being 'active' learners and empowered to make their own decisions

Our second principle concerns children being active participants in their learning rather than just passive recipients, and having opportunities to

Figure 3.4 *Authentic work processes: Robert uses a computer graphics package to design his T-shirt*

make their own decisions about their learning. An 'active' style of learning is an intrinsic aspect of enterprise projects because the children are actually experiencing adult activities first-hand, and not simply being told about them. What goes along with this is that we must always be open to the children taking the initiative. A good example of this was a poster designed by one of the children. This was done in the evening at home, inspired by a day of designing the role-play area to accompany the fashion show project, and was proudly brought into school the next morning. On another occasion, during the puppet theatre project, a child on her own initiative brought into the class a large cardboard box which had contained her family's new washing machine. She explained that this was to be made into a puppet theatre. The provision of opportunities for imaginative play is also an important aspect of this 'active' involvement of children, and we will come on to this next.

What is significant here, however, is the opportunities enterprise projects offer, because of their intrinsically open-ended and problem-solving character, for children to take decisions and so develop feelings of empowerment. Tizard and Hughes (1984), among others, have pointed out how so much of what happens between adults and children in the home is child-initiated, whereas this is often very much not the case in the classroom. The consequent loss of feelings of control, self-efficacy and self-esteem for the young child can be very damaging. Research has consistently shown that self-esteem is whittled away by the difficulties many children face in relation to school learning. The strong relation between self-esteem and school achievement is well documented.

All the projects were set up in such a way as to allow the children considerable opportunities to make decisions and develop a real feeling of ownership and empowerment. The children made choices collectively about such matters as the name of the cake stall they set up and ran, which story to do as a puppet play, how to spend the profit made by their enterprise, and so on. Individually and in small groups they made a whole range of sophisticated decisions – about what to charge for postcards on sale in the museum 'shop', about the content and layout of their page in the class newspaper, about how many tickets to print for the puppet show, what information to include in the programmes, and so on. Many of these decisions involved considerable research and discussion. The mechanism of company board meetings was also used within some of the projects as a way of helping the children to review progress, and discuss and plan the work still to be done.

While, of course, they had their plans for the projects, the teachers involved always attempted, as a further way of empowering the children, to respond to and support initiatives coming from them. This is sometimes referred to as the 'dead bird' model of the curriculum, because children are inclined to bring in this kind of fascinating object, and the skilful early years educator has always made the most of such opportunities. But it is a feature of the curriculum that has been under threat from the pressures of the national curriculum, and which it is desperately important that we preserve.

There are numerous examples of this from all the projects, but let us just mention two from the fashion show. Sometimes occasions arise because children, stimulated by their involvement in the project, bring in items with rich possibilities. During the fashion show project, a child arrived one day with a box full of Victorian hats, and the whole day was given over to examining them, finding out about how they were made, what they were made of, who wore them. Pictures were drawn, the children made their own Victorian hats, and so on.

Other occasions arise when an activity introduced by an adult is developed by the children in unexpected ways. An example of this arose when, as part of the fashion show project, an activity was introduced involving making a 2D scale drawing of the catwalk. This activity, which was planned to take about an hour, lasted for two days, as the children transformed it into a 3D modelling activity. Having completed the 2D drawing, children began to add stand-up proscenium arches, which needed buttresses. Then they raised the catwalk plans onto box bases to show the height, added model pot plants, audiences on seats and delight-fully accurate paper puppets of themselves in costume (initially on straws, but later on strings to facilitate twirling). With their models complete the children then gave miniature performances of the show to a tape of the music.

Opportunities for imaginative play

This last example leads us into our third curriculum principle. Once again, as was reviewed in Chapter 1, there has been renewed interest in the ways that children's natural playfulness, usually given full rein in the home but very much curtailed within the school context, enhances the quality of their learning. Learning through play supports the strategies developed under the previous two headings. It helps children to derive meaning from their experiences. One of the main factors in the efficacy of play is also its self-directedness; play gives children control over their own learning.

Figure 3.5 *Role-play: the museum office*

The play corner in the classrooms during the pro-jects was transformed into an imaginary cake shop, a practice puppet booth, a box office, a newspaper office, a museums office (see Figure 3.5) and a boutique. These were designed and largely built by the children, and played in to the point of destruction. During the puppet theatre project, for example, following the visit to the theatre, some of the children suggested that they turn part of the classroom into a box office. The teacher set about discussing with the class how they would go about rearranging the classroom to accommodate this. Tables were moved, chairs piled up and carpets rearranged. A table was needed for the booking lady, a door for people to walk in, somewhere to display the puppets, a noticeboard for the posters and so on. When the general environment of the box office had been created, discussion followed of what was needed to equip it. A telephone was installed, a computer, paper, pencils, pens, diary, tickets and a telephone book. From then on, throughout the project, there were always children in the box office, busily taking telephone calls, writing messages, issuing tickets, taking money, making programmes and posters, putting up notices and signs and generally becoming thoroughly involved in the exciting new world of theatre management!

This kind of play was engaged in by the children throughout each of the projects with energy and enthusiasm. As the projects developed, it was notable the extent to which new elements of the project, and new information which had been made available to the children, was incorporated in their play.

Integrating the worlds of school and community

The final feature of the projects was the extent to which the divisions between the school and the outside adult community were broken down. As we have discussed, there is an important aspect of this to do with styles of learning, but continuity and good communication between the worlds of home and school is also a vital component in providing young children with emotional security in the classroom.

There were a number of aspects of this attempt at integrating the worlds of school and adult community within the projects:

- The children visited an adult place of work, and often one where adults they knew worked; our observations of the adults explaining their work to the children suggested this was an intense and satisfying experience for both parties.
- Adults visited the classroom to explain their work to the children, and also to work alongside the children with their enterprises; this also, of course, supported the authenticity of the children's enterprises (see Figure 3.6).
- The children interacted with adults in the local community in a business-like manner (formal letters requesting sponsorship, selling advertising space, inviting local dignitaries to open the Grand Launch, giving interviews to the local press about the projects, etc.).
- The projects generated an enthusiasm that led to an enormous involvement of the parents and the wider community in all kinds of ways – loaning resources (exhibits for the museum), helping with

Figure 3.6 *Adults working alongside the children: the local museum warden discusses one of the class's collections with Sam*

making (puppets, costumes, cakes), helping with research (important people being interviewed for the newspaper, and as a source of local history for the museum), attending the Grand Opening or Launch, providing expertise (photographs of the children as models for the fashion page, and the village policeman setting up a mock robbery, both for the newspaper), offering sponsorship, providing ideas and moral support.

The involvement and enthusiasm of the children and of the local communities for these enterprise projects has been particularly rewarding. An atmosphere of real teamwork was generated in which young children, parents, teachers and community shared the pleasure of cooperative purpose and achievement. The museum exhibitions, for example, were so popular that, when they were taken down in school, they had to be immediately remounted within the local museum, which received large numbers of interested visitors, many of whom purchased some of the postcards designed and made by the children (see Figure 3.7). The video of the fashion show quickly sold out, with copies being sent as far away as the Orkneys and northern Norway!

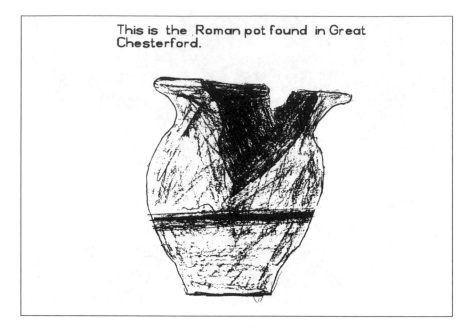

This is the Roman pot found in Great Chesterford.

Figure 3.7 *Alexander's postcard: one of half a dozen which sold like hot cakes at the local museum*

Planning and assessment

Carrying out the kind of projects described in this chapter with young children can be an enormously rewarding and effective way of organising and developing the curriculum. As with any high-quality teaching, however, it depends vitally upon detailed planning based upon careful assessments of the children's needs and abilities. We therefore need to conclude with some remarks about these crucially important aspects of the early years educator's work.

Progression

The topic-based approach to the curriculum has commonly been criticised because of the lack of progression in activities. One argument for teaching a more subject-based curriculum has been that it enables concepts and skills to be introduced and then built upon more systematically. It is, however, perfectly possible to build progression into the activities within a topic, given careful task analysis and planning. As part of the planning for the kind of enterprise projects described in this chapter, for example, it is important to analyse the planned activities in terms of different areas of the curriculum (see Figure 3.8). This ensures that a good range and balance of skills is being addressed. It also leads on to an analysis of the nature of the skills and understandings to be taught. That the activities are placed in the meaningful context provided by the topic or project, however, enhances the children's understandings about their purpose and thus supports

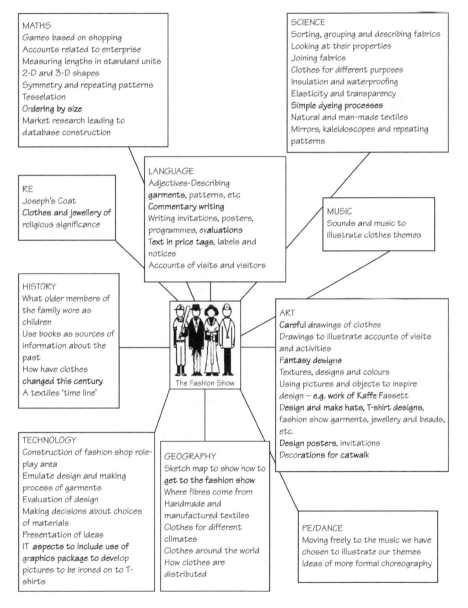

Figure 3.8 *Analysis of planned activities for the fashion show project by subject*

rather than detracts from the real progression in learning. Here are a couple of examples from the fashion show project:

Letter writing

> **Introduced** with letters to Father Christmas (not part of the project), which were chatty, informal, and concluded with 'love from . . .'.
>
> **Developed** within the project with formal thank you letters to some people from Marks & Spencer's children's clothes department who had been in to school to talk to the children about the design process; these letters had a more formal layout with the school address, proper indentation, the date, began with 'Dear Sir' and concluded with 'Yours sincerely . . .', but the content was very straightforward.
>
> **Concluded** with formal letters with more complex content; these involved applying for sponsorship, inviting special guests to the fashion show, sending a charity donation (to Radio Cambridgeshire's Send-a-Cow appeal on this occasion!) and so forth (Figure 3.2 is a good example of this stage); invariably replies were received to these letters, also written very formally.

Tessellation

> **Introduced** by looking at patchwork patterns on fabrics and tessellating squares, rectangles and hexagons of different patterns; all these shapes tessellate with themselves in any orientation.
>
> **Developed** by looking at pattern cutting for various shapes which tessellate when the shape is rotated, for example, T-shirt, sock, skirt (see Figure 3.9).
>
> **Concluded** by looking at real dress-making patterns that did not tessellate and attempting to fit them onto rectangles of fabric in the most economical way (i.e. fitting in the most patterns with least waste, as we had seen at the clothes factory we visited).

Assessment

Early years educators have always placed great emphasis on making careful observations and assessments. In order to make assessments of an individual child's understanding or level of skill it is important to plan activities that will enable the extent to which a child has made the new understanding or skill their own to be seen. This involves another kind of progression from *structured or closed activities* to introduce the new skills or

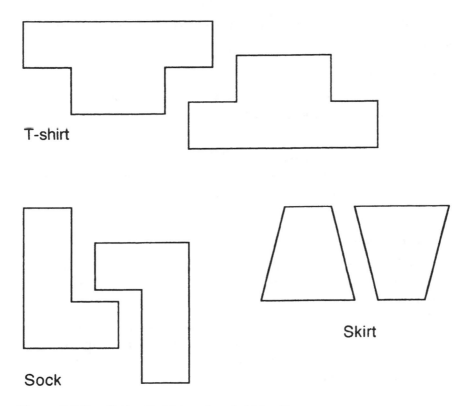

Figure 3.9 *Tessellating T-shirt, sock and skirt patterns*

concepts developing on to more *open-ended activities*, which give the child opportunities to use what they have learnt in their own innovative ways.

It is entirely possible to build this kind of progression of activities into enterprise projects. The meaningful context, furthermore, provides a real purpose to the activities, and the child's real level of skill or understanding can be much more validly revealed than when they are carrying out an activity simply for its own sake, where the child's motivation and under-standing of the requirements of the task are sometimes open to question. More open-ended activities reveal a child's thinking and abilities much more clearly than closed tasks, particularly of the *Blue Peter* variety, where all the child has to do is follow instructions. They also provide children with opportunities to express themselves, to gain feelings of ownership and to have a more memorable, first-hand experience. This is of course often what is happening, as we have reviewed, when children engage in imaginative play related to significant new experiences, and their play can be an important source for observations and assessments for this reason.

Within the enterprise projects many of the activities were planned with this kind of assessment in mind. Here are two examples, both from the fashion show project:

Measuring materials for costumes

> **Structured or closed activities** in which the children were taught various techniques for measuring themselves, including the use of appropriate measuring units and instruments.

> **Open-ended activities** where the children were required to use their measurements of themselves to measure out materials so that their costumes would be the right size; choice of method of measurement left to the children.

Emergent writing

> **Structured or closed activities** in which the children were taught the names of different garments, how to write out sizes, amounts of money, addresses and so forth.

> **Open-ended activities** in the role-play area, the 'Clothes R Us' boutique, including, for example, the provision of an order book in which children, role-playing as shop assistants, could write out orders taken from other children role-playing as customers (see Figure 3.10).

Differentiation

Having planned for a progression in the children's understandings and skills, and made assessments of their responses to the various activities, it is, of course, vital to differentiate the activities so that each child can succeed at an appropriate level. There are numerous ways in which this can be done, and once again this needs to be planned. Below are some suggested means of doing this and some examples from the enterprise projects.

- **Outcome**: perhaps the simplest form of differentiation is to set up an activity so that the requirements are the same for all the children, but it is so open-ended that they can respond at their own level; *examples*: designing a poster, making a model catwalk.

- **Support**: once again, the requirements can be the same, but the level of the outcome needs to be similar, so this common level of achievement is reached by means of variable levels of adult support; *examples*: making a costume, baking a cake.

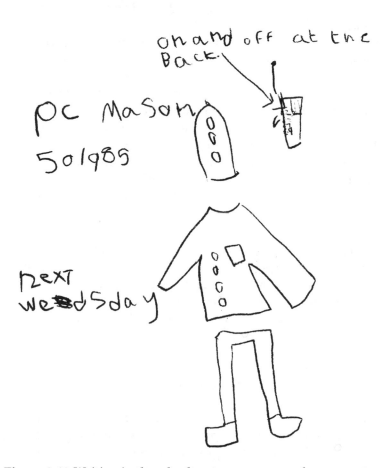

Figure 3.10 *Writing in the role-play area as a means of assessment: orders placed in the 'Clothes R Us' order book*

- **Recording method**: the activity may be the same for everyone, but the children may be required to record what they have done in more or less sophisticated ways; *example*: a science activity on the qualities of different textiles recorded by sticking samples of the textiles on paper, by drawings or by descriptive writing.

- **Complexity**: finally, the children may be given tasks to do that are all related to the same skill or concept, but which are at different stages in the progression of work planned; *example*: mapwork related to the destinations of different garments made at the clothes factory involving activities at three levels:
  - countries located on world map and drawings of garments attached;
  - journey of garments to Hong Kong investigated and a list made of the continents they travel through;
  - journey of garments through the UK to the port investigated; compass directions, road numbers and towns travelled through recorded.

As suggested above, differentiating the presentation and demands of a task by these means should lead to its successful completion by every pupil. In planning for this, one approach is to think about the various 'subtasks' involved and to then view them in reverse order. It is the actions needed to complete the task, the fastening of the final button on the coat, that children must be encouraged to complete without aid, however small this step may be. Once that step is mastered the starting point for the task can be moved back until the child is managing all the steps from start to finish.

Thus, in writing a story there is little joy for a child with difficulties in meeting the differentiated expectations of a teacher by managing the scribing of 'Once upon a time . . .' and no more. It is the satisfaction of writing 'and they all lived happily ever after' which offers the real sense of achievement. The learner has independently added the last piece of jigsaw, and hence has ownership of the completed puzzle.

Conclusion

Within education there currently is growing interest related to developing more experiential, problem-solving approaches to teaching and learning across the curriculum (Fisher, 1987, provides a good review of work in primary schools). We have attempted to show that enterprise projects can provide an excellent basis for this kind of development. There was an intensity of 'real' learning for the children within these projects that was very special. The enthusiasm with which the children, their teachers, parents and other members of the local communities still recall the projects, in some cases now after several years have elapsed, is a testimony to their significance for all who participated in them. We have attempted to demonstrate in this chapter that such projects form an excellent basis for organising an appropriate and effective early years curriculum. Through this kind of project it is possible to meet the needs of young children. They arrive at school confident and expert learners in the informal context of their home environment. Through the kind of curriculum organisation proposed here they are enabled to make the transition to becoming equally effective and assured in the environment of the school.

Pointers for organising the early years curriculum

- With thought and imagination, it is possible to organise the early years curriculum in ways that are compatible with the demands of the national curriculum, and with our understandings about how children learn
- Young children's learning will be enhanced when:
    1 the content of the curriculum is 'meaningful' to them and related to their existing knowledge and interests;
    2 they are active participants in their learning rather than just passive recipients – they should have opportunities to make their own decisions about their learning;
    3 they are encouraged to indulge their natural inclination to engage in imaginative play related to significant life experiences;
    4 they are emotionally secure because there is continuity and good communication between the worlds of home and school.
- These principles can be embodied powerfully within 'enterprise' projects
- The success of this model of curriculum organisation depends upon:
    1 clearly identified progressions of related activities;
    2 assessment of children's level of understanding or skill using open-ended activities;
    3 differentiation of activities so that each child can succeed at an appropriate level.

References

Anning, A. (1991) *The First Years at School*, Buckingham: Open University Press.

Atkinson, S. (ed.) (1992) *Mathematics with Reason*, London: Hodder & Stoughton.

Bennett, N., Desforges, C., Cockburn, A. and Wilkinson, B. (1984) *The Quality of Pupil Learning Experiences*, London: Lawrence Erlbaum.

Blenkin, G. and Kelly, V. (eds) (1994) *The National Curriculum and Early Learning, an Evaluation*, London: Paul Chapman.

Bruce, T. (1987) *Early Childhood Education*, London: Hodder & Stoughton.

Cleave, S. and Brown, S. (1991) *Early to school: 4-year-olds in infant classes*, London: Routledge.

Coltman, P. and Whitebread, D. (1992) The little bakery: an infant class develops EIU, *Economic Awareness*, 5, 1, 3–9.

DES (1985) *The Curriculum from 5 to 16*, Curriculum Matters 2, HMI Series, London: HMSO.

DES (1990) *Mini-enterprise in schools: some aspects of current practice: a report of HMI*, London: HMSO.

DfEE (1998) *The National Literacy Strategy: Framework for Teaching*, Suffolk: DfEE.

DfEE (1999) *The National Numeracy Strategy*, Suffolk: DfEE.

Drummond, M.J., Lally, M. and Pugh, G. (eds) (1989) *Working with Children: Developing a Curriculum for the Early Years*, Nottingham: National Children's Bureau/Nottingham Educational Supplies.

Early Years Curriculum Group (1989) *Early Childhood Education: The Early Years Curriculum and the National Curriculum*, Stoke-on-Trent: Trentham Books.

Early Years Curriculum Group (2002) *Onwards and Upwards: Building on the Foundation Stage*, Early Years Curriculum Group.

Fisher, R. (ed.) (1987) *Problem Solving in Primary Schools*, Oxford: Basil Blackwell.

Hall, N. (1989) *Writing with Reason*, Sevenoaks: Hodder & Stoughton.

Hughes, M. (1986) *Children and Number*, Oxford: Basil Blackwell.

ILEA (1987) *The Early Years: A Curriculum for Young Children*, London: ILEA Centre for Learning Resources.

OFSTED (1993) *First Class: The Standards and Quality of Education in Reception Classes*, London: HMSO.

Palmer, J. and Pettitt, D. (1993) *Topic Work in the Early Years*, London: Routledge.

QCA (2000) *Curriculum Guidance for the Foundation Stage*, London: QCA.

Tizard, B. and Hughes, M. (1984) *Young Children Learning*, London: Fontana.

Whitebread, D., Coltman, P. and Farmery, J. (1993) 'Project file: a puppet theatre', *Child Education*, 70, 6, 31–8.

Whitebread, D., Coltman, P. and Bryant, P. (1994) 'Project file: a class museum', *Child Education*, 71, 12, 27–34.

Whitebread, D., Coltman, P. and Davison, S. (1995) 'Project file: infant newshounds', *Child Education*, 72, 1, 29–36.

CHAPTER 4

'I'm putting crosses for the letters I don't know'

ASSESSMENT IN THE EARLY YEARS

Rachel Sparks Linfield, Paul Warwick and Christine Parker

For those concerned with developing children's learning in the early years, assessment has always been seen as: 'an integral part of the educational process, continually providing both feedback and feedforward' (DES, 1987, para. 4).

Early years educators monitor children's development to inform their day-to-day teaching and to allow them to report learners' achievements. They use formative assessment, where the emphasis is on planning the next steps to be taken with a child, and summative assessment to provide a snapshot of the child's achievements and abilities at a particular stage. In doing this they have made assessment all-embracing, attempting to build a picture of the 'whole child', believing that:

> The process of assessing children's learning – by looking closely at it and striving to understand it – is the only certain safeguard against children's failure, the only certain guarantee of children's progress and development.
>
> (Drummond, 1993, p. 10)

In this chapter we use case study evidence to illustrate some of the assessment principles and practices adopted by successful early years educators. In doing so, we make a distinction between assessment *for* learning (formative assessment), which involves the use of classroom assessment to improve learning, and assessment *of* learning (summative assessment), which measures what pupils know or can do. Underpinning all assessment practices is the role and value of observation as a tool for informing the early years educator. We will focus on observation techniques in the second half of this chapter. To begin with we will describe assessment for learning, central to which are the following principles.

Assessment for learning:

- is embedded in the teaching and learning process of which it is an essential part;
- shares learning goals with pupils;
- helps pupils to know and recognise the standards to aim for;
- provides feedback that leads pupils to identify what they should do next to improve;
- has a commitment that every pupil can improve;
- involves both teacher and pupils in reviewing and reflecting on pupil performance and progress;
- involves pupils in self assessment.

(QCA website, 2001)

Assessment *for* learning in the early years

The findings of Black and William (1998), developed by Shirley Clarke's work with thousands of primary school teachers (2001), provides a series of strategies for developing effective formative assessment. Key points for early years educators include:

- the necessity of sharing learning intentions with children;
- the need to use questioning and discussion to support learning;
- the desirability of encouraging children to make assessments of their own work;
- the importance of positive feedback and marking;
- the need to develop individual target-setting;
- the vital requirement to adjust teaching to take account of learning.

We will now consider each of these strategies.

Sharing learning intentions

Educators understand the necessity of defining clear learning objectives to ensure that both teaching and assessment are focused. However, it is also essential that these 'learning intentions' are shared with the children, in terms that help them to make sense of the purpose of the task. Giving instructions for how a task is to be carried out is different from stating the learning intentions of the task, and children need both if they are to feel the sense of success that accompanies learning. For example, the following instructions, might be given for painting a rainbow:

> Today I want you to paint a picture of a rainbow. Here is a chart of the rainbow colours that we have been looking at this week. You should have a piece of white paper, a long, flat-headed brush and some paints. Paint the most beautiful rainbow that you can.

While there is nothing really wrong with these instructions, they do not give the learning intention of the task. The instructions are likely to lead pupils to ask a number of questions such as:

- Must I fill the paper?
- Must I only do a rainbow?
- What does beautiful mean – really bright or soft colours?

These questions reflect children's uncertainty about what the teacher is looking for. Typical manifestations of this uncertainty include:

- Children asking for the instructions to be repeated.
- Time-wasting tactics.
- Do nothing, wait until a neighbour starts and then copy.

The essential adjunct to the instructions is therefore a statement of learning intentions for the task. For example:

> I would like you to show that a rainbow is made of different bands of colour, and that those colours go in the same order no matter how big or small the rainbow is that you paint.

Educators should, as far as possible, avoid including the learning intentions *within* the instructions as this can be muddling for a child. Where educators and children have a clear, shared understanding of the learning intentions assessment will have greater meaning.

Using questioning and discussion to support learning

Educators are adept at using a variety of questions for different purposes. Early years pupils benefit from questioning that will allow them to articulate *their* ideas. Only then can this information be used in teaching that is targeted to develop learning.

The following two transcripts illustrate clearly how questioning and discussion can be used to ascertain different starting points for teaching and learning for different children. A class of 4–5-year-olds was working on a project entitled 'All Around Me'. Children had been on walks and collected items for their 'interest table'. They had looked at the local countryside and had made drawings of all that they had seen. The teacher became aware that children talked about living things but was uncertain that all her class used the phrase 'living thing' to mean the same thing. During an afternoon of 'All Around Me' activities she showed the picture reproduced in Figure 4.1. and asked children to pick out living and non-living things. Transcripts of two of the conversations are given. The children had all been in the reception class for two terms.

Conversation 1 between teacher (T) and a girl aged 5 (G).

T   What in the picture is living?
G   Nothing, it's only a picture.
T   Pretend it isn't a picture but it's outside.
G   It's all living. The hedgehog, the sun, the tree, the apple, the mummy, the smoke – it's moving.
T   Is the car living?
G   Yes, it's all real. Not pretend. It's real.

This conversation indicates that this child believed 'living' to mean 'real'.
Conversation 2 between teacher (T) and boy aged 4 years 7 months (B).

T   Can you see two things in this picture that are living?
B   Mmm. The butterfly?
T   And?

Figure 4.1 *A picture containing living and non-living things*

B   The children.
T   Can you see anything that is not living?
B   The hedgehog might be dead. The car might have gone over it.
T   Is –
B   But I don't think so. I think it's happy.
T   Is the house living?
B   People might live in it.
T   Is the tree living?
B   No.
T   Why not?
B   It just grows. It's not 'alive'.
T   How do you mean, 'It's not alive'?
B   It can't walk.

In this conversation the boy readily identified humans and animals as living. Trees, however, were not viewed as alive. As a result of these, and similar conversations, the teacher realised that within her reception class the word 'living' held many different meanings. The majority saw animals and humans as living but did not view plants in the same way. For some 'living' was synonymous with 'can move'. The teacher followed up the conversations with more experiences of 'living things'. The discussions provided clear evidence of understanding and misunderstanding of a concept. They demonstrate the importance of listening to children in order to assess understanding.

While considering the use of questioning and discussion in obtaining evidence for formative assessment, it seems sensible to go further and to consider how both the products of children's work and observations of children at work can be used in combination with questioning and discussion to build a more rounded profile of the learner.

In the following example (taken from Sparks Linfield, 1994) a class of 5–6-year-olds was asked to observe a straw in a glass of water and to draw what they had observed. The teacher hoped that the children would notice that the straw appeared to bend. The teacher let four children at a time observe and draw and to use the drawings as evidence of observing the bent straw. The following conversations, however, again show the importance of talking to children and watching them at work. The drawings produced by one group of pupils appear in Figure 4.2.

The drawings produced by Lucy and Elizabeth seem to reflect knowledge that the straw appears to bend. Edmund, though, seems to have only seen a straight straw. Observation of the children at work, and discussion with them, however, showed otherwise.

The teacher was, in the words of Clayden and Peacock (1994), observing

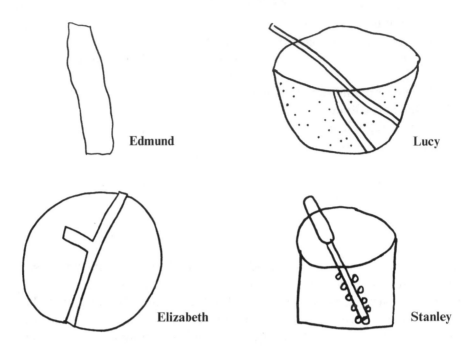

Figure 4.2 *Four children's drawings of a straw in a glass of water*

'with a purpose'. While watching the children she realised that Stanley was not drawing what he had observed. Instead, he tried to copy Lucy's drawing and then decided to draw the pipette he had used in a previous experiment. The teacher was most impressed by Lucy when she saw the elliptical bowl. They discussed her finished picture:

T   What have you drawn?
L   The straw.
T   What's under the straw? [*She pointed at what she imagined was the straw's reflection.*]
L   It's that mark on the table. I did it when I was colouring.
T   And the dots? [*She thought they were bubbles.*]
L   That's pen on the table. Shall I get a cloth to wipe it off?

   This conversation showed that what the teacher was seeing in the picture was not what Lucy had intended. The final surprise came through talking to Edmund.

T   Can you see the straw in the glass?
E   Yes.
T   Does it look like the one out of the water?

E   No, the one in the water's bent.
T   Why haven't you drawn it bent?
E   'Cos it's only pretend. Really the straw is straight.

Edmund had not only observed the bent straw but also knew this was just an optical effect. Without discussion, this knowledge would not have been evident. The experience of watching the children at work, and of discussing their drawings, raises the question of how often through looking at 'written' evidence we make the assumption that children have understood a concept when discussion would prove otherwise. Equally, how often do we think children have not understood when actually they do? Frequently children perceive things differently from adults. Many children use drawings to record what they 'know' rather than what they 'see'. Clearly discussion has much to offer here to validate assessment.

Child self-assessment

It may seem that a call to involve early years children in the assessment of their own work is an unnecessary burden on the already over-loaded educator. However, we believe that self-assessment by pupils 'far from being a luxury, is in fact an essential component of formative assessment' (Black and William, 1998, p. 10). If sharing learning intentions with pupils is likely to promote learning, encouraging pupils to respond to how well *they* feel those intentions have been met is surely equally important. The role of the educator is to train children to look for specifics related to learning intentions and to comment on these, however simply. Much is written and discussed on the subject of allowing pupils to take ownership of their work. Modelling by the educator of the process of commenting on a task is one way that self-assessment can be encouraged, and allows for a substantive development for children in adopting such ownership.

Positive pupil attitudes to work are clearly essential if motivation is to be maintained, self-esteem is to be enhanced and learning progress is to be made. Many children's enjoyment of assessing their own performance is enhanced if they feel they can convey how they feel about the work they are undertaking, as well as commenting on their progress. While simply talking to children can provide evidence of positive or negative attitudes, the example in Figure 4.3 shows a 'smiley face' assessment, completed by a 6-year-old boy, forming part of a review of work. Self-assessment such as this can help children to take responsibility for their own learning and to develop their autonomy. Children who are unable to complete such sheets unaided enjoy working with an adult or older child to scribe for them.

Another means of children themselves contributing to an assessment of

Name: Jonathan

Science Record for the Summer Term 1993

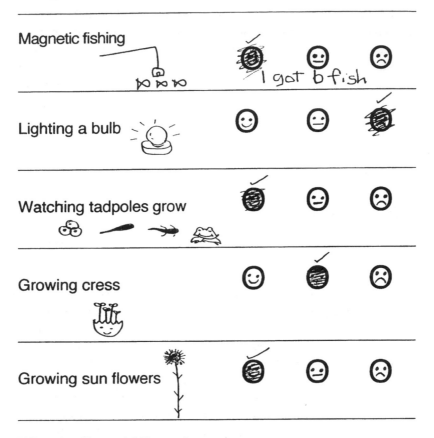

Magnetic fishing — I got b fish

Lighting a bulb

Watching tadpoles grow

Growing cress

Growing sun flowers

What I still would like to know is....

Where do tadpoles get the legs from
I want to lite a bulb My bulb
dident werk

Figure 4.3 *Self-assessment by Jonathan, aged 6*

their understanding comes through the use of concept mapping. Many educators will already be familiar with concept maps as a means of assessing children's knowledge prior to an activity. As envisaged by Novak and Gowin (1984) they are a method of constructing hierarchies of concepts, with 'propositional links' showing how those concepts are related. With young children, however, it is more sensible to simplify concept mapping, making it a method of showing links between concepts but ignoring the hierarchical structure of those concepts. To give an example, consider the words 'tree' and 'water'; how are these related? Using an arrow to show the nature and direction of the relationship, the simple map illustrated in Figure 4.4 might be produced:

This simple idea can be extended by the educator to establish the initial understanding that children have of key ideas they will encounter in a lesson or through a topic. The concept maps in Figures 4.5 and 4.6 were drawn by two 6-year-old children prior to carrying out some work with plants. They were based upon the following words provided by the teacher – seed, flower, bulb, water, light, bud, stalk:

The understanding expressed by the children in the two maps is substantially different. This suggests that even if similar activities were carried out by these children the educator would have different expectations of them and would be likely to question them in a manner more focused to their level of understanding. This technique is an important one for any educator with a broadly constructivist view of learning, where the notion of children constructing their own sense of the world is central (see Chapter 1). For the constructivist 'what is already in the learner's mind matters' (Ollerenshaw and Ritchie, 1993) since it will provide a basis for subsequent teaching and for the conceptual change that results. Harlen (2000) points out how easy even very young children find the technique, and in assessing pre- and post-teaching maps the educator is able not only to see how the child's concepts have developed, but also to assess the effectiveness of the work that has been carried out.

It will be apparent that children need to be taught this technique and

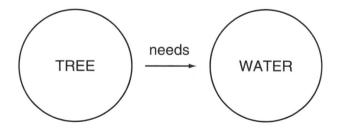

Figure 4.4 *A concept map showing the relationship between 'tree' and 'water'*

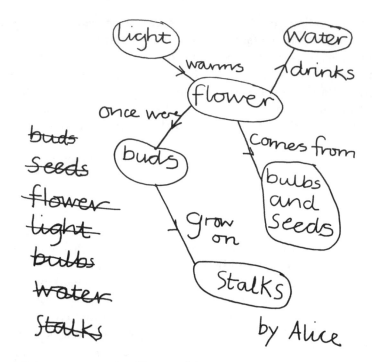

buds
seeds
flower
light
bulbs
water
Stalks

Figure 4.5 *A concept map by Alice, aged 6*

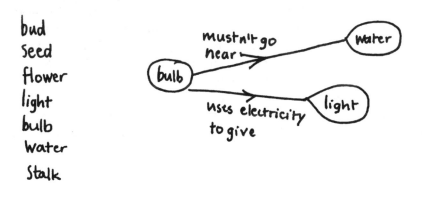

bud
Seed
flower
light
bulb
Water
Stalk

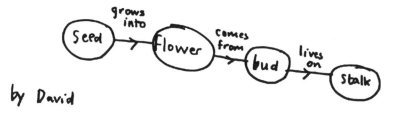

Figure 4.6 *A concept map by David, aged 6*

need to understand particularly how important the 'joining words' are in making the whole thing have meaning. It will also be apparent that concept maps used with children after work on a topic provide just one more method by which they can, with help, reflect upon their own learning. As with all methods used for recording children's thoughts, it should not be used too frequently. This is not just to prevent fatigue on the part of the children; concepts maps are time-consuming for the educator and the children to analyse and should be seen as only one tool in the assessment armoury.

Feedback, marking and individual target-setting

Feedback for very young children will inevitably be oral, with written feedback being incorporated as children are increasingly able to interpret symbols, such as smiley faces, and read comments used by the educator. There are, however, several important principles that should be applied to all feedback, some of which relate to target-setting.

Feedback needs to be provided as promptly as possible, and for young children this can often mean during the course of an activity. It needs to be positive, reflecting on success in relation to the learning intentions of the task. Stating the next achievable target should also be part of the purpose of feedback. Obviously, with young children, any targets will be stated in very simple terms and children will need to be reminded of them in future work. This is where recording of assessment information is so important, as no educator can expect to hold essential 'next steps' for all children in their head. Equally important, however, is the view of assessment as a sampling process, whereby the focus shifts from child to child and from one area of the curriculum to another. It is impossible to give detailed feedback and targets to all children for all work undertaken, just as it is impossible to engage all pupils in self-assessment for all tasks. Provided that the key issues we have discussed relating to effective assessment for learning are borne in mind, however, children's learning is likely to be promoted in any educational setting.

Adjusting teaching to take account of learning

There is an intimate and unbreakable link between effective teaching and effective planning and assessment. The three, together, form a cycle of action that should lead to the curriculum being increasingly refined for the child. When working with early years children it is vital that the assessments and subsequent changes to the curriculum consider the whole child. A child who is assessed as having weak fine motor skills may be unable to

complete a practical activity but have the conceptual understanding to follow what is happening. At such times, the careful matching for both skills
and understanding can lead to more productive and enjoyable learning.

Assessment *of* learning in the early years

To restate, assessment of learning or summative assessment, shows us what
children know or can do. In the early years summative assessments
acknowledge the holistic nature of how children learn and that children
learn through play; they are planned at key times and are informed
through observation.

Observations are on-going throughout the child's early years experience
and the early years educator's role is to make sense of this data, share it
with each child's parents and carers, and involve the child in the assessment process and therefore personalize their learning. Nutbrown talks of
how:

> Close and systematic observations can identify the threads of
> children's thinking, their patterns of development and interest. More
> complete pictures of children's knowing are only obtained when
> educators are concerned for children as a whole.
>
> (Nutbrown, 1999, p. 124)

A further description of the value of observation follows, concluding
with two practical examples of observation in action. The chapter ends by
recognizing the need sometimes to plan specific tasks to ensure children's
knowledge, understanding and skills of a specific learning outcome.

The value of observation in the early years

Observing children at play informs us about what they have learnt through
the taught curriculum, their interests and what makes sense to them. The
observation process enables early years educators to identify appropriate
ways to further support and extend the children's learning, and to signpost
progress in their learning and development. Observations need to be
collated for each child and the use of a document such as a 'Record of
Achievement' (Caverstede Early Years Centre, 2000) enables adults to
ensure that observations cover all aspects of the early years curriculum.
The possibility of developing child ownership is made easier when Records
of Achievement are accessible on a daily basis.

Observation is the key to unravelling and supporting children's learning, and celebrating each child's achievements. Drummond (1993) clarifies the depth to which we can go in terms of developing our understanding of children's achievements and how children frequently exceed our expectations. Through observation of children's play, early years educators can assess what each child is capable of independently. When children are engaged in play they frequently show high levels of well-being and involvement (Laevers, 1997). Observation provides an insight into each child's world. Susan Isaacs, an early years pioneer in the first half of the twentieth century, explored and articulated the value of observation.

> If we watch him when he is free to play as he will, the child shows us all that he is wishing and fearing, all that he is pondering over and aiming to do. He shows us what the grown-ups are to him, what attitudes he perceives in them, what his feelings are about them, and what are the happenings in the physical world which stir him to seek understanding and control.
>
> (Isaacs, 1954, p. 6)

However, it is not enough to gather observations. What is required is the theoretical knowledge to analyse the observations effectively and efficiently. From this knowledge base we are able to create a learning environment that will support each child's self-initiated learning within meaningful contexts.

Observation in action

Observations include snapshots of achievements, often recorded on post-it notes, and longer narrative observations which provide a different perspective on a child's development and learning

Snapshots

In a busy early years setting, it is not always possible or desirable for the early years practitioner to be writing lengthy observations. Writing short notes enables us to capture key learning events, whether they are planned by the adult or occur spontaneously. These snapshots can be organized within the different areas of learning as defined in the early years Foundation Stage (DfES, 2007, p. 11), the guidance for children aged from birth to 5 years in England. For ease of organization, a grid on the wall defining each area of learning can help early years practitioners to decide where the observation best fits, and to see whether one aspect of learning needs to be a specific focus for snapshot observations. This is a strategy frequently used in reception classes and helps all team members to identify the gaps.

The example in Table 4.1 shows a page of one child's achievements in 'communication, language and literacy' (DfES, 2007, p. 13). The child, Alex, is in a Year 1 class in a primary school in the east of England.

Narrative observations

Narrative observations provide the early years practitioner and the child's parents/carers with a more in-depth insight into the child's achievements and a consideration of their future learning needs. Quality not quantity is the key; for example, in a reception class between three and six narrative observations maybe completed over the academic year. A narrative

Table 4.1 Snapshot observations to support Alex's learning and development in communication, language and literacy.

07.11.06 Alex tried to join in with the phonics session, when listening for initial sounds and even recognized 'n' as a final sound.	05.12.06 Alex made a telescope with a piece of A4 paper, at his own initiation. He could describe how he had made it and wrote his name on it with confidence. Alex was proud of his achievement.
11.01.07 Alex used a full stop in his writing assessment. He said, 'That means I've finished.'	14.03.07 Alex said, 'I can draw fish, now I'm going to colour it – pink! Yellow! And then that bit, his tail is just yellow.' 'He's jumped out of the sea to make big waves and there's going to be more even bigger waves.' Alex used talk to inform, describe and to tell a story.
01.05.07 Alex was motivated to create his own book about whales. He uses non-fiction books to develop his knowledge of sea-life. Alex wrote a short story and the content is more imaginative than factual. See his Record of Achievement for a photocopy of his representational drawing and writing.	14.06.07 Alex joins in when spelling words and he joined in positively and then said 'I'm putting crosses for the letters I don't know.' He is able to recognize sounds in words.

observation can emphasise the holistic aspect of children's learning and development, and indicate clearly how the child's interactions, actions and words support all aspects of the early years curriculum. The first of two examples provides assessment evidence for one child (see Table 4.2).

The second example, in Table 4.3, describes a group of 5- and 6-year-old children playing in the role-play area. The role-play area is organized as a travel agency, airport and aeroplane. The focus of this observation is in the aeroplane.

Planning summative tasks

From time to time it is necessary to assess for summative purposes some aspects of child development. This may result from the educator's desire to 'run a check' on the appropriateness of their own formative assessments, or it may be built into a school's assessment procedures. The experience in England is certainly that many schools link intermittent summative tasks to a rolling programme of analysis linked to national curriculum levels of attainment. Whatever the reasons for embarking upon what might be seen as more formal school-devised assessments, there are a number of principles and procedures that we feel should be adopted.

The first of these is that, for these summative assessments, the focus should be limited. The activity that the children are carrying out is likely to allow them to use a range of skills and concepts, yet for assessment purposes the educator should focus on just two or three assessment objectives, which in England may or may not relate to the Foundation Stage curriculum 'stepping stones' or to national curriculum Programme of Study statements. For example, in an activity on changing materials, the teacher may have an assessment question related to science processes:

Assessment question: Can the pupils recognise when a test or comparison is unfair?

Having defined what is to be assessed it is now possible to sort out some precise evidence, related to the specific activity, that will give a guide to whether the child is achieving the objective. In relation to our example it may be:

Evidence: Child is able to articulate why items selected for melting must be the same size.

Having established up to four assessment questions to be answered (no more!), the educator will then give the task to the children and, working

Table 4.2 Observation notes to support Bethany's learning and development

CHILD: Bethany Jackson   DATE: 25/4/06   YEAR GROUP: F/S Blue
Baby Clinic/Role Play

TIMES	OBSERVATIONS MADE
9.20 9.50 Bethany was very interested and motivated through this activity. She interacted well with the others and took turns. She enjoyed herself and was engaged for about 25 minutes. She understood the role play well.	Bethany went into the baby clinic and immediately picked up a doll. She told the others, Katie and Rebecca, that she would like to be the mum coming to the clinic. She pushed the pushchair around the classroom saying 'good morning'. She then arrived at the 'clinic' and sat in the waiting area. She waited for the 'Receptionist' to call her name and then handed over her form but asked for help to fill it in. She told the babies name and then answered questions about her age and weight and asked for her to be weighed again. She carefully undressed the baby and put her on the scales. After looking at the scales she spoke more about feeding bottles and said the baby liked milk. She 'washed' her baby with baby wipes. She struggled a bit putting nappy on but persevered getting sellotape to stick to it. Finished the role play by saying she was taking her baby home.

Evidence for Achievement Towards the Early Learning Goals (DfEE/QCA, 2000 p26, DfES/QCA, 2003)
Personal, Social and Emotional Development: Dispositions and Attitudes: Displays high levels of involvement in self-chosen activities; selects and uses activities and resources independently; continues to be interested, motivated and excited to learn; is confident to try new activities and initiate ideas; maintains interest and concentrates.
Personal, Social and Emotional Development: Emotional Development: Responds to significant experiences, showing a range of feelings when appropriate; has a developing awareness of own needs, views and feelings and is sensitive to he needs, views and feelings of others.
Communication, Language and Literacy: Language for Communication and Thinking: initiates communication with others, displaying greater confidence in informal contexts; talks activities through, reflecting on and modifying actions; uses language to imagine and recreate roles and experiences; interacts with others in a variety of contexts, taking turns in conversation; uses talk to organize, sequence and clarify thinking, ideas, feelings and events.
Communication, Language and Literacy: Linking Sounds and Letters: links some sounds and letters; names and sounds letters of the alphabet.
Communication, Language and Literacy: Writing: Represents some sounds correctly in writing; writes own name and other words from memory.
Knowledge and Understanding of the World: Identifies obvious similarities and differences when exploring and observing.

Table 4.3 Observation notes in the role play area

Area: Role Play   Children: Six   Adults: 1

Observation

There are six children playing in the area. Laura and Hannah are passengers and Amy, Leanne and Sam are a members of the cabin crew and Dylan is a pilot.

Sam says, 'Take off!'

Dylan explains, 'I'm driving.'

Laura says, 'I'll just get my passport.'

Amy has a clipboard and says, 'Here's your beans and chips, it's Hannah's beans and chips, what can I get you? Leanne we need these on . . . . we have to work together.'

Sam informs everyone, 'There's one more space, we've only got two persons.'

The children continue to role play their different roles.

Sam says, 'Laura needs some Cocoa Pops . . . Frosties, no more.'

Amy organizes roles and directs Leanne, 'You do the passports and I'll do the food.'

Leanne tells the passengers, 'We need passports.'

Sam intervenes, 'I need the passports, I need another passport.'

Amy says, 'Another beans and chips please.' She turns to the adult present and says, 'You haven't got your seatbelt on madam.'

Sam asks, 'Whose holiday is number 6?'

Dylan informs, 'We're going down.'

Sam asks the passengers, 'Who ordered India? Going to India? Because we are there now, no it's India.'

Dylan reiterates, 'The plane's stopping and going down!'

Analysis

The children are using talk to describe actions, inform, direct each other, imagine, ask questions and to keep the narrative flowing. They are able to play collaboratively, roles are allocated and they have an understanding of the different parts they play. The children use their personal experiences of air travel to inform their play but also change some sequences of travel, e.g., asking to see passports on the aeroplane.

Sam refers to India, one of the countries the children have been learning about.

Future Actions

For an adult to model the different roles to unravel some of the confusion about when you have to show your passport.

For the children to create more props to use in their play, including tickets, boarding cards and menus.

Support the children in making a seating plan.

with them, will assess their performance. Again, in England, what the teacher at Key Stage 1 will need to consider is the extent to which pupils have made progress. In national curriculum terms, this may mean a movement within a level of attainment.

Hurst and Lally have commented:

> Assessment of young children must cover all aspects of a child's development and must be concerned with attitudes, feelings, social and physical characteristics. . . . Learning is not compartmentalised under subject headings for young children.
>
> (1992, p. 55)

Many early years educators show clear ability and commitment to assessments that involve the whole child. The following points are, we believe, central to effective assessment in the early years:

Pointers for assessment in the early years

- Be aware of the wide variety of opportunities for formative assessment.
- Plan for and take time to listen to and observe children.
- Appreciate that discussion holds the key to much effective assessment.
- Keep a notebook with a page for each child for formative assessment; jot down useful observations and discussion points, dating each entry.
- Feed assessment information into planning for future teaching.

References

Black, P. and William, D. (1998) *Inside the Black Box: Raising Standards through Classroom Assessment*, London: King's College.

Caverstede Early Years Centre (2000) *Record of Achievement*, Peterborough: Caverstede Early Years Centre.

Clarke, S. (2001) *Unlocking Formative Assessment: Practical Strategies for Enhancing Pupils' Learning in the Primary Classroom*, London: Hodder & Stoughton.

Clayden, E. and Peacock, A.(1994) *Science for Curriculum Leaders*, London: Routledge.

DES (1987) *National Curriculum: Task Group on Assessment and Testing – A Report*, London: HMSO.

DfES (2007) *Statutory Framework for the Early Years Foundation Stage: Setting the Standards for Learning, Development and Care for Children from Birth to Five*, Nottingham: DfES Publications.

Drummond, M.J. (1993) *Assessing Children's Learning*, London: David Fulton Publishers.

Harlen, W. (2000) *Teaching, Learning and Assessing Science 5–12*, London: Paul Chapman.

Hurst, V. and Lally, M. (1992) 'Assessment and the nursery curriculum', in G. Blenkin and A. Kelly (eds) *Assessment in Early Childhood Education*, London: Paul Chapman, pp. 69–92.

Isaacs, S. (1954, reissue 1981) *The Educational Value of the Nursery School*, London: Headley Brothers Ltd.

Laevers, F. (1997) *A Process-oriented Child Follow-up System for Young Children*, Belgium: Centre for Experiential Education, Leuven University.

Novak, J. and Gowin, D. (1984) *Learning How to Learn*, Cambridge: Cambridge University Press.

Nutbrown, C. (1999) *Threads of Thinking*, London: Paul Chapman.

Ollerenshaw, C. and Ritchie, R. (1993) *Primary Science: Making it Work*, London: David Fulton Publishers.

QCA (2000) URL: http://www.qca.org.uk

Sparks Linfield, R. (1994) 'Straw Assessment', *Primary Science Review*, 35, 17.

CHAPTER 5

'This is the best day of my life! And I'm not leaving here until it's time to go home!'

THE OUTDOOR LEARNING ENVIRONMENT

Christine Parker

Observation: play in the nursery garden

Jason and Jack are playing in the nursery garden. Jason runs up to Jack. Jack says, 'You're the monster.' Jason runs away and says, 'I'm not the monster, I'm not.' They enter the willow tunnel and sit on the tree stumps. Jason asks, 'How shall we get out?' and squeezes through a gap in the willow tunnel. Jack suggests, 'Let's go to the park.' Jason responds, 'This one here,' and points to the climbing pod. As they pass the sand pit Sophie offers Jason some sand cake. He says, 'No thank you.' Jason and Jack run off to the climbing pod. They follow each other along the climbing ropes. Jason looks at a loose tree stump and says, 'Me need this,' and attempts to move it. Jack helps him and then tries to move an even bigger tree stump. He says, 'I can't move it. Can you help?' Jason responds, 'No, it's too big for me.' They both return to the sand pit and observe the other children making sand cakes. Jason goes off to the resource shelf and returns with a large bucket and a plastic scoop. He fills the bucket with sand, using two hands to lift each full scoop. Jason asks, 'Where's some water for me?' Jack replies, 'There's a bucket.' Jason picks up the bucket of sand and struggles to carry it to the bucket of water.

In this observation a 3-year-old child decides whether he is a monster or not, finds out how to escape out of a willow tunnel, follows his friend's suggestion to go to the park, exercises on climbing ropes, tests out his muscular strength, takes cues from other children around him and asks meaningful questions, all in minutes.

Jason's key worker notes, 'Jason demonstrated high levels of involvement (Laevers, 1994), interacts effectively with his peers, displays lots of collaborative play, independence in accessing resources and engages in imaginative play.' I would like to add, Jason enjoys a physical challenge.

The purpose of this observation is to highlight the value of outdoor play. It has now been widely acknowledged (Edgington, 2004, p. 2; Garrick, 2004; QCA, 2000, p. 25) that young children need access to the outdoors, in their early years in pre-school provision and primary school. Children benefit from developing their play and learning in environments where they can move from the indoors to the outdoors, and vice versa, freely. Currently, more children have access to the outdoor environment in reception classes; and an increasing number of Year 1 children do too. *Continuing the Learning Journey* (QCA, 2005) supports this development to provide frequent opportunities for outdoor play.

To restate, we know the outdoor environment offers young children an abundance of play and learning opportunities. How can we capture their engagement and fascination for the outdoors? This chapter is an attempt to support early years educators to:

1 appreciate how the outdoor learning environment enhances and extends children's development and learning;
2 define the areas of provision;
3 observe and plan for the outdoor learning environment;
4 provide practical solutions to the organisation of the outdoors;
5 be inspired and motivated to ensure the outdoor environment is embedded in the early years curriculum.

1. How the outdoor learning environment enhances and extends children's development and learning

Emotional development

For many young children, the daily opportunity to access the outdoors impacts on their levels of well-being (Laevers, 1994). Some children prefer to be outdoors, feel better about themselves and become more adventurous and playful in their learning (as discussed in Chapter 1). Having different types of spaces enhances their emotional development – having a place to hide, to be quiet and sometimes alone, is equally as important as sharing the joy of the outdoors with others. In considering our mental health, we know the appreciation of the outdoors supports our emotional and spiritual development (Jenkinson, 2001, pp. 34–6, 100–1).

Social development

Children learn most effectively within a social context (Vygotsky, 1978, pp. 89–91). The outdoor environment offers many opportunities for children to share their play and learning with another child, a group of children, an adult or all adults present outside. Children's outdoor play and learning has the potential to support complex narrations within social dramatic play; to support planning, preparing and enjoying the outcomes of growing vegetables, herbs and fruits; to support time to meet, discuss and enjoy each other's company (see Figure 5.1).

When early years educators are finding children's superhero role-play challenging the boundaries of acceptable behaviour, the children can learn to identify their rules for this type of play and learn to protect each other. At Caverstede Early Years Centre the rules, identified by the children were:

Outside – not inside
You don't hurt anybody.

Figure 5.1 *A child who loves to be active and loud has the opportunity to be energetic within space where these qualities are appreciated by others*

No fighting.

Just battling swords together, not on someone's body.

Play with children who want to join in, if they're busy they might want to play later.

Don't push anybody.

Tell your friends the rules.

Physical development

Having the space and freedom to practice running, jumping, climbing, balancing, lifting, carrying, transporting, pushing, pulling and swinging ensures children's healthy physical, mental and intellectual development. Experiencing physical challenge is a risky enterprise but is essential in supporting and developing the child's own sense of what is safe and what is not. As early years practitioners, it is our role to provide situations that will help children to deal with testing the surface, judging whether the ladder will wobble or daring to explore a dark space behind a hedge (see Figure 5.2).

Continuous daily access to PE equipment enables children to develop their skills to throw and catch, retrieve, handle a range of tools with skill, agility and confidence. Children's fine motor skills are also appropriately

Figure 5.2 *Climbing a ladder to explore a different view of the willow tunnel*

enhanced and developed through gardening activities, role-play dressing-up, the provision of mark-making materials and equipment to use with natural materials. Children have a wonderful fascination for mini-beasts and learn to handle creatures with care and respect.

Sensory integration is well supported through the provision of different surfaces to move on. It is the normal neurological process our brain uses in order to organise sensation in our everyday lives. We receive information from our senses, including the movement senses. This information tells our brains about balance, movement, gravity and what our muscles and joints are doing. We know we need to provide different surfaces and a range of physical experiences to support each child's sensory integration. In our nursery garden children experience walking, running and jumping on grass, concrete pathways, bark chippings, Astroturf, rubber surface, gravel, logs and wooden pathways; including a change in gradient. These experiences enable the children to feel comfortable about accessing other learning opportunities.

Intellectual development

Children relish the grandeur of the problems they need to solve outdoors. How do we transport this pile of leaves, these large blocks or these wooden planks? How do we save the planet when we're superheroes? How can I make this fit? How can I make the water flow in the direction I want? Through the children's exploratory and imaginative play, they have problems to solve, roles to negotiate, knowledge to acquire and much to remember, and many questions to ask. In Chapter 1, David Whitebread explains Bruner's description of language as a 'tool for thought' and the child's need for meaningful social contexts to learn as identified in Vygotsky's work. The outdoors provides endless opportunities for the children to express their thoughts and learning, and to share these with other children and adults (see Figure 5.3). Some children are more confident and relaxed when expressing themselves outside.

Highly involved in the bog garden project the children demonstrated lines of enquiry through their questioning:

Will we wake all the plants up?
Can we splash in the bog garden?
Will the birds come?
Do spiders crawl really fast?
Can I ask about the butterflies?
Do seeds die because they are not planted properly?
Do worms make the plants nice?

Figure 5.3 *At Caverstede Early Years Centre the children planned and created a bog garden with their key workers' support*

The bog garden inspired list-making (Figure 5.4).

The Key Stage 1 science curriculum has the potential to be fully supported through quality outdoor provision; enhancing and providing challenges within the four programmes of study – 'Scientific Enquiry', 'Life Processes and Living Things', 'Materials and Their Properties' and 'Physical Processes'. There are key scientific themes to explore outside, such as change, weather, seasons, properties of materials, growth, living things. Close observation is key to developing scientific investigative skills.

2. Defining the different areas of provision for the outdoor learning environment

It is as important to define the different areas of provision in the outdoor environment as it is in the classroom. As early years educators we need to ensure we have given time to considering what is appropriate and beneficial outdoor provision. Helen Bilton explains:

> For the outdoor area to be a learning and teaching environment, it cannot be left as an empty space. It has to be treated in the same way

Figure 5.4 *A list of what was required for the bog garden, including the creatures that may visit*

as a classroom and what is provided in the outdoor area and where activities are positioned all need careful consideration.

(2002, p. 36)

So, from my own experience as a nursery teacher and from reading a range of literature (Bilton, 2002; Garrick, 2004, pp. 66–7; McMillan, 2000, pp. 8–9; Ryder Richardson, 2006, pp. 2–10, p. 46), I have decided to consider the organisation of the outdoor environment under the following areas of provision. I see these areas of provision as being continuous, that is, they are available daily and a consistent level of provision is maintained.

Areas of provision

- The natural environment: wildlife and vegetation;
- Gardening;
- Physical challenge and sensory integration;
- Role-play;
- Transporting;
- Natural materials;
- The construction site;
- The creative arts;
- Meeting places.

Bilton (2002, p. 41) suggests versatile resources that allow a whole range of learning opportunities and outcomes. This continuous provision is then further enhanced, following observations of the children's play and learning, and identification of development and learning needs for individuals, groups of children and the whole class.

The natural environment: wildlife and vegetation

The national curriculum in England becomes subject-based for children aged 5 and above, beginning with Key Stage 1. Key Stage 1 science supports children's knowledge and understanding of the living world, and what better place to develop children's acquisition of key concepts than outside? Outside we can inspire and motivate children to investigate mini-beasts, bird life and small mammals. Scientific investigations lend themselves to be well supported through core stories in literacy sessions. In this way, we can make meaningful links in the children's learning between science and literacy, for example, *The Very Hungry Caterpillar*.

The children at Caverstede Early Years Centre take full advantage of the shrubs and we always ensure that it is possible to tunnel through. The shrubbery allows children to have small enclosed private spaces and also inspires wonderful imaginative play.

Good planting provides children with a wealth of learning about plants (Bilton, 2002, p. 61). Considerations may include planting that supports children's sensory development; our herb garden is a constant reference for both children and adults. Plants may be of different heights or leaf types, or flower at different times; children can hide behind shrubs and trees provide much-needed shelter.

Gardening (vegetables, fruit, herbs and flowers)

The *Every Child Matters: Change for Children* (DfES, 2004) framework provides guidance for all professionals working with children and young people, across all sectors, for example, education, health and social care in England. The document emphasises the requirement to develop the child's sense of citizenship. Gardening offers great potential in developing knowledge and understanding of sustainability, especially where gardening is well supported by an interested adult. Children can acquire first-hand experience of what it means to grow your own food. This is a strong seasonal experience and has the potential to develop a sense of belonging to a community. In Margaret McMillan's open air nurseries of the 1920s, she emphasises the provision of 'the herb garden' and 'kitchen garden' (McMillan, 2000).

Providing gardening tools that allow the children to be successful in their efforts is an essential requirement. In small restricted areas good use of unusual containers can be made, for example, tyres. From our experience, we advocate retaining an area for digging and immersing yourself in the mud. The children soon learn that one area is for freer exploratory play and another is for the specific purpose of growing food (Figure 5.5).

Figure 5.5 *Preparing the bed for the herb garden*

Children are keen to make waterproof labels and to inform others that this is not a place to dig!

The recommendation is to start small, and let it grow! Again, there are endless opportunities for cross-curricular links in literacy, numeracy, creative development and physical development. The garden inspires interest in stories, for example *The Enormous Turnip*, which include references to numeracy and comparisons of size and weight; inspired by growing their own turnips and other vegetables, children can create pictures and re-enact the stories. Physical development can be enhanced through opportunities to pull and push like the characters do in the story.

Physical challenge and sensory integration

As previously stated, the outdoor environment provides children with great opportunities for physical challenge, on a daily basis, and to meet their sensory integration needs. Children benefit from learning to ride two-wheelers, climb up ladders, roll down hills, balance along logs and planks, swing freely, walk on different surfaces and experience impact safely (Figures 5.6, 5.7).

Figure 5.6 *Children love to construct their own obstacle courses and are good at ensuring that they are presented with safe challenges*

Figure 5.7 *Meeting physical strength challenges by pushing a tree stump up the slide*

At Caverstede, PE equipment is provided as part of the continuous provision. The expectation is that the PE equipment will be used for the purpose it is designed for. A range of balls and bats, hockey sticks, goal posts, bean bags and hoops are all accessible.

Role-play

If as a young child, you want to be a police officer or a fire fighter, what better place to be than outside, where you have the time and space to develop your narrative? It makes more sense to extend active role-play outside, where children can make a lot more noise. Role-play, often strongly influenced by real-life experiences, becomes more involved where children are able to recreate a sense of time and place. They can walk to the 'shops', run to the 'emergency' and visit several relatives. Superhero play can be supported in ways that are non-threatening but provide children with a wonderful release of energy and sense of purpose.

Transporting

Young children frequently demonstrate an interest in transporting materials (Athey, 1990). In the classroom this can cause anxiety due to a lack of space and resources. Opportunities for transporting can be well supported outside – and the more real the experience, the greater the levels of involvement and learning; for example, the provision of wheeled vehicles to transport leaves in the autumn.

Natural materials: water, sand, mud, rocks, pebbles

The exploration of natural materials is a messy business but is so easy to provide outside. With suitable clothing, the whole experience can be so much more meaningful. The provision of all-weather suits allows children to literally immerse themselves. 'Kernow Woodland Learning' is a wood-land project in Cornwall (Callaway, 2005). The concept of the project is to support children's need to experience the outdoors in all weathers. One project aim is to 'encourage children to respect the outdoors: diverse weather conditions, the beauty and forms of nature and the changing seasons' (Callaway, 2005, p. 3).

Observations in the sand pit show us the opportunities for parallel and social play, great cooperation is required to fill all the containers. The provision of a range of graded containers enhances the quality of play and there are more opportunities to make those important comparisons of weight, size and capacity. Rigging up a pulley adds a scientific dimension to children's play and learning.

Natural materials enhance the quality of the children's small-world play. In creating their imaginary miniature worlds, children are enabled to empathise, create narratives and share understandings. Play with natural materials inspires imaginative play on both a small and life-size scale (Figure 5.8).

The construction site

Combining sand and water often naturally leads to an interest in building. The opportunity to build on a large scale offers children a real challenge and a great sense of satisfaction. Large materials, such as planks, tyres and crates, require a large space and the opportunity to construct for a purpose.

Nutbrown explores notions of children's rights in *Children's Rights and Early Education* (1996) and asks the question, 'Is children's privacy respected?' She refers to aspects of communication, but it is also important that children have the opportunity to construct a private space where they

Figure 5.8 *Concocting magic spells*

can be undisturbed by an adult (Figure 5.9). We can supervise with sensitivity.

The creative arts

The creative arts can be developed in exciting and innovative ways outside. There are places for large-scale art work, to explore sound and music outside and areas can be designed for performance.

Andy Goldsworthy inspires sculpture using collections of natural materials, allowing children to explore the visual elements of pattern, space, shape, colour and texture. Jackson Pollock's art work can be fully explored outside, where children can experiment splattering paint and admire their efforts on a larger scale than indoors. Children delight in making marks when provided with large paintbrushes and containers of water and large pieces of playground chalk. Provision of art materials can enhance the development of construction and role-play, to include drawing maps and plans.

It is important to provide opportunities for outdoor art that are also soothing and calm, for example, children will respond to the provision of watercolour paints with explorations of colour, the effects made with

Figure 5.9 *Constructing dens for private meetings*

watery paint running, mixing, blending. Again, inspiration from past and living artists can be introduced in a way that is meaningful for the children (Figure 5.10).

Children enjoy experimenting with music outside, where organised sound provides a different experience. Visiting musicians have played in our nursery garden and the children are able to respond spontaneously, moving their bodies to the rhythms and melodies.

Core stories (Barrs and Ellis, 1998) are greatly enhanced by being presented outside: for example, the stories of 'The Gruffalo', 'We're Going on a Bear Hunt' and 'The Billy Goats Gruff'. The children will then initiate their own narratives, when adults have modelled the story-telling process.

Meeting places

The outdoor environment has the potential to offer children spaces where they can be alone in a safe and secure place, as well as special places to meet. These places include under a willow dome, in a tunnel in a hedge, in a wooden shed or in the sand pit. Children congregate and socialise. These are places where children's role-play will be initiated – children will travel to 'Spain', 'the moon' and 'the shops down the road'.

Figure 5.10 *An adult modelling watercolour painting to encourage care and attention to detail*

The analysis of our observations is key to providing well-informed planning to further enhance and extend the children's development and learning. We now move onto planning the outdoor learning environment.

3. Observing and planning for the outdoor learning environment

Observing children outside

Why do we need to observe children outside?

If we truly value children's outdoor play and learning then we have to give it equal status in terms of the need to highlight, capture and document the children's development and learning – we cannot leave this to chance because then it will not happen. There are challenges because of the weather – so photographs, using digital cameras; come into their own. Here are two examples.

Observation 1

Joshua is in the reception class and it is the autumn term. He has built a tall tower using the large plastic bricks. Joshua decides to use the sticky labels, which have been provided alongside them, to record the corresponding numeral and sticks them onto each brick. He refers to the numberline, which has also been provided, when he is writing numerals above 10. Joshua focuses on this activity for 20 minutes.

The space outside gives Joshua the confidence to engage in a numeracy activity, which he otherwise would not have self-selected (Figure 5,11a and b).

Observation 2

Carl is putting the doll on the slide and sliding it down. He slides down after it. He transfers the doll to another slide and again follows it down – (the plastic one allows him to go faster).

Carl – 'Wheeee!'

He picks up a scooter nearby, scoots around in a circle and comes back past the doll on the floor, slowing to look at it.

He scoots on and stops by an adult who is talking about moving on to the next school.

Appears to listen, but keeps moving around a bush in a circle on the scooter.

Conversation shifts to 'friendships'. Facial expression and smiling from Carl. Leaves scooter and twizzles in three circles.

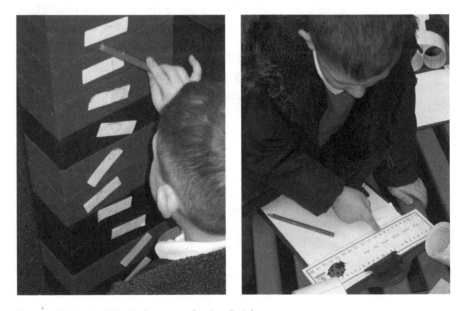

Figure 5.11a and b *Joshua numbering bricks*

Carl – 'You got hiccups?' – to peer.
Chases peer around big bush.

Displaying a need for movement (possibly rotational schematic play), evidences a desire, interest and appreciation in social interaction. Carl dips in and out of it, beginning to create social situations imaginatively with the doll to reinforce and 'prepare' himself for real ones.

Planning the outdoor learning environment

Planning the outdoor learning environment is a dynamic process that has to evolve over time. It deserves frequent revisits in order to monitor the quality of play and learning that is occurring for the children.

In creating plans for the outdoors, it is important to give serious consideration to the precise experiences and learning opportunities desired for the children. The areas of provision need to be clearly defined and understood by everyone involved. Matching the areas of provision to the potential development and learning is a key activity to revalidate the value of outdoor play and learning and ensure a shared understanding is embedded.

The examples in Tables 5.1, 5.2 and 5.3 show a long-term plan, followed by an extract of a medium-term plan and an overview of the nursery garden during one week, that is, the short-term plan.

4. Provide practical solutions to the organisation of the outdoors

To be inspired and motivated by the outdoor environment, and to give it value, early years educators need to acknowledge that there can be barriers to quality provision. Below is a brief summary of the common difficulties and barriers that may be experienced:

- Safety issues/supervision/adult expectations/sun safety/rules and boundaries
- Storage/time to set up
- Access/restrictions due to design of building and size of area
- The weather – inclement weather can be discouraging, particularly for some adults but generally not for children
- Adult attitudes towards children playing outside/not sharing the understanding of the value.

Table 5.1 Long-term planning: continuous provision

Outdoors

The outdoor area provides the opportunity for active learning across the whole curriculum, allowing children to access varied learning experiences.

Learning experiences/activities

Personal, social and emotional development

- Sharing and taking turns with equipment
- Working on collaborative projects
- Developing independence
- Being excited by outdoor world and being motivated to learn

Communication, language and literacy

- Exploring mark-making, using large and small equipment
- Making and using signs such as road signs
- Using fiction and non-fiction as a starting point
- Making and exploring sounds
- Talking, negotiating and communicating ideas

Mathematical development

- Counting
- Number games
- Matching numbers and numerals
- Looking at and making patterns and shapes
- Measuring and problem solving
- Comparing quantities

Knowledge and understanding of the world

- Investigate, observe, explore and compare using a range of resources including ICT
- Building and constructing on a large scale

Physical development

- Developing gross motor skills and spatial awareness
- Developing fine motor skills
- Becoming aware of and talking about changes

Creative development

- Making large murals
- Making mobiles
- Making music and dances in all weathers
- Setting up role play areas, with suitable clothing

Adult role

- Recognising, valuing and building on children's interests
- Sensitive intervention
- Modelling of skills
- Sharing of information

- Asking challenging questions
- Engaging in play alongside children
- Providing additional resources as appropriate
- Supporting close and accurate observations

Resources

Suggested resources could include:

- Selection of wheeled toys to ride and push and pull
- Gardening equipment
- Mark making equipment-large paintbrushes, playground chalk
- Throws, tents, tunnels, clothes airers, washing lines and pegs
- Bubble solution and bubble wands
- Wellies
- Guttering, pipes, funnels, water tray, set of small trays
- Skipping ropes, various balls, basketball net, goal
- Large wooden blocks
- Easel/chalkboard
- Sand and water toys
- Selection of small world equipment
- Resources to support role play, e.g. emergency services, the construction site
- Art resources to support large scale painting and sculpture
- Resources for outdoor music and sound making
- Items for movement play
- Toolbox and workbench
- Selection of reclaimed materials
- Trampoline, balancing boards, stilts, seesaw, plastic barrel
- Selection of natural resources

Fixed resources

- Climbing frame/equipment
- Picnic table and benches
- Play house, kitchen
- Swings and slide
- Tyres and inner tubes
- Storage

Planned areas

- Areas set up as they might be indoors e.g. sand, water, paint, role play
- A space large enough for children to run, skip and jump
- A designated area for wheeled toys
- An appropriately resourced climbing and balancing area
- A quiet area
- A free digging and exploration area
- A garden area

cont'd.

Key prompts/questions
- What's happening here?
- What's going to happen next?
- Seasonal changes
- Large movement – speed, direction, type and quality of movement
- Mathematical concepts – area, measurement, quantities
- Scientific concepts – 'change' 'living things' 'growth'

Vocabulary
- Words to describe weather, questions to support exploratory play, correct vocabulary for vegetation, wildlife, minibeasts. Words to describe movement and speed, run, skip, jump, hop, crawl, roll, leap, twist, turn, fast, faster then, fastest, slow, slower than, slowest, rapid, swift
- Vocabulary to support imaginative role play

Holding on to the vision is vital! Do not be discouraged, the outcomes are of great benefit to the children. Table 5.4 illustrates solutions to these common dilemmas.

5. Be inspired and motivated to ensure the outdoor environment is embedded in the early years curriculum

Provision for early childhood education has embraced the potential of the outdoor environment for many years. I am often inspired by the work of the pioneers of nursery education. The first open-air nurseries were opened in the 1920s by Margaret MacMillan, who was a strong advocate for the benefits of outdoor play. She provides advice that remains current. Here she explains the benefits of providing a kitchen garden and apparatus in the garden.

Kitchen Garden. Here vegetables for the table should be grown.

Potatoes, cabbages, parsnips, beetroot, parsley, onions, radishes, carrots, rhubarb and marrows. They are needed as part of the children's food, and nothing trains the mind and fills it with wholesome memories better than the carrying out of all this work in their sight, and with their help. Even the toddlers want to help. They follow our gardener, Mrs Hambleden, down the paths, and into the drills; and very early and without formal teaching of any kind they learn to know the names of things. 'Where is the beetroot?' visitors say, 'Where are the parsnips?' and the three year olds walk to the right bed or point to the right place.

Table 5.2 Medium-term plan: Autumn 2 – Cultures, Festivals and Celebrations

Area of learning: PD

Aspect: Movement

Notes/comments	Learning priorities (B-3, FSCG)	Adult initiated	Resources
	A Healthy Child *Growing and Developing* • Being active, rested and protected • Gaining control of the body **A Competent Learner** *Healthy Choices* • Discovering and learning about his/her body *Being Imaginative* • Imitating, mirroring, moving and imaging • Express themselves with action and sound • Are excited by their own increasing mobility and often set their own challenges • Move spontaneously within available space • Respond to rhythm, music and story by means of gesture and movement • Can stop • Move freely with pleasure and confidence • Move in a range of ways, such as slithering, shuffling, rolling, crawling, walking, running, jumping, skipping, sliding and hopping	Listening to music from other cultures Video of cultural dance and celebration Moving in response to music, vibration and visual stimulus e.g. firework dances- jumping, spinning, bouncing, in response to poems, percussion, singing and clapping. Banging, stamping, jumping, and marching to African drums. Moving fast and slow, turning, twisting to Indian music. Jabadeo movement play to range of music Moving and chasing with ribbon and floating materials. Party music and games – statues, dancing	Videos e.g. • Cultural dancing • Ballet • Ice skating • Swings

(cont'd)

• Use movement to express feelings	Children preferred sensory integration techniques, e.g. the swings crashing.	**References**
• Adjust speed or change direction to avoid obstacles	Finger Rhymes	Birth to three framework
• Negotiate space successfully when playing racing and chasing games with other children	Floor play – mark making, stories, sand tray	Foundation Stage Curriculum Guidance
• Go backwards and sideways as well as forwards	**Enhanced Provision**	Every Child Matters
• Experiment with different ways of moving	Space and opportunities created indoors and outdoors for movement to music and sound	– enjoy and achieve
• Initiate new combinations of movement and gesture in order to express and respond to feelings, ideas and experiences	Scarves/heavy and light material	– make a positive contribution
• Jump off an object and land appropriately	Percussion	– Economic well being
• Move with confidence, imagination and in safety	Photographs of children moving on display	Continuous provision document
• Manage body to create intended movements	Stimulus pictures:	Nursery Garden Document
• Combine and repeat a range of movements	– Fireworks	Sensory Integration Booklet
• Sit up, stand up and balance on various parts of the body	– Dancing	Schema Leaflet
• Demonstrate the control necessary to hold a shape or fixed position	– Athletics	Jabadeo Plan
• Mount stairs, steps or climbing equipment using alternate feet	– Sport	Firework poems
• Manipulate materials and objects by picking up, releasing, arranging, threading and posting them	– Wind pictures	Link with CD
• Show increasing control over clothing and fastenings	– Climbing	Music and PD Movement 2
• Move with control and coordination	– Parachuting	
• Travel around, under, over and through balancing and climbing equipment		

Table 5.3 Short-term plan: nursery garden

Continuous Provision: Week beginning . . . .

Art	Mark Making	Sand	Water	Tactile
A group of boys gained a lot from creating 'splats' like Jackson Pollock's art. They dropped sponges loaded with paint from a height and became proficient in knowing how forcefully you should aim the sponge.	Luke and Aaron looked at sheep as they made marks. Luke said, 'I'm doing down and across there' (Pointing to the Δ) Aaron said, 'mine is round. Now it's along, look.' (made curves and wiggles)	Jay and Daniel used the boats in the sand, making tracks, talking about oceans and docking.	It was raining and the undercover was leaking. The children lined up buckets to catch the rain from the leaks. The group of children observed the rain filling up the buckets. Once full they emptied the buckets.	Aaron, Corben, Ben and Rosie were smelling, touching and tearing little bits off herbs. Rosie said: 'I've smelled that before.' Ben and Aaron know the different names of herbs.
Reflections	**Personal, Social and Emotional Development**	**Communication, Language and Literacy**	**Mathematical Development**	**Construction/Blocks**
Lots more 'hide and seek' going on. Could develop as a focus. We have managed to go for walks with all children over lunch on two different days. The second day we linked up with the Ladybird class. The children	• Being able to express feelings • Knowing when to ask for help • Strive for responses from others • Growing awareness of self • Feel safe and secure	• Communicating meaning • Creating and experimenting with one's own symbols and marks • Begin to bring together hand and eye movements to fix on	• Making patterns, comparing, categorising and classifying • Notice changes in groupings of objects, images or sounds • Gain awareness of 1–1 correspondence	A group of children placed the wooden reels in a line. They then stepped on each reel, counting as they stepped on each one, 1–8. Increased interest in the blocks as builders start laying bricks. Children

(cont'd)

enjoyed looking at and collecting leaves. The walk was a significant marker in the day to those staying all day.		are using sand and scrapers to mix and spread cement. Alfie said: 'These are the bricks. I'm going to build with them. All round the edge. It's finished'. Den building: Groups frequently initiate constructing enclosures with roofs.
	and demonstrate a sense of trust • Have an awareness of, and show interest and enjoyment in, cultural and religious differences • Have a positive self-image and show that they are comfortable with themselves • Make connections between different parts of their life experience	through categorising belongings • Show curiosity about numbers by offering comments or asking questions • Use mathematical language in play • Show an interest in shape and space by playing with shapes or making arrangements with objects
	and make contact with objects • Use action, sometimes with limited talk, that is largely concerned with the 'here and now' • Use talk to connect ideas, explain what is happening and anticipate what might happen next • Use language to imagine and recreate roles and experiences • Draw lines and circles using gross motor movement	
Literacy Songs and singing filtering through into all aspects. Children are singing on the spinning board, climbing frames and along the	**Physical Development** • Gaining control over the body • Imitating, mirroring, moving and imaging • Are excited by their own increasing	**Knowledge and Understanding of the World** • Developing competence and creativity • Are curious and
	Creative Development • Exploring and discovering • Exploring and sharing stories, songs, rhymes and games • Create and experiment	**Equipment** Slides: Children are exploring friction. They have noticed that they travel at different speeds depending on what clothes they are

pathways. They could distinguish between a number and a letter. Manjeet found lots of letter 'M's'.	mobility, setting their own challenges • Use tools and materials for particular purposes • Explore malleable materials by patting, stroking, poking, squeezing, pinching and twisting them • Respond to rhythm, music and story by means of gesture and movement	interested in making things happen • Are interested in others and their families • Realise tools can be used for a purpose • Express feelings about a significant personal event • Begin to try out a range of tools and techniques safely	with blocks colour and marks • Show an interest in the way musical instruments sound • Respond to sound with body movement • Begin to describe the texture of things • Begin to differentiate colours Work creatively on a large and small scale	wearing and how they lifted their legs. Hills: Children are enjoying rolling down hills. Tom copied the more confident children.
Role Play Children from all three classes participating in 'waiting for the bus/train' (trolley) and paying for the ticket.	**Digging** We emphasised the appropriate use of different tools.	**Natural world** A group of children were collecting stones and placing them on the floor of the tree house. One child said, 'Put the eggs in the tree house.'	**Music/Sound** Rhythmic play and sequential visual clues coming to the fore – e.g. marching, banging drums and placing stepping stones. Children following each other in a line sequence of activity has a beginning and an end.	**Climbing/Sensory** Rosie and Alice instigate a turn taking game on the spinning board. They were singing 'Sandy Girl' then choosing the next one to have a go.

Table 5.4 Practical solutions to common dilemmas

Common Dilemma	Practical Solutions
Safety/rules and boundaries	• Confidence building amongst the team. • Ensure all risk assessments are in place and are revisited. • Visit other settings/schools where staff are confident with outdoor safety. • Ensure everyone knows the safety policies and procedures. • Involve the children in discussions about playing safely. • Invite the children to decide on their rules for outdoor play.
Storage and time	• Plan to acquire appropriate storage over time, set achievable goals. • Look at good examples in other settings/schools. • Involve the children in transporting resources. • Build up the availability of resources, as everyone becomes more confident. • Identify provision that can remain in site, particularly natural materials, the garden and add to the vegetation.
Access	• If you are in a school, negotiate for the classroom with the best access to the outdoors.
Weather	• Weather boxes • The weather is a great learning resource which supports the Foundation Stage and Key Stage One Curriculum.
Attitudes	• Find a like-minded colleague! • Documentation of the children's play and learning extends our confidence to demonstrate to the children, their families and colleagues the value of the children's achievements. • Whole team involvement in developing policy and procedures. • Shared learning and understanding. • Information booklets to support policy.

Table 5.5 The opportunities for meeting the five *Every Child Matters* outcomes available in the outdoor learning environment

Every Child Matters Framework Outcomes	Opportunities to be Provided Outside
Be Healthy	• To appreciate the fresh air in all weathers. • To have the freedom to move around in many different ways. • To develop gross motor skills, muscular strength and whole body coordination. • To support children's emotional wellbeing and therefore their mental health.
Stay Safe	• The provision of a safe and secure outdoor environment is essential experience for children in the early years. • To experience physical challenge with the support of qualified adults; to understand one's own limitations through experience rather than a lack of opportunity, for example, the provision of ladders, climbing. • To assert oneself within an environment that is supportive, for example, through role play, sharing wheeled toys.
Enjoy and Achieve	• To experience the pleasure of play outside and share this with others. • To problem solve, for example, with the provision of construction play and play with natural materials. • To involve children in planning the outdoor space, consult, and ask them how they perceive different outdoor environments. • To revisit resources and utilise resources in a wide variety of ways. • To develop story telling outside and re-enact familiar stories that a particular suitable for the outdoors, for example, 'We're going on a Bear Hunt', 'The Gruffalo'.
Make a Positive Contribution	• To negotiate. • To develop narratives through role play, small world play, imaginative play.

cont'd.

	• Involvement of children in planning. • Some children are more confident outside and therefore are more able to contribute and learn.
Economic Wellbeing	• To grow vegetables and fruit and take responsibility for them. • To prepare and eat the produce. • To share produce with families. • To understand different work roles, for example, the emergency services, shop assistants, staffing a petrol station.

Apparatus in the garden. This is always very simple, and is often improvised. A student leans a plank for instance against a box or seat, and up this plank our little ones go. At first holding a hand on each side, then letting go one hand, and at last walking up and down alone, always, it is true, watched and prevented, but allowed to go alone!

(McMillan, 2000 [1919])

The adult's role in supporting children's development and learning outside goes far beyond supervision. We do need to ensure there is adequate cover; but it is paramount that we show the children we are just as interested in their outdoor learning as we are in their indoor learning.

Through quality outdoor provision, it is possible to impact significantly on supporting children in the five *Every Child Matters* outcomes: 'Be Healthy', 'Stay Safe', 'Enjoy and Achieve', 'Make a Positive Contribution' and 'Economic Wellbeing' (DfES, 2004). Table 5.5 illustrates just a few of the opportunities.

It is important for early years educators to maintain an holistic view of child development. Reflecting on and applying the five *Every Child Matters* outcomes supports this endeavour.

Pointers for the outdoor learning environment

In the early years, the outdoor learning environment:

- enhances and extends children's development and learning;
- should include a range of areas of provision;
- requires careful observation and planning;
- should be embedded in every area of the curriculum.

References

Athey, C. (1990) *Extending Thought in Young Children: A Parent-Teacher Partnership*, London: Paul Chapman.

Barrs, M., Ellis, S. (1998) *The Core Booklist*, London: Centre for Language in Primary Education.

Bilton, H. (2002) *Outdoor Play in the Early Years: Management and Innovation*, 2nd edn, London. David Fulton Publishers.

Bilton, H., James, K., Marsh, J., Wilson, A. and Woonton, M. (2005) *Learning Outdoors: Improving the Quality of Young Children's Play Outdoors*, London: David Fulton Publishers.

Bruce, T. (1997) *Early Childhood Education*, 2nd edn, London: Hodder Headline.

Callaway, G. (2005) *The Early Years Curriculum: A View from Outdoors*, London: David Fulton Publishers.

DfES (Department for Education and Skills) (2004) *Every Child Matters: Change for Children*, Nottingham: DfES.

Edgington, M. (2004) 'The outdoors curriculum', *Nursery World*, 2 September.

Garrick, R. (2004) *Playing Outdoors in the Early Years*, London: Continuum.

Jenkinson, S. (2001) *The Genius of Play: Celebrating the Spirit of Childhood*, Stroud, Glos.: Hawthorn Press.

Laevers, F. (1994) *The Innovative Project: Experiential Education 1976–1995*, Leuven, Belgium: Research Centre for Early Childhood and Primary Education, Katholieke Universiteit.

McMillan, M. (2000 [1919]) *'Can I Play Out?' Outdoor Play in the Early Years*, Bradford: Bradford Education.

Nutbrown, C. (1996) *Children's Rights and Early Education: Respectable Educators – Capable Learners*, London: Paul Chapman.

Qualifications and Curriculum Authority (QCA) (2000) *Curriculum Guidance for the Foundation Stage*, London: DfES.

Qualifications and Curriculum Authority (QCA) (2005) *Continuing the Learning Journey*, INSET package. London: QCA.

Ryder Richardson, G. (2006) *Creating a Space to Grow: Developing Your Outdoor Learning Environment*, London: David Fulton Publishers.

Vygotsky, L.S. (1978) *Mind in Society: the Development of Higher Psychological Processes*, Cambridge, MA: Harvard University Press.

Play and language

CHAPTER 6

'You're supposed to tell me your name now!'

SPEAKING AND LISTENING IN THE EARLY YEARS

Dominic Wyse and Helen Bradford

By the age of 5, provided they do not have language difficulties, all children have acquired the adult grammar for the main constructions of their native language (Peccei, 2006). This is true across all cultures and in all languages. The term 'acquired' in this context is important because linguists make a distinction between *emergent* language constructions and ones which are fully acquired.

Nature versus nurture arguments are still a potent force in discussions about how child language develops. One of the most famous advocates of the idea that language development is natural was Noam Chomsky. In his early work he hypothesised that children made use of a Language Acquisition Device (LAD). This device, he argued, is a special capacity of the brain that enables children to use the rules systems of their native language. Jerome Bruner countered that Chomsky's theory correctly identified this aspect of the child's capacity but that this was only part of the process of language acquisition:

> The infant's Language Acquisition Device could not function without the aid given by an adult who enters with him into a transactional format. That format, initially under the control of the adult, provides a Language Acquisition Support System (LASS). It frames or structures the input of language and interaction to the child's Language Acquisition Device in a manner to 'make the system function'. In a word, it is the interaction between the LAD and the LASS that makes it possible for the infant to enter the linguistic community – and, at the same time, the culture to which the language gives access.
>
> (Bruner, 1983, p. 19)

Messer (2006) shows the ways that such debates have continued to be an important part of thinking about children's language acquisition. Chomsky's later work involved theories of *minimalism*. One of the important features of minimalist theory is the idea that many aspects of grammar are contained in the vocabulary of a language, and its semantic information. Previous theories proposed that grammatical representations were independent of the vocabulary. Minimalist ideas and other developments in the field have resulted in language development theorists focusing on the way that the human brain operates more generally. Neuroscientists have defined the brain's activity in terms of connectionist networks, neural networks or parallel distributed processes, which are terms describing the same phenomena. Connectionist networks have been explored by encouraging computers to learn grammatical features such as the past tense. Computers have had success with both regular and irregular past tense forms. The point of such work is to research the extent to which language features are innate, or can be learned. However, as Messer (2006) cautions, there has also been a welcome resurgence of interest in how adults speak to children and scepticism about all-encompassing grand theories.

One of the important ideas in relation to children's language acquisition was the concept of *motherese*. This is now called Child Directed Speech (CDS) in recognition of the fact that it is not just mothers who modify their speech when talking to young children. Peccei (2006) points out that there is no clear evidence that CDS should be seen particularly as a teaching tool. She accurately observes that CDS is probably just a natural response to the fact that young children use talk which is semantically and syntactically simple; therefore, if an adult is to communicate effectively with them, they need to use a similar kind of language. This perhaps suggests that *natural* forms of communication between adults and children, commensurate with the child's language at different stages, are beneficial.

Language acquisition

One of the most important aspects of learning to talk is the ability to hold a conversation. Discourse development requires the learning of many sophisticated understandings. In education settings, the ability to take turns, and having to signal that you want to speak by putting your hand up, is one of the important areas that differs significantly from the home language environment. There are also many conventions, such as manners, that have to be learned. Children also learn that language differs according to who they are talking to. So a conversation with an adult will be different

to talk with their peers. Discourse development, which is a particularly important aspect of language, is served by development in all other areas of language development. Table 6.1 is a summary of Peccei's (2006) introductory chapters on children's language development. It shows the typical ages where significant developmental milestones occur in the areas of syntax, morphology, vocabulary, sense relations and phonology; these are described below.

Children's syntactic development begins with single words and then moves on to two-word phrases. After this, children's syntax develops rapidly and on many fronts. Negative sentences such as 'I am not walking' and the use of complex sentence types will be areas that develop during the nursery stage. The ability to ask questions is another aspect of syntax that develops at this time.

The word morphological comes from *morpheme*. A morpheme is the smallest unit of language that can change meaning. For example if we take the singular 'apple' and turn it into the plural 'apples' then the letter 's' is a morpheme because it changes the meaning from singular to plural. Morphemes that can stand alone, such as 'apple', are called *free morphemes*, and those which cannot, such as the -*s* in 'apples', are called bound morphemes. Children's development of morphological understanding can be seen in their capacity to invent words, such as 'carsiz' (cars).

Lexical development is concerned with the development of vocabulary so is not something that has a particular end point, because we continue to add vocabulary throughout our lives. One of the features of children's lexical development is over-extension. An example of over-extension is where children call all meats chicken because they are familiar with that word but not others such as beef, pork, etc. Another feature of lexical development is learning about the way that the meaning of words relates to each other, something called *sense relations*. Synonyms such as 'happy/joyful' and antonyms such as 'happy/sad' are part of this. This means that children can learn about vocabulary from words that they know without having to *directly* experience the concept of the word in question.

Phonological development has been much studied, partly because of its link with learning to read. As far as talk is concerned, there are some understandings and skills that have to be acquired before those that are beneficial for literacy. For example, the young child learns to control their vocal cords. The sound/airflow which passes from the vocal cords is obstructed in various ways in order to form phonemes (sounds). The place of articulation involves use of the teeth, lips, tongue, mouth and glottis. The manner of articulation involves obstructing the airflow to varying degrees, such as completely stopping it or allowing some to pass through the nose.

Table 6.1 Summary of stages of children's language acquisition

Age	Phonological Development	Sense Relations	Vocabulary	Morphological Development	Syntactic Development	Discourse Development
Birth to 2 months	Vowel-like sounds such as crying and grunting					
2 to 4 mths	Cooing					
4 to 6 mths	Vocal play including rudimentary syllables such as /da/ or /goo/					
6 mths	Babbling such as /ba/ba/ba/ or /ga/ ba/da/do					
1 year	First meaningful words					
9 mths to 1 yr 3 mths						Prelinguistic directive such as speech sounds and pointing

Age				
1 yr 6 mths to 1 yr 8 mths	First 50 words acquired			Telegraphic directives: e.g. 'that mine', 'gimme'
1 year 3 mths to 2 yrs				
2 years	Average vocabulary = 200–300 words		Begin to put words together in sentences. Noun phrases with pre-modification of the noun: e.g. more biscuit. Pronouns appear: e.g. 'me want that'	
2 yrs 3 mths		Past tense inflection appears		
2 yrs to 2 yrs 4 mths				Limited routines: 'Where's my X?', 'What's that?'
2 years 6 mths		Starting to acquire rules for inflecting nouns and verbs: e.g. 'breaked it' or 'mouses'	Multiple pre-modification of nouns: e.g. that red ball	

(cont'd)

Age	Phonological Development	Sense Relations	Vocabulary	Morphological Development	Syntactic Development	Discourse Development
2 yrs 8 mths					Compound sentences: e.g. 'The dog bit the cat and then he ran away.'	
2 to 3 yrs		Refer to all members of category as the same: e.g. all flowers as flower				
2 yrs 9 mths						Greater precision of articulation in self-repairs, increased volume and use of contrastive stress: e.g. 'It was on the chair!' (not under it)
3 yrs					Post-modified phrases: e.g. 'the picture of Lego town'. Complex sentences	Can cope with non-situated discourse
2 yrs 4 mths to 3 yrs 8 mths						Embedded requests: 'Can I have big boy shoes?'

3 yrs 8 mths to 4 yrs	Conversation consists largely of initiation/response (I/R) exchanges
4 yrs	Elaborate oblique strategies: 'We haven't had any sweets for a long time.'
4 yrs to 4 yrs 7 mths	Acquisition of auxiliary verbs (might, may, could) and negation. Child's response itself increasingly becomes R/I
4 yrs 7 mths to 4 yrs 10 mths	Greater ability to encode justifications and causal relationships allows for longer exchanges

(cont'd)

Age	Phonological Development	Sense Relations	Vocabulary	Morphological Development	Syntactic Development	Discourse Development
4 to 5 yrs		Spontaneously use category names: e.g. rose or daisy				
4 yrs 6 mths					Coordination with ellipsis: e.g. 'The dog bit the cat and ran away.'	
3 yrs 8 mths to 5 yrs 7 mths						Advanced embedding: 'Don't forget to buy sweets.'
6 yrs old			Average vocabulary understood = 14,000 words. Average spoken vocabulary = 6,000 words			

Speaking and listening in educational policy and practice

Prior to the 1960s the idea that talk should be an important part of the English curriculum would have been greeted with some scepticism. However, in the 1960s, educational researchers became increasingly interested in the idea that learning could be enhanced by careful consideration of the role of talk. Andrew Wilkinson's work resulted in him coining the new word 'oracy' as a measure of how important he thought talk was, a fact confirmed by the *Oxford English Dictionary*, which lists Wilkinson's text historically as the first entry:

> 1965 A. WILKINSON *Spoken Eng.* 14 The term we suggest for general ability in the oral skills is *oracy*; one who has those skills is *orate*, one without them *inorate*.

The establishment of a new word is perhaps the most fitting sign of Wilkinson's legacy. The work of Wilkinson (e.g. 1991) and other educationists resulted in *speaking and listening* becoming part of the national curriculum programmes of study for the subject English.

Although the speaking and listening requirements of the national curriculum remained statutory from 1997 onwards, the implementation of the national literacy strategy (NLS) in 1998 in England and Wales meant that, in practice, speaking and listening was neglected due to a powerful focus on reading in particular, and writing to a lesser extent. It was not only the fact that speaking and listening programmes of study were not addressed by the NLS *Framework for Teaching* (FFT; DfEE, 1998), but also that the teaching methods that were strongly advocated by the NLS also resulted in weaker oral work, as a series of strong research studies has shown. English, Hargreaves and Hislam (2002) found that there was a conflict between the achievement of short-term lesson objectives that are a feature of the FFT and the fostering of extended pupil contributions. In 2006, an attempt was made to address the absence of speaking and listening by including strands of objectives for speaking and listening in the new literacy framework. In view of the discussion about the importance of oracy, the title *literacy* framework when describing the inclusion of speaking and listening objectives seems nonsensical.

Few would argue that speaking and listening is not an important feature of early years and primary teaching and learning, but there are still a number of questions that need to be asked. One of the key questions concerns the balance between speaking and listening, reading and writing. To answer this question there is a need to separate the content to be covered from considerations of teaching style. It seems to us that most of the debates about oracy, and the recent considerations of talk in teaching and learning, have more to do with teaching style than a careful consideration of programmes of study. If national curricula are present, as they are in England, then it is appropriate that they should specify the content of the curriculum. This can apply to communication/speaking and listening just as it can apply to reading and writing and other subjects in the curriculum. However, there is a need for clear thinking about what this content should be. We would argue that if teachers' practice more routinely encouraged things like exploratory talk and *dialogic teaching* (Alexander, 2006) then it may be appropriate to reduce the overall content of the programmes of study for speaking and listening. This would require renewed thinking about what the content should be and might lead to more of a focus on some of the kinds of language exploration quite rightly advocated by the Language in the National Curriculum (LINC) project of the 1980s.

By examining the stages of language acquisition and beginning to understand the theories of how and why this process takes place, it becomes clear that pre-school experience is an important factor in the child's language development. The significance of the way that adults interact with the child at this time should not be underestimated. It has been acknowledged that adults provide a number of important conditions for the child as they:

- Provide access to an environment where talk has high status;
- Provide access to competent users of language;
- Provide opportunities to engage in talk;
- Provide responses which acknowledge the child as a competent language user.

(Wray *et al.*, 1989, p. 39)

In addition, adults model (in an unplanned way) the conventions of language; provide natural feedback on the effectiveness of a child's ability to communicate; scaffold the child's language learning; and enable the child to test their current hypotheses about how language works. The ability of the adult to take into account the limited abilities of the child, and adjust their language accordingly so that the child can make sense of them, is intuitive for most parents.

The degree to which a rich language environment assists language development has been well documented. Research studies have established a correlation between home language experiences in the pre-school period and children's literacy progress at school, for example Tizard and Hughes (1984) and Wells (1986). Both document the influence of home language experiences from birth on a child's ability to use language and communicate effectively. Wells' study, for example, found a direct correlation between children's rates of progress in language learning and the amount of conversation experienced with their parents and other members of their family circle. The quality of social experience and interaction will vary greatly between children, and during the early years teachers need to be aware that some children will arrive at school appearing to be confident, articulate masters of the English language, whereas others seem less comfortable language users. However, teachers should beware *deficit models* and remember that it is too easy to label a child's spoken language as 'poor', or even to say that they have 'no language', without sufficient thought. Bearne (1998), for example, offers a transcription of a discussion including Sonnyboy, a 6-year-old boy from a Traveller community, demonstrating his ability to 'translate' language for other children:

Emily:	I loves them little things.
Sonnyboy:	Yeah . . . I loves the little sand things – that tiny wee spade . . . and this little bucket . . .
Teacher:	Do you think it would be a good idea to ask Cathy to get some? [*Cathy runs a playgroup for the Traveller children on their site.*]
Emily:	What for?
Teacher:	So that you'd have some at home.
Sonnyboy:	And who'd pay for them? Would Cathy pay?
Teacher:	No, it would be part of the kit.
Emily:	I don't know what you mean. Kit – who's Kit? Me Da's called Kit – would me Da have to pay?
Sonnyboy:	Not your Da – it's not that sort of kit, Emily. It's the sort a box with things in that you play with . . . like toys and things for the little ones.

(Bearne, 1998, p. 154)

It is important then that teachers understand about language diversity and the ways in which judgements are made about speakers in the classroom. From this perspective it is equally important that teachers recognise their own histories and status as language users, and resist the temptation to impose their own social criteria on the child's ongoing language development. As Bearne goes on to point out:

Language diversity is . . . deeply involved with social and cultural judgements about what is valuable or worthy. . . . Judgements are often made about intelligence, social status, trustworthiness and potential for future employment on the basis of how people speak – not the content of what they say, but their pronunciation, choice of vocabulary and tone of voice. Such attitudes can have an impact on later learning.

(Bearne, 1998, p. 155)

Language development and the Foundation Stage

Siraj-Blatchford and Clarke (2000, p. 20) argue that 'language involves more than learning a linguistic code with which to label the world or to refer to abstract concepts; language also involves learning how to use the code in socially appropriate and effective ways'. From a very early age, children are learning through language, they are learning to use language and they are learning about language. In the early years setting children:

- develop their knowledge and understanding about how language works;
- develop a range and variety of vocabulary to use;
- develop awareness of their audience – whom they are speaking to. (There is some evidence to suggest that, by the age of 4, children have learned to adjust their speech according to different audiences);
- think about the appropriate language to use according to the circum-stances of the situation;
- learn to speak coherently and with clarity to make themselves understood;
- learn to speak with confidence.

Purposeful language situations must be planned in order for children to practise their language skills and become aware of what is appropriate or suitable for a specific context. The way that talk is valued and the recogni-tion that what children say is important is illustrated in the following example of the way an early years setting worked with one of their children.

Jemima's language journey

Jemima, a highly articulate child aged 3 years and 6 months had recently moved house from one part of the country to another. She was an only child and both her parents worked long hours. She spent most of the day with Sarah, her nanny, and usually saw her parents only briefly each evening. She joined the nursery in September at the beginning of the academic year.

Following detailed observations of children's movements during the course of a session early on in the term, it became evident to the practitioner that, although Jemima was regularly visiting different areas of the setting, she was doing so as an observer rather than as a participant. She would only play with a resource if no-one else was using it. If another child came along and tried to talk to her she would walk away. Further, if a key adult was focusing on a particular activity with one or more children Jemima would often try to draw that adult's attention away from them by making a statement such as, 'When I woke up this morning I shouted, "Mummy! Mummy!" but guess what? Mummy didn't come! Sarah came upstairs and helped me get up.'

It became apparent that Jemima had found the house move difficult and was unsettled by it. She talked about the fact that she had lived in a large house before but now she lived in an 'enormous' house. She missed her parents. Jemima was able to express how she was feeling. At the same time, while what she was saying was not inappropriate, the context of the situation was a concern to staff.

As a result of a discussion between key adults in the setting the following plan of action was agreed. Jemima would be given time to talk with one of the adults about her new routines at home. She would then be helped and supported to understand that these routines were permanent. In addition to addressing the issue, this would give her some of the individual attention she needed. The practitioner would invite Jemima's parents to come in for a progress report. Positives would be discussed such as their daughter's use of language and her artwork to provide a balance to the consultation, which would also serve to raise her parents' awareness of her insecurity. A series of adult-focused activities involving children working in groups would be planned over the period of a month. Jemima would then experience being part of a group with adult support on a regular basis. If Jemima was spending time with one of the key adults in the setting, for example, listening to a story, the adult would invite another child to come and listen too. Jemima would then come to understand that other children needed, and indeed were entitled to, an adult's time and attention as well. Comments would be made by the key adult such as, 'Who can we invite to come and listen to the story with us?' Should Jemima be introduced to another child by a key adult and start to play alongside them, the adult would subtly withdraw and leave them to play together. Names were important to Jemima so it was agreed that all key adults would introduce Jemima to other children she was with and vice versa.

As a result of the action plan, Jemima gradually needed to talk about home life less and less. Being given the opportunity to talk things through each day with an adult she knew would listen to her helped her to work through her unsettled feelings to ones of understanding and acceptance. Jemima's parents appreciated greatly the practitioner's time and obvious care for their daughter. Her mother started to go to work later one day a week so that she could drop Jemima off at the nursery, and her father came home early twice a week so that he could pick her up. Sometimes he would try to work from home. Jemima became more and more relaxed in the company of her peers. She started to enjoy their company. At first she relied on a key adult inviting her to join in with small groups, indicating her willingness to be asked by standing close and trying to make eye contact with the adult. She no longer tried to draw their attention away from other children.

Jemima loved stories. Soon she was inviting children to join her being read to without any support from key adults in the setting. Jemima eventually became confident enough to introduce herself to children whose names she was not sure of. One day she wanted to play in the water tray alongside a male peer. 'My name is Jemima,' she said. 'What are you called?' When the boy did not reply she put her hands on her hips, leaned towards him ensuring she made eye contact with him and said, 'You're supposed to tell me your name now!' By the end of her first term, Jemima would greet key adults only briefly when she entered the setting, preferring to seek out the company of her peers straightaway. She started to regularly invite one or two special friends to her home to play and to have tea.

One of the things that this example illustrates is the way that purposeful language contexts must be planned in order for children to practise their language skills and become aware of what is appropriate for a specific context. Children need to learn to take turns, negotiate, share resources, listen to and appreciate another person's point of view, and function in a small group situation. Opportunities for purposeful language situations are many; in role-play areas, for example, or round a talk table. Collaborative interaction can be encouraged round the water and sand trays. If there are two chairs by the computer, one child can discuss with another the programme they are using and children can also learn to wait for their turn (the use of a sand-timer to make the waiting time fair can help). The practitioner can skilfully draw children into various activities and discussions in the setting, both indoors and outdoors.

Children need to know that the setting is a place where emotions can be expressed but that there may be undesirable consequences for expressing emotions in particular ways. It is the ability to manage some of these emotions through talk that is the challenge both for the individual child and the practitioner. For example, young children experience an intense sense of injustice if they feel they have been wronged. Consider the scenario where one child hits another who immediately responds by hitting back. The practitioner must aim to support the child to use language as a tool for thinking by encouraging the child to ask the following kinds of questions: Why did they hit me? Did I do anything to provoke or upset them? Why am I upset? How should I respond to being hit? What should I do if this happens again? A strong early years setting will provide guidelines for children to follow or appropriate support systems if they find themselves in this kind of situation.

Non-verbal language such as facial expression, effective eye contact, posture, gesture and interpersonal distance or space is usually interpreted by others as a reliable reflection of how we are feeling (Nowicki and Duke, 2000). Mehrabian (1971) devised a series of experiments dealing with the communication of feelings and attitudes, such as like/dislike. The experiments were designed to compare the influence of verbal and non-verbal cues in face-to-face interactions, leading Mehrabian to conclude that there are three elements in any face-to-face communication, visual clues, tone of voice and actual words. Through Mehrabian's experiments it was found that 55 per cent of the emotional meaning of a message is expressed through visual clues, 38 per cent through tone of voice and only 7 per cent from actual words. For communication to be effective and meaningful, these three parts of the message must support each other in meaning; ambiguity occurs when the words spoken are inconsistent with, say, the tone of voice or body language of the speaker.

Young children are naturally physically expressive, for example, when tired, upset or happy, yet they do not always understand straightaway the meaning another child is conveying, and sometimes need support or reinforcement to encourage more appropriate behaviour. In a situation of conflict, for example, it can be useful when practitioners point out the expression on a 'wronged' child's face to highlight the consequences of someone else's actions. Conversely, if a child is kind to another child and that child say stops crying or starts to smile, then this too can be highlighted.

Similarly, the practitioner needs to be aware of the messages they are sending out to a child via their use of non-verbal language. It is important to remember that whenever we are around others we are communicating non-verbally, whether we want to or not, and children need to feel comfortable in the presence of the adults around them. According to Chaplain (2003, p. 69), 'children are able to interpret the meaningfulness of posture from an early age'. Even locations and positions when talking can be important. For example, it is beneficial when speaking with a young child to drop down to their level, sitting, kneeling or dropping down on one's haunches alongside them. This creates a respectful and friendly demeanour and communicates a far more genuine interest in the child and what they are doing than bending over them from on high.

The way practitioners communicate with children is therefore a very important part of their role. Some pointers include:

- Talking with children so that they feel that you respect them, are interested in them and value their ideas.
- Giving children your full attention as you talk with them; use direct eye contact to show that you are really listening.
- Finding ways of encouraging children to talk in a range of contexts.
- Using specific positive praise such as 'I really liked the way that you waited patiently for your turn on the computer.'
- Smiling!

Practical activities and techniques to encourage speaking and listening in the early years

Jemima's experience as she settled into her nursery class and coped with the many changes in her life at so young an age highlights the fact that speaking and listening skills must be taught in order for children to use language appropriately. It also highlights the fact that the impact of what is happening in any child's home life should never be under-estimated and it is important for the practitioner to take the time to get to know individual circumstances in order to respond supportively. Once children begin to feel emotionally secure in their early years setting, the scene is set for further learning to take place. Here are some ideas:

- Read story books aloud to children and ask questions to enhance their understanding of the text. Talk with them about what they think is happening in the story. Ask open-ended questions to encourage predictive skills such as 'What do you think is going to happen next?' Include poems as part of your reading repertoire.
- Sing action songs and nursery rhymes with the children so that they experience role-play and music and develop their awareness of rhyme.
- Use story sacks in your setting. A story sack is a large cloth bag containing a good quality storybook with supporting materials, such as puppets and soft toys that act as visual aids to tell the story. It includes a non-fiction book related to an aspect of the story and there is also a game to stimulate language activities. Finally, there is a cassette tape with the story recorded onto it so the children can follow along.

- Make puppets a part of your setting or classroom. Most young children lose their inhibitions with puppets and talk to them as if they were real. Use them to gain children's attention and as part of your teaching during a whole-class input; put out a puppet theatre in your setting or classroom and observe the children's collaborative play; or put a puppet in your book corner and observe the children reading to him!
- Set up areas of the setting or classroom to support and encourage collaborative talk, such as role-play areas that reflect children's life experience and interests such as a Post Office or a café.
- Include a talk table in your setting or classroom. Put out the visual aids from the story sack you are using, for example, and encourage the children to retell the story.
- Use show and tell, where children talk to the rest of their peers about an object that they have brought in from home.
- Plan specifically for adult/child interaction, for example devising adult-focused activities where children work with the practitioner on a one-to-one basis.
- Have a listening area in your setting or classroom, where children can listen to stories or music via headphones.
- Use talk partners to encourage children to verbalise and clarify the thoughts in their head during whole-class discussion and before independent writing.
- Play board games with the children to encourage turn-taking.
- Use role-play drama. Drama is one of the prime ways of addressing speaking and listening. When drama work is linked with a text it can deepen pupils' understanding and interpretation of texts. Using the example of the traditional tale 'Goldilocks and the Three Bears', the following drama techniques can be used with the children and easily adapted for use with other texts:

Freeze frame: pupils in groups of four create the opening scene of the story, when Goldilocks enters the Three Bears' cottage and the Bears go for a walk in the woods and hold their position.

Speaking thoughts: select pupils in role to break from the freeze frame and voice the thoughts of their character, for example, 'What is Daddy Bear thinking of as he leaves his porridge behind?'

Talking partners: Half of the class (in pairs) discuss why Goldilocks should go into the house. Half of the class discuss why she should not. Take this to whole-class discussion.

Mime for whole class: Making and eating porridge; walking through the wood; entering the house; going to bed.

Mime for small groups: Goldilocks being discovered by the bears

Hot seating: Practitioner pretends to be one of the characters from the story and dresses as that character. The children come up with questions for that character. When children are familiar with this technique, the children can play the characters in the 'hot seat'.

Finally, as children become slightly older, speaking and listening is still an integral part of the whole curriculum and still needs to be explicitly planned for. This can be done in English but is also a valuable cross-curricular tool, for example:

- Using drama techniques in history, geography or RE.
- Explaining how a problem has been solved in maths or a conclusion drawn in science.
- As a group, deciding on rules for a game the children have invented in PE.

Littleton *et al.*, in their work with 6- and 7-year-old children, suggest that *exploratory talk* is particularly desirable and something that teachers should encourage:

Exploratory talk demonstrates the active joint engagement of the children with one another's ideas. While initiations may be challenged and counter-challenged, appropriate justifications are articulated and alternative hypotheses offered. . . . Progress, thus emerges from the joint acceptance of suggestions.

(2005, p. 173)

Conclusion

Children's language acquisition is likely to be stronger if they are encouraged to become active participants in conversation, if they are encouraged to be questioning (despite how frustrating this can be for some adults to deal with), to hypothesise, imagine, wonder, project and dream out loud, to hear stories and to tell stories to others, experiencing a range of telling techniques that illustrate the potential power of the spoken word. The social and cultural aspects of language development are equally important at this time, as children learn, through talk, to place themselves within a specific social context, and in this way the development of language and identity are closely linked.

Pointers for speaking and listening in the early years

Even though most of the language acquisition process is complete as children enter school, there is much that the teacher can do in the early years to consolidate and develop these skills.
Young speakers and listeners need:

- to feel safe and secure in their early years environment;
- to build relationships of trust and understanding with their key worker or practitioner;
- to have access to a wide variety of resources and activities to encourage, develop and support speaking and listening skills;
- to have constancy and consistency in terms of opportunities and situations in which to develop their speaking and listening skills – consider a whole setting policy;
- to participate in an environment rich in speaking and listening opportunities.

References

Alexander, R. (2006) *Towards Dialogic Teaching*, 3rd edn, Cambridge: Dialogos.

Bearne, E. (1998) *Making Progress in English*, London: Routledge.

Bruner, J.S. (1983) *Child's Talk: Learning to Use Language*, Oxford: Oxford University Press.

Chaplain, R. (2003) *Teaching without Disruption in the Primary School*, London: RoutledgeFalmer.

DfEE (Department for Education and Employment) (1998) *The National Literacy Strategy Framework for Teaching*, London: HMSO.

English, E., Hargreaves, L. & Hislam, J. (2002) 'Pedagogical dilemmas in the national literacy strategy: primary teachers' perceptions, reflections and classroom behaviour', *Cambridge Journal of Education*, 32(1), 9–26.

Littleton, K., Mercer, N., Dawes, L., Wegerif, R., Rowe, D. and Sams, C. (2005) 'Talking and thinking together at Key Stage 1', *Early Years*, 25(2), 165–80.

Mehrabian, A. (1971) *Silent Messages*, Belmont, CA: Wadsworth.

Messer, D. (2006). 'Current perspectives on language acquisition', in J.S. Peccei (ed.) *Child Language: A Resource Book for Students*, London: Routledge, pp. 110–18.

Nowicki, S. and Duke, M. (2000) *Helping the Child Who Doesn't Fit In*, Atlanta, GA: Peachtree.

Peccei, J.S. (ed.) *Child Language: A Resource Book for Students*, London: Routledge.

Siraj-Blatchford, I. and Clarke, P. (2000) *Supporting Identity, Diversity and Language in the Early Years*, Buckingham: Open University Press.

Tizard, B. and Hughes, M. (1984) *Young Children Learning*, London: Fontana.

Wells, G. (1986). *The Meaning Makers: Children Learning Language and Using Language to Learn*, London: Hodder & Stoughton.

Wilkinson, A. (1991) 'Evaluating group discussion', *Educational Review*, 43(2): 131–41.

Wray, D., Bloom, W. and Hall, N. (1989) *Literacy in Action*, Barcombe: Falmer.

Annotated bibliography

Bearne, E. (1998) *Making Progress in English*, London: Routledge.

While this is not purely a book about speaking and listening, it contains wonderful examples of children's talk (often with teachers) and provides keen insight into the way in which this talk is related to reading and writing development.

Dawes, L. and Sams, C. (2004). *Talk Box Speaking and Listening Activities for Learning at Key Stage 1*, London: David Fulton Publishers.

A helpful practical guide to a particular approach to speaking and listening.

Maclure, M., Phillips, T. and Wilkinson, A. (eds) (1988) *Oracy Matters*, Milton Keynes: Open University Press.

Andrew Wilkinson coined the term 'oracy' and this collection is an important record of the work that was done before and during the National Oracy Project.

Norman, K. (ed.) (1992) *Thinking Voices: The Work of the National Oracy Project*, London: Hodder & Stoughton.

A collection of voices which includes children, teachers, project coordinators, LEA advisers, academics and researchers, combining to present a readable and comprehensive introduction to speaking and listening issues.

Qualification and Curriculum Authority (QCA) (2003) *New Perspectives on Spoken English in the Classroom*, London: QCA.

There is a series of excellent contributions to this publication, which summarises various kinds of work on speaking and listening.

CHAPTER 7

'It is only a story, isn't it?'

INTERACTIVE STORY-MAKING IN THE EARLY YEARS CLASSROOM

Lesley Hendy

Children are born as storytellers. We have an innate need to tell, act out and listen to stories in order to shape our lives and give them meaning. As Bettleheim (1995) reminds us: 'Today, as in times past, the most important and also the most difficult task in raising a child is helping him to find a meaning in life.' Children's story-making is often hurriedly dismissed as either being appealing but rather shallow or lacking in coherent construction and limited in meaning. But, as Engel suggests: 'Children's stories can be vital to us as parents, teachers and researchers because they give us insight into how children of different ages experience the world, and how a specific child thinks and feels' (1995, p. 3).

One of the activities that can be observed in early childhood is the ability to play in the 'as if'. When you ask a group of adults what games they played as children they often reply, 'mummies and daddies', 'doctors and nurses', 'cowboys and Indians', 'shops', 'hairdressers' and so on. All these games require children to substitute the real for the fictional; the play is about working 'as if' you were someone else, somewhere else, doing something else. This ability to use 'pretend play' begins before nursery age and often continues into puberty and sometimes beyond.

Children actively engage in story-making from as early as 12 months old. They are able to use 'pretend' play to act out their stories, either by themselves or with others. Small children at play will often speak their thoughts aloud and provide actions to support them. As their lives change, the stories of their lives change accordingly. Many parents and teachers have experienced the 'make-believe' tea party or the imaginary friends.

It could be said that the beginnings of drama can be found in these early types of story-making activities. These stories are 'played out' and the 'scripts' children use come from their experiences. Drama as used in early education, however, concerns the making of meaning rather than the making of plays. Young children are not creating 'roles' in the theatrical sense but enter these 'pretend' situations as themselves. As Hendy and Toon (2001, p. 22) state: 'Pretend' play could be described as children engaging with a series of different behaviours and events. It is about trying out ideas, motivations and reactions to events in make-believe situations.' Pretend play, in this regard, has a very important part to play in a child's development. The introduction of the national curriculum sadly brought about a decline in 'pretend' play and especially the role-play area as an integral part of the curriculum. It is hoped that the establishment of the Foundation Stage will reverse this trend.

The phrase 'role-play' is a problematic term. It is often used to describe what children are doing in 'pretend play'. There are inconsistencies and individualised understandings of the term 'role-play' that make it complicated. In the theatrical sense, the actor who is in 'role' has to take on board all the characteristics of the character they are playing. They need to know about a character's past history, emotions and relationships with others.

When young children engage in 'role-play' they play as 'themselves' being a doctor, nurse, shopkeeper, etc. They take on the generic nature of a 'role' as they are not able at this stage to play a fully rounded character. I prefer to describe young children who are engaged in 'fantasy play' as using their 'pretend-self'. We are not asking them to 'act'.

As schooling progresses, personal response through play and pretend-play is often regarded as unreliable and self-indulgent. By adulthood the wonderful spontaneity and creativity found in small children, has been replaced by feelings of inadequacy and social foolishness. Mention the word 'drama' to gatherings of trainees or practising teachers and a perceptible apprehension travels through the group. 'I hope she isn't going to make us get up and do something' or 'I'm not making a fool of myself' are common comments often heard at the beginning of drama courses. For many, the memory of reading Shakespeare around the class or participation in performance, requiring the learning and delivering of lines, has caused their adult misgivings.

In the last ten years or so, business and industry have rediscovered the use of role-play as an important constituent of management training. There are now few courses in which there is not an element of role-play used for team-building, the exploration of difficulties in groups or as a means of engaging in problem-solving and decision-making. These are precisely the things that the good early years specialist wants to encourage in her children's learning and development.

In this chapter, I shall outline some ways in which drama in the early years can be used as an effective learning medium, from adult intervention in play in the 'home/role-play corner' to actively making stories with children. I shall also discuss the use of 'drama strategies' as a way of providing time for reflection and widening experience within story-making. In doing so, I hope to ease anxieties about drama and provide early years educators with a strong rationale for including drama as a teaching tool within the planning of the curriculum.

Why drama is important in the early years

As an integral part of the natural development of children's play, pretend-play offers us a ready-made medium in which we can engage with our children. Through the 'as if', that is, the ability to function in an imaginary environment, children are given a different viewing point from which to consider, discover and make meaning of the world.

However, 'pretend-play' as a feature of children's play needs careful examination. We need to be aware that small children function in the 'as if' in two distinct ways. The first is *socio-dramatic play*, in which they act out 'scripts' from their real lives and the second is *thematic-fantasy play*, where they create stories from their imagination. It is important we provide opportunities for both, as each requires a different mode of thought.

It was Bruner (1986) who first defined these two ways of thinking. His 'paradigmatic' mode, which he described as being involved with logic, sequencing and the ability to be analytical, can be detected in the socio-dramatic play of 'homes', 'hospitals', 'offices', etc. Bruner's 'narrative thinking', on the other hand, can be found in the creativity and construction of 'make-believe' events found in thematic-dramatic play.

The inclusion of dramatic activity in speaking, listening and learning at Key Stages 1 and 2 (Core learning in literacy) would appear to be for the encouragement of purposeful language. Some significant research has shown the importance of role-play in the development of early language (Hutt, 1989; Kitson, 1994; Sylva *et al.*, 1976) and an OFSTED report, *First Class*, indicated that where 'drama and role-play were used effectively' there appeared to be 'better overall standards in literacy' (1994, p. 8).

In spite of this, the use of drama should not be seen as exclusive to the development of language. The socio-dramatic aspects of 'pretend' play should be extended across the curriculum and used in any circumstances that require children to describe and communicate their findings and observations. All aspects of the curriculum can be enhanced when children are given a fictional, 'as if' context in which to discuss and communicate what they know. They will need to use their logical and analytical abilities in 'as if' contexts that require natural laws to apply. The 'narrative' skills provided by thematic-dramatic play will develop creative thinking and strengthen work in the other arts.

Drama work, as well as giving opportunities to explore the curriculum in different ways, can also provide the teacher with the opportunity for group activity that involves social interaction and the exchange of ideas. Through such activity the core skills as identified in the Foundation Stage literature can be addressed. Children pose and solve problems, reason, make decisions, use numeracy, engage in communication, extend their personal, social and emotional skills, and use their knowledge and understanding of the world. There are also opportunities to develop creativity and physical ability.

By bringing into the classroom the dimension of action, drama enhances learning through the use of PEOPLE–SPACE–TIME. Through the creation of a fictional world, children are given the opportunity of being who they like, where they like and when they like. For example, they could enter a fictional world, as themselves, trying to find solutions to such matters as how to clean up their village as part of a project on the environment. They might be mice trying to reach the moon in order to see whether it is really made of cheese as part of a topic on the sun and moon. They could be a group of servants worried about the disappearance of Snow White, or, alternatively, farmers trying to work out how you can remove milk from a broken-down milk tanker.

The use of fictional contexts puts children in control, casting them in the role of 'experts'. By making use of their existing language, experience, motivations and interests, the teacher can intervene in the play to bring new shape and fresh ways of looking at things. These opportunities provide the teacher with a wide range of potential contexts otherwise unavailable in the normal classroom situation.

The overall purpose of drama as a way of learning should be to effect *change*, which may occur in a number of ways. For example, it may bring about:

- a change in the level of knowledge and understanding;
- a change in ways of thinking;
- a change in attitude;
- a change in the expectation of what pretend-play can offer;
- a change in existing language;
- a change in awareness and the needs of others.

There may also be a change in the relationship that exists between language use and the control of knowledge. By providing opportunities for children to set the agenda and to learn about things that interest them, the teacher has access to a wider curriculum. This can be achieved even within the constraints of existing curriculum requirements.

The general characteristics of drama as a learning medium can be described as:

- a method of teaching that helps present information and ideas within a different form of communication (sometimes children are the experts, the teacher the one who needs to be taught);
- a means of giving children some control over their learning, thereby giving them greater access to knowledge and ideas (children are given opportunities to choose the problems that have to be solved and the decisions to be made);
- a method of giving children a fictional situation in which they can respond outside the structure of the ordinary classroom (the shy child is given a context in which to act as someone else);
- an alternative means of describing and communicating, which allows pupils to bring their own knowledge about the world into the classroom (children with specialised knowledge such as fishing or horse-riding are able to make a fuller contribution);
- a method of learning that allows pupils and teachers to function as equals;
- a method of providing a 'need to know', which can heighten the learning that has taken place or will take place back in the classroom (children often want to research into something that has arisen within a story).

If drama activity is about anything, it is about the learning and turning-points in life. Such moments can cause the participants to reflect on their actions and to rethink some of their ideas from within a safe environment. To sustain the action the players have to use both their factual and subjective knowledge. They will also be introduced to new material, both factual and objective, that they can use to help them solve problems and take decisions. This is where the teacher plays such a crucial role. As Readman and Lamont (1994, p. 16) reflect:

It is the responsibility of the teacher to:
- resist any assumptions about the kind of role(s) children might adopt;
- select content areas which reflect genuine cultural diversity;
- enable children to adopt roles which challenge any stereotypes;
- offer children opportunities to work collaboratively.

Out of the home corner

In the early years classroom, the most obvious place for a teacher to introduce new ways of using the 'as if' is in the 'home/role-play corner'. 'Home/role-play corners' in the classroom are usually the province of children only and sometimes it is important to allow the children to play alone. But, there are other times when an adult could enter the fantasy situation and play alongside them.

Knowing when and how to intervene constructively, without the children feeling that the teacher is intruding, takes sensitivity and watchfulness. Initially just passing by and engaging in short conversations in role will help build trust. On a recent visit to an infant classroom where the teacher had set up a seaside cafe in her 'home corner', I was encouraged to buy chips and join a complaint about the lack of salt and vinegar!

When you gauge that the children are ready to accept you, an adult, into their 'make-believe' world, more time can be spent with them in their 'home/role-play corners'. By dropping 'home' and renaming it 'role-play' area, many more possibilities become available. 'Role-play' corners should be seen by the children as more than just places for dressing up and pushing the doll's pram. A 'home corner' can confine the activities to socio-dramatic play only. By providing different types of environment, the children are given scope to engage in both socio and thematic-dramatic play.

The creation of a 'role-play' area could involve the class in making things to go in it and might require knowledge of number and shape, making things or the use of IT. Often sterile play comes from the fact that the children have had no input into the design or management of the area.

Intervention by adults

Having joined the children at play and adopted a pretend persona within their make-believe, we can both initiate or respond in order to facilitate learning. Each intervention by the teacher varies the learning opportunities and the possible learning outcomes (Baldwin and Hendy, 1994). It is particularly effective if the teacher identifies and makes use of learning opportunities that arise naturally and are offered by the children themselves. It is important for children to feel some ownership of the story and that their contributions to the dramatic play are valued. The teacher may enter the story as the patient or the customer but they must treat the 'doctor' or 'dentist', 'travel agent' or 'greengrocer' with the same respect as in real life. This will help to develop the shared fiction in a more open way, and, as other children hear the conversations, they can be encouraged to join in. The teacher's intervention will also help the child in role to become more committed to their part in the fiction. By using this approach, we are able to indicate to the children that their dramatic play is valued and highly regarded. We communicate that it is important to us and is a respected form of activity.

Types of role-play area

'Role-play' areas do not always have to represent familiar locations: any place and any time is possible. Some examples might be:

- places that take children back in time, such as castles, sailing ships, pirate ships, old houses, to begin to give small children a sense of the past;
- time travel settings, such as a space ship or a time machine;
- fairy story places, such as the Three Little Pigs' brick house, Little Red Riding Hood's cottage, Cinderella's kitchen or the Seven Dwarves' house;
- places of the imagination, such as the all green room, the upside down room, the room of dreams.

All these possibilities develop children's speaking and listening and allow exploration of other areas of the curriculum. What we choose to provide for our children will determine the learning opportunities we can exploit.

By entering children's dramatic play in this way, we are able to build up trust and commitment. We are able to add dimensions that children are usually unable to sustain for themselves. The ideas can be extended later, when bigger group or whole-class drama is undertaken. Our interventions can add the dimension of persistence and consequence: what children do and say can be challenged, questioned and analysed, not just by the adult but by the children themselves.

The Greek word for drama means 'living through' and the action of the drama needs to be lived through by players using 'make-believe' to create the setting for their pretend existence. Within this fantasy world, it is important that all agree to take part and share the same action. Adults must be careful never to begin in role without telling the children that they are doing so. Saying 'Can I play?' informs children of our intentions. All the players must employ knowledge they have brought with them from their real lives to help them in the pretend world. Life experience and factual knowledge are applied in an active way, frequently providing a genuine 'need to know'. It is important that children and adults are always aware that they are playing. They must be able to 'hold two worlds in their head at the same time' (Readman and Lamont, 1994, p. 27). All should be aware that at any time the 'make-believe' can cease, which paradoxically creates the safety. Vygotsky described this ability to live in these two worlds as the 'dual affect'. Aristotle also described this phenomenon as 'metaxis' – the real world and the fantasy world of the drama coming together in the mind of the player.

Drama helps children to communicate in a more significant way and allows them to think more deeply about the consequences of their actions. The random 'play' shooting of the playground, for instance, can be challenged – shooting hurts people and this can be explored. Also, drama allows children to have new experiences and to test out their reactions in a 'safe' environment. Children are repeatedly asked to interpret the actions of others, often in unfamiliar ways, and are given the opportunity to replay, change and reflect upon different parts of the action.

Using improvisation as the medium for dramatic activity

The term *improvisation* as the medium for dramatic activity often appears in documents and books. Within most groups, either students or early years educators, there is some common understanding as to what this term means, but less understanding of how it works. It could best be defined as an active method of working which requires both children and teachers to enter a fictional world in which – sometimes as themselves or sometimes as other people – they will be able to:

- explore human relationships and behaviour;
- have a first-hand experience of events and ideas;
- have a genuine need to talk and listen;
- solve problems and make decisions.

In this fictional world, both dialogue and non-verbal action between participants is made up as the situation proceeds, as with ordinary conversations and actions in real life. The group does not have a pre-written script that is learnt, spoken and acted. Through the fictional context, the dialogue and non-verbal action can be steered to include anything the teacher or the children want to discuss or explore. This activity is known as 'continuous improvisation' as it carries on as long as all participants are able to sustain it. Drama in the classroom uses elements that are also to be found in theatrical action: human relationships and situations driven by tension and suspense caused by complications in the plot linked through place and time, using movement and language.

It is very difficult to sustain continuous improvisation for long periods of time. Young children can quickly become disengaged from it, either because they feel their contribution is not being heard or they become absorbed in their own story-making. Maintaining improvisation with very large groups may not be easy and, with ever-increasing class size, drama needs to be carefully planned and organised.

Drama strategies/conventions as a tool for planning

A drama strategy/convention is a structuring device that helps the teacher focus the children on certain aspects of the story being made. Over recent years, the use of drama strategies/conventions has become an important aspect of drama planning and structuring. A teacher can interrupt the story by using a drama strategy/convention to:

- help build a shared environment – are we all in the same wood? What common understanding do we have about circuses? As we look at the island what do we all see?
- move the plot on through teacher narration if the story is not going anywhere or has become rather circular in its development;
- look at something that has happened to help build group identity about the dilemma – this stops children's insatiable desire for 'what happens next'.

In some instances the group can go back and re-run a section which might be leading the children somewhere they do not want to go. 'Unlike real life', as one student observed 'you can re-wind and change what has just been done.'

Some useful drama strategies/conventions that work with early years

Most good books on educational drama contain descriptions and uses for drama strategies (Baldwin and Hendy, 1994; Neelands, 1990; Readman and Lamont, 1994; Toye and Prendiville, 2000; Woolland, 1993). The ones I have included are those I personally have found most suitable for work with early years children.

Teacher-in-role is possibly the drama strategy/convention most familiar to educators. This is a very powerful tool as it allows the teacher to enter the fictional world alongside the children and to structure the story from within. When first introduced to this strategy, teachers-in-training can find the prospect of entering into the context with the children rather daunting; organising the action from the outside seems a much safer option. Those who are willing to undertake teacher-in-role and participate fully in the story-making find that this is one of the most effective and adaptable roles they can employ. To engage children in a known story, use the drama strategy/convention **My Story**. Here, the teacher in their role tells the story of their predicament, for example, Mother Pig cannot find her children, the park keeper has lost all the animals, the Sandman's grandchild doesn't know where to find the right sand.

Other strategies/conventions include:

- **still-image** – the group or smaller groups take up a pose to construct a picture to describe what they want to say;
- **continuous role-play** – all the children are involved in creating the story by taking on the role of a generic group, e.g. farmers, office workers, friends of the three pigs, children who know how to fly;
- **circle time** – the whole group gathers in a seated circle to discuss events and make group decisions. A useful device for calming and controlling the group;
- **collective role-play** – several children take on the role of one character and support each other in what they say;
- **what can you see?** (more suitable for Key Stage 1) – each child describes an environment, an event, a person to build a group image;
- **thought-tracking** (more suitable for Key Stage 1) – individuals say aloud what they think and feel about an event, character or idea;
- **small-group work** (more suitable for Key Stage 1) – a small group of children are asked to create a small scene, with or without dialogue, to show what might have happened during an event or what might happen if an idea is carried out.

Planning dramatic activity

By using the elements of theatrical action, improvisation and drama strategies/conventions, teachers have the tools to plan and structure story-making. The dramatic activity is based on creating a context for improvised situations to take place, which can be enhanced by the use of other dramatic strategies/conventions when needed. As has already been suggested, using drama for educational purposes is about making meaning for children rather than making plays.

The structuring of the story-making must provide a strong dilemma (tension and suspense) from which the children can build belief; in other words something must happen to engage their interest. The children need to be able to enter the role behaving 'as if' it were so. To work, the activity must provide enough stimulation for the children to have a common willingness to 'suspend disbelief'.

Young children possess an innate ability to understand the structuring of stories. They instinctively know that once the story of the drama has started something is going to happen (Hendy, 1995). They know that the protagonists in the story will come across complications and dilemmas that have to be solved – Red Riding Hood meets a wolf who wants to eat her, the Three Little Pigs are chased by a wolf intent on destroying their homes and eating them. These dilemmas are strong and life-threatening. This does not mean to say that all drama must be about life-and-death situations. But something must be happening that creates a powerful tension to hold the interest and create contexts in which new knowledge and understandings can take place.

Choosing the context

Choosing the context is an important factor in the planning for interactive story-making. Well-known children's stories are a good basis for starting as they often have interesting settings that capture the imagination of small children. Having selected the context it is worth identifying some of the learning areas that could be explored as the story develops. Stories set in woods or the outdoors might lead to environmental issues or aspects of knowledge and understanding of the world. Stories set indoors might provide a context for communication, language and literacy, and problem-solving, reasoning and numeracy.

After the theme has been selected, key learning areas should be identified. These can be universal ideas such as:

• How do we find out about what people are like?
• How do we deal with people who are different?
• How do we deal with the things that frighten us?

Or they can be more curriculum-based, such as:

- How do we describe similarities and differences between materials? (Knowledge and understanding of the world)
- How do we design something which will carry us on the wind? (Problem-solving, reasoning and numeracy)
- Can we recount a story from our past? (Communication, language and literacy)
- How should we treat these new people that we have found? (Personal, social and emotional development)

To answer some of these questions the story can be structured, through the use of improvisation and drama strategies/conventions, to explore key learning areas. Using 'The Sandman' as an example (see detailed plan, Table 7.1), the universal question from this story might be: how do we cope with difficult problems?

The teacher needs to decide whether the story-making is going to be used to develop 'paradigmatic' or 'narrative' thinking. Stories that involve children pretending to be in familiar surroundings can be effective vehicles to introduce information or assess their ability to problem-solve, reason and use numerical understanding, communicate with each other and work together socially. Such stories could be termed 'home' stories as they are based in reality and all the activities are controlled by natural laws, in other words there is no magic. Such interactive stories are a useful way of helping young children learn more about their world.

Fantasy stories, on the other hand, have a different feel and are rooted in the imagination. This kind of drama work can extend children's narrative thinking and imaginative powers, allowing the possibility of all worlds and ideas, however bizarre and extraordinary.

Planning must take into consideration the children's willingness to:

- adopt the 'pretend';
- make-believe with regard to actions and situations;
- make-believe with regard to objects;
- maintain the make-believe verbally;
- maintain the make-believe through movement;
- interact with the rest of the group;
- keep to the structure and the rules of playing.

Teachers must also plan with a commitment to their own participation in mind. Children are not able to engage in effective learning through drama unless the adult has:

- a genuine desire to work in this medium;

Table 7.1 Interactive story-making session planner : using a nursery rhyme . . . 'The Sandman Comes'

The Sandman comes
The Sandman comes.
He brings such pretty snow-white sand
For every child in the land
The Sandman comes.

Learning Objectives:
Speaking, Listening and Responding:

- enjoy listening to and using spoken language and readily turn to it in play and learning
- sustain attentive listening, responding to what they have heard by relevant comments, questions or actions

Drama:

- explore familiar themes and characters through improvisation and role-play
- adopt appropriate roles in small or large groups and consider alternative courses of action.

Learning Intentions	Planning	Making the Story
To encourage attentive listening	Teacher as herself teaches the nursery rhyme and makes contract with the children	Gather children into sitting circle. Teacher reads the nursery rhyme 'The Sandman comes' and teaches children to say the rhyme. Teacher asks 'Who is the Sandman? What does he do? When does he come? What does he bring?' Encourage answers. (Set up the story by making the contract) Tell the children they are going to make a story together. Teacher tells the children she will leave the circle and when she comes back she will pretend to be the novice 'Sandman' who comes every right and they are to be children who can't get to sleep.

To provide information to set the context for the story	Teacher uses 'T-I-R' & 'My Story'	You are a novice 'Sandman' who comes every evening with the snow-white sand and you sprinkle the magic sand into the eyes of little children to make them sleep. You are very new because your grandfather who has been the Sandman for many, many years wanted a holiday from flying around the world every night and he has asked you to take over while he is away. What he didn't tell you before he left on his long, long holiday is where you go to get the snow-white sand. You have run out and you have come to the children to ask for their help
To use language to imagine and create roles and experiences	**Continuous improvisation** to build the context	Children prepare with T-I-R to get ready for their journey. T-I-R asks 'What do we need to take with us? How long will it take to get there?' Children will provide answers and solutions to problems set. T-I-R assesses the options and decides with the children the most likely solution. Begin the journey.
To develop communication and social skills	**Continuous improvisation** to create the tension	The journey could take you anywhere. T-I-R should bear in mind you are looking for places where sand can be found. Keep asking questions 'Where can we find beautiful white sand?' 'Has anyone been on a beach lately?' 'How will I know it is the right sand? The stuff my Grandpa uses.'
To develop problem solving and reasoning	**Circle time** to reflect and re-engage	From time to time take time out by gathering in a group to discuss what has happened and what is going to happen. Discuss actions and decisions.
To develop personal and emotional skills	**Still-image**	To restart the story, ask children to take up position as if in a photograph of what they are doing just before they were called into the circle. Ask them to close their eyes and think about how they feel about the journey. Ask the picture to come to life and very slowly ask children to find a friend and whisper how they feel to their partner
To work in small or large groups and consider alternative courses of action	**Continuous improvisation** to develop the story and build to an acceptable conclusion	Allow the story to develop following children's ideas until you reach an acceptable conclusion. In the case of this story the children should return home and the apprentice Sandman should sprinkle the sand in the children's eyes and they finish all going to sleep.

- an eagerness to enter the child's world, to believe in what they are doing and to take their work seriously;
- an understanding of how improvisation and drama strategies function and can be used;
- knowledge of the learning potential of any particular story together with ability to keep this to the fore;
- techniques to introduce problems for the group to solve;
- the willingness to take risks;
- the willingness to work beside the children and allow the group to make decisions.

Making the contract

It is important that before engaging in interactive story-making both children and adults enter into a contract that makes clear the plan of action, the expectations and the responsibilities of how to proceed when the story-making has begun. As has already been advised, never begin a story until all participants know what they are expected to do.

Some examples of active story-making

Working with a modern children's story

A trainee teacher recently decided to use Nick Butterworth's 'After the Storm' as the basis for her drama. This story has the setting of a wood in which a storm has taken place and the animals have been left homeless. This story provided a richness of learning possibilities she could explore with her reception class. The class topic was 'animals' so this story fitted well into the overall curriculum planning.

She began to examine her areas of learning. The wood setting would allow her to test out the children's knowledge of trees and animal habitats, work that they had already undertaken in the classroom. She wanted to discover how much knowledge the children had of life processes and living things. She wanted to see whether she could introduce some information about shape, space and measures as the children in their role as animals started to think about the design of their new homes. Design and making would be a strong feature of the story. Knowledge and understanding of the world could be discussed as the children made observations about their damaged habitat. By asking the children to remember what it was like before the storm, and sequence events before they heard the great wind, she hoped to increase their sense of the past. Gradually, through careful planning, she was able to build up the learning potential inherent in the story.

Throughout she was keen to let the 'animals' tell their own story, but, by participating herself in the role of a water rat, she was able to question, pose problems and expand their understanding. Almost immediately, the children introduced 'tension' by the introducing the idea of the wolves. These animals were never seen but were present throughout, driving the 'animals' to find a new home quickly before they were eaten. Not having the right tools or materials also became a major problem and slowed up progress on the new homes. Rescue came in the role of 'Wise Owl', a character again introduced by a child, who invited all the animals to his home in the tree and gave them tea.

Most of the story was created through 'continuous improvisation', but the trainee introduced some other strategies to increase reflection and commitment. At the very beginning, the children were asked to stand quietly in a circle and look at the tree. The trainee went round to each child in their role as an 'animal' and asked them what could they see. Gradually, they built up a group picture of the tree fallen in the wood. She then asked each of them to go and rescue something from their home. They returned to the circle and showed the others what they had rescued and what it meant to them. Many of these items were then used in the story. At the end of the story, each child was asked to pretend to be a photograph (still-image) of their animal standing outside their new home. She subsequently read them the story and it became a big favourite with the class.

Working from children's ideas

When working from children's ideas the teacher has to be able to 'think on her feet' and to seize learning opportunities as they arise. Such work is ideal for building group cooperation and extending children's ability to solve problems and to take decisions. This does not mean that there is no previous planning involved, but the planning will be of a more fluid nature, predicting beforehand what learning could be achieved if certain situations arise. With experience, teachers can engineer situations whatever line the story is taking. The following example comes from a story developed by a vertically grouped class who had been working on the theme of castles.

The session commenced with circle time. The children sat together with the adults and decided where they were, who they were and what they were doing. They wanted to be servants to a King and they were to be preparing a grand banquet. To start the action in a controlled manner, each child was asked to enter the story space and take up a pose of the job they were doing (still-image), as if someone had painted a picture of them. When all the children were assembled the action began.

The story began slowly, with all the children 'acting out' mixing and peeling and roasting, etc. In my role as a new servant I asked for jobs to do and was told where everything was. I created problems by not doing my work well and was helped by the other servants. From this, I learnt a great deal about the children. Their knowledge of food preparation was very good and we had a long discussion about the best way to cook the potatoes. I asked questions about what I thought I knew about cooking and checked whether I was correct. In this instance, the children were the 'experts' and I was the novice.

Before long the first major complication, the one that changes the course of the story-line, occurred. A child shouted 'fire' and before long we were running about trying to put out the flames. This was an opportunity to talk about the dangers of fire: how did it start? What happens when you get too near the flames? How do you deal with burns? etc. Having dealt with this complication another arose. A second child told us that it was not the servants' carelessness that started the fire but a dragon the King had locked in the dungeon for burning people. The dragon was now crying and its tears had put out the flames.

As we sat down amongst the ruins of the King's banquet we discussed how we could help the sad dragon. Could we trust it not to burn us? How do you learn to trust people who have done you harm? Was the dragon really fierce or was she just afraid? Why might she have been burning villages and people before she was captured? After the discussion each 'servant' was asked to say aloud what they thought and felt about the dragon (thought-tracking) and the bravest were dispatched to release her from her prison. Questions in such stories are endless and can lead to many learning opportunities of a kind that are difficult to discuss in normal class-room situations as they do not necessarily arise.

To describe all the events in this story would take too long here; suffice to say, some 90 minutes later the dragon had been taken home to her babies and the 'servants', complete with cooked banquet, returned to the castle to feed the King. Many areas of the curriculum were covered, including prob-lem-solving, reasoning and numeracy – how big will we need to make our magic carpet to hold all the servants and the dragon? How can we measure the length of the dragon without a tape measure? Knowledge and under-standing of the world – do dragons eat the same things as people? How fast did we need to run to get our magic carpet to fly? Where in the world do dragons live? What sort of terrain will we be walking through if we land in the mountains? Creative development – let's make up a quiet song to sing to the dragon's baby to make her sleep.

The stories made up in this way are very special to children. I always make a point of telling children at the end that no-one has ever heard this story before, it is new and it belongs to them. By writing these stories into book-form, they can make their own popular addition to the book corner.

Making use of a fairy story

Through the employment of teacher-in-role the teacher became the Mother of the Three Little Pigs and asked the children-in-role as the little pig's friends to help her find them. By placing the context (the who, where, what and when) outside the events in the story already known by the children, the teacher gave herself more scope for exploration. It avoided the some-times unproductive 'acting out' of a familiar story. The children's know-ledge of the original story helped them create a sequence of events, but more like detectives piecing together evidence on their journey.

The story began with circle time, where the teacher told the children who she was going to be. She said when she returned to the circle she would be in role as the Mother of the Three Little Pigs and that they, the children, would be some of the pigs' friends. She asked them to close their eyes while she went out of the circle.

On returning she began to tell them about her children and how worried she was as they had been away for a very long time and she had received only had one letter since they had left home. She reached into her pocket for a letter (which she had prepared earlier). She read it to the children. The letter said 'Hello Mum, We are fine. We have built a house made of straw and we are very proud of it. We have heard there is a wolf about so we will take care.' She asked the children questions about wolves and what they are like – should she be worried? Should she go and look for them? Would the children like to join her?

In small groups they drew maps of the landscape around the pigs' home, using pictures and symbols to represent different places. These maps were used on the journey. Questions were asked about the locality – which way did they go? Did they go north, south, east or west? Did they go over the hills or through the woods? The path through the woods was chosen. As it grew dark they thought about a shelter for the night. Where will be the best place? How will they protect themselves from the wolf? Where will they find something to eat?

As the session progressed, the children's interest was sustained by the teacher in her role as Mother. By introducing challenges and problems through effective questioning and leading discussion, and by allowing children to direct the story and make it their own, she was able to exploit much of its learning potential. Through skilful use of drama strategies she created moments of reflection on events, people or ideas when and where they were needed.

The session ended as it had begun, in a circle time. The pigs had been found, the wolf was vanquished and all the participants were ready for bed.

Drama as a time saver

Contrary to popular thinking, teaching through drama is not a drain on precious classroom time. Through working in this active way teachers are given a powerful method of teaching and learning that is not always available in other forms of classroom organisation. Learning by doing, through the use of this interactive method encourages the retention of information. Recently a 7-year-old was able to tell me, in great detail, the events of an interactive story she had made two years previously in her reception class. Through the different modes of thinking and talking that story-making promotes, children are able to articulate what they know. With careful planning and structuring, drama, in the form of interactive story-making, provides a time-saving method of introducing children to new learning, challenging their assumptions and ideas and testing their existing knowledge within different contexts. This type of activity makes a significant contribution to children's social, emotional and cognitive development in their early years.

Pointers for early years drama

Some points to remember when using drama in the early years classroom:

- Story-making is a natural activity in early childhood.
- Drama in education is about making meaning rather than making plays.
- Drama is a useful teaching tool across the curriculum and not exclusive to speaking and listening.
- The teacher as well as the children must be willing to 'suspend disbelief' and participate in the 'as if'.
- Planning for drama is strengthened by effective use of drama strategies.

- The context of the story must contain interesting complications and dilemmas.
- The context of the story should provide powerful learning situations.
- By its nature drama is an efficient and time-saving method of introducing new learning or testing old knowledge.

References

Baldwin, P. and Hendy, L. (1994) *The Drama Box*, London: Harper Collins.

Bettleheim, B. (1995) *The Uses of Enchantment: The Meaning and Importance of Fairy Tales*, Harmondsworth: Penguin.

Bruner, J. (1986) *Actual Minds, Possible Worlds*, Cambridge MA: Harvard University Press.

Engel, S. (1995) *The Stories Children Tell*, New York: W.H. Freeman.

Hendy, L. (1995) 'Playing, role-playing and dramatic activity', *Early Years*, 15, 2, 13–22.

Hendy, L. and Toon, L. (2001) *Supporting Drama and Imagination Play in the Early Years*, Buckingham: Open University Press.

Hutt, C. (1989) 'Fantasy play', in S.J. Hutt, S. Tyler, C. Hutt and H. Christopherson (eds) *Play, Exploration and Learning*, London: Routledge, pp. 99–116.

Kitson, N. (1994) 'Fantasy play: a case for adult intervention', in J. Moyles (ed.) *The Excellence of Play*, Buckingham: Open University Press, pp. 88–98.

Neelands, J. (1990) *Structuring Drama Work*, Cambridge: Cambridge University Press.

OFSTED (1994) *First Class*, London: HMSO.

Readman, G. and Lamont, G. (1994) *Drama: A Handbook for Teachers*, London: BBC Education.

Sylva, K., Bruner, J. and Genova, P. (1976) 'The role of play in the problem-solving of children 3–5 years old', in J. Bruner *et al.* (eds) *Play: its Role in Development and Evolution*, Harmondsworth: Penguin, pp. 55–67.

Toye, N. and Prendiville, F. (2000) *Drama and Traditional Story for the Early Years*, London: Routledge.

Woolland, B. (1993) *The Teaching of Drama in Primary School*, London: Longman.

CHAPTER 8

'Is there a seven in your name?'

WRITING IN THE EARLY YEARS

Sally Wilkinson

The aim of this chapter is to look at ways in which we as educators can provide opportunities that will nurture children as writers. Young children are constantly exposed to print in the environment in which they live, whether at home, at playgroup, in the street or at school. They see adults and older children writing notes to each other, lists for a shopping trip, letters and e-mails. They begin to realise that these marks on paper and screen are regarded as important by those around them and can have many uses. Just as they learn to talk by experimenting with spoken language and imitating those around them, children will often experiment with marks on paper and on the computer screen. They will try out patterns and attempt to communicate through this medium themselves.

These independent marks are often referred to as 'emergent writing'. This term encompasses the vast number of ways in which young children use marks and letters to make meaning. As Yetta Goodman (1986) described, from a young age children engage in writing tasks for a wide variety of reasons and by the age of 2 most children have begun to use symbols to represent real things. Therefore, by the time children enter a nursery or reception class, they may already be very experienced emergent writers. They may be mark-makers or they may be aware of the alphabetic nature of print. It is our job, as educators, to build on these skills, and the knowledge and understanding of writing that the children have. This involves adopting a developmental approach to writing, whereby the children's emergent writing is acknowledged and they are encouraged to 'have a go' rather than copy from an adult model. The implications this has for how writing is approached in school, the contexts in which it happens and ways of encouraging children as independent writers will form the basis for this chapter.

Understanding children writing

Ann Browne, in her book *Helping Children to Write* (1993), correctly says that before we undertake the planning of a writing curriculum for young children we should have some understanding of what writing is for, how it is used and how it looks from the child's point of view. In his nursery class Josh has been looking at snails. Part of his response to this experience (see Figure 8.1) is to make sweeping circular marks across his paper which he says, as he does so, are the snails, and to make dots under this which he says is his writing. Josh is clearly showing, even in this early stage of his hand coordination development, that he knows that drawing and writing are formed by different sorts of marks.

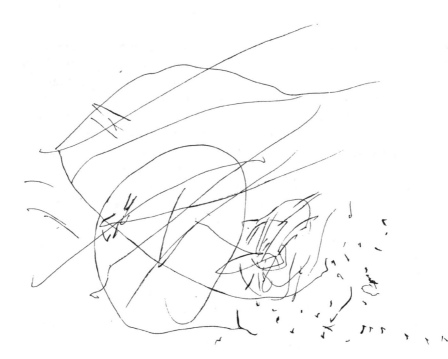

Figure 8.1 *Drawing and writing about snails by Josh, aged 3*

Other children of a similar age might respond with:

- marks mostly horizontal
- zig-zags
- single or linked round shapes
- straight and round marks imitating letter shapes

- large circular shapes
- one letter from their name repeated
- assorted letters from their name.

How children respond in these early stages varies greatly and is not part of a rigid hierarchy of stages. As the many examples of children's writing collected by teachers involved in the National Writing Project (1989) showed, some children experiment with all of the above, others with only one or two.

It does seem to be true, however, that the appearance of the marks in general reflects the children's cultural background, with marks being formed in the direction and following the orientation used by adults around them. Therefore, a child used to seeing adults using a Chinese script may well emphasise vertical marks in their writing. It is also often the case that children who prefer writing with their left hand, or who have not yet shown a preference, may start much of their mark making from the right-hand side of the paper.

Children whose mother tongue is not English may also include characters from their home language in their writing. In the piece of writing shown in Figure 8.2 Fatima is experimenting with a wonderful array of letter and character shapes based on written forms found in English and Bengali. The way that writing is approached and organised in her class has meant that she is confident about herself as a writer and is willing to take risks with her writing. This piece of writing was in response to a story read by the class teacher who then wrote down what Fatima told her that the writing said. She praised Fatima for using so many different letters and characters and they talked about the ones Fatima liked the best.

Young children often develop knowledge and understanding about print long before they are able to demonstrate this through the marks they make on paper. Alex completed the two examples of writing shown in Figure 8.3 in the same week. The marks on the left were completed one morning in his nursery class. When making the marks with his pencil, he showed an understanding of one-to-one correspondence as he told his teacher the letters as he wrote his name. However, his fine motor skills were not sufficiently developed to allow him to represent actual letters. Later that week, when Alex was writing using a computer at home, he was able to demonstrate the full extent of his knowledge about print. First, he chose to type the alphabet in capital letters. (After typing the first 'a' he selected the Caps Lock, as he preferred capitals.) Writing the alphabet involved much concentration as he sang an alphabet song after he typed each letter to help him remember which letter came next. He knew the name of each letter and could find them on the keyboard, but was not sure about all of

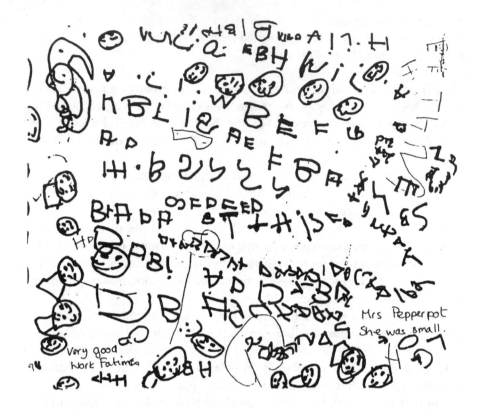

Figure 8.2 *Letter shapes drawn by Fatima showing the influence of English and Bengali written forms*

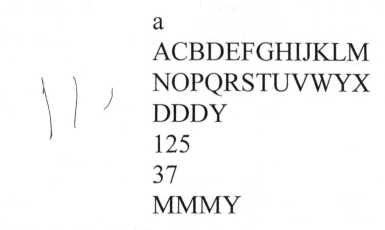

a
ACBDEFGHIJKLM
NOPQRSTUVWYX
DDDY
125
37
MMMY

Figure 8.3 *Alex's writing by hand and using a word processor*

the sounds they made. He could remember the visual appearance of 'mummy' and 'daddy' and write the numbers of two of his favourite types of train.

This opportunity to use a word processor, whether at home or in his nursery class, was very important to Alex for developing both his knowledge about writing and his belief in himself as a writer. As with many young children, boys in particular, Alex did not yet possess the physical skills to form the letters that he already knew. The computer therefore provided a very important avenue for his developing literacy skills.

The role of the educator

As can be seen from the examples so far, by encouraging children to write independently from the start, the role of the educator is altered significantly. Instead of spending time writing sentences for children to copy or answering requests for help with spelling, the educator has a more active role. Time can be spent talking with the children about their writing, observing the skills and knowledge they are using and joining with them as a fellow writer. As can be seen from Figure 8.4, the ways in which an educator can support and interact with children engaged in the writing process are many and varied.

What is certain is that the educator is at the centre of what happens in the classroom. We make decisions all the time, which influence not only the opportunities children have for writing in our classrooms but also how they perceive the task of writing and themselves as writers. Writing needs to be presented as part of the whole language environment, a way of initiating or responding to communication, and as something which can give pleasure for its own sake. The ways that activities are set up in the classroom should recognise that: 'reading, writing, talking about writing and talking in order to write must be continual possibilities; they overlap and interlock' (Smith, 1982, p. 202).

Talking about writing

Making time for talk at various stages of the writing process is one way of improving the quality of the content of the writing that the children produce. The importance of children being clear about what they want to say before they are asked to write is stressed in *Developing Early Writing* (DfEE, 2001). Encouraging children to tell their stories to a friend who would:

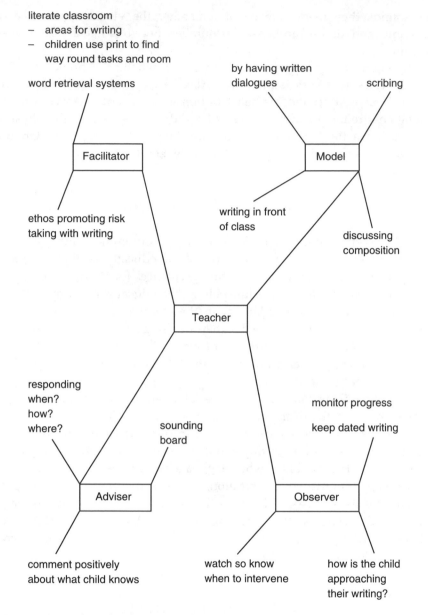

literate classroom
– areas for writing
– children use print to find
  way round tasks and room

word retrieval systems

by having written
dialogues

scribing

Facilitator

Model

ethos promoting risk
taking with writing

writing in front
of class

discussing
composition

Teacher

responding
when?
how?
where?

sounding
board

monitor progress

keep dated writing

Adviser

Observer

comment positively
about what child knows

watch so know
when to intervene

how is the child
approaching
their writing?

Figure 8.4 *Modes of interaction of the educator with children engaged in the writing process*

- say which parts they liked;
- ask questions to clarify their understanding;
- make suggestions of additions or parts to alter.

means that a story is well-established in a child's mind before a pen or pencil has been picked up. There is therefore less chance of the writer coming to the mental block of what to write next, as they have already rehearsed it orally. Using talk in this way asks the children to draft their writing orally. This is an important stage on the way to them being able, when they are more experienced writers, to alter and improve their work on paper and respond to written comments given by peers. The latter idea, which involves partners responding to each other's work, is perhaps usually thought of as only being appropriate for older children. However, as was demonstrated during the National Writing Project (1989), with the support of an educator, young children are able to use talk and writing to comment on a partner's work in a way that extends that child's ideas or encourages them to develop their writing further.

Known texts and writing

As well as recognising the importance of talk to writing we also need to encourage children to draw on the stories, poems and factual texts that they have heard or have read for themselves. This knowledge, coupled with real-life experiences, forms the nucleus of the store of ideas which they tap when involved in writing. Adult writers constantly use ideas that have their basis in something they have once read. So we should value examples in children's writing (such as that by Dale in Figure 8.5), which show through the language used or the ideas expressed that they have drawn on known texts or forms of writing.

Shared writing

One of the ways that the educator can support and develop children's use of the language and formats of known texts is through shared writing with a group of children or the whole class. This methodology is emphasised in the National Literacy Strategy (DfEE, 1998) and consists of:

- demonstration and modelling of writing by the educator;
- scribing and developing ideas given by the children;
- supported composition by the children.

One day Sylvester was resting. Some
beans rolled to Sylvester's basket.
He was a cat.
The beans grew and grew and grew
into a Giant beanstalk. Sylvester
woke up and suckering suckertash and
he climbed the beanstalk . He
climbed and climbed and climbed
and climbded to the giants castle
and when he went down he got knocked
into China.

Figure 8.5 *'Sylvester the Cat' by Dale: writing showing the influence of known texts*

These elements may not all be present in one shared writing session and the educator may choose to develop a piece of writing over two or more days.

A group of children in a Year 2 class had been reading a talking book on the computer of the 'The Tortoise and the Hare'. Following on from the shared reading of the story, the group made up their own fable with their own chosen characters, a spider and a cheetah. In shared writing, the teacher began by demonstrating how to begin the story in the same style as 'The Tortoise and the Hare' and then scribed the group's ideas for the story, helping the children use the story language they had heard in the talking book. Once the story was complete it was read several times by the teacher and children together. Then pictures were drawn to go with each scene and scanned into 'Clicker 4', a computer programme with a book-making facility. Each child then wrote the part of the story that they had illustrated, with the support of word grids, to go on to the screen opposite their picture. Once all the pages were complete they were linked by the teacher to create the children's own talking book. Figure 8.6 shows one page from their finished book.

Writing areas

Careful thought needs to be given to the balance between the children writing in response to a stimulus initiated by the educator and providing

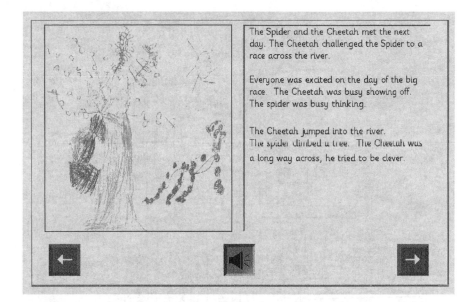

Figure 8.6 *A page from the talking book The Spider and the Cheetah*

opportunities for them to decide on the reason for writing. By setting up a writing or graphics area in the classroom we are providing time and space for children to experiment with a variety of writing materials. They will also be able to make decisions about what they would like to write and how it will be organised. Setting up an area does not require a large space or a major cash outlay. A table against a wall with a notice board for children to display their writing if they wish is fine. A plan of a typical area is shown in Figure 8.7. If the demand is great, the children can always spill over on to neighbouring tables. Equipping the area with a variety of writing implements is more important than having large quantities all the same. The same is true of the materials that are provided for the children to write on; old envelopes, a pad of forms, different shapes, sizes and colours of paper can all be gathered through requests to businesses, shops and parents. The writing area can also reflect topics going on in the class. For instance, a topic on giants could mean that the writing area had giant size envelopes, paper and markers. A Year 1 class was helping to plan the planting for a flower bed in their school grounds, so the materials in their writing area included forms from seed catalogues, labels and diagrams of the school grounds for them to annotate. In settings where space is very limited a writing box can provide the same resources as a writing area. A plastic open toolbox with a carrying handle works well as children and educators can take it to where the writing will take place.

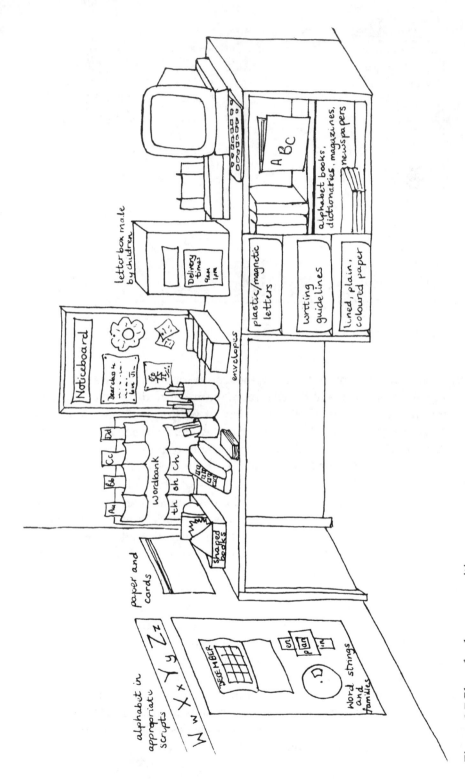

Figure 8.7 *Plan of a classroom writing area*

The writing area provides a low-risk environment in which children can rehearse favourite ways of writing, try new ideas and have control over the whole process from deciding on the purpose of their writing to whether they will make a final neat copy. Sayarun, a Year 2 whose first language was Sylheti, often spent her time in the writing area writing letters to other children in the class. She would choose as her recipients those whom she thought needed cheering up, someone she wanted to congratulate, or someone who had not had a letter from the class postbox for a while. As her letter to her teacher shows (Figure 8.8), she understood many of the functions that letters could fulfil.

Notes

To Mrs Wilkinson I like your
dress do you like my Long dress
I got it from Bank glesd and my
sister got one has well it coloeur is
orgen and like the Palgrave school
Miss did you saw eveytwing yes or No
from sayarun

Figure 8.8 *Sayarun's letter to her teacher*

The postbox was an important feature of the writing area as it provided an authentic opportunity for writing to others, something which definitely motivated the children to write and influenced the quality of the writing that they produced.

Another child in the same class wrote his first truly independent piece of writing in the writing area. He had joined the Year 2 class from another school and was convinced that he could only write by copying an adult's model. At first much of his time in the writing area was spent drawing or on the phone to his grandmother. After a few weeks he posted his first letter and sent it to his teacher (Figure 8.9).

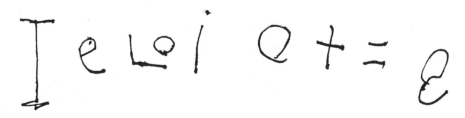

Figure 8.9 *Lee's first letter*

She was overjoyed to receive it and was also able to see from it what Lee understood about print. He had used letters from his name and had included mathematical signs as well. His drawing also began to include examples of environmental print, such as car registrations, street signs and shop names. Lee spent time at weekends out with his father on his ice-cream van and was very interested in and knowledgeable about cars. It was not surprising, therefore, that these examples of environmental print were an important part of his first independent writing attempts.

Writing and role-play

Letters and postboxes also became an important focus for a Year 1 class who had been watching videos and listening to and reading stories about Postman Pat. An area of their classroom became Greendale Post Office and letters from the writing area and home corner were brought from the letterbox to the post office for sorting. The children also took on the roles of post master or mistress and customers, providing opportunities for form-filling, marking of parcels and list-making. Since the post office also sold cards, envelopes, writing paper and pens, these could be purchased and used in the writing area or home corner to generate more post for Greendale staff to collect, sort and deliver.

In role-play situations, it is important that the children have some understanding of the context in which their writing takes place and the forms of writing that might be expected to take place there. Therefore, setting up some types of role-play area might involve the children being taken on a visit to see what sort of things are needed in the area and what people do who work in, for instance, a vet's surgery. Prior to setting up a travel agency in their classroom, one reception class visited a local travel agency and saw all the brochures, forms and computers that were used when people came to book a holiday. They asked the staff what they said to the customers and watched while information was filled in on the computer and forms. Back in the classroom they equipped their travel agency with the following:

telephone	booking forms	pens
computer	tickets	pencils
diaries	timetables	ruler
note pads	labels	stapler
fax machine	posters	envelopes

(cardboard box with slits in)

When the children were playing in the travel agency, an adult some-times joined in with them, taking on the role of a customer or one of the staff. The way in which the children were able to use writing in their play was expanded both by their visit to the travel agency and by an adult modelling the ways in which writing could occur. The children acting as customers would fill in forms on brochures and write notes in the home corner to remind them of what they wanted to ask the travel agents. Those being staff in the travel agency would type details into the computer, make notes, complete forms and fill in information in their diaries.

Providing authentic writing experiences, such as those above, in role-play means that the children are more likely to base their writing on realistic models of writing. The example in Figure 8.10 is from a nursery class and shows Chloe making the choice of an appropriate piece of paper for writing a shopping list from a selection of paper of various sizes avail-able to them. She then wrote her list in the home corner (notice how many of their chosen letters are from their names) and took it with them when they went shopping in the class shop.

Figure 8.10 *Chloe's shopping list*

Purposes and audiences for writing

The importance of children having real reasons for writing in a range of forms and for a range of audiences has been a major topic of discussion in recent years. The English National Curriculum (DfEE, 2000) sets out very clearly the range of purposes and audiences that children should have experience of during Key Stage 1.

When considering who the audience is for a piece of writing, it may be that for children writing in the writing area the answer could be a friend in the class who will receive their card or letter, someone at home or themselves. The value of the latter should not be under-estimated, as providing an opportunity for a child to write without any obligation for them to show their writing to anyone else can contribute immensely to their writing development. The relaxing environment of the writing area can free some children to write in ways that they are not able to do when an educator has expectations of their achievement. Daniel was in Year 2 and his teacher felt that even though he had mastered the technical side of writing, she did not often succeed in motivating him to want to write. For Daniel, the freedom to write for himself and about whatever he wanted was essential. His story (Figure 8.11) began from a blank flap book that was part of the stock of the writing area and represents his greatest writing achievement during his first term in the class.

The examples of children writing during role-play showed how important it is for children to write in authentic situations, so that their play echoes the purposes for which writing is used in the real world. They can also gain much from writing to imaginary audiences, such as when a reception class received a letter from Roger the robot that they had made from junk materials. They corresponded with 'Roger' – in fact their class teacher – for several weeks, with the children asking Roger many questions about himself and responding to enquiries from him about themselves. The way in which children respond to their audience in this situation can vary. Some are happy to believe that Roger can write while others may be more sceptical. Even children from the latter group are usually still willing to enter into correspondence if they know their letters will receive a reply.

Another way of providing opportunities for children to experiment with forms of writing that they do not usually have the opportunity of using is through writing in role to an imagined audience. Excellent stimuli for this are picture books such as *The Jolly Postman* and *Each Peach Pear Plum* (both by Janet and Allan Ahlberg). The former contains many examples of different reasons for writing, which can lead the children to develop their own letters, catalogues and postcards. In the example in Figure 8.12 Darren's letter to BB Wolf draws directly on one in *The Jolly Postman*, from Red

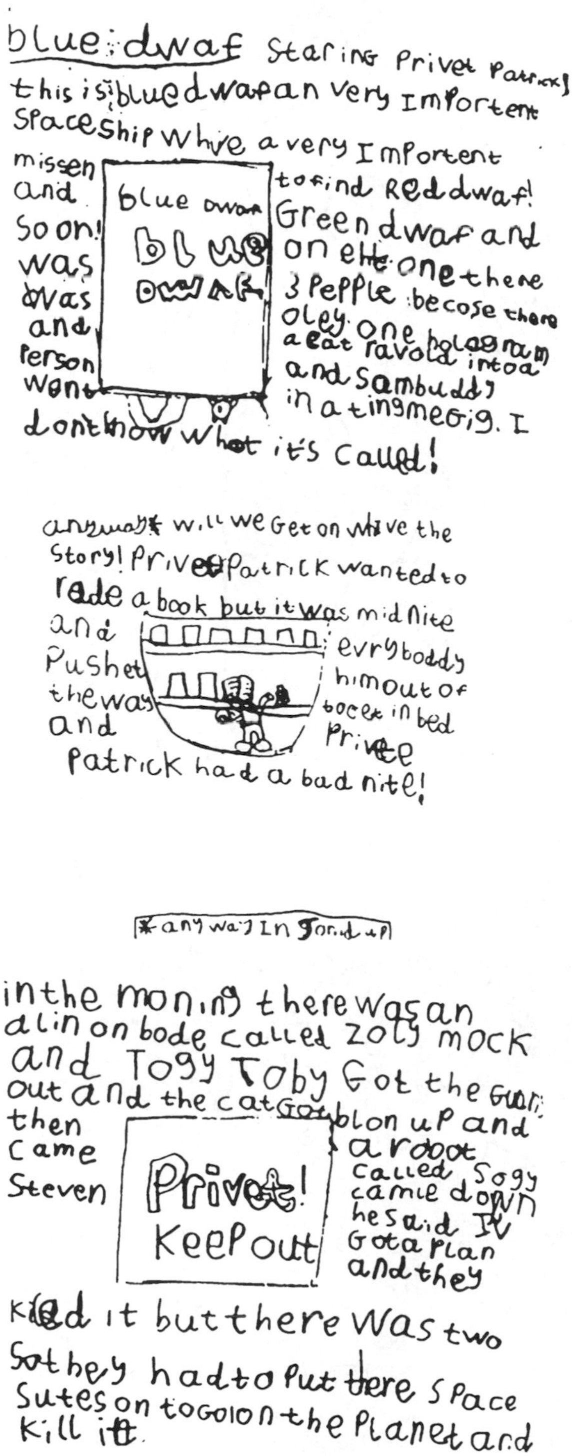

blue dwaf Staring Privet Patrick!
this is blue dwaf an very Importent
Spaceship whive a very Importent
missen   to find Reddwaf!
and   Greendwaf and
So on!   on eht one there
was   3 Pepple becose there
bvas   oley one holog ram
and   a cat ravold into a
person   and Sambuddy
went   in a tingmecig. I
dontknow what it's called!

blue dwar
BLUE
DWAR

anyway will we Get on whive the
story! PrivetPatrick wantedto
rade a book but it was midnite
and   evryboddy
Pushet   himout of
the way   bocet in bed
and   Privet
Patrick had a bad nite!

*anyway In gone up

in the moning there was an
alin on bode called Zoty mock
and Togy Toby Got the Gun
out and the cat Got blon up and
then   a robot
came   called Sogy
Steven   camie down
   he said Iv
Privet!   Got a plan
KeePout   and they

kiled it but there Was two
So they had to Put there Space
Sutes on to Golon the Planet and
Kill it.

Figure 8.11
*Daniel's story on a
self-chosen theme!*

Figure 8.12 *Letters to BB Wolf and Bo-Peep by Darren and Simon*

Riding Hood's solicitors. Simon's, on the other hand, shows him devising the whole scenario for himself. He was invited to write something that could have been posted to one of the characters in *Each Peach Pear Plum* and he chose to write a postcard to Bo-Peep from her lost sheep. The way that he manages to express succinctly all that is necessary is just right for a postcard and the explanation of where the sheep have gone is so appropriate!

Making books

Book-making gives children an excellent reason for writing. Seeing their book published, either within the class or for a wider school audience, is tremendous for developing children's self-esteem and their image of themselves as writers. Often the books made by themselves and their peers are the ones that are the most popular in the book comer and are returned to over and over again. The actual recording of the text of a book can be done in several ways and does not have to be completed by the children. The role of the educator may be to lead the composition of the text in shared writing sessions, or to act as a scribe for a group of children, rereading for them what they have composed so far and encouraging contributions from the whole group.

Collaborative writing

Sometimes being alone with a piece of paper is a daunting experience. Young children can feel that they don't have any ideas or are unsure of committing them to paper. Collaborating with other children means they can build on each other's ideas, discuss possible options and make adjustments together. It is another way in which talk becomes central to the writing process. The actual recording of the writing could be carried out:

- by the educator acting as scribe for the group;
- jointly by all the children in the group;
- by one or two children decided on by the group;
- by a child nominated as scribe by the educator;
- by an older child working with a younger child.

Children in a nursery class took turns to put their hands in a feely bag containing fruit and vegetables, such as a pineapple, fennel and broccoli.

As they told the educator about the contents of the bag he encouraged them to build on each other's comments. John began by describing the leaves of the pineapple as being like monster nails, so the educator encouraged the next child to extend from this by posing the question: 'Which part of the monster can you feel?' As a picture of the 'monster' was built up by the group, the educator showed how he had recorded their ideas and read them back to the children. They then drew the monster, working in pairs on large sheets of paper.

In this nursery class, the educator modelled not only how ideas could be recorded in writing but also how to combine ideas from several people. This modelling is appropriate with all age groups of young children and is one way in which educators can support the children's learning. Another way in which this support can be given by educators is through 'scaffolding' writing situations, so as to reduce the scope for failure within them. A Year 2 class, in self-chosen groups of three, embarked on a project involving composing a story around the theme of space. The first stage involved them in making a pictorial plan of their story on a large sheet of paper. They then taped their story, with members of the group taking on the role of specific characters or of the narrator. From this point the children's stories developed in many different ways. Having produced a story communally, a process which had supported those who found composing a story difficult and had allowed others in the group to act as educators, the children then produced their own versions of their taped stories singly. Several of the children in the class were now able to write more freely and in greater detail than they had ever done before. Vygotsky (1978) says this shows children working within their 'zone of proximal development', the latter being the distance between their achievements when working alone and their potential as shown when working with the support of an educator or more capable peers.

Peer tutoring

Another way of organising collaborative writing, which can also provide support for young writers who lack confidence, is by pairing younger children with older children. The example of a Year 2 class paired with a Year 6 class illustrates the variety of ways in which these partnerships could work:

- older child acting as secretary for the younger child;
- older child encouraging the younger child to expand on their initial ideas;

- joint decision-making on content of writing;
- sharing the task of writing;
- younger child developing the ideas of the older child;
- younger child doing most of the writing, asking questions of the older child.

The educators involved set up the pairings very carefully so that the children working together were able to relate to each other socially. Where the older children were leaders in the partnerships they provided invaluable one-to-one interaction, developing their own skills as encourager and questioner as they sought to extend their younger partner's ideas. This can be seen in an excerpt of conversation between Ruby, a Year 2 bilingual speaker and Seema, Year 6:

Seema: What do you think should happen next?
Ruby: It flies. He [the bird] eats the food.
Seema: [writing] The bird flies up to the tree and eats the food. What happens to the two girls?
Ruby: They go home.

Conclusion

This chapter has considered young children writing in a variety of settings and for a range of purposes and audiences. Central to all these has been the understanding the educator has of the sorts of responses to expect from the children, which reveal the knowledge, skills and understanding they have about writing. The educator provides writing opportunities which build on these, involving the children in using writing in play situations, writing areas, and when working collaboratively with others. These and other experiences will allow children to develop as confident, motivated writers. willing to take risks with their writing. So instead of classrooms where children ask educators:

'Can you write that for me?'

what can be heard are enthusiastic emergent writers saying:

'I can write that myself!'

Pointers for writing in the early years

Young writers need:

- an environment to write in which provides real purposes for writing
- to have ownership of their writing
- to be able to choose what to write about and for what reasons
- to have their attempts valued whatever their stage of development
- to have experiences which link writing with talking and reading
- to see adults writing
- opportunities to write in collaboration with others.

References

Browne, A. (1993) *Helping Children Write*, London: Paul Chapman.

DfEE (Department for Education and Employment) (1998) *The National Literacy Strategy: Framework for Teaching*, London: DfEE.

DfEE (Department for Education and Employment) (2000) *National Curriculum for English*, London: DfEE and QCA.

DfEE (Department for Education and Employment) (2001) *Developing Early Writing*, London: DfEE.

Goodman, Y. (1986) 'Writing development in young children', *Gnosis*, 8, March.

National Literacy Strategy (1998) *Framework for Teaching*, London: DfES

National Writing Project (1989) *Becoming a Writer*, Walton-on-Thames: Nelson.

Smith, F. (1982) *Writing and the Writer*, London: Heinemann Educational.

Vygotsky, L. (1978) *Mind in Society*, London: Harvard University Press.

Further reading

Czerniewska, P. (1992) *Learning about Writing*, Oxford: Blackwell.

Hall, N. (ed.) (1989) *Writing with Reason*, London: Hodder & Stoughton.

CHAPTER 9

'What's that dog thinking, Mrs Bromley?'

PICTURE BOOKS AND LEARNING TO READ

Helen Bromley

Supporting young children with their development as readers should be an exciting prospect for all those working with children in the early years. Building on the knowledge of reading that they bring with them, sharing well-loved favourite texts, introducing and discussing new authors and titles, and, most of all, watching the children's excitement grow as the world of the reader opens up to them (see Figure 9.1).

My own memories of school reading are not exciting. I can vividly recall being sent to the headmistress' study to read some of my *Happy Venture Reader* book to her. Although I can remember Dick, Dora, Nip and Fluff, it is not with any particular affection. They are remembered more as distant relations who had to be tolerated, rather than as good friends. The books with which I formed the closest ties had been introduced to me at home, courtesy of the local library: *Little Bear* (Minarik Holmelund, 1957), *Fox in Socks* (Seuss, 1965) and many others. This was in the late 1950s. Since then there has been an explosion in the publishing of books for children, providing educators with a rich and varied selection to use in the classroom.

Liz Waterland (1992) talks about the difference between 'free range' and 'battery' books. The difference between these is that free range books are written by authors and illustrators who have had freedom to carefully choose and compose their books from the imagination, while 'battery' books are products of a factory-type approach to literature: 'There is a hint of unnatural practices, of confinement and restriction . . . even a suggestion of the mechanical and the automatic' (pp. 160–61).

This is a pitchure of Mrs Bromerloy and some pepole children Lisning to Her read a storey.

Figure 9.1 *The excitement of reading!*

Books as children's friends

In order to explore this difference further, I will return to the analogy of friendship. Children need friends that they can interact with time and time again, they need to share the good times and the bad. Books described as 'free range', that is high-quality, multi-layered texts, provide such opportunities. Amelia, aged 4, sat with a copy of *The Teddy Robber* (Beck, 1991), every morning before school, for six months, just as she might have depended on one child for friendship. She read it over and over again, taking great comfort in its familiarity, and the happy ending. Eventually, she was able to make other 'friendships', but in times of stress, she always returned to *The Teddy Robber*. Developing favourite texts is a key experience that all young readers should have, and is closely linked to the devlopment of tastes and preferences.

Brooke, whose aunt had recently died, took *Granpa* (Burningham, 1984) home, not for herself, but for her mum. As she explained to me, 'It's so mummy will see that everything will be all right in the end.' An example of one friend helping another, and an example of how the youngest children can develop an understanding of how reading can support all of us. I have used many reading schemes during my career and cannot recall examples of any which would have provided such support. 'Battery' books do not provide the sort of friends that stick around for long. They are with you for a short period of time, before you leave them and move on to the next. Lasting ties are not encouraged.

One of the important parts of friendship is the shared conversations that can exist. With your friends you laugh, cry and build a collection of joint memories, while all the time finding out more about yourself. Children's literature can provide such experiences. Alyck took *Owl Babies* by Martin Waddell (1992) home repeatedly, because he thought that Bill, the baby owl, was so funny. Other young children that I have taught have enjoyed *Owl Babies* because they feel that 'missing their mum' is legitimised in the story, and they strongly identify with Bill.

Children need friends that will help them learn, without fear of failure and with the knowledge that risk-taking is a worthwhile activity. Friends encourage you to 'have another go', whether trying to ride your bike without stabilisers or to read *Each Peach Pear Plum* (Ahlberg and Ahlberg, 1980) for yourself. Books such as those I have mentioned invite re-reading because they offer opportunities to see the familiar and unfamiliar juxtapositioned in such a way as to make you want to read them again and again. Just like visiting an old friend, but playing a new game. Texts constructed especially for the teaching of reading may not provide such friendly support, especially if reading does not come easily. It is often difficult for children to recognise themselves in the text (or illustrations) and there may be no chance of trying out a new game until you have mastered the old one.

There is no doubt that the best friends are those that grow and change with you, not just those that were suitable for you when you were 5 or 8. This is also true of children's reading material. Liz Waterland (1992, p. 161) quotes Jim Trelease, 'If a book is not worth reading at the age of fifty, then it is not worth reading at the age of ten either.' Look at the books that you use in the classroom as if you were looking for friends. If you do not find them interesting and want to get to know them better, then why should the children? This is not to deny that there will be differences in opinion and in taste, but it's a good place to start.

I would hope that, encouraged by the adults with whom they work, children would develop a rich collection of good friends, to be remembered with affection and pleasure. Friends who teach them that reading is a pleasure for life, not a series of hoops through which they must jump. This chapter intends to introduce activities for using meaningful texts with children that have been successful in my own early years classroom. It is not intended to be a definitive list of suggestions. Far from it! I hope rather that people would try one (or all) of the ideas out for themselves and be inspired to go on to discover more.

What young children need to learn about reading

It is important to accept that young children already know much about reading when they enter our classrooms. The activities outlined in this chapter, therefore, are designed to allow children to demonstrate what they already know, as well as educating them in new lessons about reading. Henrietta Dombey (1992, pp. 12–15) summarises the lessons that she feels children need to learn about reading; this is an abridged version of her list:

Attitudes

- Pleasure and satisfaction: to see books as a powerful source of enjoyment, information and understanding.
- Confidence: a firm belief that they will learn to read.
- Concentration and persistence.
- Toleration of uncertainty.
- Tentativeness: a readiness to correct error.
- Reflexiveness: a readiness to look with a certain detachment at what they can do and have read, and at what they need to learn.

Knowledge and strategies

Children need to understand:

- that the text is the same on each re-reading and that the marks on the page tell you what to say;
- that language is composed of separable words;
- the conventions of the English language system;
- that words are made up of individual letters;
- the rules of English spelling.

And children must:

- have reliable sight vocabulary;
- know how to use their knowledge of the world and the content of books to aid word identification;
- know how to use the information from the pictures (Figure 9.2);
- know how to use all these various devices together – orchestration.

HaNNaH andrstus The words Becos of The Pichets.

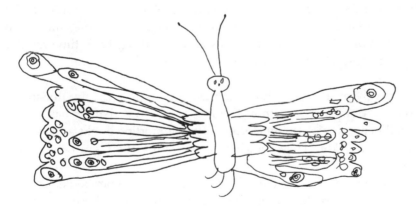

Figure 9.2 *Using information from the pictures*

I feel that the best way for children to learn these vital lessons is through the provision of a variety of rewarding experiences, provided by an educator who is enthusiastic about reading. Some lessons will, by necessity, be more explicit than others, but all will be crucial to the development of the children as readers. There is not room within this chapter to document all the ways in which it is possible to support the emergent reader. I feel that the activities outlined below show a variety of meaningful contexts in which most, if not all, the above lessons could be learned, both implicitly and explicitly.

Big Books

The theory behind using Big Books is well documented. Holdaway (1979), for example, working in New Zealand in the 1970s, looked at children who were already reading when they came to school, to find out what had made them successful. Many of the children had favourite stories that were read to them repeatedly. Gradually, the children were able to take on more of the reading for themselves, first by remembering the text and eventually being able to match words and phrases to the known text. Big Books were devised as a way of making stories available to a wider audience. Holdaway noted that all children were able to be successful at their own level with this approach. Large groups were able to be involved in the shared reading of a familiar text. They provide a shared context for discussion and make it easy for all the children in a class to focus on the chosen text.

A favourite Big Book in my reception class was *This is the Bear* (Hayes, 1995). The children already knew the text extremely well, having heard the small version read out many times. The text rhymes and has marvellous pictures, features which help support the developing reader. Using this story in its outsize version helped to create a situation for the children to learn both explicit and implicit lessons about reading. Each time the Big Book is used, a similar format can be followed:

- Look closely at the cover, find features such as title, author, illustrator, publisher, publisher's symbol. If this is done on a regular basis, then the children will pick up the vocabulary surrounding books and authorship very quickly. They then use these terms for themselves, quite naturally.
- Have a look at each page, ignoring nothing. Some books contain beautifully constructed endpapers and in some cases, these tell part of the story (*Farmer Duck*, for example, Waddell, 1991).
- Look for dedications. Who would the children dedicate a book to?
- What initials would they use?
- Do the cover and the preceding pages tell the reader anything about the story that is to follow?

Developing comprehension skills

The teacher can then follow one of several paths. Skills of prediction and authorship can be encouraged by reading the story part of the way through and asking the children to decide what happens next. To extend this activity, ask the children to justify their reasons for suggesting particular outcomes. This provides an excellent opportunity for formative assessment of their ability to make deductions and create their own hypotheses.

Alternatively, the story can be read to the children, not necessarily without interruption, but with as little as possible, so that the children can get the most meaning from the story. This will be the first of many readings, so there will be plenty of opportunities for discussion. The idea is not to encourage passive listeners, an audience powerless to interrupt the reading instructor, but rather to encourage the children to join in and to question what they see and what they hear. This is more effective, however, when the children have heard the whole story through once and have a shared context for discussion.

There are many ways in which Big Books can be used to stimulate discussion. One of the most effective ways I have used is to organise the children into small 'talk groups' and ask them to devise questions to ask about the story. This gives all children some opportunity to be involved in discussion about the text, and provides a safe context for talk for those who prefer not to speak in front of a large group. It also promotes close scrutiny of the text in a collaborative way, providing an ideal opportunity for children to discuss their reading and learn from one another.

As well as promoting comprehension skills, Big Books can be used to look carefully at features of print.

Looking at features of print

- Choose a particular letter. How many of this particular letter can the children find on one page, on a double page spread?
- Can they find any words within words, e.g. 'is', 'in', 'the', 'and'?
- Can they find two words with similar endings? (Particularly useful in a rhyming text.)
- How many capital letters can they see? Whereabouts do they appear in the text?
- Introduce the children to the notion of the silent letter. Can any of these be found?
- Use the children's own names as a basis for the print search. Can Jodie find any words beginning with J? Can Matthew find 'at', 'the' or 'he'? My experience has shown that children especially enjoy the activities

that involve their names and quickly learn features of not only their own, but also other people's names.
- Children can also be encouraged to devise similar questions of their own, so that this can become an independent as well as an adult-led activity.

Obviously, there is far more to becoming a critical and highly motivated reader than studying metalinguistic features of print! As educators, we want children to know that reading is pleasurable and that there is much to be gained from the re-reading of old favourites. Again using Big Books, it is possible to demonstrate all of this to children and, at the same time, allow them space to air their opinions and perceptions about the books that they are reading. This is achieved by a combination of teacher questioning and, most importantly, providing the opportunity for the children to ask their own questions.

Looking beyond the text

- Children can be put into groups of two or three and asked to devise one question about the story (illustrations included).
- Encourage the children to focus on how the illustrations might be telling a different story to the pictures.
- Look carefully at the body language of the participants.
- Follow the actions of one character throughout the whole story. Use this tracking as a basis for studying character, motive and plot!

Looking beyond the text is especially exciting, as even with numerous readings of the same text, the children always spot something new. This was demonstrated when I discussed *This is the Bear* (Beck, 1991) with a class of 5-year-olds. Briefly, this is the tale of a teddy bear who is pushed into the dustbin by a dog and mistakenly taken to the dump. He is found after a long search, by the same dog, and driven home to a hero's welcome! Questions devised about the story included:

Why did the dog push the bear into the bin?
How does the bear feel about being in the bin?
How would you feel if you lost your teddy and couldn't get it back?
Do you think that the dog is jealous of the bear?
Do you think that the bear likes the dog?
What's that dog thinking, Mrs Bromley?

I think that it is important to note that there were no questions of the type

'What colour is the van?' All the questions generated by the children were looking deep into the story, to try and find out more about the characters in it.

Games and play

Whenever I have carried out such activities with my class, I have always told the children that it is part of a game; sometimes them against me, sometimes a collaborative guessing game. For example, individual words can be covered up with a small piece of card, while the children close their eyes. When they open them, they have to guess which word is covered. This promotes close scrutiny of the text and finger/voice match. Then, when the large group session is over, I would always make the suggestion that, if they wanted to play the games themselves later, then they could do so. All that needs to be provided is a Big Book, clipped to an easel, four chairs placed in a semi-circle around it and something to be used as a pointer.

This game was a particular favourite with Eleanor, Hannah and Rebecca, who would often take the opportunity to persuade other members of the class to come and take part as pupils, while they operated their own version of team teaching. Rebecca, the most experienced reader in the group, would ask questions like 'Can you find "the" on this page?' Eleanor, who was particularly skilled at memorising texts, would read the book to the rest of the group, pointing with the ruler as she did so. That left Hannah, who had an excellent grasp of initial sounds and was able to devise questions such as 'Can you find a word on here that begins with the same sound as "apple"?' I think that the pupils in the game were getting some excellent teaching from three young experts.

From watching the children play what in my class has become known simply as 'schools', it is apparent that the children reproduce and therefore reinforce the types of behaviour demonstrated by the teacher. Each time the game is played, it is never an exact copy of the previous game, new ideas are added and children negotiate and discuss the questions and the answers.

Developing children's awareness

The children in my class have also had the opportunity to share the Big Books available with their reading partners, children from a Year 2 class. At one session, I asked the children to reflect, in their pairs, on how Big Books might help them with their reading. Here are some of their comments:

I like Big Books because you can always see the writing.

I think and my friend thinks that a Walker Big Book is good because you can see them better than you can see an ordinary book and you can see the pictures better.

Big Books help you to read properly because they have big words to help you read. (See Figure 9.3.)

It will help you write better. Reading will help you think better. It will help you to learn. It will help you think about the pictures.

Figure 9.3 *'Big Books help you to read properly because they have big words to help you read'*

As you can see, the children are very much aware of how the large format of the books encourages them to become participants in the shared reading process, allowing them to become even more involved than in a normal storytelling session. Talk is central to all the activities outlined above. They are operating in the zone of proximal development (Vygotsky, 1986) alongside a more experienced reader, and their own knowledge and learning potential will only become apparent if they are allowed to explore their knowledge through conversation. Through role-play (such as the game of 'schools') they are able to have the opportunity to act as the more able other, in the company of their peers. Self-esteem and confidence is built up this way, as well as there being room for errors to be made, away from the ever watchful eye of an adult.

Group reading

Big Books are not the only way in which children can be encouraged to play with their reading! Group reading around multiple copies of the same text provides similar opportunities, if the right atmosphere for learning and risk-taking is created.

Maisie Middleton (Sowter, 1994) is the story of an ordinary little girl who gets up one morning and, despite attempting to rouse her parents, eventually has to prepare breakfast for herself. It is a story which appealed to all the children in my class, possibly because they too would like to share some of Maisie's independence, however transitory. It was because of the popularity of the book that I chose it as a subject for group reading. All four children in the group had heard the story an equal number of times and could therefore bring some previous knowledge to the group situation.

During the session, the children listen to the story read out loud first, joining in if they wish. They then take it in turns to ask questions about each of the pages of the book, either to each other or to the adult present. I was surprised at how involved the children became with this particular text. I soon realised that I had under-estimated it's potential. The first page shows the exterior of Maisie's house, framed in an arch with a flower on the top. Eleanor began. 'I wonder who sleeps behind the blind with the stripes on?' she asked, and immediately the others joined in, speculating on the possible occupants of the house. Brooke was trying to imagine herself at the front door, stroking the cat and bringing in the milk. What to me had appeared to be a fairly simplistic picture provided the children with a rich source of discussion for at least 15 minutes. I thought that we were never going to get any further into the book. Much knowledge was revealed in this discussion, and many questions asked and answered. It's wrong to assume that it is always the adult that provides the answers. Thomas wanted to know why the milk was still on the doorstep; he was worried in case the sun turned it sour. It was Brooke who pointed out to him that as the blinds were still down, it must still be early in the morning. Eleanor also pointed out that the stars were still in the sky, so 'That's why the milk hadn't been taken in.' This discussion clearly demonstrated the children's speaking and listening skills, as well as their powers of reasoning and their ability to apply their knowledge of the real world to the imaginary world of the book. It also allowed them to develop ways of taking pleasure from the text that were in addition to those intended by the author.

While we were still considering the first two pages of the book, the children started to do something that I can clearly remember doing as a child. That was to pretend that they were in the book themselves. They began by deciding which room was which in Maisie Middleton's house and dividing them up among themselves. Space was also made for siblings and pets, ensuring links between the real world and the imaginary one. I felt that this incident demonstrated an enormous amount, not only about the children's understanding of the book, but also of their awareness of the possibilities that exist for any reader. (Another description of a child talking about *Maisie Middleton* can be found in Jordan, 1992.) I feel strongly that these lessons are as important as the lessons on sight vocabulary and decoding of text. It was very rewarding when, a few days later, Eleanor asked: 'Can we play that pretending game again? You know, that one when we were in the book. That was really good.' Following the success of this activity, I built it into further group reading sessions, although the children did not need much direction from me. It was as popular with non-fiction texts as with stories, with children taking on the roles of knights and soldiers in one particular book.

Group reading of texts

- Try to provide a range of texts for this activity – include non-fiction, comics, etc.
- Use groups of texts by one author/illustrator, so the children can identify similar features.
- Promote discussion about the characters – who would the children most like/not like to be etc.?
- Encourage and promote the use of puppets and props with the groups of books. A group of zoo animals with *Dear Zoo* (Campbell, 1985) for example, or some astronaut and alien puppets with *Children of the Sun* (L'Hommedieu, 1996).

Reading out

This activity was actually devised by my class themselves, and was to provide a source of pleasure to them for many weeks, as well as giving me the opportunity to listen to them read, checking their sight vocabulary, acquisition of known texts and their understanding of what they were reading. Reading standards in the class improved dramatically, as did listening skills and concentration spans. It was such a worthwhile activity that I would definitely introduce it to any new group of children that I taught.

The activity began when Rebecca came in one morning and asked if she could read out *Daley B* (Blake, 1992), her favourite book of the moment, to the rest of the class. It was agreed that she could and, later in the day, she read the book, with great expression and obvious understanding. The reaction from the rest of the class was extremely positive. Not only did they all, including the most restless children, listen attentively and with keen interest, but many of them offered to read out too. In fact, the whole activity snowballed. Children were allowed to 'read out' either on their own, with a friend or in a small group. This was to allow some of those children who were not quite brave enough to read by themselves to have the opportunity to participate in what became a very highly regarded activity.

The most popular grouping for the activity was a threesome. Within this group there would be one child who knew the text extremely well, one who knew it quite well, and one who was in the group to gain confidence and add to their knowledge of that particular text. This was a very good example of how children are able to achieve more when in the company of others than they could possibly achieve on their own. It provided great opportunities for the rest of the class to practice texts that were known to them already and add new texts to those that were familiar. Because the children were copying behaviour that they had seen in adults, many of them became adept at reading with the book held next to them, teacher-like, showing the pictures and questioning their very attentive audience.

I tried not to appropriate this activity, although I found this difficult, desperately wanting every one to 'have a turn'. One child in particular, Alyck, could not be encouraged to read out, however hard I tried to persuade him. This situation changed when his friend Sebastian wanted someone to read *Each Peach Pear Plum* out with him. He chose Alyck, who found it impossible to refuse his friend, even though it had been quite easy to refuse my requests. Alyck did read the book out with Sebastian, extremely well, and this provided an enormous boost to his confidence and self-esteem. After this occasion, he frequently read out to the class.

Although I was involved in the activity as a non-participant observer, the children regulated the whole of the sessions themselves. Everyone who wanted to read out would leave their chosen book, with a named post-it note on the front, on a special chair, waiting for reading out time. They would question each other about the books that were read out and would comment on each other's reading. This was delightful to hear, and was only ever positive. Comments such as 'Your reading's coming along very well, Hayley', were never patronising, but well meant.

The teacher's role

It is important to realise that the three activities outlined above should not be young children's only experience with good quality picture books. They should exist as part of a well thought out set of experiences designed to give children a myriad of opportunities to engage with the literacy heritage that surrounds them. As educators, we have the power to excite and inspire the children in our care and this should not be under-estimated. Early years educators should make good use of, and familiarise themselves with, the rich variety of books that are published for young children, developing favourites of their own in order to be able to demonstrate to children, that it is OK to have tastes and preferences that are different from one another.

I believe quite passionately that the picture books of today will provide far more 'good friends' for the children that I teach than *The Happy Venture Series* ever did for me. However, in order to become known to children, these friends must first be invited into classrooms and introduced to children in ways that make them want to 'play with them', time and time again. As Henrietta Dombey states:

> All children need the skilled help of informed and sympathetic adults, who appreciate their strengths and weaknesses, have a clear idea of the goal ahead and engage the children's interest and commitment. They also need to encounter texts that are involving, manageable and satisfying, and give them a clear sense that they are making progress. If all this occurs in ways that are exciting and inspiring, then young children will certainly acquire many 'friends for life'.
>
> (1992, p. 20)

Pointers to supporting the emergent reader

- Take time to get to know a wide range of children's books yourself.
- Act as a role model for the children, demonstrating enthusiasm for and an interest in books and other reading materials.
- Encourage children to talk about what they have read, to you and each other.
- Plan for a wide range of reading experiences which include incorporating reading into children's play experiences (puppets, props, etc.).
- Develop effective and informative ways of monitoring the children's progress that truly reflect all aspects of the reading process, not merely the acquisition of sight vocabulary.

References

Dombey, H. (1992) *Words and Worlds: Reading in the Early Years of School*, Sheffield: NATE.

Holdaway, D. (1979) *The Foundations of Literacy*, Sydney: Ashton Scholastic.

Jordan, B. (1992) 'Good for any age – picture books and the experienced reader', in M. Styles, E. Bearne and V. Watson (eds) *After Alice*, London: Cassell, pp. 113–25.

Vygotsky, L. (1986) *Thought and Language*, Cambridge, MA: MIT Press.

Waterland, L. (1992) 'Ranging freely: The why and what of real books', in M. Styles, E. Bearne and V. Watson (eds) *After Alice*, London: Cassell, pp. 160–71.

Children's books mentioned in the text

Ahlberg, J. and Ahlberg, A. (1980) *Each Peach Pear Plum*, London: Picture Lions.

Beck, I. (1991) *The Teddy Robber*, London, Picture Corgi.

Blake, J. (1992) *Daley B*, London: Walker Books.

Burningham, J. (1984) *Granpa*, London: Cape.

Campbell, R. (1985) *Dear Zoo*, London: Puffin Books.

Hayes, S. (1995) *This is the Bear*, London: Walker Books.

L'Hommedieu, A.J. (1996) *Children of the Sun*, Swindon: Child's Play (International) Ltd.

Minarik Holmelund, E. (1957) *Little Bear*, New York: Scholastic Book Services.

Seuss, Dr (1965) *Fox in Socks*, London: Collins.

Sowter, N. (1994) *Maisie Middleton*, London: Diamond Books.

Waddell, M. (1991) *Farmer Duck*, London: Walker Books.

Waddell, M. (1992) *Owl Babies*, London: Walker Books.

The wider curriculum

CHAPTER 10

'We are passing the smile around.'

PERSONAL, SOCIAL AND HEALTH EDUCATION IN EARLY YEARS

Helen Broomby and Sue Bingham

Introduction

When a young child goes to school, becomes a member of a class or goes out into the playground at break time, before he or she can even begin to be ready to take in any formal learning of any prescribed curriculum, a huge amount of personal, emotional and social learning has to take place.

Fundamentally, the child needs to become comfortable with, get to know, and relate to one or more key adults. He or she has to become familiar with finding their way around strange buildings and rooms, with new routines and rules. And he or she has to become used to being with lots of other children, who are probably strangers at first, in the main, but potentially will become more familiar and friendly over the academic year. These are all new experiences for the child and require special learning of particular 'rules':

- Rules for behaviour within a group; what is acceptable or unacceptable behaviour here with other children in the classroom may be quite different from at home.
- Rules for behaviour within a classroom; what does 'tidying up' mean here and why can't I run inside when I want to?
- Rules for behaviour within a school; what is 'assembly' and why do I have to put my hand up?

In essence these 'rules' form a basic framework for ways of behaving in general life, in any group, where the needs and desires of others as well as oneself have to be taken into account and reflected in behaviour. Early years teachers are pivotal in shaping a young child's first experiences of being in a society outside the family and in scaffolding their learning to adapt, cope and succeed in emotionally and socially demanding situations. The implementation of an appropriate PSHE curriculum is a crucial base from which all other learning and development is built, from which children can flourish or flounder. Without personal, social and health development, all further layers of learning may be skewed and thwarted. For here, we are talking about the child's basic social and emotional needs, their self-worth and self-belief. It is now accepted that, whatever cognitive powers we inherit, they cannot be utilised fully if our personal and social health needs are not nurtured.

Additionally, the realisation of the child's development in PSHE enables children to play an active part in their world and to form a sound basis for citizenship. They develop the competence and motivation to 'make a difference'. They learn to contribute to the world in which they live.

We know from a wealth of research that children learn best through 'active learning', through physical engagement with materials and through engaging with people. There is nothing more potent in this experiential learning than that which is negative: a damning word, an experience that suggests failure, a gesture that underlines rejection. On the other hand a friendly smile or a kind word can be very effective.

The nature of the interactions between child and carer/adult is a crucial and controlling factor in that child's development.

Babies are acutely sensitive to every move and gesture made by the people around them, they depend on this instinctively for their survival. They study the moves and read the signs that tell them who they are and what is expected of them. Babies and children learn through this method from the moment of their first breath. They learn from every move, every glance and every word. They learn about how to be and how to behave, they learn what you think of them, how important they are, how they fit into the family and later into school and society. They learn both the positive and, unfortunately, the negative.

Adults respond differently to the realisation of the weight of this responsibility, especially when their involvement is with young children still in the formative stages of their development. For some adults, the tendency would be to ignore it and others may become over-anxious about their handling of young children. Neither is a good option. Both reactions are based on the adult's own experiences and these experiences need to be considered if they hamper effective working with young children. These considerations underlie a need for an approach that takes account of adult's responses and children's needs. We discuss in this chapter the need for a whole-school approach that supports both the children and the adults.

Context

In addition to the above thoughts, the contrasting theories of the Nature versus Nurture debate, the political dimension of women in society and mothers' role within the home, the personal and private versus the public and the political have swung back and forth over the years. The blame for the 'poor upbringing', low self-esteem and anti-social behaviour of the children has often rested within the personal dimension of the home and primarily with the mother. At other times it has rested with schools and society. We need to take regard of this and be mindful to accept responsibility and to avoid blame. People as parents, guardians, teachers or carers all come with their own histories and experience, but they also come from within a culture, a society that for that period in time has fostered a particular aspect or approach. As a teacher or carer of children we are working within an establishment with particular social constraints, the schools are an element of the society that we are creating for children. They are also highly significant in the development of those children.

If the above observations are taken as given, PSHE must be seen as an on going developmental partnership between the family, including the child, and the school or pre-setting. This includes *all* those engaged with the children during the normal course of the working day. It refers not only to the relationships taking place within the classroom but also those relationships between the child and non-teaching staff.

In what follows, we will first consider the importance of and some practicalities in, developing a whole-school approach and then turn to considerations as to how PSHE can be embedded both as day-to-day practice and as a discrete curricular subject.

The benefits of a reflective style should not be underestimated. Too often we are preoccupied, not able to make the time. Nonetheless, it helps to work within a reflective style and, most of all, a style that avoids much of the blame that can be used to absolve schools of their responsibility. The systems, the policies and procedures we set up need to reflect the acceptance and inclusion of all children, an appreciation of difference and enhancement of the self-esteem of the children. It is as part of that society and the expected socialisation of the children that we are considering within this chapter.

The whole-school approach

In adopting a reflective style it helps first to examine the nature of your own personal history and that of the society and its expectations that you are part of, especially in relation to assumptions about children and child-care practices. An exercise of this sort is the opening to the development of a whole-school approach. These considerations need a personal response from all members of staff and, after discussion, a whole-school view.

- What future, what type of society, what sort of people to we want to develop?
- What sort of school, what sort of teacher and what sort of children?
- How can we establish an ethos and values that will achieve this future?

It is crucial that schools allocate time to discussing, establishing and agreeing the ethos and values to which the whole team feel they can work towards. This must be done with everyone in the school including the classroom assistants, caretaker, secretaries, school meals staff, playground supervisors, school nurse, parents.

> *I overheard a conversation between a small group of reception class children who were talking about the order of who was in charge, who told who what to do. The group agreed that the teacher tells the children what to do and the headteacher tells the teacher what to do. When I asked then who tells the headteacher what to do, the answer was 'the school caretaker'.*

The people who make a difference to the school as perceived by the children are often not the same as those that the adults think of first. Good practice in the classroom will be undermined if the experience is not carried throughout the whole school day, through the meal time into the playground and through all of the school years. Many of the problems experienced by children happen in the playground.

What is a whole-school approach?

Once established, the ethos, values and policy need to be what informs every aspect of the settings. The messages related throughout every aspect of school life need to project a consistent ethos of respect, consideration, inclusion and equality. The notices on the wall, the letters home, the manner in which different types of families are treated and the way in which children are spoken to in the playground are all part of this work.

The policy is undermined by the actions of those not subscribing to the ethos of the whole-school approach. The policy will need to be reviewed regularly as new members of staff join the team or there are new government requirements. Creative ways need to be found to safeguard this way of working to ensure that full account is taken of the children's needs. A school that has discussed this fully and developed the ethos of a whole-school approach will be in a better position to protect it.

In the absence of this an ad hoc system will emerge. With basic philosophical gaps in the system fragmentation will occur, with a consequent of lack of consistency of approach. Individual teachers will bring to bear their own particular agendas and methods of working. This may work within the four walls of the classroom but will need to be re-negotiated as the children move into the shared space of the playground or the dining hall. This is where many of the difficulties of the lack of policy will emerge.

With a set of agreed principles embedded in policy, practitioners have a framework within which to work.

As part of this whole-school approach, PSHE needs planning for progressive incremental steps throughout the school. The importance of the subject will be severely undermined if the exact same format is repeated each year. Valuable as it is, how many times can children engage with a project about Me and My Family? Schemes of work for progression need to be agreed across the whole school and, if at all possible, with the pre-school settings.

Circle time

Early years settings have for many years understood the value of circle time as a sociable activity for children. This time is used to encourage children to talk to the group and to listen to each other, to sing and read stories together. This practice has in recent years been developed into practice for group discussion and PSHE activities for older children. Jenny Mosley (1996) in her book *Quality Circle Time in the Primary Classroom*, provides extensive circle time activities on, for example: feelings, being kind, friendship and cooperation. Mosley promotes circle time as part of a whole-school approach, with every class participating in their own circle time meeting, and extends this idea to encompass the notion of a school circle time. Circle time is one part of developing the time to work on the issues of this programme. To be effective the learning needs to be integrated and applied consistently across the school day using a variety of different activities and methods.

In a school where all children, whatever their background, are valued and have a clear understanding of and respect for one another, appreciation of differences and an understanding of acceptable behaviours and ways of relating to each other; the aim is that they will begin to adopt the values underpinning this approach as a framework for social interaction.

Circle time activities

The magic box

Tell the children there is a picture of a very special person inside. Each has a look inside the box but must not say anything and pass the box on until every child has had the chance to look inside the box. They are then asked who was the special person. What the children see inside the box is a mirror.

'I am good at . . .'

Ask the children to think about all the things that people may be good at and give some examples to get them started. When you have a lots of suggestions introduce the self-portrait activity. Children paint self-portraits and label them. Use smaller pieces of paper for drawings and descriptions of all the things they are good at. Glue the pictures around the edge of their self-portraits. In the circle time each child holds their picture and in turn names the things they have drawn around their self portrait, 'I am good at'.

Guess the feeling

One child leaves the circle, the rest of the class choose one emotion, for example, happy, sad, cross, excited, etc., and think of ways to show this emotion. The person comes back and has to guess which emotion has been chosen.

Pass the smile around the circle (see Figure 10.1)

Personal development

Curry and Johnson (1990) offer a useful description of four areas to take account of in personal development: acceptance, power and control, moral worth and competence. Children need to feel accepted for who they are, first by the important people in their lives and, later, by their peers, friends and teachers. Young children experiment with power and control over their immediate environment, their relationships and they eventually develop

Figure 10.1 *Circle time: 'We are passing the smile around' by Becky, aged 6*

self-control. Moral worth is about the development of a sense of right and wrong and the emergence of conscience. Competence is about the child's increasing skills and abilities to achieve in all aspects of their development. There are significant considerations that will be developed further under the following headings: self-esteem, behaviour and the development of independence.

Self-esteem

The concept of self is being developed during the first and second year of life. Initially the baby is not aware of the different and separateness of the adult feeding her. The child has to discriminate between what is 'me' and 'not me'. Where do I begin and others end? The physical nature of what the boundaries are begins with this experience and develops into more involved complex and sophisticated ideas about the self. In this very early interaction there are three important lessons being learned. One is about acceptance, essential for self-esteem; the second is about boundaries; and the third is about the relationships between themselves and others that will run throughout the whole of their lives. Acceptance is essential to self-esteem.

The development of positive self-esteem is, in my view, the most valuable gift you can give to a child. This will affect their capacity for development in every aspect of their lives: the personal, social, intellectual, emotional and physical, at home, at school, at work and at play. Children need to feel sure of themselves in order to fully engage in any activity. They need to feel confident of their self-worth to be able to take risks and face challenges (see Figure 10.2). They need to be given permission to make mistakes and to know that this will not destroy them. They need to feel totally accepted for who they are, no more, no less. They need to feel tolerated when their actions push us to the limits. They need to know that we can separate who they are from any unacceptable behaviour.

At this point it is worth taking note of the work of Goleman (1996) and Rogers (1961). Goleman argues that our view of human intelligence is far too narrow and that what he refers to as 'emotional intelligence' is closely linked to success in later life. He presents a powerful argument that asserts that the emotional lessons a child learns actually sculpt the brain's circuitry. It seems to me that we cannot afford to ignore this aspect of development. Rogers says that not only is the development of self-esteem central to all other forms of learning, but also that people will only learn if they feel that the learning helps to construct or maintain their sense of self. He

Figure 10.2 *'I can do it. Look at me.' Physical skills help increase confidence*

makes a strong case that people will reject or block learning that is perceived as threatening to themselves.

If we accept these arguments, the remit for our work is set. We must ensure that children's emotional well-being is taken account of for them to make full use of their cognitive abilities to becoming thinking beings.

We would be well advised, concludes Goleman, to pay more attention to this aspect of children's development, which will cascade into every other aspect of human development and life. What can we do that will help a child fare better in life?

How do we enhance children's self-esteem?

There are a number of books that are particularly good on this subject, one of which is *Self-esteem and Successful Early Learning* by Rosemary Roberts (1995). In addition, we offer a few general principles:

- Avoid using raised voices, put-downs, sarcasm and humiliation – even those glares used to silently make children feel bad about themselves.
- Be open, clear and simple about what is expected.
- Children on the whole want to please, use that as a starting point.
- Offer realistic praise for effort and achievement.
- Offer encouragement.
- Provide opportunities for children to comment on the things they have done well.
- Make sure the tasks you request are within the capabilities of the children; build on success.
- Practise the use of positive language.
- Develop full use of drama and role play to develop confidence.

Behaviour

A happy and accepting atmosphere in the classroom helps children to learn. If you are positive about your work and enjoying what you are doing this will emanate to the children. There is nothing so infectious as an atmosphere either good or bad. It is unrealistic to think people are happy all of the time but a genuine interest in the children and in what you are doing will go a long way in producing positive results.

How can we help children in dealing with powerful emotions?

Young children experience very powerful emotions. Sometimes these feelings can be uncontrollable, unpredictable and frightening for the child. Children's lives can be traumatic and life can demand a lot from them. We know that it helps children to be able to talk about their feelings, but this demands a good deal of sophistication and maturity. It is important to introduce children to the language of emotions: happy, sad, angry, frustrated, disappointed, afraid and so on, and to help them to identify their feelings. When children experience strong feelings it can be difficult for them to understand what is causing the feelings but they are uncomfortable with the sensation. Identifying feelings and naming them helps provide a context for understanding and expression of the feelings, and offers a sense of control. There are lots of card games and books produced now along these lines, for example, 'Angry Arthur'. As with all other aspects of learning the adult's role is then to work with the children to extend their emotional language. This is by far the most crucial aspect of emotional development.

- observe children to note any changes in behaviour;
- listen to what children say;
- develop active listening skills in the children;
- provide games that extend emotional language;
- provide books and stories that identify and express feelings;
- allocate time for children to engage in pretend play;
- provide sensory play materials which can be either soothing, for example, water, or a release of tension, for example, clay;
- provide therapeutic experiences, for example small world play to re-enact situations;
- verbalise your own feelings and thinking, helping children to understand the process you use.

It is difficult for a child, in isolation, to deal with feelings of rejection, pain, separation and loss. These can be the result of a family breakdown or a bereavement. At such times, when the whole family needs support, the child is often left struggling to understand what is happening. Schools and settings may be the only consistency in their lives. Children react differently to these life situations. With some children we will be in no doubt that something is wrong, but with others we may need to watch more closely to notice the quiet withdrawing. We will need to think about how best to approach this at a time of crisis with a particular child, but, as the class develops in terms of language and expressive skills, children will have some useful tools when difficulties arise.

Children who are not allowed to express their negative feelings may be in danger of what Roberts (1999) calls a kind of 'emotional helplessness'. Feelings do not cease to exist simply because they are denied. The tendency is for them to become more powerful. Emotional development is about learning how to accept and manage feelings, and how to respond appropriately.

Very young children experiment with their ability to control; they play with situations that help them understand the control they exert over their environment. They also do this in relationship to the adults and other children in their lives. This is developed further into helping them to deal with their emotions. For a child to develop self-control they need to have these feelings acknowledged.

How do we help children to deal with difficult behaviour and manage conflict?

Consider the following two everyday classroom situations and the actual learning which takes place.

Scenario A
A child hits another, in an argument over whose turn it is to have the 'digger' in the sandbox and the aggrieved party ends up crying loudly. The teacher approaches, takes hold of the 'digger' and holds it up out of reach saying 'That's not very nice! Say sorry Jack! Stop crying Joseph! You need to share and play nicely boys! You can have the first turn Joseph and you can have a turn in a minute, Jack.'

Scenario B
A child hits another in an argument over whose turn it is to have the 'digger' in the sandbox and the aggrieved party ends up crying loudly. The teacher approaches, bends down to the children's eye level and as she asks what is happening, gently removes the 'digger' into neutral territory. She listens attentively to both children's points of view, one at a time, 'containing' (describing and acknowledging) each child's feelings as she perceives them, if they are unable to label them themselves. She asks each child to look at the face of the other and describe what feelings they see on their friend's face. She asks why their friend is feeling like this. She asks the children how they can make each other feel better and how they can both sort out the problem of the 'digger' sharing.

In Scenario A the children are learning that loud shows of emotion produce results in terms of attracting a teacher's attention – Joseph has not learned that he needs to express his distress in a more appropriate way. They are both learning that they need an adult to sort out their problem, rather than trying to find a solution to the sharing issue independently. Both boys are learning that they have done something wrong for which

Jack is expected to apologise (insincerely?), but it is not clear what 'playing nicely' means. Joseph is made to feel that crying is unacceptable. The boys make no choices and solve no problems, they simply follow an adult's instructions and will probably just tug at the digger hard again next time, rather than think about alternative ways of sharing.

In Scenario B, the children are given an opportunity to distance themselves from their raw emotions of anger and frustration over whose turn it is to have the 'digger' and are given time to express their feelings in alternative, more socially acceptable ways. They are led to identify their own feelings and those of their friend and to think about the causes. The teacher leads the children to take a degree of responsibility for having caused these negative feelings and at the same time provides an opportunity for them to demonstrate their independence in planning to do something to make them both feel better. She also asks them to think about what they will do next time to share, so that the situation can be avoided in future.

The methods used by the teacher in the second scenario pivot not only on providing children with opportunities to solve issues independently, but also on fostering a sense of empathy between members of the class. The teacher is scaffolding the children's emotional and social learning, providing guidance and support to a child until he is able to take over the task for himself. The child is not passively absorbing the strategies of the adult, but takes an active, inventive role, reconstructing the tasks through their own understanding, while the adult makes the process of learning explicit to the child en route – handing the children a high degree of control of the situation. The children are learning that disciplining our own feelings or desires involves us in doing things that we don't always want to do, but is an important aspect of independence. As teachers, when we support children in acquiring self-discipline, we help them to understand that they, and not other people, are responsible for what they do and for carrying out certain obligations. This is a subtle area and one that all too often we leave to chance. However, if children are to learn self-control and self-restraint then they need our thoughtful and deliberate support and they particularly need us to be consistent and explicit.

Conflicts are common in 3- and 4-year-olds peer relations (Parker and Gottman, 1989; Shantz, 1987), but they are rarely terminal to relationships and children of this age do not regard conflict as incompatible with friendship (Shantz, 1989). Because cooperative play occupies an increasingly central place in social relations, pre-schoolers tend to regulate their squabbles so that they do not undermine the broader purposes of working together. In this respect, peer social relations appear to evoke certain types of behaviour more frequently than do family contexts. Dunn (1988), for example examined the use of reasoned argument by 3-year-olds at home

Figure 10.3 *'Can I help you?' Encouraging children to look out for others*

with mother and siblings, and by the same children when alone with a close friend. It was found that conciliatory, reasoned argument was more common in peer conflicts (at 22%) than in domestic strife (at 9%). Not only does emotional understanding with peers enhance the incentive for prosocial behaviour and reduced aggressive conduct among pre-schoolers, it also contributes to the quality of social skills that elicit peer acceptance or rejection and fosters the emergence of lasting friendships in early childhood (Dunn and Herrara, 1997). In this sense, rather than being an entirely negative experience, conflicts between young children can be an important source of emotional and social learning.

An example of conflict: the problem of 'lining up'

During a recent piece of classroom-based research conducted by one of the present authors, the following methodology was developed to help children learn from a conflict situation:

- detailed observation and analysis of the conflict situation, and the children's conflict behaviour;
- presentation of the problem to the children;
- consultation with the children, leading to some proposed solutions;

- further consultation and evaluation with the children of the success of the revised procedures.

Observations

Video recordings, tape recordings and observations were made of the lining up routines and the types of conflict observed were categorised, including 'power struggles' (e.g. wanting to be the 'leader' of the line), 'possession disputes' (e.g. 'I was there first' or 'That's my space') and 'mild physical aggression' (e.g. pushing or barging into the line).

Analysis of the observations of these behaviours revealed that children seemed to be confused about the objective behind lining up as well as the process of doing so. Some children evidently did not realise that they were supposed to go to the end of the line, some did not understand the concept of the 'end of the line', some children seemed to think they were being sensible by 'filling in' a gap in the line, not realising that others may see this as 'pushing in', and other children simply left huge spaces within the line for no discernible reason. Moreover, it was clear that, although the children used the term 'the end of the line' quite freely in telling each other how to queue up, many children had not yet grasped the concept of finding the intangible 'end', which led to many instances of 'pushing in'!

Presentation of the problem to the children

Within the 'Feelings' circle time of the two weeks leading up to the 'Discussion Week', the focus had been upon 'being fair', in terms of treating other people as they like to be treated themselves. During lining up time after circle time one morning, a situation was stage-managed, where the teacher commented on how many faces displaying 'negative feelings' could be seen and heard; some children looked cross, some sad and some children were even shouting or crying in the line. The question was posed 'What does this show?' One or two children said that it showed that there was a problem, so the teacher asked what could be done about it. The children suggested talking about it, so everyone went back into the classroom and re formed the circle.

Consulting the children

Analysis of the transcript of the consultation reveals that initially, the focus of the discussion time was on clarifying the objectives behind lining up. The reasons for going to the end of the line, what in fact constitutes 'the end of the line' or 'a gap' in the line, and the term 'pushing in' were all clarified through discussion.

JT: We could all go to the back of the line and if there's too much people, some people could go over there [*pointing*] so we could have a bigger line.

Teacher: Good idea, James . . . I think you said you didn't want the line to be too squashy, so we could make the line longer, with enough space for everyone. Was that your idea, James?

JT: Yeah.

Teacher: So people aren't squashed?

JT: Yeah. We could leave a gap if someone wants to be in the middle.

Teacher: Hmmm. Gaps in the line make us muddled up. Sometimes when children come out from the loo, they see a gap and go into it. They think it looks like the end of the line and they get muddled up.

IS: Then some children might tell them they are pushing in.

JT: But we don't want our friends to be squashed.

Teacher: No, we don't.

HW: How about if we just made a little space in between each person?

[*General 'yes' noises.*]

Teacher: Shall I write that on our page of ideas? OK . . . just a little space between each person in the line, so we aren't squashed.

IS: Not big gaps though.

Teacher: OK. [*Writes*] No big gaps in the line.

Emc: When we squash people we might fall over.

FC: We might fall over when we're walking. You might bump your head or get blood.

IS: I hear people saying 'OW that's squashy'.

In response to the issue about 'pushing in', one boy suggested having an 'end of the line person', to point out where there were gaps in the line and direct those children joining it where to stand. The children also decided that they wanted a line on the floor in the corridor, to mark where the front of the line was. It was agreed that the fairest way would be take turns at being 'the leader' of the line. The children asked that a list of the class be put on the wall and the names ticked off as each child had a turn, day by day, so that they could see whose turn was next.

Evaluation

After several days of trying out the new system of lining up, a second, impromptu consultation took place in which the ideas the children had come up with were assessed in the light of their implementation. This discussion came about when one of the adults spotted the 'leader' of the line for that day, walking along the line counting the children. When she asked what he was counting, he replied that he was counting 'smiley faces'! The idea of counting 'smiley faces' as a measure of the successful implementation of the new system was stunning in its simplicity and logic! The assessment of there being a problem with lining up in the first place had been to look with the children at how many faces were showing 'negative feelings' within the line-up. Counting faces showing happy feelings was a direct extension of the same idea and one that the children themselves could effect, making the measuring of success immediate and relevant.

In line with recent work concerned with developing a pedagogy for self-regulation in young children (Whitebread and Coltman, 2007) the present project supported the view that, given the opportunity and appropriate support, 3–4-year-olds show a clear capacity for considerable emotional and social self-regulation. Key to the success of the intervention developed here was the identification, through careful observation, of a problem that was meaningful to the children, and the development of a process that supported the children themselves in articulating the nature of the problem and devising strategies aimed at its resolution.

Through the process of consulting with children about their attitudes and behaviour, some of the autonomy and responsibility that adults recognise as being critical within the domain of the emotional and social development of young children was handed directly to them. In the process, the children learned that rules can protect as well as restrict, and help a community to regulate itself. The consultation process also appeared to bind the children together emotionally and socially, creating a real sense of community. The children also listened well to each other during each consultation process, which gave everyone time to reflect on what was being discussed. On several occasions, for example, one child endorsed and developed and idea or point of view expressed by another. Underlying the success of this whole approach, however, and perhaps most importantly, was the building of a relationship of trust and genuinely shared control between the adult educators and the children.

Social development

Social development includes issues that are both general and specific. Our considerations here need to extend to the wider community that we are preparing children for. Providing them with the knowledge, skills, attitudes and understanding for creating a healthy society and a positive view of the diversity of people within it, we hope to generate a tolerant and inclusive school and future. We need to foster this by providing a positive view of children from a variety of different backgrounds, families, cultures and dis/abilities.

In what follows we consider the need to create a welcoming environment and agree the rules with the children. This is followed by three main threads: working together, relationships and citizenship.

Setting the scene

Children need to feel valued, safe and secure among the adults and children around them. They need a sense of belonging, to feel they have a place in the group and that they are important. They need to know they can trust the adults to take care of them in every aspect of their being. Adults are very powerful in this situation and the atmosphere we establish will set the framework for how the children behave towards one another and develop an understanding of what is acceptable and what is not.

Creating a welcoming environment

Most schools now have a settling in policy for working with children new to school, which reflects the importance of the partnership with parents. Many schools will visit the children at home or at their pre-school setting prior to their first day. This visit is invaluable. It establishes a strong link with home and acknowledges the child's prior experiences as important. It also provides the teacher with an opening for conversations with the child. Many settings have a staggered intake for new children and call upon the established children to assist with the new children and to help them to become familiar with the setting, to show children around and take them to lunch. It is an excellent two-fold venture: in addition to the obvious benefits to the child who is new, it provides a real opportunity for children to help a younger child and in turn, enhances their self esteem.

- Make sure every child has a place in the group. Having their photograph included on a welcome poster instantly gives the child a place in the group.
- Provide a welcome in different languages.
- Provide a welcome that lets children and parents feel that you really are pleased to see them.
- Give yourself time to prepare the classroom in advance of the children arriving so that you can focus your attention on the children and parents.
- Look after yourself so that you can make sure you are fresh and ready for the day.

- Be sure to talk to all of the children as they arrive.
- Show respect for all children and their parents.
- Make sure that you have a good range of multicultural resources and check the images portrayed within books and on posters.

Remember that children learn from watching us. They are very good at reading body language and will follow our signals. If we are seen to respect all children and all families it will establish important messages from the outset.

Agreeing the rules with the children

Children need to feel safe and secure both in themselves and in the group. This is provided by the boundaries that we operate within, which give us a feeling of being in control and equally provide a certain element of predictability with regard to the control of the group. This way it is not so threatening (see also Chapter 1). Rogers (1995) identifies the following three rights that apply to children and adults: the right to feel safe, the right to learn (and to teach) and the right to be treated with dignity and respect.

Additionally, children need to know and understand what is expected of them and for what reasons. They will engage with this better if they have a part in thinking it through. If the children have had the chance from the outset to consider the options, think about what is important and what sort of class they want to be part of, it will make more sense to them. It offers children a framework in which to understand and be part of creating the boundaries of the group.

Children for whom this approach of discussing and negotiating is similar to their experience at home will find it easy to adopt. For other children it will be much more difficult and you can see them struggling to understand the new approach. However, the more open, defined, verbalised and repeated the messages are, the more it will begin to make sense and assist with developing reason.

One model for establishing the principles and guidelines is through a class discussion.

Activity

Discuss with the children and develop ways of working. Ask the children some guiding questions in order to draw out some guidelines for them to agree.

- What do you think makes a classroom feel friendly? What could we do?

- What do you think we could do to make sure everyone gets time to talk and for us to listen?
- How do you think it would feel if some children in the class made fun of you? How do you think we should behave to each other?
- What do you think could happen if you run in the classroom? How can we make sure people don't get hurt?
- What would you like to happen if . . . you fall over, you are having trouble tying your shoelace, you feel upset, you cannot reach the toy you want?
- What do you think would be a good way to help a new child to settle in the class?
- If someone was being mean to you, what do you think you should do? What do you think others around you could do to help you?

The outcomes from this discussion should be recorded in simple statements and displayed in language accessible to the children. Get the children to draw pictures and illustrate their own posters to depicting their statements.

Possible outcomes for example, might be:

- We work together.
- We listen to each other.
- We take turns and share. (see Figure 10.4)
- We walk in the classroom.

Figure 10.4 *'Sharing' by Rosie Alsop, aged 7*

- We help each other.
- We are kind to each other.
- We look out for each other.
- We are friendly to one another.

The way we work with the children from here on in will be based on this initial task. This is just a starting point. For this to be fully adopted as a way of being in the school it needs to be followed up by activities throughout the year. The verbalisation of the agreement and the reasoning behind it will help the children to become familiar with this way of thinking. If the group of children hear the same messages repeated when they go into assembly, the playground or the dinner hall, they will begin to feel a sense of security in the consistency and fairness this offers. The discussions need to develop in complexity and become more sophisticated as the group moves through the school.

Working together/cooperation

How do we help children to develop the skills of cooperation?

We are as human beings essentially sociable. Children are interested in each other and social interaction can be encouraged and facilitated by the way the teacher sets the scene and manages the classroom. However, for some children this is not so easy. This lack of ease may be developmental.

We must take into account the maturity of the child, and their experience. Some theories show a child moving from solitary play through to cooperative play (Piaget, 1896–1980). Critics of this view have since argued that the stages are not so clearly defined or distinct. Babies certainly are sociable beings and from a very young age will play turn-taking games in passing you a toy and taking it back. This is clearly evident in conversation with babies where the baby has learnt, long before words are formed, that there is a sequence taking place. They gurgle in response to the carer and then wait their turn. The baby is playing sociably.

Between the ages of 3 and 8 years, there is a huge development of fantasy/dramatic play/imaginative play which involves children in playing out a whole scene together. This is a very elaborate form of cooperative play. Children learn significantly from these interactions (see Figure 10.5).

It is well documented that when children are experiencing shock or trauma they will revert to the things that give them comfort and are less demanding. This may involve becoming more solitary for a period.

Figure 10.5 *Children playing out a scene together and learning to cooperate*

Classroom organisation

The organisation of the day and the classroom need to be considered for their added value in social interaction. This may be through organising for close proximity or ease of eye contact. This is best done by providing:

- seats set facing diagonally opposite, round or square tables;
- play equipment chosen to encourage cooperation and positioned to take into account what the children can see to encourage them to talk and think together, for example, painting easels side by side, water tray positions opposite (see Figure 10.6);
- a well-resourced role-play area with lots of opportunities to move freely and play cooperatively;
- floor space for construction, rail tracks, large puzzles;
- comfortable book corner and communal listening bay for sharing stories;
- opportunities for joint creative projects;
- comfortable, sociable meal time.

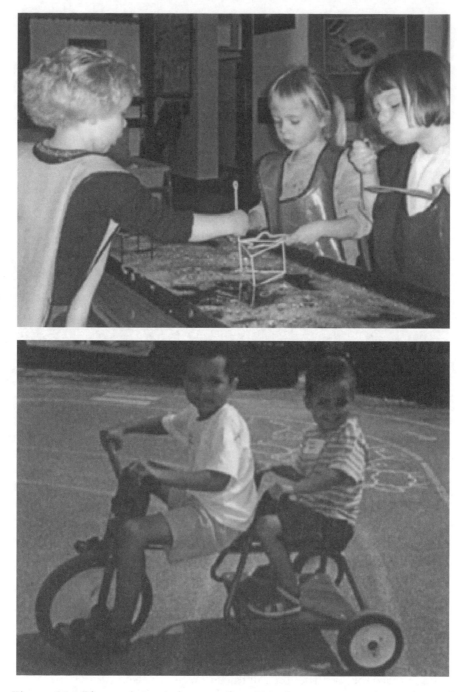

Figure 10.6 *Play equipment chosen and positioned to encourage cooperation and social interaction; sharing a tandem and standing around the water tray*

There appear to be fewer opportunities now for children to engage in unsupervised play in their free time. Increased amounts of time allocated to organised activities (e.g. music lessons) or in isolated activities such as watching TV leave less time for engagement in cooperative play and less opportunity to test out their social skills. We need to ensure that this is happening during the school day by making sure the opportunity exists and engage children fully in group activities, games and lessons. Some activities that support cooperation are listed below:

Working things out together	Cooperative play	Taking turns
Building/construction	Parachute game	Card games
Large puzzles	Role-play	Computerised toys
Playing music	Drama	Bikes
		Skipping
		Team games

Relationships

What part can we play in helping children to make friends?

Goleman (1996) states that social intelligence is crucial for our success and levels of fulfilment in virtually all aspects of our lives, from making friends to holding down a job. When children are asked to comment on what is important to them at school it is friends they talk about. Peers are important to us.

> Friendships provide us with a sense of ourselves and our self-worth. For some children making friends does not come naturally. One child in ten has a social learning deficiency. They do not know how to act in social situations and have limited and isolating responses to others. They are basically not fun to be with and do not know how to make others feel good. They are more likely to brag, sulk, cheat, and give up when losing. They have poor empathy skills.
>
> (Wear, 2000, p. 95)

We have considered the need for children to have a sense of belonging to a group that comes from feeling accepted for who they are. Belonging can then be difficult if a child has already developed 'social learning deficiencies'. We have to accept that some children are not as easy to like as others. Children in the group will watch your response to these children and will learn from how you are with them. You will need to find positive ways of working with all children. Some of the social lessons need to be explicit and reinforced.

How do we encourage friendships between children and assist in the development of social skills? One significant aspect of our practice should be the positive reinforcement of friendly actions and social skills amongst the children (see Figure 10.7). Here are some examples:

Salim was kind to me when I fell over.
Carol helped me to do the puzzle.
Beth lent me her pencil.
Jason said he liked it when I said thank you.
Nadia looked after the rabbit.
Afsi asked if I wanted to have a ride in the cart while she pulled it.
Paul let me have a go with his new toy.
Ben invited me to play with him in the skipping game.
Kate saw what a mess I had made with the paints and offered to help me to clean it up.

Figure 10.7 *Friendships provide us with a sense of self-worth: we should encourage and praise friendly actions*

Encourage children to see what others need and prompt them to offer support.

> Jess, look, Sam is trying to put the rabbit back in the hutch, do you think he could do with some help? 'I'll hold the door open for him.'

Systematic approaches to teaching social skills are often highly effective in changing behaviour. Wear (2000) found that social skills training that included the teacher modelling behaviours and giving clear and positive feedback on children's attempts to practise them worked better than attempts to teach attitudes and values alone.

Citizenship and involvement

How can we help to develop the citizens of the future?

Children need to have an active part to play in their world. Each is an important member of the group and each has a useful contribution to make. Children who are damaged by lack of self-worth will have difficulty in believing this message. Children need to learn that they can make a difference and that their contribution counts for something for them to develop a sense of responsibility towards the social classroom and the people around them.

Where children have been engaged in putting forward their ideas for making the classroom, school or play area better and they have been taken seriously, they have learned some very valuable lessons in social responsibility. There are lots of examples to draw on to illustrate this, from children's suggestions on how to make a better cage for the classroom pet to live in, to a better play space in the playground, to how to prevent bullying. In some schools, children as young as 7 are actively involved in formal meetings of the school council, being elected by the class to represent their views at the meeting and reporting back. The most popular topic for discussion always seems to be the toilets! Maybe the planners could learn something from this.

The degree to which children will take responsibility will be incremental, but even the smallest task needs to be seen as important, whether it is watering the plants, helping to clear away or listening to a younger child read.

Health education

It is well documented that much can be done during these early years to positive effect. In the UK, the White Paper *Excellence in Schools* (DfEE, 1997) outlines the government's intention to help all schools to become healthier schools, and that education has a role to play in promoting better health and emotional well-being for all children, in particular those who are socially and economically disadvantaged. A healthy school is one that is successful in helping pupils to do their best and to build on their achievements. It promotes physical and emotional health by providing accessible and relevant information, and equipping pupils with skills and attitudes to make informed decisions about their health (DfEE, 1999).

- So what do children need to know about health and keeping safe?
- How can we best promote an understanding of these issues with children in the early years?
- How can we assist them to develop the skills to make decisions about healthy living and keep safe?
- What role do the parents and families have?

What do children need to know about health and keeping safe?

There is a wealth of texts on what children need to know about health and keeping safe in the primary years. *Health for Life Ages 4–7* by Noreen Wetton and Trefor Willians (2000) is particularly well considered about these issues in the early years, and full of ideas for activities. To summarise, children need information that is appropriate to their age. Children aged 3 to 8 years are very capable of absorbing huge amounts of basic information about their bodies, naming parts of the body and differences between people: hair, skin colour, gender, what we put into our bodies, for example, food, drinks, medicine, etc., and what we put on our bodies, for example, clothes, hats, sun cream. Children need to know that their bodies need good food and exercise to be healthy. They need to know that there are dangers and they will have a better understanding of some of these dangers more than others. They need to know what things feel like and what makes them feel good, what makes them feel bad and what is that strange feeling when you are not quite sure, but you don't feel comfortable. This sense is one that we need to work on with young children to help them to take notice of and to trust their instincts.

We are laying the foundations of an understanding of good health by providing information and encouraging decision-making skills that assist in children's ability to make healthy lifestyle choices.

How can we best promote an understanding of these issues with children in the early years?

Children need guiding into thinking about what are good things that the body needs and what are not good things (see Figure 10.8). They will have an understanding of what it feels like if they hurt themselves/their body and will be able to make suggestions about how to protect themselves from danger, for example, from sharp objects, traffic, falling.

The best way to promote this understanding with young children is to make sure that what we do starts from what they know, for example, themselves. Start with the feelings they have and can identify and develop from this (emotional literacy again). We need to make sure that the work we do with children is developmental and progressive. We would do well to acknowledge Bruner's notion of the 'spiral curriculum' here. The curriculum and information needs to be progressive, but also needs to be repeated at different levels of understanding to a greater depth and packaged differently. The youngest children need to work things out by

Figure 10.8 *Good things that the body needs: 'Would you like some fruit?'*

repeatedly playing through ideas. They need the opportunity to repeat games themselves in order to make sense of them. We know that the more tangible and hands on the activities are the greater their assimilation of understanding.

Ideas for health education activities

- Circle time rounds: 'I am healthy when . . .', 'Being healthy is . . .', 'What do healthy people do?';
- Change places if . . . (teacher calls out examples of healthy things, for example, if you had cereal for breakfast, if you brushed your teeth this morning) – children stand up and change places;
- Draw pictures of themselves doing something healthy;
- Sort out pictures of food into healthy and not so healthy and make a collage;
- Keeping safe: My name is . . . and I live at . . . (name of the road or town); make a card with their name address and phone number on; paint pictures of their front door with the number on and make a class display;
- Ask the children to name all the things they feel they have to keep safe from and talk about them; add to the list to make sure they include fire, water, sun, road and home safety. Ask the children to draw pictures. Back in the circle, lay three large sheets of paper on the floor each with a title in the middle: 'things', 'people' and 'places'. Discuss with the children the pictures they have drawn and get each one to place their picture on the poster;
- Books and stories;
- Role-play area, dolls etc., hospital;
- Card games of body parts;
- Road safety tracks;
- Swimming pool safety;
- Naming feelings: what makes me happy/sad angry/upset is . . ;
- Puppets;
- Small world play;
- Visitors, traffic control, fire brigade, police, nurse;
- Circle time discussion on:
  - What happens when you are tired? . . . Your body needs sleep.
  - What happens when you are hungry? . . . Your body needs food.
  - What happens when you stay underwater for a long time? . . . Your body needs air.
  - What happens when it is a rainy day and you cannot go out to play? . . . Your body needs exercise.
  - Saying No!

We could also help children to practise the skills they need to deal with difficult situations and to call on others to help them. This is part of developing a caring environment. This can be particularly helpful if we as adults take a stance against bullies. The whole staff approach is important here. The days have gone when it was considered character-building to leave children to deal with bullies on their own. Many schools have effective anti-bullying policies in place. Bullies can only operate if everyone turns a blind eye. If the culture of the school is to take this seriously and to develop a supportive ethos, then the bullies will eventually lose their lifeline. We need to develop in children an ability to ask for help. This needs playing out and re-enacting. Role-play and drama are very useful here. Some children will need lots of experiential rehearsal of this situation to be able to assert themselves.

How can we assist children to develop the skills to make decisions about healthy living and keeping safe?

We need to give children the resources to deal with life situations. Decision-making is a key skill here. Children need to feel they have power to make decisions. They need to use their knowledge, and their understanding and they need to be able to make the decisions to promote their health. We need to develop decision-making at a basic level before this can be drawn into play at more complex levels. Lorna Farrington (2000) talks about children in the early years spending 75 per cent of their day in making decisions, but higher up the school, only 5 per cent of their time. We need to turn this around. We know that this is an important skill to develop and we need to reconsider the school day to ensure we are extending this skill as children move through the school.

What role do the parents and families have?

Parents/carers need to be fully aware of the issues that are being discussed with the children. It is a good school policy to state, prior to children's entry, that certain issues will be part of this curriculum and to engage parents in this from the outset in the interest of informing and protecting children.

The lives and culture of families will play a significant role in the lives of the children in regard to healthy lifestyles or otherwise. Children are not easily in control of what they eat, the types of food bought for the family, the approaches to exercise, the use of leisure time, the ability to express individual preferences, or to reject what parents do themselves. However, most parents want what is best for their children and are delighted when the school takes some responsibility for this. Many parents have had to battle with schools to take these issues seriously, especially over the provision of school meals. Parents have a huge job on their hands to compete with advertising which becomes ever more invasive in enticing children to want things that we know are not good for promoting health and are delighted that schools will support them in this. There is no point in teaching good nutrition and good eating habits in the classroom and then providing children very poor and unhealthy food at lunchtime.

Some parents may need to understand why the programme encourages children to think for themselves and to question when they would prefer that children simply learn to do as they are told.

Families need to be aware when children will be considering issues relating to children keeping safe. This may include dealing with some delicate issues. This really needs a specific meeting with parents to discuss the issues, let them know how the subject will be approached and what will be discussed. It is important that parents are involved in this discussion. They may have to pick up on issues or questions with the child at home and need some preparation for this.

Conclusion

Children learn as much, if not more, from the way in which we behave towards them as from the content of the lessons and activities. The approaches we use and the attitudes and respect we show children in their early years will affect their ability to learn and their growth into effective citizens.

Pointers for PSHE in the early years

- The links between PSHE and children's learning has been well established by research.
- The quality of the relationship between the adults and children is crucial.
- The partnership between the family and school is important.
- The benefits of a whole-school approach to PSHE cannot be underestimated.

Personal

- Personal development is best founded on a firm basis of positive self-esteem.
- Adults need to help children to identify, understand and develop skills to cope with powerful emotions.
- Conflicts can be a positive learning experience.
- Even very young children can learn to solve emotional and social problems independently.
- An atmosphere of trust between adults and children is vital to support children's emotional learning.

Social

- Creating a welcoming environment and agreeing the rules sets the scene.
- The processes involved in developing these principles are learning experiences in themselves.
- There are vital aspects of the social component of the PSHE programme and approach that help children to cooperate, to develop friendships and to develop citizenship skills.

Health

- A healthy school enables children to give their best and build on their achievements.
- The safety of the child is paramount.
- A major goal is to develop children's understanding of health issues as a precursor to their making informed and important decisions.
- In health, as in all other social and personal development issues there is a need for continuing dialogue with the children's families.

References

Curry, N. and Johnson, C. (1990) *Beyond Self-esteem: Developing a Sense of Human Value*, Washington, DC: NAEYC.

DfEE (1997) *Excellence in Schools*, White Paper, Nottingham: DfEE.

DfEE (1999) *National Healthy Schools: Standard Guidance*, Nottingham: DfEE.

Dunn, J. (1988) *The Beginnings of Social Understanding*, Cambridge, MA: Harvard University Press.

Dunn, J. and Herrara, C. (1997) 'Conflict resolution with friends, siblings and mothers: a developmental perspective', *Aggressive Behaviour*, 23, 343–57.

Farrington, L. (2000) *Playground Peacemakers: Peaceful Conflict Resolution for*

Schools Using the Mediation Way for Teachers in Key Stage 1, Plymouth, UK: Loxley Enterprises.

Goleman, D. (1996) *Emotional Intelligence: Why It Can Matter More Than IQ*, London: Bloomsbury.

Mosley, J. (1996) *Quality Circle Time in the Primary Classroom*, vol. 1, Wisbech, Cambs: LDA.

Parker, J.G. and Gottman, J.M. (1989) 'Social and emotional development in a relational context', in J.M. Gottman, L.F. Katz and C. Hooven (eds) *Meta-Emotion: How Families Communicate Emotionally*, Mahwah, NJ: Erlbaum.

Roberts, R. (1995) *Self-esteem and Successful Early Learning*, London: Hodder & Stoughton Educational.

Rogers, C. (1961) *On Becoming a Person*, London: Constable.

Shantz, C.U. (1987) 'Conflicts between children', *Child Development*, 58, 283–505.

Wear, K. (2000) *Promoting Mental, Emotional and Social Health: A Whole-school Approach*, London: Routledge.

Further reading

Laishley, J. (1987) *Working with Young Children*, 2nd edn, London: Hodder & Stoughton.

Roffey, S., Tarrant, T. and Majors, K. (1994) *Young Friends: Schools and Friendship*, London: Cassell.

Wetton, N. and Williams, T. (2000) *Health for Life, Ages 4–7*, Cheltenham: Thornes Nelson.

Whitebread, D. and Coltman, P. (2007) 'Developing young children as self-regulating learners', in J. Moyles (ed.) *Beginning Teaching: Beginning Learning in Primary Education*, 3rd edn, Buckingham: Open University Press, pp. 154–68.

CHAPTER 11

'How do I do this better?'

FROM MOVEMENT DEVELOPMENT INTO PHYSICAL LITERACY

Patricia Maude

How do you like to go up in a swing
Up in the air so blue?
Oh, I do think it is the pleasantest thing
Ever a child can do!

(Robert Louis Stevenson)

Introduction

The early years are exciting times both for children's physical development, as they grow, changing in shape and size, and for children's movement development, as they gain in body awareness and as they explore the vast range of available movement experiences within their environment. Through experimentation, trial, error and success, young movers progress towards coordinated, mature movement knowledge and performance. Not only is movement the main medium of exploration for the young child, but also physical activity is essential for normal growth, providing the necessary stimulus for normal development. As young children develop other abilities, including language, observation skills, knowledge of the environments in which they live and understanding of movement contexts, so they also become increasingly physically literate.

We, as educators, have a responsibility for ensuring that the children we teach are exposed to the widest possible world of movement. Within that world of movement children need to experience a varied programme of activity which both balances the demands made on different parts of the body and takes into account the maintenance and enhancement of strength, mobility and endurance, helping to ensure the development of sound physique and posture. Giving children worthwhile movement experience will also develop motor-competence and encourage motor-confidence and creativity. Confidence in movement is vital for self-expression, and articulate coordinated movement ability greatly enhances the development of self-esteem. One of the challenges for the early years educator is to capitalise on the vast movement experience that children have accumulated prior to starting school. Educators can then expose children to a rich and rewarding movement vocabulary from which they can increase physical knowledge and skill, build on that past experience and broaden their physical literacy.

In this chapter we shall examine some of the processes of physical development from birth through infancy and early childhood; we shall then explore motor development by looking at ways in which the acquisition of fundamental motor patterns and movement experiences are achieved by the young child. We shall also consider the role of the child as a movement learner through play, the role of the educator as a facilitator and provider of movement knowledge, and some suggestions as to what might constitute quality movement learning for children in their first years at school. In exploring what might constitute physical literacy in the life of the young child, we shall also consider some aims and content for the physical development and physical education curriculum in the early years, including the Foundation Stage and Key Stage 1 of the national curriculum in England.

Readers are encouraged to:

- review their knowledge of children's early physical development and motor skill acquisition;
- consider ways of extending children's movement vocabulary and movement memory;
- extend their ability to observe and analyse children's movement in order to give informed feedback on performance;
- provide an appropriate curriculum which emanates from children's play and which raises standards in children's movement-competence;
- guide children in their entitlement to physical literacy.

Some processes of physical development

Pertinent to the learner and educator of movement are three key factors in the early physical development of infants, namely the principles of:

- cephalo-caudal development;
- proximo-distal development;
- differentiation.

Cephalo-caudal development

This first principle of physical development is so named because it stems from the Greek word for 'head' which is *'kephale'*, and the Latin word for 'tail' which is *'cauda'*. It denotes the principle that development occurs from the head downwards towards the feet. This seems obvious, since the head houses the brain which is the chief controller and regulator of all bodily functions. The brain also regulates the growth and development of the body. The head is the most developed part of the body at birth, having already achieved half of its adult length and the upper limbs, the arms, being near the top of the body, are quite well developed. The lower limbs, however, are relatively undeveloped and of relatively little importance, lacking in musculature, having achieved barely a fifth of their adult length. This principle of 'top-down' development will influence our planning and teaching when we are looking to ensure that the children we teach have acquired all the fundamental motor skills to enable them to be articulate movers in both the upper and lower limbs. For example, to help children to know and understand about efficient use of the ankle joint, we should refer to ankle extension and flexion, rather than to talking about 'pointing toes', since the neural message relates to movement at the ankle joint rather than in the toes.

Proximo-distal development

The second principle refers to growth from the centre of the body outwards towards the extremities. This, too, is easily understood in the context of the significance of the central nervous system which controls all messages from the brain, running down the spinal column and managing all the life functions of the infant. The vital organs, essential to survival, are housed in the centre of the body, with maximum potential for protection. By comparison, the early activity of peripheral limbs such as the hands is relatively insignificant! For example the hands, the most distal elements at the farthest extremity from the centre of the body, are relatively inactive and non-instrumental in early life. Indeed, at this stage they are not structurally ready for action, since, for example, not all the bones in the wrists are differentiated. Before the wrists are fully prepared and ready to service the complex variety of movement demands that will be placed upon the hands when older, some of the wrist bones will separate and will develop appropriate musculature.

As with the principle of cephalo-caudal development, the principle of proximo-distal development is also important for the educator in creating a movement programme that takes account of the length of time necessary to achieve movement competence in those parts of the limbs that are relatively more distant from the centre of the body. Classroom learning can also be significantly dependent upon this principle, where, for example, the learner may not have achieved the moment of readiness to hold a pencil with the pincer or tripod grip (between the thumb and index finger) and feels more comfortable using the palmar or power grasp (pencil gripped between the palm and the fingers). The product of work produced using the palmar grasp is usually less accurate than that of the pincer grip with which it is possible to achieve greater control. However, the muscles of the hand need to be sufficiently strong to enable the child to sustain the more demanding pincer grip.

Differentiation

The third principle is that whereby the newborn child offers an apparently global response, whereas the more mature child is more discriminatory in response. For example, in response to a pin prick on the hand, the infant cries, pulls the limb away and generally thrashes about, whereas the older child will withdraw the limb and may cry, but the adult is unlikely to do more than consider withdrawing the affected limb. As neurological development takes place and the child matures, so the ability to differentiate responses grows. This developing ability to discriminate responses with increasing maturity is an important element of learning for the early years child in school.

These three principles not only provide us with many insights into the process and rhythm of development of the infant, but also underpin many aspects of child development. They are particularly relevant as we move on to consider the movement (motor) development of young children. Movement is the lead area of functioning for the infant in acquiring information about the environment and in learning about self. The principles and processes of movement development therefore, hold many of the keys for the educator, in developing an appropriate movement curriculum for children.

Some processes of motor development

Motor development, along with other areas of development, follows the principles of cephalo-caudal, proximo-distal development and differentiation.

In relation to **cephalo-caudal development**, success is achieved in movement involving the upper part of the body before that involving the lower limbs. Control of the head, as in turning to look towards a stimulus and later lifting and holding the head, precedes management of the shoulders, as in pushing up from front lying to raise the head. Thereafter further control of the trunk and hips enables the infant to learn to sit. This in turn precedes control of the hips, knees and ankles, and later the feet, and the increase in strength required for weight-bearing on the feet and for achieving the standing position, prior to learning to take the first step and later to walk.

The sequence of learning to walk, then, is significantly influenced by the principle of cephalo-caudal development. While it is very rare that the mainstream educator of young children needs to be involved in teaching locomotion, this is a very significant sequence of development for some physically and mentally delayed and disabled children, and for children with delayed movement development who are integrated into mainstream schooling. All early years educators will, however, be involved in developing and enhancing the efficiency and quality of this fundamental movement pattern and of the motor patterns that emanate from it, such as running, jumping and all other locomotion skills. The significance of cephalo-caudal development and its influence upon children's success in movement is of great importance both in the planning of the movement curriculum and in the general education of young children.

The equally logical principle of **proximo-distal movement skill development** can be observed as the infant explores the immediate environment and subsequently gains control over the arms, starting at the shoulders as the central or proximo part of the limb, before gaining controlled movement in the hands, the more peripheral or distal elements of the arms. Early exploration of the environment takes place through movement. Even from the relatively still supine lying position, the infant is seen to use the entire arm, flailing in the air, as if to swipe out and later to reach for objects in sight. In a similar way, apparently indiscriminate movement of the arms results in the infant discovering the mouth with the hands and subsequent success is achieved in grasping at objects with both hands, followed by trying to put them into the mouth.

Much movement experience is gained using the entire arm as a single lever, with relatively little **differentiation** between the arm joints. It is not until distance from an object becomes significant that flexion of the elbow is used to shorten the arm, for example. Much later, when one hand rather than two is required to achieve a movement task, the infant is dependent upon the development of the wrist joint and the joints of the fingers and thumb having acquired appropriate structure and musculature. Significantly, the principle of 'readiness', by which the child is unable to attempt a more advanced procedure until the structure and musculature are sufficiently mature, dominates motor development. We thereby do not see the infant progress from two-handed grasping to the use of one hand until that readiness is in place.

The sequence of growth and development

This leads us on to consider the sequence of growth and development, including motor development, which is invariable, from one infant to the next. Helpfully for us as educators, the order in which all infants acquire movement skills is the same – every child follows the same sequence. Normally, for example, infants learn to roll over, then to sit and later to stand before learning to walk (see Figure 11.1).

Similarly, in terms of sequential development, prior to acquiring the skill of hopping, children must gain the strength to fix the pelvis so that it

Figure 11.1 *The regular sequence of motor development in infants*

remains horizontal when holding the body balance over one foot. They then need the balance and coordination to transfer the body weight to that single foot before learning to take off and land on the same foot, usually to hop along before hopping on the spot.

The fact that all children follow the same sequence of movement development is very helpful. However, the challenge for the educator comes from the knowledge that the rate of development is unique to each child; no two children, even in the same family, follow the same pace of development. In preparing movement programmes, therefore, we must take account, particularly in the Foundation Stage and Key Stage 1, of the need for children to complete their learning of fundamental motor skills.

Gross and fine motor skills

Linked with the three preceding principles of motor development is another invariable and not-surprising feature of child development, that of 'gross' and 'fine' motor skills. The child achieves greater control in large (gross) body movement before managing control in smaller (fine) movements. For example, walking, jumping and running are more advanced in their performance and control at a relatively younger age than are drawing, cutting or colouring-in, where detailed management of the developing muscles of the wrist and hand can be extremely challenging for the young child. Much learning activity in the classroom involves drawing, painting, writing, measuring, cutting, sticking, etc., and the more mature the child's wrist and finger development and the stronger the musculature, the more successful will be the practical elements of the product, with the least inhibition experienced due to muscle fatigue. Some children's classroom behaviour may be observed to be off-task or to demonstrate a lack of concentration, when the true inhibitor is lack of maturity in the structure and functioning of the wrist and hand, thereby disqualifying them from maximum participation. Since gross motor competence serves as a springboard for developing efficient fine motor skills, it is incumbent upon educators to provide frequent opportunities for young children to practise both gross and fine movement activities.

The importance of physical play

How better can provision for frequent gross and fine motor activity be made than through physical play?

In developing a movement curriculum for young children, the notion of building upon play is a compelling aim. Physical play is important for:

- encouraging discovery of movement abilities;
- allowing for exploration of the movement environment;
- offering practice time to enhance fundamental motor skills and strengthen the cardio-vascular system and the muscles.

The provision of a stimulating environment, both for children's pre-school play and for developmental play during and after the school day, is a matter for detailed planning for parents and educators of young children. In providing for gross motor competence, this might include:

- an adventure playground;
- a secret garden;
- a playground with suitable markings to encourage challenge in movement;
- a tarmac area with wheeled toys including trucks, go-carts, scooters, tricycles, bicycles and other ride-on and push-along toys;
- an indoor space with soft-play and gymnastics apparatus;
- grass and hard areas with balls of various sizes and textures, beanbags, hoops, bats, velcro-catchers, targets, skipping ropes, ribbons and scarves.

These and other home and school provisions can significantly enhance the movement-learning experience for young children.

The importance of play involving gross and fine motor skills is of paramount importance in children's movement development and must underpin the devising of the physical development and physical education curriculum. Indeed, the school curriculum should be founded upon the natural movement vocabulary of the playing child.

We rely on children arriving at school already articulate in movement, with mature movement patterns already established in the fundamental motor skills. On arrival at school, with a wealth of pre-school movement experiences, children should expect to draw from their existing movement vocabulary, using established and efficient movement patterns to enable them to participate fully in the activities on offer, to enjoy their learning and to be successful. My own experience suggests that even where articulate movers arrive in school, reinforcement of mature movement patterns should continue to be a part of the curriculum, as the child grows, as body levers lengthen, strength increases and body awareness is enhanced. The child is in a state of readiness to become even more skilful and to acquire an even greater movement vocabulary and movement memory.

Developing an appropriate movement curriculum for young children

As a starting point for devising a movement curriculum we may ask ourselves what constitute the most useful movement skills that children bring with them to school. Certainly efficiency in all daily living tasks, including feeding, toileting, dressing and moving safely around the environment will enable the child to operate independently in school. Additionally, children bringing a range of the gross and fine motor skills that are needed for full participation in class activities, such as those previously discussed, have an advantage over children who are less experienced or whose gross and fine motor skills are less developed.

Many children also bring with them a rich movement vocabulary developed through play. The importance of play as a basis for all aspects of education, cannot be overestimated, as has been ably discussed in this and other chapters within and beyond this book.

Aims of the physical development curriculum

Before deciding on the content of the physical development curriculum, we should explore what we might consider to be the aims of that programme. In order to enhance the child as a learner and to ensure that you, as the educator, offer the best possible provision for that learner, the following broad aims for the physical development curriculum for early years children need to be developed. These relate to physical and movement development, movement skill acquisition and confidence in movement as physical literacy develops.

Physical development

- to stimulate growth;
- to enhance physical development;
- to provide healthy exercise.

Movement development

- to build on existing movement vocabulary;
- to develop coordination, body tension and control;
- to extend movement vocabulary.

Movement skill acquisition

- to develop fundamental motor skills to the mature stage;

- to introduce new motor skills;
- to increase knowledge of dynamics of movement;
- to develop coordination;
- to teach accuracy and efficiency in movement.

Movement confidence development

- to teach movement observation skills;
- to develop movement experimentation and expression;
- to enhance self-expression;
- to enhance self-confidence, self-image and self-esteem.

Other aspects of provision for physical literacy might be to:

- teach appropriate vocabulary for describing, explaining, discussing, assessing and improving the quality of movement;
- stimulate thought processes that feed into motor development;
- expect quality work from children;
- encourage independence in, confidence in and ownership of learning;
- learn respect in cooperation and competition;
- enhance positive attitudes towards health-related exercise;
- provide experiences that teach children to plan, perform and evaluate their movement learning;
- sustain feelings of enjoyment and well-being in physical activity.

Are there other aims that should underpin a curriculum plan for early years children in movement development and physical education, such as providing stimulating, challenging and imaginative learning experiences for children? These can be built into the curriculum, to ensure children's entitlement to be physically educated and to be physically literate.

The physical development curriculum, therefore, should contain an extensive, broad and generic movement vocabulary of learning experiences for all children, from which, specialisation can later develop most successfully.

The development of skilled movement

The route to the acquisition of skilled movement has been plotted by Gallahue & Ozman (2006). They name three progressive stages in skill learning:

The initial or rudimentary stage
This is the emergent movement pattern, or early experimentation stage.

The elementary stage

At this stage, in which coordination is improved, the movement is still incorrectly performed and incomplete, perhaps lacking in strength, mobility, balance or speed.

The mature stage

Finally the child achieves the mature stage, in which all the elements of the movement pattern are integrated and in which the movement includes appropriate preparation, followed by the accurate action and ends with efficient follow-through and recovery. At this stage the movement pattern also becomes integrated into the movement memory, to be called upon with ease.

Watch a professional cricketer throw the ball in from the boundary and compare that action with the overarm throw of the average 5-year-old and your mind's eye will no doubt provide ample evidence of potential for further development in the young child's achievement (see Figure 11.2)! Note the trunk flexion, rather than rotation.

Figure 11.2 *A beginning thrower*

Figure 11.3 illustrates the movement development between a beginning and an advanced runner. With the advanced runner there is a much fuller range of leg motion and the thighs and arms drive forward and back rather than swinging out slightly to the side.

Bearing in mind that the elementary and mature movement patterns are normally achieved during the primary school years, the educator has considerable responsibility for recognising the three stages in the various fundamental motor skills of locomotion (walking and running), jumping (including taking off and landing) and projection (throwing, kicking), and in analysing the child's achievements in order to improve performance.

Recognising the moment of readiness in the child is a skill in itself to be acquired by the educator. Spatial and body awareness as well as

Figure 11.3 *A beginning and advanced runner*

appropriate maturing of the body structures and brain functioning are influential in attaining that moment of readiness. Have you ever tried to teach a child to ride a bicycle before readiness has been achieved? Holding the saddle, you walk or run along behind the bike growing ever more exhausted, as the child tries to stay upright and pedal, without success as far as independent balance is concerned. Put the bike away for a matter of weeks (or months if you or the child had been over-ambitious!) and then notice that when the child gets the bike out again she climbs on and rides away unaided. The frustration of anticipating readiness too soon is outweighed by the satisfaction of helping a child to be successful in enhancing a partially learnt skill or in acquiring a new skill!

The early years physical development

So, what should we include in our physical development curriculum that will meet our selected aims and provide satisfaction and rich movement experience for our young learners? In England, *The Early Years Foundation Stage* (DfES, 2007) shows children learning through movement in almost every area and also focuses on developing children's movement capabilities. The emerging physical literacy curriculum (www.physical-literacy.org.uk) promotes the development of generic movement ability and skill for children in the early years. At Key Stage 1, physical education in the national curriculum currently promotes experience in dance, games and gymnastics, with swimming as an option in either Key Stage 1 or Key Stage 2. These activities seem entirely appropriate for children whose early years physical development and movement experience has been made up of broad-based and varied play. Dance, games and gymnastics are also appropriate activities for children aged 5–7 years, as between them they offer the learner extensive movement vocabularies, opportunities to develop creative as well as functional movement, and opportunities for exercise and the stimulus for physical development and growth. Through dance, games and gymnastics, the child can achieve the mature stage in fundamental movement patterns and can derive challenge, enjoyment, confidence and movement competence.

The range of movement vocabulary on offer can also be advantageous to the child with delayed movement development, who, with support from knowledgeable adults, can work within personal constraints and push out the boundaries of those limitations.

The child illustrated in Figure 11.4 has acquired by the age of 6 a sophistication of skill in kicking that is rarely seen in Key Stage 1.

The child seen in Figure 11.5, who is also aged 6 years, has achieved a quality of body and spatial awareness in leaping that should be our aim for all children in Key Stage 1.

For the normal child there need be no constraints beyond those imposed by the limitations of the developing body and brain, the confidence of the learner, and the bounds of reasonable safety imposed by the environment, the equipment to be used and the other children sharing the same space.

For me, the early years programme must be one of discovery and achievement, of valuing the learner, with evidence of excitement and

Figure 11.4 *An advanced 6-year-old kicker*

Figure 11.5 *The leap*

Figures 11.4 and 11.5 copyright PCET Publishing

satisfaction in learning. Can you recall an experience similar to that quoted above by Robert Louis Stevenson? Do you remember the effort of getting the swing started and then of discovering the knack of leaning back and then forward to increase the height of the swing and then the fear of going over the top, having seemingly swung too high? Do you also remember the pleasure derived from such play activities, as are recalled here by A.A. Milne?

> He played with his skipping rope,
> He played with his ball.
> He ran after butterflies,
> Blue ones and red;
> He did a hundred happy things –
> And then went to bed.
>
> (from 'Forgotten' in *Now We Are Six*,
> Milne, 1927, p. 98)

Perhaps it is here, in the young child's physical play that we should start observing in an attempt to discover the 'lifeworld' of physical literacy for young children. If we are to provide worthwhile learning experiences that challenge children, give them ownership of their learning and enable them to build on pre-school play experiences, we must seek out appropriate starting points. From these we can build upon:

- the fantasy and exploratory expressive play that can become **dance**, as in twirling, galloping, leaping, reaching up and away and pausing;
- the **games**-like play that involves chasing, dodging, catching, throwing, kicking and hitting;
- the **gymnastics**-like play that involves rolling, jumping, climbing, swinging and balancing.

We may need to take a closer look at what children actually do when they engage in physical activity and, from our observation, put ourselves in touch with the nature of children's physical development, before proceeding to influence that development by the pedagogical framework that we provide.

The role of the educator

One area of educator competence that is essential, in addition to that of children's physical and movement development, is knowledge of the progressions for, and techniques of, the basic skills to be developed in physical education. The remainder of this chapter attempts to illustrate what is involved here using an example from each of the areas of dance, games and gymnastics. Enabling children to leap, to catch, or to do a forward roll, which are our three examples, requires a minimum level of technical knowledge, which can be acquired from observation, from personal experience, from demonstration or from videos, pictures or books.

Learning to leap

Learning to leap involves transferring the body weight off the ground, from one foot to the other. Lead-up skills for children who cannot leap include the basic jumping skills of take off and landing on two feet and on one foot (hopping), as well as focusing on stepping from one foot to the other. Striding (taking very long steps), trying to push off and make the knees straight to extend the stride length, is also an important lead-up skill. Many children who find leaping difficult take a run and then take off and land on the same foot, i.e. they do a sort of long, fast hop. Encourage these children to take long strides and to try to push off the floor, taking off from one foot, to do the step through the air and land on the other foot. Once the child can leap through the air from one foot to the other, the quality of the technique can be developed. Look for an upright body position, arms swinging to help elevate the leap, and then extending, probably sideways and symmetrically, to help control the shape in the air. Finally, look for, height, distance, a clear shape in the air and a controlled landing.

Learning to catch

Learning to catch is best achieved by using a range of progressions, rather than by repeating experiences of failure if it is clear that the child cannot catch the object being thrown. Progressions can be considered in at least two aspects:

1 **missile used** – size, weight, texture, shape, surface; encourage the child to choose a missile that is easy to catch, for example. a velcro catcher, a soft bean bag or a foam ball;
2 **receiving activity** – the progressions here are as follows:
   • receive from a slow roll sent along the ground towards the two waiting hands of the receiver;
   • receive from an underarm feed with bounce so that the ball comes up to the waiting hands of the receiver;
   • receive from an underarm throw.

The technique of the catch involves three phases:

1 **the preparation** – including the stance, arms extended towards the missile, the open-palmed ready position of the hands and the eyes watching the missile rather than the sender;
2 **the action** – the hands closing around the ball, the arms bending or recoiling to control the impact of the missile;
3 **the recovery** – in which the catcher regains a controlled position.

Learning to forward roll

As with the catch, there are many progressions that can precede practising the forward roll for children who cannot readily perform this complex roll. (The forward roll is made up of at least 17 flexions and extensions of joints of the body and limbs as it is performed!) Give children a vocabulary of other rolls that they can practise on the floor, on mats and on and from apparatus. Start with the log roll in which the child lies in a straight line and rolls over sideways. This roll can also be practised tucked. Rolling forward from front-lying on a low platform, by placing the hands on a mat to control the descent of the body onto the back of the shoulders, is often a helpful progression.

Teaching the ending of the forward roll, prior to the whole roll can greatly encourage the less experienced child. By learning how to stand up from rocking on the back in a tucked shape, often encourages the child to try out the complete roll. To do this the learner should keep the knees bent and rock forward to place the feet on the floor near the seat, while reaching forward with the hands and arms to help transfer the weight from the seat to the feet. The child is then ready to learn how to transfer the weight from standing on the feet to the hands and then onto the shoulders in a complete forward roll. This is best learnt going down a soft, gentle incline, such as a foam ramp onto a mat, before practising the whole roll on a mat. Early forward rolls on a mat are also easier when started with the legs in a wide (straddle) position, thus lowering the body and making space to tuck the head under, in transfer of the weight from the feet to the hands and to the shoulders.

These are some of the main teaching points for three basic skills. Other texts provide greater detail of these and other skills (see list at the end of this chapter).

What else should be included within the pedagogical framework is a question to be answered by the competent curriculum planner, in devising an appropriate developmental physical development programme for young children?

Satisfying the 'skill-hungry years' of children in primary school and answering the myriad questions of these same children, such as 'How do I do this better?' – the key question asked by children – is a constant and often insatiable challenge for the educator.

My own view is that this is not an insurmountable challenge. The educator who first observes and studies the lifeworld of physical activity as experienced by the young learner engaged in natural movement development, is well on the way to success. If the child is put at the centre of the learning experience, then the educator can ensure that the joy of indulging in physical activity is sustained and enhanced as children mature and engage ever more skilfully and knowledgeably in the wide range of physical activities available.

Pointers for physical development, physical education and physical literacy in the early years

An effective physical development and physical education curriculum for the early years will help to cultivate in children movement that is skilful, articulate, creative and satisfying. In order to help young children to acquire motor skill competence, to be confident and articulate movers and to develop their physical literacy, they need teachers and carers who have:

- acquired knowledge of the physical development of young children in relation to motor development and the achievement of mature motor patterns;
- learnt and understood the progressions for and techniques of movement skills;
- developed observation skills to enable them to assess progress and to give appropriate developmental feedback on the child's performance;
- built the physical development and physical education curriculum from natural movement and play;
- provided children with rich and frequent opportunities to explore movement and to practise and develop their movement vocabulary, movement memory and the quality of their movement.

Children will then be able to achieve their entitlement to full physical development, to be physically educated and to enhance all aspects of their physical literacy.

References

Maude, P.M. (2001) *Physical Children, Active Teaching*, Buckingham: Open University Press.

Maude, P. M. (2003) *Observing Children Moving*, CDRom: www. observingchildrenmoving.co.uk

Milne, A.A. (1927) 'Forgotten', in *Now We Are Six*, London: Methuen.

Further reading

Movement development

Gallahue, D. and Ozman, J. (2006) *Understanding Motor Development: Infants, Children, Adolescents, Adults*, 6th edn, Boston: McGraw-Hill.

Haywood, K.M. (2001) *Life Span Motor Development*, 3rd edn, Champaign, IL: Human Kinetics.

Macintyre, C. (2000) *Dyspraxia in the Early Years*, London: David Fulton Publishers.

Rathus, S.A. (1988) *Understanding Child Development*, New York: Holt, Rinehart and Winston.

Physical development, physical education and physical literacy

Davies, M. (1995) *Helping Children to Learn through a Movement Perspective*, London: Hodder Headline.

DfES (2007) *The Early Years Foundation Stage*, Nottingham: DfES.

Hopper, B., Grey, J. and Maude, P.M. (2000) *Teaching Primary Physical Education*, London: Falmer.

Maude, P.M., Wetton, P. and Whitehead, M. (2006) *2Move*, London: Central Council for Physical Recreation.

Maude, P.M. (1997) *Gymnastics*, London: Hodder & Stoughton.

Physical Literacy: www.physical-literacy.org.uk

Portwood, M. (1999) *Developmental Dyspraxia*, London: David Fulton Publishers.

Weinstock, M. (2007) *Gymnastics*, www.mwgymnastics.co.uk

Youth Sport Trust. (2000) *TOP Tots, TOP Start, TOP Play, TOP Sport*, Loughborough: Youth Sport Trust, www.youthsport.net

Youth Sport Trust (2000) *TOP Dance, TOP Games, TOP Gymnastics*, Loughborough: Youth Sport Trust, www.youthsport.net

CHAPTER 12

'Can I play the drum, Miss?'

MUSIC IN THE EARLY YEARS

Jane Edden

The task ahead

It would be altogether too easy to be deterred from teaching music to children. After all, in an investigation carried out in a College of Education, it was discovered that 'By a wide margin . . . music is the subject in which most students have the least confidence as teachers' and that 'Some students thought that they needed to have musical skills customarily associated with music specialists, e.g. piano playing, fluent music reading and an inside-out knowledge of the Classics' (Mills, 1989). This somewhat gloomy picture is offset, however, by those who have faced the challenge head on and, in one case, emerged with recommendations from the county music adviser as providing good practice in the classroom. A teaching head in Warwickshire (Dancer, 1991) who had 'never been on a music course of any kind' began her written guidelines with the words: 'You don't need a piano, a guitar, a wonderful singing voice or a special room to enjoy music making with children.' Her commitment to 'bringing children into contact with the musician's fundamental activities of performing, composing and listening (DES, 1985, p. 2) in order that they 'can best discover something of its nature, its vitality, its evocative power and the range of its expressive qualities' (DES, 1985, p. 2), serves as an illustration for this chapter, which aims to outline the ways in which the world of sound can be presented to young children in an exciting, meaningful and yet non-threatening way. It is also hoped and expected that, during this endeavour, students and other early years educators may very well rediscover the key to their own previously lost world of sound. As such, the chapter will address the following:

1 the recognition, exploration and manipulation of sound and the beginnings of composition;
2 integrating musical activities into a broader framework;
3 the question of singing;
4 introducing rhythm and movement;
5 listening as part of a wider curriculum.

Exploring sound: starting points

The simplest way of beginning an exploration of sound in the classroom is by helping children to develop the art of listening.

> Learning to listen – both to sounds around them and sounds that they can make themselves – is fundamental to children's music making. By encouraging children to think about these sounds, to be aware of them, to talk about them and to experiment with and manipulate them when they are in groups or by themselves, we provide a framework within which musical activities can take place and a real musical awareness can develop.
>
> (Davies, 1985, p. 8)

Through a series of questions, children can be introduced to some listening games in order to help them focus on the sound world around them.

What sound?

Listening game: what can you hear?

1 Ask the children to close their eyes and to listen to any sound they can hear within the room. Discuss with the children.
2 Next, ask the class what they can hear outside the room, but inside the building. Discuss.
3 Finally, ask them to listen to any sounds they can hear outside the building. Discuss.

As will be discovered, children will initially talk about any sound they hear, regardless of its origin, but on repeated exposure to the game (it can be used as an infill at the end of a session, or as a contrast to a lively activity – no two playings will ever be the same!), it can be seen that the children are developing not only their powers of concentration, but also the ability to discriminate – two vital ingredients of the listening act.

The whole notion of games to explore musical learning is of significance.

Storms (1983), suggests that games are nothing new, but they are increasingly recognised as a valuable preparation for music education. He believes, moreover, that games are a way of overcoming barriers for children and their educators alike – they can aid the personal, social and creative development of the children, while perhaps allowing the person lacking in confidence to explore ways of delivering music in the classroom.

It is important to give young children the opportunity on a regular basis to play some of these earliest listening games in order to develop their listening skills. It is worth remembering that an ability to listen is a crucial part of a child's whole development and essential for day-to-day life in the classroom! Something as simple as asking the children (with eyes closed) to wiggle their fingers when they hear keys being shaken will sharpen their concentration while aiding their motor skills.

Listening tape

Collect together on tape some household sounds, for example, a tap running, a clock ticking, a kettle boiling (it may be appropriate to group them together in order to enhance a topic – Water/Machines/Myself – early morning routine).

This could be used as a 'Guess the sound' game by itself as a classroom activity, or 'Match the picture to the sound' by providing visual representations of the sounds on the tape (such as those in Figure 12.1).

This could then become an individual listening task, which could be set in an area with a small tape recorder and the picture cards – an activity which would contribute to the development of children's autonomy,while at the same time acquainting them with the operation of simple technology.

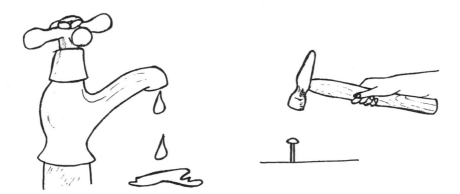

Figure 12.1 *'Match the picture to the sound'*

Once children have been given practice in listening skills, it is time to move on to ask the next question.

What kind of sound?

Listening game: Listen to my sound!

1 Gather together a collection of percussion instruments (if possible, an assortment of tuned and untuned, wood and metal).
2 Seat the children in a circle with an instrument in front of each child.
3 Ask the children to take turns in making one sound on their instrument, but only playing when they can no longer hear the sound made by the previous instrument.
4 Go round the circle, avoiding as far as possible any comments from the children. In this way full attention will be given to the sounds made and a sound picture will emerge.

A slightly different version of this game – How long does my sound last? – can be found in *Soundwaves* (Davies, 1985).

The discussion that follows the game can include a variety of questioning. A good way of beginning is to ask the children if they noticed if everybody waited until the sound had finished, thus focusing on their previously acquired skills (it is worth remembering however, that an early entry may very well have more to do with over-enthusiasm than an inaccurate hearing!). Other questions might be:

1 Who thinks they had a longer sound? (e.g. metal instruments). Invite those children to play their sounds again.
2 Who had a shorter sound? (e.g. wooden instruments). Ask the class to listen to the differences between the two.
3 How do the materials affect the sound?
4 Can anybody change the sound they made? It may be necessary to demonstrate at this juncture. A particularly good point to make is how a drum can be played very quietly indeed (even with finger tips), thus putting paid to any preconceived ideas that it is always to be beaten as loudly as possible! It is also worth showing more imaginative transitions, for example, how a long ringing note on a glockenspiel can be changed into something much duller and shorter by dampening it with one's hand.
5 What kind of sound is that? Can you describe it?

This last question is central. In setting up opportunities and games in which they can experiment and play with sound possibilities, children can be encouraged to respond in a variety of ways. For example, from the simple shaking of a maracca comes initially a recognition of the sound of a shaker. Through questioning, they can come to understand that they are making a series of 'fast' sounds. Furthermore, in encouraging them to talk about any related feelings or images that come to mind – 'It sounds like rain', 'It makes me scared 'cos I think of mice running' – they can use their imaginations to invent their own sound images.

Thus it can be seen that the exploration of sound with young children can elicit both a cognitive and an affective response, in addition to working hand in hand with the acquisition of language. Through this playful, experiential process with the raw materials of sound emerges a new vocabulary, neatly set out as the list of musical elements in the music national curriculum document:

> **pitch** – higher/lower
> **duration** – longer/shorter; steady pulse, beat, rhythm
> **dynamics** – louder/quieter/silence
> **tempo** – faster/slower
> **timbre** – different types of sound
> **texture** – different ways sounds are combined

and the use of the above within:

> **structure** – different ways sounds are organised.

Some of this technical vocabulary may seem daunting, but it is much less so, for educators and children, when the concepts have already been explored and described. The word 'timbre', for example, might be threatening in isolation, but when known to be dull or bright and, most importantly, recognised as the difference between the clashing cymbal or the one which falls with a thud to the floor, it is much more acceptable as part of a new vocabulary. Sound must be experienced before symbol to sow the seeds of joyous musical discovery. Gone are the days when the stave was taught in a vacuum without any meaningful purpose.

What makes the sound?

The third question addresses soundmakers, and it is important to remember that the child's first resource is his or her own body.

Listening ideas: my body

Get the children to listen to the sounds that they can produce themselves – this may well come out of a topic on 'My body', for example:

- playing with hair
- fingers on cheek – mouth open/mouth closed
- fingers in cheek – pops
- tapping/scraping teeth
- tongue clops/clicks

See Baxter and Thompson (1978) for further ideas.

This only goes as far as the head! What can they think of for the rest of their body? What kind of sound are they making? What words can they use to describe the sounds they make? Encourage the children to listen firstly to their own sound, but then to the effect of the same sound made by the whole class – what do they think of when they have their eyes shut but are listening to the sound of 30 arms being lightly rubbed? Talk about the sound images that emerge.

Can they invent their own words for their very own soundmakers? If children are given permission at a young age to think creatively this will serve them well in every other area of life.

Listening game: Tropical storm

1 Stand the children in a circle.
2 Ask the children to very lightly rub the palms of their hands together. Gradually get louder.
3 Change to tapping two fingers against their palms.
4 Increase the volume and use the whole hand to clap.
5 Use the hands to slap the thighs.
6 Move the feet in quick succession.

The object of this game is to achieve a continuous increase and decrease in volume (no sudden lurches!) to represent the appearance and disappearance of a storm. It is an ideal opportunity to discuss dynamics with the children, and in particular the meaning of a **crescendo** and **diminuendo**. (It is only meaningful to do this because the children are experiencing it.)

Once the class have a grasp on the sequence of the actions, divide the circle up into four groups. The conductor (it could eventually be a child) then points to a group at a time to indicate when they start and move onto the next sequence. In this way the storm gradually increases in ferocity and will ultimately die away. Voices can be used (only use a few children at a time!) depending on how tropical the class want the storm to be. Keep this in reserve, however, for when the game has been played before, or possibly as an introduction to a discussion on the possibilities of the voice.

The voice

The voice of course, is a very important soundmaker in its own right. Children should be given ample opportunities to use their voices inventively in order for them to appreciate that each one has their own very special instrument with its own wealth of possibilities (Chacksfield and Binns, 1983, have some interesting ideas). The author appreciates that there are some among us who may feel very uncertain about exploring this area, but it is to be remembered that young children are a very uncritical audience and only welcome the opportunity to be allowed to make their own discoveries. As will be seen later, the larynx is a muscle that needs developing like any other.

Other soundmakers

Once children have been encouraged to use their voices, bodies and instruments in inventive ways, they can broaden their horizons by recognising that anything is a potential soundmaker. They might be asked to bring in any discarded packaging from home which can then be explored in exactly the same way as any other resource. An instant listening and response game can be conducted around different kinds of paper for example. This may well fit into any kind of work on conservation or be linked with a blitz on litter!

'The freedom to explore chosen materials' (Paynter, 1978, p. 7) gives children the vocabulary with which to express themselves. If the word 'composition' (potentially threatening to some!) is to be seen as 'a way of saying things which are personal to the individual' (Paynter's definition of 'creative music' – an earlier description of the composition process), then by this stage children are ready to compose.

Combining sounds

Having had the experience of playing with sound, manipulating it to their own ends and realising that there is no right or wrong way, it is now time to give the children a framework in which to explore further. John Paynter has clear ideas about the role of the educator which might well be encouraging to many: the educator's role 'is to set off trains of thought and help the pupil develop his own critical powers and perception . . . as far as possible this work should not be controlled by a teacher' (Paynter, 1978, p. 7).

The simplest 'trains of thought', useful as starting points for composition are action-packed pictures or picture books with a few words on the page (e.g. *Rosie's Walk*, Hutchins, 1968; *Dinnertime*, Pienkowski, 1980). After two or three readings of the story, the children can be asked to suggest some ideas for sound effects as illustration. This can emerge from discussion on characterisation and events, and use any sound sources the children consider appropriate (they may need to be reminded about their voice and body possibilities due to over eagerness to play instruments!).

'The processes of composition in any art are selection and rejection, evaluating and confirming the material at each stage. It is essentially an experimental situation!' (Paynter, 1978, p. 7). So it is that the educator becomes an enabler and facilitator to help children explore, discuss and select the sounds they want. It is a case of constantly checking that they are happy with their choices. If, for example, they felt that the woodblock didn't sound 'bad' enough for the fox, the educator could open up a line of questioning on what kind of sound might sound more menacing – longer, shorter, metal, wood, vocal even? It is important to take time and for the class to listen with care to each other's suggestions (an ongoing reinforcement of the skill of listening). Maybe someone might favour some longer sounds on the cymbal. This might be a forerunner of the processes of discrimination and refinement – 'Could we get louder then quieter?' Time will then need to be spent in fine tuning, until the children are satisfied with their results.

In the initial stages of this work, one would need to make this a whole-class activity, but ultimately small group work is desirable, as independent learning and social skills can come into play. The finished product can be committed to tape and played back to the children for appraisal. A series of questions can elicit to what extent the class are satisfied with their piece. Did it sound as they wanted it to sound? Is there anything they would like to change/improve upon? An opportunity for them to make further refinements is empowering and helps them to adopt the ownership of the work. Part of the role of the educator is to assist the children in taking a pride and a sense of responsibility for their creative acts. Encouraging positive comments to begin with before accepting constructive criticism can give the children a model with which to work.

We as educators can, during this critical listening time, be open to opportunities to reinforce any musical elements that might have been used. For example, Rosie walking over the haycock might have served well as an illustration of pitch, or a blend of voices/instruments and other soundmakers could have created a particularly interesting texture. If we can heighten children's awareness of what they have produced, we are making a substantial contribution to their musical development

What then has the learning been in this compositional process? Over and above John Paynter's key summary, we can list the following:

1 **Social skills** and **cooperation**: taking turns, working together and sharing would have been in evidence (even more so when group work is begun).
2 **Motor skills** and **coordination of hand, ear and eye** would have been practiced, for example, holding a beater and playing at the right time.
3 **Imagination** would have been heavily engaged.
4 The children have been involved, not only as **performers** and **composers**, but as three different kinds of **listeners**: as composers – 'Which sound is better for the splash?'; as performers – to each other; and finally as audience listeners – when they stand back and listen to the tape (and ultimately to their peer groups).
5 They have been introduced to the first stages of **appraising** their work.

Recording the sound

The final stage of the compositional process – finding a way to store the information on paper, can be an important breakthrough for adults and children alike in discovering its accessibility. In helping children explore pictorial representations of sound, the word '**notation**', threatening for so many in the past, can have new meaning when expressed graphically. Figure 12.2 shows some early examples of starting points.

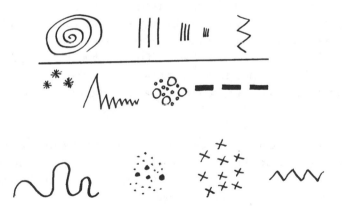

Figure 12.2 *Young children's graphical notation for music*

Figure 12.3 shows a full score in graphical notation, entitled 'Red Dragon's Cave', from *Dewi the Dragon* by Gill Wilson (Edden *et al.*, 1989).

Before performing this, the children could look at, discuss and play each line separately, noting the obvious changes in pitch and dynamics, for example. For further reading in this area, see Gilbert (1981).

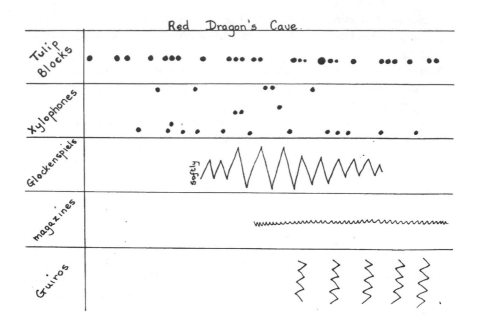

Figure 12.3 *'Red Dragon's Cave' – a full score in graphical notation*

An holistic framework

It has been seen that composing, performing, listening and appraising skills can sit together very comfortably under the developmental umbrella of exploring sound. Such integration can be viewed as a model for working in an holistic fashion. Not only does this make sense from the child's perspective, but it can be most reassuring from our point of view to realise that music can be approached from any angle and in particular from our own strengths.

> Good primary school practice is based on teachers recognising the opportunities to fertilise work in one part of the curriculum with work in another. The unifying and integrating aspects of the arts give them a particular value in this respect.
>
> (Arts in Schools, 1982, p. 53)

Let us take an example. *Rosie's Walk* (Hutchins, 1968) can be read to the children as part of a topic on journeys. To give it musical depth two elements are pre-selected to focus on, although this does not mean that others are not acknowledged! Pitch, tempo and duration all give particular scope (but it is hoped that during the course of the year all elements will be explored in some depth through various activities). Already, attention has been paid to pitch through Rosie walking up and down the haycock. Further endorsement of this might come at another time by showing children the xylophone and working with some high and low notes. Science can be introduced by carrying out pitch experiments with levels of water in bottles which could then be played like a xylophone. Geography can be covered by recreating Rosie's journey as simple mapping work for a classroom display, and maybe helping children map out their own journeys to school, which could then be used as scores for graphic notation. Language of course, has been explored alongside the selected sounds.

Games can be played to reinforce the concepts and there are many useful books to explore. Mary York's (1984) choice is particularly appropriate in her book *Gently into Music*, and *Hi Lo Dolly Pepper* (Clark, 1991) includes a comprehensive exploration of all the concepts, together with some attractive graphic scores. Nursery rhymes like 'Hickory Dickory Dock' lend themselves ideally as a good illustration of both pitch and tempo. Stories like 'The Three Bears' and poems like 'The Four Friends' (in York, 1984) provide wonderful opportunities to consolidate the idea of pitch, but also feed into other areas of the curriculum. The flow chart in Figure 12.4 might be used not only as a model for any kind of comprehensive musical input to any topic, but as a basis for the kind of holistic framework that has been discussed.

Also not to be missed as valuable sources of topic ideas:

Topic Anthology for Young Children (Gilbert, 1991) – includes Water, Machines, Toys, Machines, Fairs and Circuses, Cowboys and Indians)
Music through Topics (Clark, 1990)

The question of singing

One of the best links that can be made between topic areas and the musical elements is singing.

> For both children and teacher, the importance of regular classroom singing is greater than realised. It can stimulate and calm the children, bring class and teacher together and provide an enjoyable controlled activity to balance the programme of a busy day. It develops the child's musical abilities and social skills while also acting as a valuable aid in reading and language development, in building basic concepts and in linking and extending other areas of the curriculum.
>
> (Gilbert, 1981, p. 15)

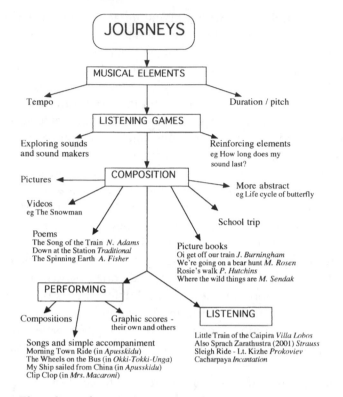

Figure 12.4 *Flow chart of musical activities related to the topic of journeys*

Ideally singing should be a daily activity and should fulfil a variety of criteria. Songs of different kinds will perform different functions

Songs with repetition and action songs

These are particularly important to young children. The action song 'Jack in the Box' (Scott Wood) with its descending scale and its final leap 'Yes I will!' in answer to the question 'Will you come out?' is a perfect example of how to illustrate pitch to children. Some children might join in with a xylophone, stepping from high to low, while others could take it in turns to be Jack, and leap from low to high. Many songs can be used in this way to consolidate musical learning through a focus. Increasingly, there are books available which use songs in this kind of broader context. Try exploring other songs used to feature pitch and other elements in:

Game Songs for Infants (Richards, 1990)
Mrs Macaroni (Tillman, 1985)

Managing Music with Infants (Edden *et al.*, 1989)
Gently into Music (York, 1984)
Hi Lo Dolly Pepper (Clark, 1991)

Two- and three-note songs

Children also need to be given opportunities to work with two- and three-note songs (e.g. 'Rain Rain', 'Bell Horses') to help them find their voices. Singing the register using the Soh Me interval, or responding to a sung question can be of great value. Nicki Bennison, in her intensive work with children at Central School Chichester, proves how valuable this kind of work can be, and the success story of her choir (Sainsbury's Choir of the Year 1990) is living proof that constant exposure to singing and making it a highlight of the school day can pay rich dividends. 'I believe that all children can be taught to sing if and only if somebody bothers to find their voice' (Bennison, 1991).

Singing with confidence

But what of those who have very low self-esteem when it comes to their own singing, and are fearful of leading children in song? There are no magic cures for this dilemma, but there are reassurances that can be given. The first of these is that young children are just grateful to have an opportunity to sing. They are not a critical audience. Be encouraged with older infants, moreover, to allow the stronger singers to assist in leading the class. There is a distinction to be made between those who are unwilling to sing in front of their peers but will 'have a go' behind closed doors, and those who have absolutely no confidence whatsoever. For the latter kind, pre-recorded tapes are a useful prop. The author has witnessed a very successful use of such a strategy in a situation where confidence was low, but a commitment to children's singing was high. Ten minutes before each break time, the teacher would gather the children from their various activities to sit together on the carpet and sing with the tape. It was a joyous sight, particularly in the light of the teacher's own perceived difficulties. It is important to realise that a willingness on the part of the unconfident educator to expose children to the joys of singing can be infinitely more beneficial than the 'expert' who quite erroneously blames a child for singing out of tune. After all, at 7 years old, only about 50 per cent of children can represent a given pitch.

Rhythm and movement

Another area which gives particular concern to early years educators is that of introducing rhythm to children. Yet simple activities can serve children well in this area. All children have had the experience of a steady beat (mother's heart beat, rocking, knee bouncing) and, by the time they come to school, many have a developed sense of **pulse**. Helping children reinforce this skill by using body percussion to accompany simple rhymes, songs, jingles or any piece of recorded music with a steady beat is a good starting point.

Rhythm game: follow my leader

1 Select a piece of recorded music with a strong beat.
2 Establish the pulse.
3 Ask the class to copy what you do – 'follow my leader'.
4 Use a variety of different body percussion to keep a steady pulse, for example, tapping hands on head, shoulders, thighs; clapping, clicking, etc.
5 Alternate the actions.
6 If appropriate, invite a child to lead.

This game is not only helpful in terms of developing a sense of pulse, but improves concentration and is fun! It can also be used as a 5-minute 'filler' for those occasions when there is time to spare at the end of a session. Maybe the music that is selected (and this is certainly an opportunity to introduce the class to different genres) is chosen as part of the holistic framework, and can thus feed into an integrated curriculum.

Simple echo clapping, where the educator claps four beats (pulse) and the children follow, can move into an understanding of 'walking' beats – walk, walk, walk, walk – and can ultimately be drawn on cards as a demonstration of simplified crotchets (this is the very beginning of staff notation). The natural progression moves to clapping patterns (e.g. names, topic words, the words of a rhyme such as 'Rain, Rain, go away'). The following example demonstrates how children can begin to understand simple rhythm patterns in terms of walks, slow walks and runs.

Big	Chief	Sitt	ing	Bull		
(walk	walk	run	run	walk)		

Hi	a	wa	tha	brave		
(run	run	run	run	slow walk)		

Pain	ted	tee	pee	Arr	ow	head
(run	run	run	run	run	run	walk)

War   drums   grave.
(walk   walk   slow   walk)

Each one of these lines forms a **pattern**, as opposed to a pulse, and a line said repeatedly becomes an **ostinato** (repeated pattern). This can be an exciting way of introducing simple song/rhyme accompaniment and the following can be used as a model for any simple song or rhyme.

Using an Ostinato:

1 Familiarise the children with the song or rhyme.
2 Select a short phrase from the words of the text which lends itself to being repeated, for example, 'Big Chief Sitting Bull' or 'Rain, Rain'.
3 Ask the children to repeat it several times in rhythm.
4 Ask a small group to continue to do this while the rest of the class say the rhyme. This is vocal **ostinato** in action!

As a progression, try substituting the phrase with either body percussion or untuned percussion, asking the children to say the phrase silently in their heads. This internalisation helps develop musical memory. Linking patterns to words is a security and a learning tool for educators and children alike! It is important to state here that it is best to only work with the staff notation with which one is comfortable. It would be foolish to topple confidence which has gradually emerged in other areas by putting too much emphasis on delivering what might well be at the heart of our fears. This is in no way intended to undervalue the traditional form of recording music, but is much more an observation on unrealistic expectations.

Rhythm through movement

Many rhythmic ideas can be experienced through movement activities. 'Music is not heard by ear alone but the whole of the body' (Mothersole, 1920, p. 23). Movement is an ideal vehicle for consolidating learning while at the same time enabling children to make creative use of their energies. Games are a perfect medium to explore movement activities. Try the following:

Movement game: 'Journey of the animals'

1 Divide the class into four groups of different syllabic animals (cat, ti – ger, po – lar bear, al – li – ga – tor).
2 Send each group into a corner of the room.
3 Tap out each of the rhythms in turn, and encourage them to move to the secret cave in the centre by stepping out their pattern, when they hear

their particular rhythm. (You may need to demonstrate first!) They must stop when they hear the pattern change.

4 When the children are secure with their rhythms, be more unpredictable in your sequencing!

5 Change the groups in order for them to experience all the patterns.

Some movement games need instrumental players: e.g. 'Charlie Chaplin went to France' and 'Punchinello' (Edden *et al.*, 1989) both need a two-note drone (i.e. the same two notes played repeatedly throughout.). Games to reinforce any of the musical elements can be led by someone without pianistic skills. With *pitch*, for example, children can be asked to 'walk tall' if they hear some high notes on the piano or move as low as they can when they hear low notes. This, of course, is further practice in listening skills.

Listening as part of a wider curriculum

In a world bombarded with sound, young children do not necessarily find listening as easy as in years gone by. There has already been discussion earlier in the chapter about the crucial role it plays in a child's musical development, and, as such, educators are encouraged to expose the child to a variety of listening activities. Affective responses can be made through the medium of paint or words (a 'journey' to South America to hear 'Cacharpaya', played by Incantation, is an ideal starting point here: 'How does it make you feel?', 'What can you imagine?'), while the cognitive response can be developed even at an early stage (Prokoviev's 'Sleigh Ride', for example, from Lieutenant Kizhe, features the sleigh bells the children may very well have on their music trolley. Can they hear them?) Attention to *tempo* can be given through Villa Lobos' 'Little Train of the Caipira', where they can hear the train increasing in speed, but they can also be asked if they think it sounds like a train, and why? We need to try and present a focus for listening and to take the 'musical' questioning as far as we are able. Recorded music, it has been seen, can be played in a variety of different contexts all within a cohesive programme. Try finding a piece of music as a follow-up to children's compositions, or something relevant to the topic that could be used for movement purposes. If children can be in touch with live music (either attending concerts or inviting musicians into school) then it becomes an exciting, living reality.

Conclusion

It is hoped that after reading this chapter early years educators will come to see that, whatever their own musical history might be, they have an important role to play as an enabler and inspirer of young children's music. If you can make music an integral part of the school day, you will be using the your own and the children's creativity to build a new way of being for yourself and the children you teach. 'Every creative act involves a new innocence or perception, liberated from the cataract of accepted belief' (Arts in Schools, 1982, p. 22).

Pointers for early years music

- Don't assume you need to have had a traditional music training in order to facilitate young children's music making.
- Use simple games as a means of reinforcing a musical idea.
- Exploring sound and sound sources can stimulate the imagination while developing language skills.
- Look for any opportunities to reinforce the elements of music.
- When planning a topic look for ways in which music can be naturally linked with other areas of the curriculum, thus making it a daily and relevant activity.
- A song a day keeps the grumps away!
- Make music fun!

References

Arts in Schools (1982) *Principles, Practice and Provision*, London: Calouste Gulbenkian Foundation.

Bennison, N. (1991) *Singing is Central*, BBC2.

Dancer, A. (1991) 'Every child has a song to sing', *Times Educational Supplement*, 8 February.

Davies, L. (1985) *Soundwaves*, London: Unwin Hyman.

DES (1985) *Music from 9–16*, London: HMSO.

Gilbert, J. (1981) *Musical Starting Points with Young Children*, London: Ward Lock.

Mills, J. (1989) 'The generalist primary music teacher', *British Journal of Music Education*, 6, 125–38.

Mothersole, A. (1920) La Rythmique est-elle une lubie? *Le Rythme*, 5, 23.

Paynter, J. (1978) *Sound and Silence*, Cambridge: Cambridge University Press.
Storms, G. (1983) *Handbook of Musical Games*, London: Hutchinson.

Source material referred to in text

Baxter, A. and Thomson, D. (1978) *Pompaleerie Jig*, Exeter: E.J. Arnold.
Chacksfield, M. and Binns, P. (1983) *Sound Ideas Books 1–6*, Oxford: Oxford University Press.
Clark, V. (1990) *Music Through Topics*, Cambridge: Cambridge University Press.
Clark, V. (1991) *Hi Lo Dolly Pepper*, London: A. & C. Black.
Edden, J., Edwards, R., Malcolm, A. and Wilson, G. (1989) *Managing Music with Infants*, Cambridge: Cambridgeshire County Council.
Gilbert, J. (1991) *Topic Anthology for Young Children*, Oxford: Oxford University Press.
Hutchins, P. (1968) *Rosie's Walk*, London: Bodley Head.
Pienkowski, J. (1980) *Dinner Time*, London: Orchard.
Richards, C. (1990) *Game Songs for Infants* (available from Acorn Percussion Ltd., Unit 34, Abbey Business Centre, Ingate Place, London SW8 3NS).
Tillman, J. (1985) *Mrs Macaroni*, London: Macmillan.
York, M. (1984) *Gently into Music*, Harlow, Essex: Longmans.

Other source material

Birkenshaw, L. (1974) *Music for Fun, Music for Learning*, Toronto: Birk – Holt, Rinehart & Winston.
Farmer, B. (1982) *Springboards*, Melbourne, Australia: Nelson
Gamper, E. (1986) *Music with Mr Plinkerton*, Woodford Green, Essex: International Music Publications.
Maddocks, A. and Stocks, M. (1991) *Growing Up with Music KS1*, Harlow, Essex: Longman.
Mills, J. (1991) *Music in the Primary School*, Cambridge: Cambridge University Press.
Wheway, D. and Thomson, S. (1993) *Explore Music through . . .* (9 subject areas), Oxford: Oxford University Press.

CHAPTER 13

'Oh . . . I'm just IN LOVE with those pots'

YOUNG CHILDREN'S ART

Jane Bower

Introduction

It took me a lifetime to learn to draw like them.

(Pablo Picasso, in old age, at an
exhibition of children's drawings)

Why is art taught in schools? Why is it considered so important that it is a compulsory part of the curriculum?

Wherever you are as you read this, stop for a moment and look around you. If you are in a room, it is likely that everything in it has begun with an artist. Your clothes, the furniture, the weave of curtain fabric, the clock and other objects, the carpet pattern, and even your hairstyle have all been conceived, designed and executed by an artist of one kind or another. If you are sitting outside, the same applies – street furniture, benches, gardens and architecture have all begun in the mind of an artist. Without the creativity of art and design we would not only be static, but unable to function, and this form of creativity is inbuilt in every human from birth.

By the time a child begins attending school this inbuilt creativity is already being influenced by adult attitudes. It is for this reason that the teaching of art in the early years is so vital if we are to encourage children's understanding and expression of art to develop and grow richly and healthily, and not be stunted by lack of confidence, often unwittingly expressed by the most well-meaning of adults, including teachers.

Let us take drawing as an example. It is a familiar occurrence when a young child asks a parent, grandparent or other adult to draw them something, for the adult to reply, 'Oh, I can't draw', or 'I'm no good at drawing.'

The same statements are frequently made by teachers or students on drawing courses, and by the time children reach the age of around 7, many are beginning to say the same thing.

I often ask adults and these older children whether a baby can draw. Most say it can. Some say a baby 'just scribbles.' I point out to them what the baby is doing. First, it has to learn to grasp a drawing tool and keep hold of it. Then it has to select the right end or part of the tool, and make and maintain contact with a surface, moving the tool along it. Finally, it has to see that this action causes a mark to be made. I ask them if they now think a baby's scribbles are drawing, and they decide that they are.

Why is it, then, that when a child first takes two steps and then falls down, we rush to tell our friends, but when this far more complex set of skills is achieved, we call it 'scribbling'? Conversely, why do we praise young children even for the most unformed drawings, saying 'That's lovely!' and yet denigrate our own efforts?

One of the first questions I put to adults is what they think drawing is. Most answers include words such as 'image', 'representation' or 'accurate portrayal.' Many also say that 'you need a pencil and paper'.

I begin to challenge their definitions. *Do* you need pencil and paper – would a finger in sand not be drawing? Does a drawing always have to look like something? Couldn't it be patterns, pleasing shapes or colours?

My definition of drawing is 'making marks with a tool on a surface', and this is how I begin with young children, just as, if you were approaching maths, you would start with learning the names and value of numbers, not try to tackle logarithms. If you happen to have a genuine talent for drawing, you must still begin at the child's level.

Who was the first artist? Many adults' and children's conception of an artist is a famous, and usually dead, male painter. But an artist does not have to be any of these. Surely the first artist was the first person – and several of the earliest people have left examples of their art on rocks and cave walls. This for me proves that art is an inbuilt instinct and need, a natural form of human expression. Cave people had no formal tuition. They simply looked, with remarkable observational skills, and recorded what they saw.

> We have long come to realise that art is not produced in an empty space, that no artist is independent of predecessors and models, *that he . . . is part of a specific tradition . . .*
>
> (Ernst Kris, quoted in Gombrich, 1987)

Children need to realise this too – that they also are artists, part of a continuing culture.

Of course, drawing is only one of many artforms, but whether you are teaching art through clay, paint, fabrics or any other medium, the same principles apply.

As well as a necessary part of human existence, art is a subject that penetrates deeper. It feeds the soul. Without the arts our whole culture would collapse. It opens up for children beauty, emotion, expression, and the huge range and magic of colour, shape, texture and form. The following examples of ways to approach the teaching of art through various media were devised to maximise in the young child not only delight in exploring a material and learning the practical skills associated with it, but the sense of wonder that comes with creating something where there was nothing before; something entirely unique.

What should be covered?

When planning art teaching in the long term, the aim should be to give children both practical experience, and a deeper understanding of artists and their work.

The practical experience should offer children as wide a range of materials and techniques as possible, so that they become adept at choosing the right media and tools for certain tasks, and begin to develop preferences and a deeper understanding. Ensure that there is a good balance between two- and three-dimensional work. The range might include:

- Drawing (pencil, pastel, chalk, wax, charcoal, crayon on different surfaces);
- Painting (powder, liquid, block; using brushes, fingers, other tools);
- Printing (inks, paints; using fingers, card, vegetables, polystyrene);
- Modelling materials (clay, Plasticine, dough, Modroc);
- Textiles (fabrics, threads, wools; cutting, sticking, weaving, stitching);
- Building (boxes, card, recycled materials, wood; various joining methods).

A diversity of stimuli should also be offered as starting points for artwork. These might include:

- Natural forms (e.g. seedpods, woodgrain);
- Made artefacts (machine parts, glassware);
- The imagination (a story, dreams);
- Tactile stimuli (a rough shell, a smooth pebble);
- Aural stimuli (recorded music, percussion instruments);
- Other artists' work (a bowl by a local potter, an Indian sari, a Monet reproduction);
- Photographs (of architecture, moving water, clouds).

This list is by no means exhaustive and should also include opportunities for children to plan, design and discuss their work, evaluating and modifying it as necessary. The emphasis at this stage should be on exploring the materials, finding out what they can do; on discovering and delighting in the process rather than always concentrating on the end product.

> The aim of art education is not the production of works of art but the unity of the entire growing personality . . . an increase in (the child's) capacity to bring forth what is within him.
>
> (Lark-Horovitz, 1967)

This practical work should be consistently supported, complemented and illustrated by the work of other artists, so that children can relate what they are doing to what is going on, and has been going on for thousands of years, in the world of art around them. 'Other artists' includes yourself, potters, sculptors, weavers, wrapping paper designers and so on, famous or unknown. For example, if a child has just learned to make a firm join with clay, a pottery jug could be used to show them how important such joins are. If printing, a photograph of an early Aboriginal handprint would form a link between their own work and that of a past culture.

The three media and activities I describe below have been chosen to complement each other and to introduce a balanced range of the examples given above. Clay provides three-dimensional experience, painting two-dimensional, and textiles the possibility of either or both, depending on how the fabrics and threads are used.

Clay

Clay is one of the most beautiful and exciting materials for children of all ages, and my preference is to introduce it to them as early as possible. It is also one of the most inexpensive resources. Although there are several self-hardening or other varieties of modelling material available (all at a higher price!), nothing can match real clay for versatility and natural beauty of texture. Used correctly, it generates no mess, and neither a sink nor a kiln are required to achieve valuable results.

Choosing subject matter

To give children a recognisable object to model, such as a cat or a house, at too early a stage can pose a threat and a high risk of feeling a failure ('Mine doesn't look like a cat'). It is important for children to first explore clay in an abstract way ('Can you make a curvy shape/a sharp shape?') to build up their confidence and knowledge of the material. The activity described below is designed to meet these criteria, and deliberately avoids any tools other than the fingers, so that children can discover the huge range of manipulation achievable with their own hands before investigating other possibilities.

Preparation

Before starting any work with clay, ask each child to apply a small dot of handcream to their palms, rubbing it in well. (I call this 'putting our invisible gloves on'). This is recommended as a health and safety measure, and should become second nature to anyone working with clay. Potters' barrier cream is probably the most effective (available from educational catalogues) but any unscented handcream is fine. Children with allergies or eczema should use their prescribed cream or wear protective gloves.

Provide a mat for each child to rest their claywork on. Deckchair canvas is by far the best, cut into 30cm squares. Hessian goes mouldy and makes an imprint; wooden boards warp easily and clay often has to be prised off them, whereas mats can be peeled cleanly from the work. One side of the mat can be used for grey clay and the other for red, and no washing or hemming is necessary. (When ordering clay, check that the two colours fire to the same temperature so that both grey and red pieces can be fired together, or mixed in the same model.)

Learning objectives

The suggested activity provides opportunities for children to learn in both practical and expressive ways:

- observing a natural form and responding to it;
- exploring a three-dimensional medium and experimenting with shape, form and space;
- expressing their feelings and ideas as they work;
- building up a knowledge of the visual and tactile qualities of clay and the vocabulary associated with it;
- using their own imagination to inspire their work;
- evaluating and modifying as they go along.

Introducing the clay

When first introducing clay to children, I make a point of bringing it in just as it comes – in the plastic bag. If it is presented to them ready rolled into a ball, much vital work is missed.

My first question is always 'What is clay?' Occasionally a child will know that it is earth or soil, but many will say 'Plasticine' or 'play dough'. There is a teaching point here not to be ignored, because clay is the complete opposite of Plasticine; it hardens in heat, whereas Plasticine will melt.

When I ask 'Where does clay come from?' they often say 'a shop' or 'the factory'. Many are amazed when I say that it is from the ground. Where was it dug from? Why isn't it full of dirt, stones and worms? Why is it so heavy? Why does it have to be kept in a plastic bag? I ask the children to consider the colour of the clay. Not all clay is the same colour, because it is dug from different areas of the country.

Children love to watch the action of the clay cutter as I carve off chunks (you can make your own from two clothes pegs joined with a length of fuse wire or plastic thread.) Any misconceptions that the clay is 'dirty' should be dispelled at this stage. It is beautifully clean, and smells of nothing. The size of the chunks should reflect the size of the pupils' hands – each chunk should be easy to control, and not too big to pick up and handle.

Never have water on the table when working with clay. It is unnecessary and should only be introduced (and then in very small quantities) when children learn to join clay, at a much later stage.

Rather than launch into making something straight away, take the time when introducing the material for the first time to let the children explore the clay and find out its potential, and simply take joy in it. One way to do this is to ask the children to wait until everyone has their own piece, and then all touch it together, saying any words that describe the clay when they first feel it.

The first reaction from anyone is almost always 'It's cold.' 'Why does it have to be cold? Why must it not be allowed to get warm?' Other words such as 'squidgy' and 'soft' soon follow. It is never too early to develop the vocabulary associated with clay, so that words such as 'pliable' and 'moist' gradually come to replace 'bendy' and 'damp'. Such preliminary explorations and discussions serve not only to teach the children the properties of clay but begin to build up their fascination in it. To the children, clay seems to have almost magical properties, and for me its fascination never abates. You can bend it, squeeze it, break it, smear it; it can be turned into pottery, change its colour . . .

Similarly, it is never too early to teach the skills needed to form a solid foundation for later work in clay. From their very first model, I teach children to wedge clay, explaining that it contains minute air bubbles, often far too tiny to see, which must be burst before any models can be made. (If left in, an air bubble can explode when fired in the kiln.) To wedge, the heel of the hand is used to knock the clay on all sides so that it forms a dense ball. After a few lessons, the children learn to put on barrier cream and wedge the clay before starting work.

A suggested clay activity – bony sculptures

Ask the children to hold their ball of clay in their stronger or writing hand. They are going to make it change its shape by giving it one, and only one, big squeeze. It is helpful if you do this too, so that you all squeeze together.

Apply as much pressure as possible and then gently peel the fingers out and place the squeezed shape carefully on the mat.

What shapes can you see or feel? Where are there shadows and which bits have light on them? Do you think any other person could make a shape exactly like this one? Point out to the children that already each person's sculpture is unique because no-one else has their fingerprints. Look closely to see them in the clay, along with the creases from the palms or marks from the nails.

Introduce a selection of clean bones to the children. Compare the shapes with the squeezed clay – are there any similarities? The shapes of our own bones in our hands have influenced the shapes of our sculptures. Now the selection of bones can be used to influence them further. Shells or fossils can be substituted for bones.

Encourage children to explore particular facets of the bones and develop their sculpture to incorporate or echo some of them. They are not changing their sculpture into a model of a bone, but rather aiming to subtly alter their sculpture to make it more bony.

For example, a ridge of clay formed between two fingers on the squeeze could be pinched thinner and sharper; a depression formed by the end of a finger could be pushed further until a hole is made through the clay. Areas could be smoothed with a thumb or left cracked to resemble the different textures found on the bones.

The finished sculptures can be displayed among the real bones, perhaps lit from one side with a lamp. Their shapes are often reminiscent of some of the work of Henry Moore, whose sculptures can provide inspiration for further sessions. The quotation in the title of this chapter was the response of a Year 1 child on being shown ceramics by Mary Rogers.

Clearing up

When the claywork has been completed, children should not wash their hands in a sink, as the accumulation of clay dust will quickly block up the waste pipe. Instead, provide a bucket of warm water and paper towels for washing. Alternatively, have a couple of cloths in the bucket and pass the cloths around the class. The handcream applied earlier allows the clay to slip off the hands easily and there is no mess. The mats can be shaken over a bin, and the tables given a wipe.

Pour the water away outside, on to the nearest soil or garden. I was delighted when a 5-year-old described this as 'the clay going home'. It made a good opportunity to mention recycling!

Cross-curricular links

Clay offers a wealth of opportunity in science (observing how materials change when heated – particularly spectacular if you are glazing the work), history (the first pots made by people, how they shaped and fired clay and what they used clay vessels for) and geography (where clay occurs naturally in the earth, its properties and how it affects the environment).

Painting

> Virtually every activity in which the child engages contains an element of magic. With paint one can change a white paper into a blue paper. That is magic . . .
>
> (*Pre-school Play*, Jameson and Kidd, nd.)

As with clay, there is a time when paints should be used by the young child for pure play, for the joy of watching paper change colour and marks appear. But the way that paints are organised, handled and presented when undertaking a structured project will have an important effect on children's management of and respect for the materials, and their understanding of colour mixing. For the project below, ready-mixed liquid paints were used.

Preparation

Provide children with a sponge, a mixing tray (or plate), chalk and two brushes. The sponge should be dampened and squeezed out. It can be used for wiping brushes, cleaning a place on the tray, mopping up any spills and as an alternative painting tool. (My aim is always to minimise any mess and to avoid the need for any child to get up to change their paint water during the lesson.) The three primary colours and black and white are the only ones needed to mix any colours you need, and therefore the only ones I ever buy, although I do order two variants of each primary, such as a lemon and a chrome yellow.

Chalk is better than pencil for drawing – it won't show through the paint. Use the palest colour that will show on the paper. I provide both a large and a small brush (such as a size 12 bristle and a size 2 soft) so that the children have to make a choice. In this way they learn to consider what they are about to paint and what to expect from each tool. Teach the children to hold the brush like a pencil, on the fattest part of the wood.

Squeeze a small amount of each paint on to the child's tray. Trays should preferably be white to show up the paint colour clearly, and are better than palettes for colour mixing with liquid paints, as the children can pull colours directly into others across the surface, often making surprise discoveries for themselves.

Learning objectives

The main points I want children to learn when introducing paint, which I make again and again over the coming weeks until they become an automatic part of the children's practice, are:

- Do not mix one colour all over the tray. Because it is thin it will dry quickly and there will be no space for other colours.
- Whenever possible, paint light-coloured areas first and move towards darker colours. This minimises the need to wash the brush.
- Wipe the brush on the sponge rather than always washing it in the water, or after doing so.
- Use as little water with the paint as possible – liquid paints are already mixed to the correct consistency.
- When eventually the water does need changing, ask the teacher to do it (have some filled replacements standing by) rather than carrying it yourself.
- Pale colours (yellow and white) are weak and you need a larger quantity of them; dark colours are strong and you need only a minute amount to change a pale colour.

The last point should be remembered when you are dispensing paint. As a general rule you need to give the child three times the amount of white and yellow, and twice the amount of red, as you do black and blue. The same amounts apply when you are ordering paint for the school – don't make the mistake of buying the same amount of each! It helps if you think of them as foods – white as milk, red as tomato puree, black as chilli powder.

As well as the above practical teaching points, there are other learning outcomes I aim to bring about:

- Good paintings are not always produced in one session; an artist will often need to work on a painting over a long period of time, rejecting, improving and developing ideas.
- An artist does not always find painting easy; it may involve struggling with problems, but there is always a way to solve them.
- You can often do something you didn't think you could do, and the feeling of pride and achievement on completion of a fulfilling piece of work makes all the problem-solving worthwhile.

A suggested painting project – snakes

This project began when a live pet snake was brought into the school. Having studied its appearance and movement, and learned about its habitat, we looked at the jungle paintings of Henri Rousseau and clear, close-up photographs of snakes, and discussed the different environments against which they appeared.

I asked the children to decide how their snake was to be positioned. We talked about placing it on the paper (in this case thick buff sugar paper, good for supporting lots of paint, about 42 × 62 cm) so that its shape was balanced. I drew a tiny snake in the corner of the paper, and then a snake which filled the space. Which looked better? The children drew their snakes in yellow chalk, and I encouraged them to take care to keep the snake's body even, only tapering at the tail. The heads were drawn after looking closely at the photographs.

I then asked them to decide where their particular snake lived. Was it on a stony, shingly desert, or hot, sparkling sand, among big rocks, deep in a jungle, in a dark cave, or under the sea? They took their inspiration from the books I had brought in and from the Rousseau paintings.

The first two sessions were devoted entirely to the backgrounds. We looked at other reproductions of paintings to see how artists had made these full of interest. I told the children they should prepare the loveliest home they could for when their snake arrived in the picture. I pointed out that rarely great artists leave blank areas of canvas – the one exception known to me being Gauguin, who at one stage was so poor he had not enough paint to fill the corners of some of his Tahitian paintings.

I asked each child to tell me the colour they had in mind and how they thought it would be mixed. I then came round with the paint bottles and dispensed small amounts of the appropriate colours for them to mix, helping them if they did not know the combination. This means a lot of walking around, but is far less of a headache in the long run. When children need more paint, they put up their hands and tell me which colour they need.

The backgrounds provided a good opportunity for putting into practice the method of painting from light to dark. For example, a sandy background could start with pale yellow blobs, then a little red could be added to make a pale orange for more blobs, then a little blue to make a beigy brown, until gradually darker and darker blobs are added to the texture, without at any time needing to wash the brush.

Only when every bit of background was filled with paint in varied textures, shapes and colours, and had become interesting in its own right, were the snakes introduced. By now the children were itching to paint them, especially as I had been whetting their appetites with descriptions of how jewelled and brilliantly patterned we could make them.

We talked about what colours the snakes should be compared to the backgrounds. Would they be camouflaged, or show up brightly against them? Clean, large brushes were used to fill in the snake shapes with the child's chosen colour. Then the tiny brushes were used to paint contrasting, intricate scaly designs over the base colour. Children should be taught to stroke and not scrub with these, pulling the brush backwards from the paper, never pushing it forwards, and never letting the metal part of the brush rest on the paper. I encouraged the most minute detail to make a direct contrast with the textured, sweeping or bobbly backgrounds.

Finally, children used gold pens, metallic wax crayons and oil pastels to add the finishing touches – ferns growing between rocks, sparkling decoration on the snakes' scales, strange underwater plants, or tiny flowers blooming in the desert sand. The children (a mixture of reception, Year 1 and Year 2) worked on the paintings during five fairly lengthy sessions over a period of three months, working on other art projects in between some of the sessions.

(a)

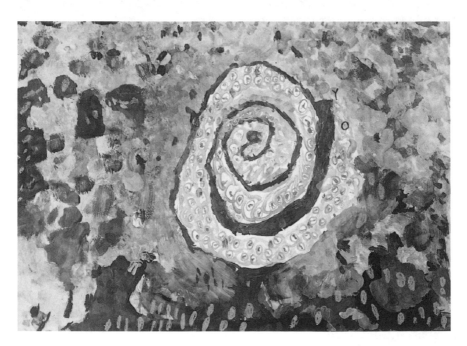

(b)

(c)

(d)

Figure 13.1 (a), (b), (c) & (d) *Snake paintings by Jenna Campbell-Butcher, Victoria Richards, Elizabeth Gunning and Miles Taylor, all aged 5 years, Horler's Pre-preparatory School, Comberton, Cambridge*

Cross-curricular links

The snake project provided valuable links with English (descriptive poems or prose about the snake and where it lives, building on vocabulary and a set of instructions for looking after art materials); geography (hot countries, different habitats); science (reptiles, what they eat, how and where they lay their eggs, what conditions they need) and maths (numberwork based on sequence patterns such as those painted on the snakes).

Textiles

I think of stitching as mark-making or a form of painting with wools and threads. With the right combination of equipment, teaching techniques and subject matter it can be taught successfully to very young children.

Preparation

For very first stitches, begin by fixing small (7 cm) circular rubber embroidery rings into a roll of stockinette (dishcloth fabric obtainable on a roll from household or car stores.) The stockinette comes doubled, and should be used like this, as a single layer is very easily ripped.

Unroll the cloth and fix all the rings you need in it before cutting. If you try to cut pieces to fit in the rings they will curl up and be impossible to manage. Cut round the rings with sharp scissors, leaving about 2cm around the edges. Any less, and it will jump out of the ring; any more and the child will catch it with the needle and sew it underneath.

Threading the needle

Use blunt-ended, large-eyed metal needles or bodkins for first stitches. You can show even the youngest children how to thread them – they will enjoy trying and will often succeed. Teach them to find the end of the ball of wool and put it on their nose. Holding the ball in their other hand they should unwind it slowly until the elbow is straight (this is good manipulative practice in its own right!) and cut the wool near the ball. Doing this, which is the traditional way for tailors to measure thread, ensures that the wool will be a comfortable length for the child to use.

Discourage licking the wool, or trying to poke it through the needle as if it were thread. Instead, fold it around the needle top, pinch it off between finger and thumb (I tell the children to try and hide it, like a little secret) and poke the eye of the needle over the almost-hidden pinched loop before pulling it through. There is great excitement when this is managed alone for the first time.

The stitching process

Show the children how to use their thumb and forefinger 'like a bird's beak' to hold the needle. All the other fingers on that hand should be used to grip the wool in the needle eye, forming a fist so that it can't escape. I call this 'trapping the mouse'. As you poke the needle through the fabric and hold it as it comes out the other side, say 'bird's beak', and as you pull the thread through and grab it with your remaining fingers say 'trap the mouse!' Children soon get used to this sequence and enjoy it.

Starting and finishing

I never tie knots in the end of the wool. It only means that queues of children will form for this to be done, and more importantly it tends to make them yank the wool, knowing the knot will stop it, rather than drawing it through carefully. Similarly, never tie the wool into the needle. Not only will it prevent the wool being pulled through some fabrics, but it also gets in the way of them learning the correct procedure for holding and manipulating the needle described above.

Instead, show children how to leave a loose end on the back when they first pull the wool through (I call this 'the mouse's tail') and this gradually teaches them not to pull too tightly. Later, teach them 'fastening off' – two tiny stitches in the same place on the back.

When first beginning stitching, select a subject which lends itself to simple mark-making with wools. For example, water or fire offer more freedom and are far less threatening than 'my initials' or 'a cat'.

Try looking at photographs of fireworks exploding, or watching a real sparkler outside (held by an adult in a gloved hand). Ask the children to choose suitably coloured wools (I store these in separate baskets, each holding a different colour range) and then make stitches on the 7cm rings of dishcloth. As they grow more confident you can give them small challenges – 'Can you make a long stitch/a tiny stitch/a stitch that is loose so that it stands up like a loop?' On one such project I showed the children how to snip these loops at the top when the firework stitching was completed. The children described these as 'jumping-up sparks'.

Learning objectives

Children should learn that:

- stitching is a form of recording from first-hand observation, and that it offers tactile and textural two- and three-dimensional possibilities which can be used to suggest or represent objects or materials;
- to take delight in the variety of colours and textures fabrics, wools and threads offer, and to begin to understand what they can expect from them;
- to learn to manipulate relevant tools correctly and safely.

A suggested textile project – pizzas

Pizzas make an excellent first project for many reasons. They are round, which means that a circular embroidery ring to hold the fabric taut forms an ideal frame, and they have a beige-coloured dough base for which the dishcloth fabric is perfect. They are not neat and tidy, but are covered in randomly shaped and positioned foods, so that even children who find cutting and sticking extremely difficult can have success, and they offer a range of textures, shapes and colours so that a variety of fabrics can be used.

The project was devised to give children a range of experiences and techniques including collage, stitching and beadwork. Initial stimulus for discussion is important – looking at photographs of pizzas from packets and in recipe books, studying a selection of raw ingredients used for toppings, a visit to a local pizza house to make pizzas, or making pizzas in school. Discuss the shapes, colours, textures and how foods change when they are cooked; how the cook chooses to place the ingredients on the pizza so that there is a bit of everything everywhere, and how the toppings overlap each other.

The pizzas illustrated began with the children choosing a fabric they thought was suitable for one chosen ingredient. A good way to do this is for them to carry a pizza photograph from the packet over to the fabrics (which, like the wools, I store in different colour ranges) and hold it against different pieces until they find a close match. There is good opportunity for developing vocabulary here – ('Is this piece paler or darker than the mushrooms? Is it shiny or matt? Do you think we need a richer brown?' etc.)

I encouraged the children to cut several examples of the same topping (e.g. sliced mushrooms, strips of green pepper) and place them in a balanced but random position on the stockinette background before gluing them. For this I gave them a small dab of Copydex on a plastic dish, and showed them how to use the glue-spreader vertically to apply the tiniest dab (we called it a 'whisper of Copydex') on to the background rather than the cut-out shape. The shape was then stuck on to the dab. The huge advantage of Copydex is that so little is needed, and although It holds immediately, the pieces can be peeled off and repositioned. There is also no washing up – the dried residue can simply be peeled off leaving a beautifully clean dish or spreader. If on the hands or table, children can just rub the surface, whereupon the Copydex turns to solid rubber and can be thrown away. But do protect clothes – it is difficult to remove from them without a chewing-gum stain remover.

The same procedure was followed for the other toppings, and gradually the pizzas filled up with red pepper, ham, pepperoni, anchovies and numerous other delicacies. The children then used wool stitching in different yellows to stitch on grated cheese. I encouraged them to bring the needle up in blank areas of the dishcloth, and keep the stitches about 2 cm in length. They enjoyed the effect of the yellow wool against other colours as they stitched over the toppings.

Thinner green thread and smaller stitches were then used to sew on sprinkled herbs. This was good preparation for sewing on the beads, because to do this a thinner needle is needed to pass through the hole in the bead, and I wanted the children to have some experience of manipulating these smaller needles and finer thread. There was great excitement over the beads. I found some real dried sweetcorn (on a necklace in a charity shop) and some oval black beads for olives. The latter had very large holes and some children were able to cut a tiny sliver of red or green felt to slip through the hole after sewing the beads on, to make stuffed olives. We decided that the beads were not shiny enough for black olives, so as a final touch the children took turns to paint them with a layer of clear nail varnish.

Finally the pizzas were removed from the frames and mounted on the backs of paper plates with the frayed edges wrapped underneath. The plates gave them a domed shapes reminiscent of a real pizza.

(a)

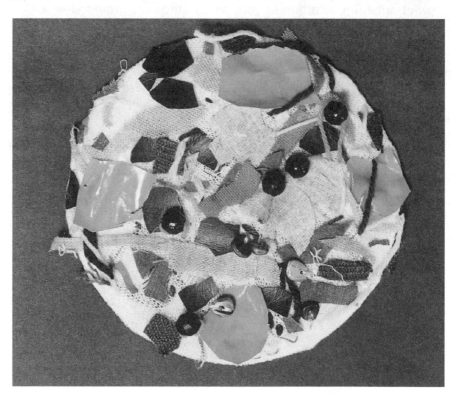

(b)

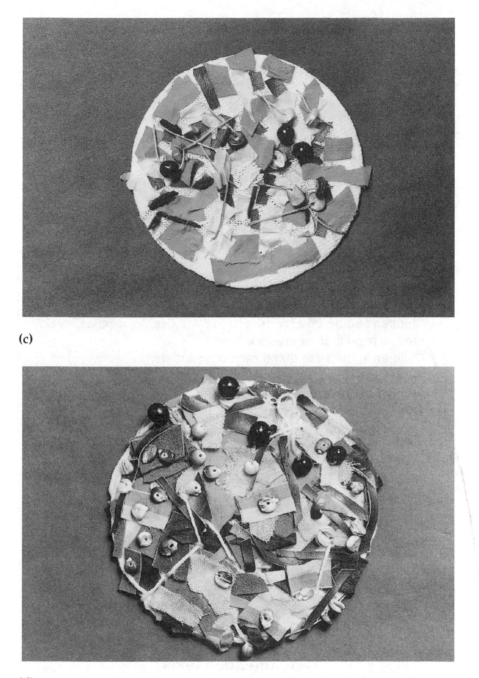

(c)

(d)

Figure 13.2 (a), (b), (c) & (d) *Sewn pizzas by Tiffany Worrall, Tatiana Hoecklin, Byron van Deventer and Sam Harrison, all aged 4 and 5 years, Horler's Pre-preparatory School, Comberton, Cambridge*

Cross-curricular links

The above project provides links with design technology (designing pizzas, cooking, designing menus), different writing styles (setting out a recipe, describing the taste and texture of a hot pizza), science (how foods change in heat) and geography (origins of pizzas, where the ingredients grow, which plants fabrics and threads are made from, where wool comes from).

Pointers for art in the early years

- Children should be helped to realise that art is a necessary part of our culture and inheritance, and that humans have an inbuilt instinct to create.
- Children should learn through as wide a range of stimuli, media and techniques as possible, exploring, discovering and delighting in their variety.
- Children should be encouraged to plan, design, discuss, evaluate and modify their artwork.
- Children should see that they too are artists.
- Sound organisation and practical management of materials bring about better results and a safer classroom environment.
- The way the teacher respects, handles, and stores art materials, and responds to art, gives a strong message to children.
- Art is interwoven with every other curriculum area.

References

Gombrich, E.H. (1987) *Art and Illusion*, London: Phaidon.

Jameson and Kidd, (1974) *Pre-School Play*, New York: Van Nostrand Reinhold.

Lark-Horovitz, B. (1967) *Understanding Children's Art for Better Teaching*, Columbus, OH: Charles Merrill.

Recommended books

Bower, J. (2005) *Practical Creativity at Key Stages 1 and 2*, London: Routledge. (Forty inspiring lessons in art, drama, dance and literacy on ten themes.)

Edwards, B. (1993) *Drawing on the Right Side of the Brain*, London: HarperCollins
(A fascinating and readable book detailing practical ways to unlock the human ability to draw.)

McQueen, D. (1998) *Art and Craft Skills: Painting* (Consultant – Jane Bower), London: Franklin Watts.
(A colourful, practical book giving a wide range of painting techniques and ideas for children.)

Mein, A. (1995) *The Art of Annemieke Mein*, Tunbridge Wells: Search Press Ltd.
(Beautifully detailed photographs of stunning 2D and 3D textile forms based on the natural world. Children find the work breathtaking.)

Rogers, M. (1984) *On Pottery and Porcelain*, Sherbourne: Alphabooks.
(Beautifully made handbuilt pots, mostly based on natural forms, to inspire children.)

CHAPTER 14

'How many toes has a newt?'

SCIENCE IN THE EARLY YEARS

Penny Coltman

Rich in first-hand explorations, science in the early years can be seen as one of the most dynamic areas of the early years curriculum. The intention of this chapter is to consider some of the factors that can support the development of secure scientific concepts and process skills in young children. The desirability of accessing and building upon existing ideas and understandings will be discussed, together with some practical implications of this approach. In addition, the aim of the chapter is to endorse the value of both real and imaginary contexts in promoting learning as they encourage children to see both purpose in their activities and usefulness in their new-found knowledge and capabilities.

On entering an early years classroom to observe a science lesson the sight encountered was of twenty something children, draped in various pieces of fabric and seated in a large circle. The initial reaction was to suppose that a mistake had been made; the class was not carrying out a science activity after all, but was engaged in a rehearsal for some sort of performance. A closer look, however, revealed that this was a lesson about observing and describing the properties of materials. The children were absorbed in a role-play activity in which they had been carried away to a distant land by a magic carpet. In true Arabian Nights fashion they had been transported to the palace of a king who had been cursed. Unable to see or feel beautiful objects, the king was dependent upon the children to tell him about the wonderful things which they had brought for him. Only by helping the king to sort the materials they had brought into various enchanted circles (each labelled with different, descriptive vocabulary) could the children help to lift the dreadful curse.

This lesson, planned and led by a talented trainee teacher, was magical in more ways than one. It showed a rare appreciation that, although science may be viewed as a progression towards an understanding of perceived realities, the teaching of science in the early years can and indeed should adhere to those principles which are understood to promote any effective learning in young children, not least of which is a substantial use of imagination.

Working with children's ideas

If we accept a holistic model of learning in the early years, then the notion of science as an independent curriculum subject becomes somewhat spurious. As children learn in a wide-ranging, multi-disciplinary manner they constantly explore the phenomena and workings of their world and make increasing sense of their findings. The interpretations that children make may be anomalous, based on literal constructions or idiosyncratic connections, but nevertheless such ideas are remarkably resistant to change, and children will hold on to them, even when subsequent experiences provide conflicting evidence (Driver, 1983).

This awareness of the potential variety of ideas that young children may bring with them to the classroom leads to a constructivist approach to the teaching of science, which involves a constant cycle of accessing and modifying children's ideas. Harlen (1999) describes constructivism as a model in which learning is seen as changing pupils' own ideas into ones consistent with the scientific view. A key element of teaching any aspect of science through this approach is consequently the range of strategies used in eliciting responses from children which illuminate existing understandings.

Rachel Sparks Linfield, Paul Warwick and Christine Parker discuss some of the ways in which children's ideas can be accessed in their chapter on assessment (Chapter 4), but it is worthwhile here to consider some additional strategies for gaining insights into children's thinking. Conversation is certainly a powerful tool, especially when children feel comfortable in the company of the interviewer. It can be even more enlightening to place children in role for the purposes of assessment. When in role children respond with confidence. In role anything is possible. In a realm of fantasy there are no right or wrong answers – anything goes. The children on the flying carpet at the beginning of this chapter were at that boundary beyond which imaginative worlds become at least a temporary 'reality', so intense was their captivation. Such scenarios allow and encourage children to venture ideas within a safe context, the bounds of possibilities are known to become elastic as anything goes in a fantasy world.

Similarly, children can be placed in role as directors. Such devices are now commonplace in mathematics lessons, in which children correct the counting errors made by a cuddly but inept puppet, thus demonstrating their own proficiencies. It is not hard to see how this strategy could be transferred to science as the same character, for example, plans his meals or plants his garden. Lesley Hendy, in her chapter about the value of dramatic activity (Chapter 7) describes a similarly effective lesson in which children give advice to Mrs Pig about the relative merits of the various materials her children have chosen to use to build their houses. The skilful presentation of this context gives an urgency to the response reminiscent of the 'It's behind you!' moments in a pantomime, guaranteed to motivate and enthuse young learners.

Collaborative storytelling can be used in much the same way. In a recent lesson the class teacher started to tell a class of 6-year-old children a story about themselves. They had gone on a school trip and become hopelessly lost, eventually finding themselves in some dark and mysterious caves. Each member of the class was woven into the story, delighting the audience as references were made to their own characteristics. The storytelling then became much more interactive, with children confidently adding details to their own adventures and at this point the assessment purpose of the activity became clear. The teacher was exploring children's ideas about the variety of light sources. As the story progressed through the gloomy tunnels, each child in turn was encouraged to find new ways of providing light:

Teacher: As the children turned around the corner they could hardly see their way, but luckily Robert found a . . .

Robert: A torch!

Teacher: This made all the difference, but unfortunately the batteries in the torch were not strong, and the children had not gone far when the torch went out. Fortunately Elli found a . . .

Elli: A candle!

Language and science

One of the difficulties in making assessments about children's understandings, is that conceptual development and language development may not be in step. Science is a discipline which is heavily dependent on precise definitions; indeed, one of the indicators of progression in science is the use of increasingly sophisticated and refined vocabulary. In the early years, children's attempts to describe or explain phenomena may well be open to misinterpretation as they search in vain for the most appropriate language to use. An example of this is often encountered when young children, playing outside on a sunny day use the word 'reflection' to describe the shape they see on the ground. It may indeed be the case that there is some confusion of concepts, and that children have the idea that the ground is somehow behaving as a mirror. Alternatively, it may be that in the search for a word to describe the observation, children have used one which they have found useful before in describing 'an image of themselves'. In other words, use of inappropriate language cannot always be assumed to indicate a genuine misconception, but may be more indicative of the problem many will have faced when trying to order a drink in a foreign language. We use the best word available in our limited vocabulary – and it may not prove to be quite as accurate as we would like! Such difficulties are evidence not of *mis*conceptions, but rather of concepts which are still unrefined. Further experience of both mirrors and shadows will be needed before the two words are understood to relate to distinct and unrelated phenomena.

Further illustrations of children's ideas can be found in the reports published by the SPACE (Science Processes and Concept Exploration) project, which was a joint project between the Centre for Educational Studies, King's College and the Centre for Research in Primary Science and Technology, Liverpool University (SPACE, 1990–94). Many examples are cited, and often the source of misconception or confusion is explored. Young children, for example, frequently expressed the idea that an object is seen because of something coming from the eyes. Osborne (1995) describes how this idea is extended by children to imagine that the eyes direct some ray towards objects to make them visible and goes on to cite examples of everyday speech which implicitly reinforce this notion; we 'look at' books, 'cast our gaze', 'have looks thrown at us' or even 'look right through people'. We might also speculate on the effect of cartoons such as those in which superheroes send laser beams from their eyes in order to see in the dark or zap the enemy.

Another example is commonly found as young children describe materials and appear to demonstrate misconceptions over the use of the words 'soft' and 'smooth'. If we try to clarify the meaning of the word 'smooth' the difficulty becomes apparent. This is a problem of definition. An explanation, for example, of the word 'smooth' is almost certain to focus on negatives. A smooth surface does not have bumps, it is not rough and it is not creased or crumpled. This is a confusion that only experience will resolve. As children handle hard pebbles which are smooth, or soft knitted fabrics which are soft but textured, the distinction between the two terms becomes less ambiguous. So, as questioning reveals a greater insight into children's understandings, the importance of language development in early years science becomes evermore apparent.

Rosemary Feasey (2000) lists three major challenges of language development in the early years which are relevant to science;

Figure 14.1 *May explores materials as she makes a batch of dough*

- to introduce language that is directly related to immediate, concrete, everyday, hands-on experiences;
- to move children on, so that they are able to use the same scientific language in a wider range of contexts that are removed by time and space;
- to develop scientific language that is conceptually based, that is, linked to ideas that may be difficult to understand, for example the movement of particles in dissolving and changes of state.

If children are to move from concrete to abstract in their thinking, or from generic to specific language, they must be given the opportunity to manipulate and experience objects, materials and phenomena and to talk about them. The basic words of naming and describing become the tools of the future. The everyday contexts of making a collage of shiny, curly or transparent materials, or of using paints of different textures and thicknesses, provide rich contexts for the development of this vital language. As adults talk about activities, explaining or questioning, the use of new language is modelled in an appropriate and secure context. As vocabulary is introduced, it is helpful to draw attention to it, encouraging children to repeat and enjoy the new words. Using new language in questions then helps to consolidate and ensure understanding:

Can you think of something which is shiny to use for the robot's buttons?

What sort of material do you think we should use for the baby fairy's bed?

Developing skills

Science is a subject with two complementary aspects. The exploration of areas of knowledge encountered – whether to do with materials, natural sciences or physical processes – provides the contexts for the development of skills, such as observation, questioning, communication and using measurement, which in turn will facilitate the acquisition of knowledge. Later in the primary phase, the skills of science will be combined to form investigations, but in the early years they will largely be developed independently. An analogy can be made with the way in which children learn to play a team game such as football. Skills such as kicking and aiming a ball, passing and receiving, must be practised before a team game can be played. Eventually these will all be drawn together, but only with a great deal of adult direction. It will be some time before children are ready to organise themselves into coherent teams. In the same way, the skills related to scientific exploration, which will eventually be woven together, need to be separately honed. Later they will be brought together as children carry out their first investigations, but the structure of these will be heavily teacher directed. Careful teacher guidance, gradually involving greater degrees of pupil initiatives, will allow the investigation process to become internalised, until by the end the primary phase, or thereabouts, children are ready to plan and carry out fair tests, with independence and confidence.

The first stage in the field of measurement, for example, is language that categorises by size: big, little, thick or thin. Progression is seen as children begin to use comparative vocabulary; smaller, taller, etc. By the end of their reception year most children have begun to use arbitrary units, introducing a quantitative aspect to their measuring skills. The length of a table can be measured in toy cars and the weight of a teddy can be determined by counting the conkers that will balance it. Stories such as that of the king whose new bed is measured by the strides of carpenters of vastly differing sizes are used to help children to under-stand the limitations of such methods, and the conkers and shells will soon be replaced by uniform units, such as plastic cubes, counters or dominoes. This is then the precursor to the introduction of standard units. Over the remaining primary years children will then become adept in measuring using increasingly sophisticated resources, to ever finer degrees of accuracy.

Daisy (see Figure 14.2) is 4 years old. She is able to count small numbers fairly accurately and knows something about measure. The newt, pictured with her, was perhaps unfortunate enough to be discovered during an outside play session. Daisy gently held the animal on her hands, carefully examining it from every perspective and expressing great delight as she noticed its tiny feet. 'I can see its toes' she said. 'I am going to count them.' Then she spotted a cardboard teaching clock on the ground nearby and carefully placed the newt in the middle of it. 'Look,' she announced emphatically, 'The newt weighs ten!'.

Figure 14.2 *Daisy investigates a newt*

The role of questioning

The brief interaction described demonstrates that Daisy is confident in making observations. She is able to look closely and to talk about what she sees. In addition she is confidently exploring the idea of quantifying her observations. She is also able to apply the knowledge she has already gained of animals, to inform her exploration of the newt, looking for legs, toes, eyes and, less successfully, ears. As Daisy makes such connections between new and previous experiences she will gradually develop and refine her understandings and will begin to be able to make reasoned assumptions.

Early years curriculum guidance tends to place great emphasis on the importance of encouraging children to ask questions. The thinking behind this is presumably to foster the sense of enquiry that will lead to cognitive and conceptual developments as illustrated by Daisy. However, children need no encouragement to be curious; they spend their lives in exploration and experimentation. Observation in an early years setting, however, generally provides fewer instances of children asking questions than might be anticipated. Part of the reason for this may be that the concepts that children are encountering and developing, by reason of their newness are rarely within their confident linguistic grasp, as previously discussed. To formulate a question also requires a degree of familiarity with possibilities gained by experiences that are as yet beyond young learners. So the role of questioner in the early years classroom could be described as one predominantly to be adopted by the educator rather than the children.

We now have to accept that children's explorations alone are not going to result in the acquisition of secure and accurate concepts. We can take a child to water, but that will not make him learn!

> Sand and water play is often promoted and justified as supporting children's learning in science, but we can easily overestimate what young children learn through these activities. In fact our expectations are often contradictory. While we fail to recognise the quality or significance of the child's observational skills in their day-to-day interaction with the world, we nevertheless expect them to discover phenomena whenever we make the relevant resources available to them.
>
> (Siraj-Blatchford and MacLeod-Brudenell, 1999, p. 33)

Learning in relation to specific objectives will only occur when the adults supporting an activity are clear about the learning intentions of that activity, and promote relevant conversations, rich in carefully framed questions. This questioning can support learning in a number of respects:

- It presents a linguistic role model, showing children how to frame appropriate questions:
  'I wonder what would happen if . . .' 'How could we . . .?'

- It can present a model of autonomous learning that is characteristic of science. If we want to find something out, then we can do something about it. Children are shown how to be pro-active learners.
  'What do you think the snails would feel like?'

- It directs children's attention to those activities and aspects of activities that will lead to teaching opportunities.
  'Where do you think the water has gone?'

- It can reinforce new vocabulary.
  'What else do you think the magnet might be attracted to?'

- It can promote thinking and problem-solving skills.
  'How could you change the bubble mix?'

- It can help children to make connections between new and existing experiences.
  'What do you think has happened to the chocolate? Think about the ice cubes we used yesterday.'

Questioning is also one way of introducing ideas that gently challenge children's existing cognition, leading children towards new understandings. This is sometimes described as creating 'dissonance', and it is particularly effective when the new thinking opens up, in a manner which is clear to the learner, new possibilities and/or explanations (Harlen, 1999).

Here is an example to illustrate this. Daniel was attempting to balance a short, flat piece of wood on top of three cones. He carefully lined up the three cones in a row and placed the piece of wood on the top of them. When the wood immediately fell down, he checked that the linear arrangement of the cones was as straight as could be, and then tried the balance again.

Daniel's teacher then replaced the piece of wood with a cube and asked Daniel whether he could use the cube and cones to build a model rocket. Both the chosen context and the constraints of the blocks available now strongly suggested that the cones should be arranged in a group under the cube rather than in a line. As Daniel arrived at this conclusion, and successfully balanced the cube on the cones he discovered the concept of a tripod. His previous understanding, that linear arrangements are generally more likely to be successful was challenged and found wanting. Armed with his new discovery, he returned to the original piece of wood, arranged the cones in a tight group and successfully managed the balance. A further element of metacognition, as Daniel showed an awareness of his learning and its potential usefulness, was seen as he was later observed taking great delight in applying the idea of tripods made from cones or pyramids to the constructions he created during free play. New possibilities had been created not only for methods of achieving balance, but for the cones and pyramids themselves, which had previously been used exclusively to decorate or punctuate the tops of towers (for more details see Coltman *et al.*, 2002).

The importance of purposeful science

Writing about ways of helping children become confident mathematicians, Whitebread (2000) cites the observation that mathematics is often bereft of any real, meaningful or supporting context as a prime feature contributing to difficulties experienced by young children. Children complain that mathematics 'isn't about anything'. Sadly, in many instances the same criticism could be levelled at the teaching of science. Too often children are taught procedures or pieces of knowledge, but are not presented with opportunities to use them in any meaningful way. They consequently have little or no appreciation of the value of their learning or the possibilities for its use. There is no notion of the model of teaching and learning suggested by a popular brand of electrical goods: 'The appliance of science'.

Failure to provide opportunities for children to use their learning prevents them from demonstrating anything other than superficial understanding. The development of secure concepts is manifest when children are able to show metacognition, transferring learning to new situations, as Daniel used the tripod. Annie, aged 6, demonstrated this beautifully when she announced after a lesson on simple circuit building: 'I know what I could do – I could put landing lights on that plane I built' (see Figure 14.3).

Creative tasks can also support learning by providing a focus for relevant conversation. As children weave with fabric samples, they will discuss texture, colour, thickness, flexibility and appearance. The selection of materials for a woven seascape or tapestry of autumn colours invites discernment and gives real purpose to discrimination. As they make salt dough models of faces children will use the vocabulary of features and expressions and will describe the feel of the dough as they manipulate it in their hands and the forces used as it is stretched, flattened and squeezed.

Figure 14.3 *Annie's drawing shows how she used her knowledge of circuits to add landing lights to a plane made from a construction kit*

Motivation and engagement and consequent meaningful learning are again promoted by the goal of the finished artifact.

The manufacture of artifacts is an underrated route to assessment. As children make things they demonstrate their knowledge not only by the conversation elicited by the task, but also by their representations. Children constructing imaginary animals, for example, will happily discuss the location in which it might be found, the appearance of its legs, head and wings, and whether or not it can run, swim or fly. Less obvious ideas are explored: Can this animal talk or sing? What other animals might it like to live with? Would you want one in your garden? In this way children are not only demonstrating an appropriate use of subject-related vocabulary as they name and describe features, but are also communicating a broader understanding of interrelationships, structure and function.

Using the outdoor environment

One particularly encouraging aspect of early years curricula is the developing emphasis on the use of the outdoor environment. By exploring the natural world around them, children encounter a wealth of constantly changing phenomena illustrating an infinitely diverse range of concepts. Science is firmly placed within a real, relevant and vibrant context, which is familiar and yet constantly changing and endlessly fascinating. It is through such explorations that the attitudes of responsibility and respect towards both the living and non-living environments can be engendered, as children learn to look closely, to 'not disturb' and to handle with care.

Simple trails can be set up which encourage children to develop awareness of a range of environmental features, and the use of different senses and methods in making observations. Sensory trails have stations which encourage children to explore experiences; 'Shuffle the leaves with your feet. What can you hear?' 'Rub a leaf between your fingers. Enjoy the lovely smell.' Other trails invite the use of apparatus: 'Use a mirror to look around the corner. Can you see the spider's web?' 'Look at the moss through a magnifier.' The joys of such discoveries are compounded by opportunities to share findings with others, and it is not hard to imagine how such ideas can be built into opportunities for children to plan and make trails for others to enjoy.

As schools develop ideas of the 'outdoor classroom', many are including permanent and semi-permanent features to encourage children to enjoy and care for school grounds. Many schools now have gazebos and outdoor working tables to facilitate outdoor learning, and mazes, tunnels and huts made from living willow wands are sprouting in profusion. Wildlife areas vary from formally designated sites, with fences, pond and seats, to a log in an unmown patch of grass with a tree swathed in knitting wool: 'What can you add to the weaving tree?'.

But desirable as these may be, environmental education is not dependent on anything so structured, and, as always, it is often the simplest of ideas that are the most effective. The construction of a 'playground for a mouse' or a 'rain shelter for a fairy' are examples of the types of activities that foster imagination and creativity and remain in memories for a very long time. Intense concentration is evident as children select natural materials for their tasks, supplementing them with sequins, twisted aluminium foil goblets or a smooth, round pebble placed as a throne, and rich and relevant conversation flows. This is 'materials chosen for their uses' in the real sense, with a purposeful context leading to autonomous and self-directed learning as children meet their own self-imposed challenges.

The following passage is taken from the book *The Hundred Languages of Children* which accompanies a remarkable touring exhibition presenting a series of projects carried out by children in municipal infant–toddler centres and pre-schools in Reggio Emilia, Italy. It epitomises a pedagogical approach which is based on an enquiring and aesthetic appreciation of the natural world, and the importance of listening to children. Both uncertainty and amazement are valued as integral to any learning and especially to learning in science. The smallest of everyday contexts is seen as rich in opportunities for scientific enquiry and deduction. The excerpt describes what happens when a group of children explore a puddle:

> The children's excitement ... becomes astonished and vociferous when they notice the play of light, of colours, of transparencies in the puddle and the reflection of their images and that immediate part of the world around them which the puddle mirrors back at them. From that moment on the game opens up and expands, changes level, and draws in all the children's intelligence. And this intelligence stimulates children's observations, thoughts, and intuitions, and leads the children closer and closer to convincing laws of physics and perception, even when – and perhaps above all – they use their intelligence playfully to contemplate situations and even worlds that are turned upside down, with everything this implies.
>
> (Malaguzzi, 1987)

Key points

- Science is a creative area of learning which can be taught through rich imaginative contexts.
- Educators must take into account the diversity of children's previous experiences and the consequent variation in their understandings.
- Language development is a crucial consideration in effective science teaching.
- Each of the process skills related to scientific investigation has its own strands of progression and should be separately addressed.
- The educator has a vital role in promoting scientific enquiry through questioning.
- Children should have opportunities to use newly acquired skills and knowledge in practical and purposeful contexts.

References

Coltman, P., Anghileri, J. and Petyaea, P. (2002) 'Scaffolding learning through meaningful tasks and adult interaction', *Early Years*, 22, 1.

Driver, R. (1983) *The Pupil as Scientist?*, Milton Keynes: Open University Press.

Feasey, R. (2000) 'Children's language in science', in M. de Boo (ed.) *Science 3–6: Laying the Foundations in the Early Years*, Hatfield: ASE Publications, pp. 28–38.

Harlen, W. (1999) *Effective Teaching of Science: A Review of Research*, Edinburgh: SCRE Publications.

Malaguzzi, L. (1996) 'Puddle intelligence', in T. Filippini and V. Vecchi (eds) *The Hundred Languages of Children*, Reggio Emilia, Italy: Reggio Children, pp. 118–19.

Osborne, J. (1995) 'Science from a child's perspective', in S. Atkinson and M. Fleer (eds) *Science with Reason*, London: Hodder & Stoughton, pp. 15–25.

Siraj-Baltchford, J. and MacLeod-Brudenell, I. (1999) *Supporting Science, Design and Technology in the Early Years*, Milton Keynes: Open University Press.

SPACE (1990–94) *Science Processes and Concept Exploration*, London and Liverpool: King's College, London and Liverpool University Press.

Whitebread, D. (2000) 'Teaching numeracy: Helping children become confident mathematicians', in D. Whitebread (ed.) *The Psychology of Teaching and Learning in the Primary School*, London: Routledge/Falmer, pp. 185–211.

Further reading

Johnston, J. (2005) *Early Explorations in Science*, Milton Keynes: Open University Press.

Oliver, A. (2006) *Creative Teaching: Science in the Early Years and Primary Classroom*, Suffolk: David Fulton Publishers.

CHAPTER 15

'How many shapey ones have you got?'

NUMBER AND SHAPE IN THE EARLY YEARS

Sue Gifford and Penny Coltman

Playing with early number: the big ideas

A nursery child asked her teacher 'How do you write three and a half?' Her attempt was to draw three crosses: + + +. Perhaps she thought the crosses looked like halves, and so did three of them.

Two boys in a reception class were supposed to be drawing their favourite story tale character: instead they drew two columns, wrote 'Esdmat' above one and 'TOT' above the other. In the 'Esdmat' column they wrote '1003', '76776', '303030' and '21268710'. Under TOT they wrote 7, then 8. The previous day they had filled in a sheet requiring them to estimate then count numbers of pencils and crayons. These boys had obviously enjoyed the activity and had chosen to do it again, but this time with ridiculously huge estimates; 1003 was their attempt at writing 103, by combining 100 and 3.

A 7-year-old was asked to put a total number in the middle of a triangle, then put numbers at the corners to add to it. He chose 1 as his total and then said he would have 'minus a million' and 'a million and one going upwards' at the corners. Zero was his third number.

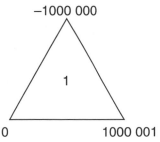

All these children were using creative logic to investigate the number system, using reasoning to push boundaries, and enjoying fractions, large numbers and the paradox of using big numbers to make a tiny one. The third child was used to playing with numbers on a calculator. For many adults, especially those for whom the mention of mathematics creates anxiety mounting to panic, it is hard to see numbers as things to play with, as these children do.

Young children can be creative and investigative mathematicians – but how do they get to be this way? What are the key ideas which develop number sense and how do children learn them?

In countries where children start school later than in the UK, they achieve more highly, pointing to the importance of informal early learning and of deferring written arithmetic (Aubrey *et al.*, 2000). Children know a lot about number before they come to school: young children can tell whether there are more or fewer objects, usually know some number words and can recognise small numbers of objects without counting. They know that numbers give status in terms of age. They learn that number symbols are significant, on doors, cars, football shirts or party invitations. They also find that counting earns praise and large numbers are exciting. However, understanding the meaning of numbers and the structure of the number system is a complex and gradual process: researchers have pointed out that children need a lot of repeated experience over time (Fuson, 1988; Munn, 1997).

Children learn a lot at home: however, this will vary according to family circumstances. One child may experience a lot of talk about time and learn to recognise number symbols from clocks and calendars. Another may learn their door, car and phone number, and possibly their height and weight too. Older siblings may sit around doing homework with impressive 'sums'. For some 3-year-olds, learning to count, whether stairs or spoons, will be part of daily life; grandmother may sing number rhymes or an older brother teach them to write numbers. Some will pick up number skills incidentally. New Zealand researchers concluded that children were number 'experts' or 'novices' dependent on the amount of number experiences they had at home. Research has also shown that the strongest predictor of mathematical achievement is parents' socio-economic status (SES), suggesting that children from poorer homes are also likely to be disadvantaged mathematically (Gersten *et al.*, 2005). Children who start behind, tend to stay behind: however, an effective home learning environment is not always determined by income, and a number focus in pre-school settings can make a difference, as UK research has shown (Sammons *et al.*, 2002).

What do we know about how children learn about numbers?

Recently, neuroscientific research has suggested the importance of different kinds of memory for learning. In learning to count, children use verbal memory for the word sequence, kinaesthetic and spatial memory for keeping track of which ones they counted, and working memory to ensure each is only counted once and to remember the final number. Children's working memory expands considerably after the age of about 6, so learning to count is challenging, especially for young children who are also developing coordination skills. Spatial memory is usually stronger than verbal memory for younger children, which explains why some respond to 'how many' questions by holding up the right number of fingers, while saying the wrong word.

Subitising

Young children often learn to recognise numbers up to five on dot dice, without counting. Using visual patterns like this is called subitising. For numbers over five, the symmetrical doubles seem more memorable, perhaps because we are symmetrical beings.

In many cultures, children will be taught to recognise numbers of fingers, and since ten is the basis of our number system, this is very useful.

Part–whole relationships

'When I see six, I see three and three.' Children who make remarks like this can see numbers as made up of other numbers, showing an awareness of part–whole relationships. Some children learn that seven can be made up of five fingers on one hand and two on the other (and also four fingers and three fingers). These visual and kinaesthetic finger images help children learn addition facts, making use of spatial memory rather than taxing verbal memory.

Linking images with symbols

Children need to learn that number words and numerals can represent a range of number images, collections of objects, sounds and  actions. Munn concluded that learning numerals, for instance when labelling a box of things, helped young children to understand number concepts, even before they understood counting.

One-more-than relationships

Four-year-olds, when asked if they would rather have five or four sweets, often cannot pick the larger number. It seems that comparing numbers which are close together is difficult, even when children have learned to count. Researchers found that middle-class children starting kindergarten in the USA could do this, but most from poorer families could not: 96 per cent compared with 18 per cent (Gersten *et al.*, 2005). This underlines the importance of home experience and also of working with parents.

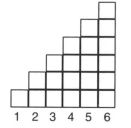

1 2 3 4 5 6

When young children learn to count, they do not realise that counting numbers are connected by size in a one-more-than relationship. The staircase image of the number system represents this: children enjoy constructing staircases from numbered sticks of cubes. Muddling them up and re-ordering helps children to realise that five is one more than four.

Gersten *et al.* suggest that failing to connect counting and relative size may inhibit children's number sense and that 'Creating such linkages early may be critical for the development of proficiency in mathematics.'

Using counting as a thinking tool

Whether a 5-year-old could count out five pencils from a potful predicted how good they would be at mathematics when they were 9, according to New Zealand researchers (Young-Loveridge, 1991). In order to understand the purpose of counting, children have to realise that the final number word gives the number in the collection.

Young children need to use counting as a thinking tool, to solve problems, according to Nunes and Bryant (1996). Children who count to get the number of plates for the table, or to check they have the right number of counters in a collecting game, understand the purpose of counting. The most challenging problems are those which require children to count to compare, for instance to see if sweets have been shared fairly. This requires children to reason about the results of their counting.

Beginning to calculate mentally

Connecting counting with number size leads to being able to add and subtract. It helps to know that one more will give the next counting number and taking away one gives the preceding number. Early subtraction experiences are provided by number rhymes like 'five little ducks', which encourage children to predict. The importance of episodic memory, for significant personal experiences, also suggests the power of drama and stories for helping children to learn mathematics.

Some older children, and even adults, rely on their fingers to calculate. They may add eight and two on their fingers by counting on from eight: 'Nine, ten'. Children who know that eight and two are ten may see that eight and three will be one more. If children see numbers as made up of other numbers, and are used to playing around with relationships between numbers, they are more likely to reason like this. Deriving unknown facts by reasoning from known facts is behaviour typical of higher achievers.

This was the method used by Daniel, who was working out the number of hidden bears: his teacher had started off with ten bears of which five were visible. He said five were hidden, so she got eleven bears, with five visible, which he readily said was six, so then she got twelve, then thirteen. When they came to fourteen bears, he said, 'Last time it was eight, so this time it has to be nine!' This practical game helped Daniel to spot a pattern.

$$10 - 5 = 5$$
$$11 - 5 = 6$$
$$12 - 5 = 7$$
$$13 - 5 = 8$$
$$14 - 5 = 9$$

Implicit in this pattern is a rule: if you increase the starting number by one, but take the same number away, then the result will increase by one. Some children will spot such short cuts, especially if they are led to them by a 'chain' like this. Teachers can help by focusing children's attention on the recorded pattern and asking 'What do you notice?' Children can go on to spot other patterns from $10 - 5 = 5$:

$10 - 5 = 5$	$5 + 5 = 10$	$10 - 5 = 5$
$10 - 6 = 4$	$6 + 4 = 10$	$11 - 6 = 5$
$10 - 7 = 3$	$7 + 3 = 10$	$12 - 7 = 5$
$10 - 8 = 2$	$8 + 2 = 10$	$13 - 8 = 5$
$10 - 9 = 1$	$9 + 1 = 10$	$20 - 15 = 5$

Asking 'If you know this, what else do you know?' is a good way of generating and spotting such patterns, and helping children to become flexible with numbers.

Groups as units

Number sense includes the ability to see numbers of objects as units. Some young children can count pairs of socks, while others insist on counting single socks. Being able to talk about three pairs leads on to answering 'How many twos in six?' and understanding multiplication and division. Children from Asian cultures who are taught to count in threes by using the segments of their fingers may have a head start in multiplying and dividing by three. Being able to count groups of ten, as with fingers (and toes), is vital for an understanding of place value.

Place value

The boys at the beginning were not yet aware of the significance of place value. For this children need to understand that the value of individual digits in a number is determined by its position relative to the others, so that in 13, the 1 is worth ten, whereas in 31, it is only worth one. In writing 1003, the boys did not realise that they were placing 1 in an invisible 'thousands' column, by writing three digits to its right. To begin to understand tens and units, children need experience of representing objects grouped in tens, such as fingers or sticks of cubes. Scenarios which involve objects packed in tens, like boxes of pens, are useful to help children think in numbers of tens. Fosnot and Dolk (2001) describe a teacher's story about a seed merchant sending out orders of expensive seeds, ten to an envelope. The children 'helped' by representing orders for different numbers: they did this in their own ways, moving gradually from drawing seeds and envelopes, to representing by written numbers. They then progressed to 'packing' hundreds of seeds by grouping ten envelopes to a box. The story context helped to develop place value understanding because it generated repeated activity and provided an opportunity to develop recording which was meaningful to the children. The extremely gradual development of abstract understanding is revealed when children record activities in their own way, because they only adopt symbols when they understand them. Some contexts like this offer simple, structured images, whereas others (for instance stories involving groups of children) will lead to distractingly detailed pictures.

Later, children can spot and describe patterns with two digit numbers, discovering, for instance, that adding ten to a number alters the tens digit, but leaves the units digit the same:

$$5 + 10 = 15$$
$$15 + 10 = 25$$
$$25 + 10 = 35$$
$$35 + 10 = 45$$

They enjoy generating their own patterns involving place value.

$50 + 50 = 100$ $500 + 500 = 1000$
$60 + 40 = 100$ $600 + 400 = 1000$
$70 + 30 = 100$ $700 + 300 = 1000$
$80 + 20 = 100$ $800 + 200 = 1000$
$90 + 10 = 100$ $900 + 100 = 1000$

Children can explore larger numbers with calculators: for instance, if challenged to find different ways of making five, they will produce patterns like the following:

$10 - 5 = 5$
$110 - 105 = 5$
$210 - 205 = 5$
$310 - 305 = 5$
$1010 - 1005 = 5$

Young children are ready to spot patterns and to recognise the significance of numbers in their everyday lives. Some need more help from number experts; all of them need time and encouragement to make the connections that will help them develop a feeling for number. If adults can also feel that numbers are interesting to play with, this will help children develop the positive dispositions which are vital to mathematical learners.

Key ideas

Young children learn about numbers in a variety of ways from their everyday lives, (including playing games outdoors).
They need to link counting skills to the meaning of numbers.
Young children are excited by large numbers and are keen to spot patterns.
Adults can help children to play with numbers.

Getting into shape

In recent years the strong focus on developing number skills in the early years has tended to place initiatives and innovation related to early studies of shape rather on the educational back burner. Anecdotally, practitioners tend to perceive shape as relatively straightforward, with well-established approaches to teaching. Indeed, a browse through an early years resource catalogue offers little evidence of new thinking as materials to support the teaching of shape remain familiar and traditional. This part of the chapter aims to explore how a fresh look at shape might offer new insights into children's developing understandings, and suggest some new approaches to supporting this development.

Looking at 2D shapes

Before further discussion about pedagogy, there is one issue linked to early experience of shape that must be addressed. When giving children experience of two-dimensional shape, most practitioners are unwittingly guilty of underpinning a key misconception. We cheat. A two-dimensional 'flat' shape, by its nature, only exists as an image; a drawing or a picture that cannot be picked up. Any object that can be handled must be three dimensional. Yet in most settings one of the most widely used resources for exploring the way in which 2D shapes 'behave' is a box of mosaic blocks. This would not be a problem if children were encouraged to look for a shape with a 'square face', but it is much more likely that, as verbal shorthand creeps in, both adults and children discuss the fact that the 'triangles' will fit together. It is similarly not unusual for even published texts to recommend that 'feely bag' activities can be used to encourage children to identify triangles, squares and circles. Again, a nonsense that merely serves to support confusion.

The key property of any 2D shape is its border. In recognising a shape as a triangle, the attributes that identify it are its three straight sides and three pointed corners, and it would be an expectation that, in describing a triangle, children would draw attention to these features. So it is only sensible in the early years to ensure that children gain plenty of experience designed to establish and consolidate understanding of this vocabulary. What do we mean by a 'straight' side? Does this have any relation to other uses of the word: 'Do it straight away', 'That picture is not straight' or 'My hair is straight'. In other words, the ability to describe 2D shapes must begin with an ability to talk about lines; wiggly lines, wavy lines, zig-zag lines, lines that go around and around, lines that curve, lines that turn corners, lines that squiggle and wriggle and, yes, lines that are straight. Explorations with paint, rope, ribbons on sticks and fingers in sand, wet clay or foam will all help to familiarise children with these basic building blocks of language.

The use of interactive software can make a real contribution to activities relating to flat shapes. This is a context in which children really can manipulate 2D images as they rotate, flip and drag them around the screen, finding dissimilar shapes that fit together in tilling patterns, or working with multiple copies of the same shape to explore tessellation.

Here there is no 'cheating', the shapes remain exactly what they are – two dimensional images that cannot be picked up.

One of the prime mysteries in relation to shape in the early years must be the almost exclusive emphasis on regular geometric shapes (which applies to both flat and solid shapes). Important as the ability to describe a triangle may be, is it really so much more important than the ability to describe the shape of a butterfly's shadow or the edge of a leaf? Developing a broad experience of shape and line through rich, practical and playful activities using real examples enables children to later work with a wealth of diverse and exotic shapes, confidently drawing on a bank of vocabulary to describe their observations.

Learning about the faces of 3D shapes

The need to manipulate 3D shapes is absolutely fundamental. Without extensive concrete experience of handling, turning and examining objects, children cannot develop the ability to imagine shapes as they begin to work in more abstract contexts. When any geometric object is placed on a table, for example, a child who has had inadequate first-hand experience cannot possibly be certain of the shape of any faces that are hidden from view (Clements and Battista, 1992). The implication for practice is that it is essential to give children time to explore the properties of different shapes as they make their own constructions using wooden building blocks, or recycled 'box modelling' materials. These activities may involve children setting their own agendas and goals or may centre on a problem posed by an adult. Observations of children absorbed in such tasks will reveal them to be engaged in both discovering and exploring properties of shapes and using the language of shape for their own real purposes as they discuss progress and share ideas (Coltman, 2006). The quotation from a child used as the title for this chapter, 'How many shapey ones have you got?', comes from a transcript of children's conversations as they collaboratively used wooden blocks to create a large house for a toy dog, Paws (see Figure 15.1). One group of children collected shallow cuboids to tile a 'carpet', while others used prisms, cylinders, arches and cones to decorate the exterior. In both instances, the group used their own words to describe the kinds of blocks that they were collecting. Shallow cuboids were referred to as 'flats' and the blocks being used for decorative purposes were referred to as 'shapey' ones. This coding system, in which children use self-generated language, can only be effective when there is a shared understanding of

Figure 15.1 *Reception class children work together as they build a house for a large toy dog, Paws*

meaning (Lampert and Blunk, 1998). In this instance, the words also indicated awareness of some key attributes of the blocks being described. The shallow cuboids were indeed 'flat', and the term 'shapey' could be interpreted as meaning essentially 'non-rectilinear'.

Julia Anghileri and Sarah Baron (1999) recognised that the development of secure understandings of 3D shapes is a complex process and pursued this idea using traditional wooden blocks. Working in classrooms they explored some of the most common tasks that young children are asked to complete. They found, for example, that children frequently experienced difficulties in correctly orientating a 3D shape so that it stood on a simple outline of one of its faces, or in reaching into a feely bag to find a given shape such as a cylinder. Building on this work, Coltman *et al.* (2002) studied individual children as they approached such tasks, identifying the particular difficulties they encountered. Findings were used to inform the design of problem-solving activities which would effectively support teaching and learning about shape in the early years.

In one investigation, observations were carried out of children undertaking the face recognition activity described by Anghileri and Baron (1999). Children were given a card of simple geometric outlines, asked to look at each in turn, and to find a block with a face that exactly matched it. The activity was essentially a work-card version of the classic 'shape sorter' toy in which children post blocks through shaped holes. Incorrect responses included the matching of shape but not size, or a failure to orientate a correctly chosen block in such a way as to match the face to the outline. In a few cases, encouragement to pick the blocks up and turn them, looking at and feeling the edges of faces, was sufficient to prompt children to 'see' matches.

To support the skills of matching faces to outlines, children were shown how to print 'footprints' with the blocks in soft dough, making impressions of recognisable shapes. They were encouraged to run their fingers around the edges of the impressions and to then feel the edges of the face of the block that had made them. The strong story context built around matching footprints to blocks gave the activity purpose and relevance.

Finally, children were invited children to help to pack a selection of blocks into a home-made 'shape sorter' toy lorry. The crucial adaptation was that the shaped openings into the lorry were packed with foam underneath so that correctly chosen blocks were held in the shaped recesses. This was done to address a perhaps under-recognised problem with many commercial shape sorters; that when a shape has been posted it disappears. There is no opportunity to talk about what has happened. Did the shape chosen go through the hole by sheer luck, or was there some careful looking and matching? Preventing the blocks from falling through the lorry holes allowed tactile and visual reinforcement of the link between the orientation of the block and the shape of the corresponding hole in the lorry.

Interestingly, when this work was repeated in Moscow, it was found that Russian children showed a greater inclination to pick blocks up and turn them around in their hands to find faces that matched 2D outlines. One suggestion to explain this came from comparing the activities routinely presented to the different groups of children. In UK settings, common problem-solving shape activities are jigsaws. In order to solve these puzzles, children need to turn jigsaw pieces around, looking at the shapes of edges and the pieces of picture visible on the upper surface. There is rarely any need to pick pieces up to examine other faces. Russian children, by contrast, are frequently offered 'picture block' puzzles that take the form of covered cubes. In order to complete a picture each cube must be picked up in turn, and rotated in all directions as each face is individually explored.

Using feely bags

Feely bag games are widely used, not only in the study of 3D shape, but also in language and science activities designed to develop the use and understanding of descriptive vocabulary. Children explore a hidden object, feeling and describing it before it can be withdrawn for 'checking'. Children may be asked to identify the 3D shape 'hiding' in the bag, or to locate a given shape from a selection in the bag. The activities are seen as enjoyable and challenging.

And in many ways they are. But their popularity belies the challenges they present to children. When feeling shapes that cannot be seen, children need to make constant translations between the tactile sensations experienced, and remembered or imagined visual images. Again, for children with insecure concepts due to a lack of first-hand experience, this procedure becomes increasingly complex, rendering the task inaccessible.

To support children in early feely bag activities, it is a good idea to ask children to 'find another block like this'. Children are encouraged to manipulate a cube, for example, before reaching into the feely bag to find another. Thus they are matching like with like; two tactile experiences. Providing the children with a block to hold in one hand while reaching in the bag to find a matching one takes this support one step further.

Identifying 3D shape 'families'

There is another hurdle in developing the skills of naming 3D shapes. This is associated with the properties of individual shape 'families'. If a group of people are asked to think about cubes, all the imagined shapes will be more or less the same. Regardless of size, the proportions and shape-related properties of cubes remain constant. Once children have met one cube, in many ways they have met them all. Similarly one sphere is much like another. But this is not true of all shapes. A cylinder, for example, might look like a wheel, a grocery tin or a drinking straw. A triangular prism might resemble a roof or a portion of well-known Swiss chocolate. How can we help children to recognise members of these more complex shape 'families'?

A useful approach is to identify the key characteristic properties shared by all shapes which share the same name. What makes a cylinder a cylinder? Children who were observed by Coltman *et al.* (2002) sorting cylinders from a selection of shaped wooden blocks, were frequently seen to select blocks that met their own criteria based on partial understandings of cylinders. Blocks were chosen, for example, that were 'tall'. To developing understandings, key knowledge was placed in a memorable story context.

The children were told about a mother 'cylinder bird', who was able to recognise her babies using two key pieces of information. Drawing on the printing strategy previously discussed, it was explained that cylinder bird babies like to jump in muddy places (represented by dough) and whether they jump on their heads or their bottoms they leave the same round shape in the mud. Secondly, young cylinders love to roll down slopes, and are good at it, rolling quickly straight down to the bottom. Again, this is readily illustrated using a tipped tray. Using these two key clues, and with access to the appropriate 'testing' resources, children were later able to confidently identify cylinders of several different proportions from a selection of blocks that included cones, brick-shaped cuboids and cubes.

Summary

In thinking about why strategies of the type described in this chapter can be so effective in supporting learning about shape, it is useful to consider the factors shown by research to enhance young children's learning in any context. Referring back to Chapter 1 in this book will remind readers of the evidence supporting the importance of using playful, imaginative contexts where possible, so that tasks are perceived by children as having both purpose and relevance. Similarly the involvement of adults in 'scaffolding' learning, in the manner described by Bruner (1983), can guide the learning experience to the point where children find solutions for themselves. These principles apply throughout the mathematics curriculum, whether the context is counting, number problems or acquiring knowledge of shapes.

Key points

- The complexities of shape as an area of mathematics are often under-estimated.
- An ability to describe 2D shapes is founded in an ability to talk about lines.
- Children need to manipulate 3D shapes, reinforcing visual observations with tactile experiences.
- Approaches to supporting the development of mathematics, as much as any other area, should be embedded in the principles known to enhance learning in young children.

References

Anghileri, J. and Baron, S. (1999) 'Playing with the materials of study: Poleidoblocs', *Education 3–13*, 27, 2, 57–63.
Aubrey, C., Kavkler, M, Tancig, S. and Magajna, L. (2000) 'Getting it right

from the start? The influence of early school entry on later achievements in mathematics', *European Early Childhood Education Research Journal*, 8, 75–85.

Bruner, J. (1983) *Child's Talk*, New York: Norton.

Clements, D.H. and Battista, M.T. (1992) 'Geometry and spatial reasoning', in D.A. Grouws (ed.) *Handbook of Research on Mathematics Teaching and Learning*, New York: Macmillan, pp. 420–64.

Coltman, P. (2006) 'Talk of a number: Self-regulated use of mathematical metalanguage by children in the Foundation Stage', *Early Years*, 26, 1, 31–48.

Coltman, P., Petyaeva, D. and Anghileri, J. (2002) 'Scaffolding learning through meaningful tasks and adult interaction', *Early Years*, 22, 1, 39–49.

Fosnot, C. and Dolk, M. (2001) *Young Mathematicians at Work: Constructing Number Sense, Addition and Subtraction*, Portsmouth, NH: Heinemann.

Fuson, K. (1988) *Children's Counting and Concepts of Number*, New York: Springer Verlag.

Gersten, R., Jordan, N.C. and Flojo, J.R. (2005) 'Early identification and interventions for students with mathematics difficulties', *Journal of Learning Disabilities*, 38, 293–304.

Lampert, M. and Blunk, M. (eds) (1998) *Talking Mathematics in School*, Melbourne: Cambridge University Press.

Munn, P. (1997) Children's beliefs about counting', in I. Thompson (ed.) *Teaching and Learning Early Number*, Buckingham: Open University Press, pp. 9–19.

Nunes, T. and Bryant, P. (1996) *Children Doing Mathematics*, Oxford: Blackwell.

Sammons, P., Sylva, K. *et al.* (2002) 'Measuring the impact of pre-school on children's cognitive progress over the pre-school period', Technical Paper 8a, London: Insitute of Education, University of London.

Young-Loveridge, J. (1991) 'The development of children's number concepts from ages five to nine', Hamilton, NZ: University of Waikato.

CHAPTER 16

'PLEASE can we have another bit?'

INFORMATION AND COMMUNICATIONS TECHNOLOGY IN THE EARLY YEARS: AN EMERGENT APPROACH

John Siraj-Blatchford

Socio-constructivist perspectives in early childhood education (Sayeed and Guerin, 2000) recognise the importance of viewing play as an activity where children are developing their confidence and capability for interacting with their cultural environment. If we are to provide for an appropriate, broad and balanced education in the early years we must first therefore think about children playing, but then we must also think about the particular subjects of that play. In recent years the application of Information and Communications Technologies (ICT) has brought about fundamental changes to our culture, and the legitimacy of its place in the curriculum can therefore be hardly doubted.

Since computers were first introduced into UK primary schools in the early 1980s an ever wider range of ICT products have been developed for use by young children. Some of these have been found appropriate for use in pre-schools, and other new products have been developed specifically for this age group (Siraj-Blatchford, 2006). But given the relatively high cost of computers and of computer software, and the even greater investment in training that is required to use them effectively, it is important that we make critical and informed choices regarding their use.

There are six commonly cited benefits in applying ICT in the early years. It has been argued that:

- Computers offer a means of teaching basic skills more efficiently.
- Computers have been widely employed in schools and industry, and it is therefore important for children to begin to develop the computer

keyboard and mouse skills that will increasingly determine their future success in these new technological environments.

- Children working at the computer benefit from the experience of collaborating with their peers.
- Programmable toys and screen images provide motivating real and virtual objects for the child to 'think with' (Papert, 1982).
- Early play and experience with ICT supports the development of enduring positive dispositions to the subject.
- Technology provides a range of powerful compensatory tools to be applied in educating children with Special Educational Needs.

Learning 'the basics'

A range of software products have been developed to support early learning in a wide range of subject areas. These include drill and practice programs designed to support the development of number and letter recognition and basic phonic skills. Popular examples include *Baileys Book House* (Edmark) and *Oxford Reading Tree*. Programs such as *My World Animal Sort* and *Freddy Teddy* also support children in developing sorting and sequencing skills. A good example of an early drill and practice program of this sort is *Millie's Math House* (Edmark). This CD includes 'Make a Bug', 'Number Machine' and 'Bing/Bong', a program that encourages children to complete patterns which the program makers claim will 'empower children to recognise other patterns in music, mathematics, art, and science and to make better sense of the world'. While an optional free-play mode is included in this program, it also provides a very clear demonstration of the behaviorist teaching approach (a learning approach based on behavior modification) that is inherent in many of the programs of this genre. If the child gets a right answer they are rewarded by some amusing action sequence and/or tune. If they make a mistake the options are gradually reduced until they are forced to make the 'correct' response. This is an approach that is widely considered inappropriate in British early childhood settings, as it runs against the grain of the dominant 'play and discovery' philosophy of early childhood education.

When children interact with this kind of software their interaction is often especially absorbing and extended. Products should therefore be carefully reviewed to ensure that they are suitable. There are flaws even in some of the most popular programs. To take one notable example of this, 'Sentence builder' (*Stickybear's Reading Room*) allows the child to create their own sentences, the computer animates them, prompts them to read it and then plays their recording back:

The program has 86 nouns and 48 verb phrases but is interesting to note that while the software refers to an astronaut, an acrobat, clown, diver, and 29 animals – there are no children included. The people that the child might identify with are therefore all adult and they are also stereotypically male – and this is compounded by the artefacts – bulldozers, garages, motorcycles, submarines and rockets that are included. There are no prams, shopping trolleys, department stores and kitchens.

(Siraj-Blatchford, 1998)

The verb phrases are restricted in that it is possible for the astronaut to move in a wide variety of ways: he can fly, jump, even skip ... but he cannot sit, talk, laugh, cry or hug anyone. The program has an inbuilt bias towards boys. As the US National Association for the Education of Young Children (NAEYC) Position Statement on Technology suggests:

The teacher's role is critical in making certain that good decisions are made about which technology to use and in supporting children in their use of technology to ensure that potential benefits are achieved. Teachers must take time to evaluate and choose software in light of principles of development and learning and must carefully observe children using the software to identify both opportunities and problems and make appropriate adaptations. Choosing appropriate software is similar to choosing appropriate books for the classroom – teachers constantly make judgments about what is age appropriate, individually appropriate, and culturally appropriate.

(NAEYC, 1996)

The use of an inappropriate teaching method can have a devastating effect upon a child's learning dispositions. There is evidence to suggest, for example, that excessive early drill and practice in the teaching of reading can undermine a child's dispositions to be a reader (Katz, 1992). Yelland (2002) usefully cites Negroponte in this context:

In the 1960s, most pioneers of computers in education advocated a crummy drill-and-practice approach, using computers on a one-to-one basis, in a self-paced fashion, to teach those same God-awful facts more effectively. Now, with the rage of multimedia, we have closet drill and practice believers who think they can colonise the pizzazz of a Sega game to squirt a bit more information into the heads of children, with more so-called productivity.

(Negroponte, 1995, pp. 198–9)

Computer keyboard and mouse skills

Many early years teachers prioritise the development of basic mouse and keyboard skills, and software such as the *Switch on Original: Picture Building* (Brilliant Computing) is often used specifically for these purposes. School suppliers and toy shops provide a range of other apparatus and equipment designed to satisfy the same needs. Yet, if we look back to the early days of educational (or industrial) computing, one of the most obvious changes has been in precisely these areas. The first computer introduced into many primary schools was the Sinclair ZX81 (see Figure 16.1). Programs were stored on cassette tapes that took a long time to load. None of the early computers had a mouse and written commands had to be typed onto the screen – the 'drag and drop' facility that was first introduced by Macintosh had yet to be developed. We have come a long way since these early days ... but they weren't actually that long ago, and that is something we really need to think about. Future developments are difficult to predict but looking back on developments so far it is clear that computing in the future will faster and easier to access.

Figure 16.1 *The Sinclair ZX81*

Touch-sensitive screens have already replaced other means of control in a variety of hand-held devices, and the likelihood of the infants of today operating a mouse in their future employment seems extremely doubtful. New technologies are constantly being developed and voice recognition systems are becoming increasingly sophisticated. The future of the QWERTY keyboard seems even more bleak. The odd layout of the QWERTY keys was initially designed to slow down the typist to avoid the typewriter 'hammers' colliding and locking together as they were thrown against the ribbon and paper. That keyboard is already a technological anachronism . . .

Children do need to access the technology that is currently available, and the point that I am making here is not that we shouldn't support them in initially gaining that access. We should provide them with the best possible access to the technological tools currently available. But what we shouldn't do is present that as a central objective of early years ICT education.

Most new desktop computers arrive with an instruction book that warns the user about some of the ergonomic difficulties associated with extended exposure to the screen and in operating the keyboard and mouse. The dangers of developing repetitive strain injuries (RSIs) and carpal tunnel syndrome have been well documented. The recommendations for appropriate posture should therefore always be followed as far as possible. Yet this is often extremely difficult to achieve in a classroom, and in pre-schools the difficulties may actually be insurmountable. Young children vary greatly in height and the provision of suitable furniture is often beyond the resources of playgroups and nurseries. In these circumstances the identification of alternative patterns of usage and means of access becomes crucial.

A major advantage of using a touch screen is that children's interactions with the computer are often relatively short, and the equipment may be set up to be accessed by the child from a standing position. This overcomes many of the ergonomic problems alluded to above. Software such as the Fisher Price's *Toyland* and the *Winnie the Pooh Toddler* (Disney) lends itself very well to these purposes. One of the games featured on the CD involves 'Popping balloons for Pooh', a game where the child is encouraged to 'help Pooh and his friends get down from an awfully high place' by popping balloons! As each balloon is popped it sounds out the letter, number, color or shape that it is decorated with. The game therefore enhances the educational environment (supporting the development of emergent literacy and numeracy) without making that the central function of the activity.

Collaboration

While the extended use (e.g. in excess of 40 minutes or an hour at a time) of desktop computer keyboards is therefore not to be recommended in early childhood, there are still a great many early years programs available that can be used to encourage collaborative activity (see Figure 16.2).

Figure 16.2 *Good early years software encourages collaboration and joint attention*

As Light and Butterworth (1992) have argued that 'joint attention' and 'children learning to share' and/or 'engage jointly' provides an important source of cognitive challenge for young children. In collaboration, children articulate their thinking, sharing their understandings and bringing to consciousness many ideas that they may still be only beginning to grasp intuitively (Hoyles, 1985). Collaboration is also considered important in providing opportunities for cognitive conflict as efforts are made to reach consensus (Doise and Mugny, 1984), and it has been recognised as important in facilitating the co-construction of potential solutions in the creative processes of problem-solving (Forman, 1989). The best of these provide context for work away from the screen. A screen 'bug' designed in 'Make a bug' (*Millie's Math House* – see Figure 16.3) may be subsequently constructed using play dough or found materials.

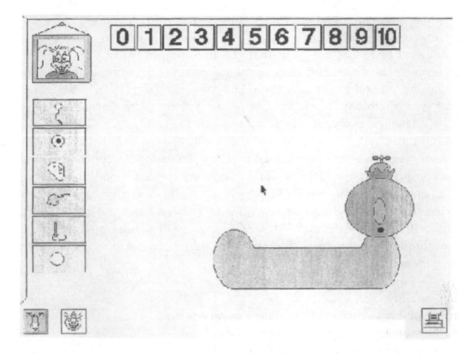

Figure 16.3 *'Make a bug' from Millie's Math House*

Adventure games and simulations are also popular and old favourites such as *Grannie's Garden* (Formation) and *Albert's House* (Links Education) are now increasingly being supplemented by programs such as *Pirate Ship* (Fisher Price). There is also a wide range of graphics programs on the market that can be applied collaboratively. Early word processing packages have also been used to good effect at times (*First Writer, My World*).

Manipulables

At one time it was thought that many of the activities associated with computers would not encourage creativity, and in fact required only that the child press buttons. The manipulation of virtual objects on a screen was seen as a weak substitute for the manipulation of real three-dimensional objects, artifacts and toys. But, as Yelland (2002) argues, the potential of computers to enable children to encounter and play with ideas has been increased, and products such as *Logo* and *Kid Pix* provide a means by which children can create and manipulate objects, playing with them in a variety of ways. In such environments the children often spontaneously discover mathematical ideas and engage in interactions with other learners in ways that would not have been possible without the technology.

Most early childhood educators believe that young children learn best by investigating with their senses, but a common concern among early childhood educators has been that children are not ready to work with computers. In discussing developmental issues surrounding the use of computers in childhood education, Silvern and McCary (1986) suggested that two conditions should be met for an activity to be considered 'concrete'. The first is that the material used in the activity should be easily manipulated and the second is that 'the results of the manipulation must be directly verifiable by the manipulator'. Using these criteria, concrete uses of the computer may be identified and effectively applied by children. But as Clements and McMillen (1996) have stated, in any event: 'What is concrete to the child may have more to do with what is meaningful and manipulable than with its physical nature' (p. 273). Clements (1994) has also highlighted the unique characteristics of computer manipulatives and suggested that they include:

- flexibility;
- the ability to change arrangement or representations;
- the storage and availability of configurations;
- recording and replaying children's actions;
- linking the concrete and the symbolic and providing feedback;
- dynamic linking of multiple representations; and
- focusing the children's attention and increasing motivation.

While most of us are very much aware of the ways in which ICT has revolutionised *communications*, its parallel effects in *control* technology is often forgotten. This is unfortunate because it's probable that the vast majority of the computers that we interact with on a day-to-day basis are dedicated to these purposes alone. Microprocessors are now routinely incorporated in a vast range of devices. They are also incorporated in a growing number of children's toys. In the UK, programmable toys are now commonly available to children as 'symbolic objects to think with' (Papert, 1982). A floor 'turtle' such as Swallow Systems' *Pixie* is controlled by the child by giving it program instructions: Forward, Back, Left, Right. These instructions make the turtle move and in the process children use their thinking skills to explore, take risks and apply their prior knowledge in new and creative ways. Many experts believe this can enhance their cognitive development. *Pixie* is exceptionally simple to control and provides a very good starting point as an 'object to think with'. The 'Jelly bean hunt' in *Trudy's Time and Place House* (Edmark) provides an appropriate and popular screen-based alternative (see Figure 16.4).

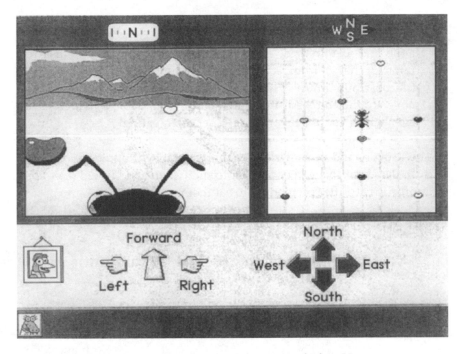

Figure 16.4 *The 'Jelly bean hunt' in Trudy's Time and Place House*

Symbolic play, and sociodramatic play in particular, is seen as a characteristic mode of activity for this age group, and by inference the most appropriate vehicle for learning (Anning and Edwards, 1999; Vygotsky, 1978; Wood and Attfield, 1996). ICT research conducted as a part of the Children's Awareness of Technology (CHAT) project (see web address p. 354) has shown that the manipulation of symbols and images on the computer screen may actually represent a new form of symbolic play, which the children seem to treat every bit as 'concretely' as the manipulation of any alternative blocks and small-world toys:

> On-screen images were 'grabbed', scolded, fingered and smacked, with dramatic effect, as part of the small-group interaction with the software. In some instances, they took on an off-screen life of their own, as children continued the game the computer had initiated, away from the machine. 'Food' items were one of the favourite symbols for adoption, particularly by the morning 'girls' group':

>> Tabitha says 'click'; Alice says 'That won't do anything'; there is group glee when they succeed. All three evolve highly physical and interactive game away from computer: for several minutes

they pretend to eat the cheese on the screen, with lots of lip-smacking and appreciative noises and role-play – 'Oh god, it's all gone and I didn't get any!' Annabelle skilfully uses mouse to remove cheese from screen into the limbo of a black border (unconscious control, very skilled). Tabitha says 'PLEASE can we have another bit?' All three are standing and role-playing: Alice even wipes her fingers on her jumper after 'eating'.

These three, and other girls, frequently 'grabbed' apples and pears from the screen, begged each other to share them, and licked their lips appreciatively after pretending to eat them.

(Brooker and Siraj-Blatchford, 2002)

Developing technological literacy and positive dispositions to ICT

'I'm a rocket scientist', one engineer complained to me. 'I design missile systems, but I can't figure out how to program my VCR.'

(Norman, 1995)

As Norman (1995) has argued it is inevitable that, as technology has developed, we have all come to know less and less about the inner workings of the systems that are under our control. This is as true of adult experiences of technology as it is of children's experience. In the face of these changes, we need to consider carefully what our educational priorities should now be. We also need to consider what it actually means to 'understand' a technological product. When technology was mostly mechanical we could see the internal workings and we could see the effects of our actions on machines. But increasingly their operation and design are invisible and abstract, so that, if we are not to be entirely alienated from the technology around us, we need to redefine what it means to be technologically literate. It is this sort of argument that provides the rationale for including educational provisions for children learning about the 'uses of technology' in the Foundation Stage curriculum.

Many early childhood applications thus provide a parallel with adult applications. Children are now introduced to a wide range of computer software on CD-Roms and in addition to all of those referred to above; they soon come to apply software encyclopedias and a range of word processors, spreadsheets and databases in school. In the early years hardware and software applications have been developed specifically with the intention of encouraging children to 'play' within adult ICT contexts. For example, the *Playskool Store* (Hasbro) checkout unit clips on to the keyboard providing a point of sale shopping simulation that incorporates a working till, bar-code reader, etc. (see Figure 16.5). When we apply technology in this way in the early years we may describe our perspective as one supporting an 'emergent technology curriculum' (Siraj-Blatchford and Siraj-Blatchford, 2006).

Figure 16.5 *The Playskool Store checkout unit*

An 'emergent technology curriculum' is in many ways just like an emergent literacy curriculum. Teachers who teach emergent literacy encourage 'mark making' as a natural prelude to writing. In emergent technology we should encourage the 'application' of technology and support the child in sustaining them over time. Teachers who teach emergent literacy *read* a range of different kinds of text to children. In emergent technology we should introduce the children to 'new applications'. We should provide them with the essential early experiences that they must have if they are to go on to understand and be empowered by technology in their later lives.

These early experiences will include playing with a range of different technological artifacts and software products (real and pretend telephones, cameras, computers, etc.). They will also include drawing children's attention to the uses of technology in the world around them. We can also encourage 'technology play' in the nursery, setting up office play environments, supermarket checkouts and bank cash points for children to integrate into their play. Teachers who teach emergent literacy provide positive role models by showing children the value they place on their own use of print. In emergent technology education we can do the same by talking about technology and involving children in the development of our own collaborative technological applications. We can set up a computer database to keep a check on the books and other resources that we use. We can use the computer for our own purposes, sharing our experiences of its use with the children. In doing so, we will encourage children to develop an emergent awareness of the nature and value of these resources, as well as positive dispositions towards the kind of technological applications that they will experience in the future.

Many of those promoting emergent literacy see parent and teacher 'modelling', that is teachers and parents providing good role models, as the most important factor in developing children's capability. They therefore encourage parents to read to their children and ensure that the children see them reading for their own purposes. This is backed up by numerous large-scale research projects that show that the single most influential factor in determining children's future academic success in the early years is parents reading to children and taking them to the library regularly (Sylva *et al.*, 2000). This in turn is related to social class and other factors – but the primary determinant seems to be the parents' behaviour: change that and it will compensate for social class differences in academic achievement! So the real challenge is to provide children with strong models of technology so that they develop positive attitudes and beliefs about the importance of the subject; that, more than anything else, is what will influence their motivation to engage in it in the future.

Play is a 'leading activity' (Leontiev, 1981; Oerter, 1993), and as van Oers (1999) has suggested, when children consciously reflect upon the relationship between their 'pretend' signs and 'real' meanings they are engaged in a form of semiotic activity that will provide a valuable precursor to new learning activities:

> . . . learning activity must be fostered as a new special form of play activity. As a new quality emerging from play activity, it can be argued that learning activity has to be conceived as a language game in which negotiation about meanings in a community of

learners is the basic strategy for the acquisition of knowledge and abilities.

(van Oers, 1999, p. 273)

From this theoretical standpoint I want to argue that we should be providing opportunities for children to play with technology and to play at being technologists. It is commonplace for children to play at being mummies, daddies, as well as a wide range of traditional roles such as soldiers, doctors, nurses and firemen. In the UK, pre-school suppliers and toy shops produce 'dressing-up' clothes to promote this kind of play. All we need to do is to provide the props and encouragement to include technology in all of this as well. For some practitioners this may seem to be prescriptive, but, as Vygotsky argued:

In one sense a child at play is free to determine his own actions. But in another sense this is an illusory freedom, for his actions are in fact subordinated to the meanings of things and he acts accordingly.

(1978, p. 103)

Special educational needs

Experience in the UK and abroad suggests that computers may actually be maintaining, and may even be exaggerating, educational inequalities. Some children benefit from having frequent use of computers in the home, and boys tend to be encouraged to use them much more than girls. Girls' and boys' software preferences differ, and it is all too easy for the children who have the most experience and capability to dominate the computer's use. ICT provides no panacea for educational inequality; everything depends upon the choices that are made to provide technology that is appropriate to each child's unique special needs, learning style and individual preferences:

For children with special needs, technology has many potential benefits. Technology can be a powerful compensatory tool – it can augment sensory input or reduce distractions; it can provide support for cognitive processing or enhance memory and recall; it can serve as a personal 'on-demand' tutor and as an enabling device that supports independent functioning. The variety of assistive-technology products ranges from low-tech toys with simple switches to expansive high-tech systems capable of managing complex environments. These technologies empower young children, increasing their independence and supporting their inclusion in classes with their peers. With adapted materials, young children with disabilities no longer have to be excluded from activities. Using appropriately designed and supported computer applications, the ability to learn, move, communicate, and recreate are within the reach of all learners. Yet, with all these enhanced capabilities, this technology requires thoughtful integration into the early childhood curriculum, or it may fall far short of its promise. Educators must match the technology to each child's unique special needs, learning styles, and individual preferences.

(NAEYC, 1996)

In our study of early computer use by bilingual children (Brooker and Siraj-Blatchford, 2002) we found that the nursery computer provided accessible language forms that were being exemplified and supported through visual cues and animations, and that these were frequently repeated:

Instances of language learning, and practice, in response to the software, were regularly recorded. The computer often provided a shared focus and experience for children who didn't share the same spoken language, and this undoubtedly contributed towards the development of the very positive, collaborative, and language enriched multicultural learning environment that we observed.

(Brooker and Siraj-Blatchford, 2002)

Conclusions

We began the chapter by identifying six reasons that might be given for introducing computers into early education: they might be used to teach basic skills more efficiently; prepare children for the future in schools and employment; encourage collaboration and positive dispositions towards ICT; provide objects for the child to 'think with'; and/or provide for special educational needs.

In the subsequent discussion of each of these areas, the UK early learning goals and statutory requirements of the national curriculum were put to one side. But if we consider the early learning goals carefully we can see that they actually address a very similar set of concerns:

- use computers to support their learning;
- find out about and identify the uses of technology in their everyday lives;

• use programmed toys to support their learning.

('Early Learning Goals', DfEE, 1999)

The evidence shows that, when they are given the freedom to play with appropriate software, young children are active in constructing their own learning at the computer, and in scaffolding each other's learning. As the UK Foundation Stage curriculum suggests, young children should be encouraged to begin to develop a knowledge and awareness of the common uses of ICT. As I have argued above, there can be few places better to start this process than in early childhood socio-dramatic play. This is also the sort of integrated ICT provision that is promoted by the Developmentally Appropriate Technology in Early Childhood (DATEC) project. DATEC has involved a two-year collaboration between practitioners and academics in the UK, Sweden and Portugal, and provides early childhood guidance and exemplar material. This information is now freely available from the project website (see p. 354).

We all have a contribution to make in providing a better ICT education for young children, and in doing so we should always be acutely aware of the influence of the wider environment, and of role models in particular, on young children. In our work and interactions with children we should demonstrate confidence and competence with technology. As Pluckrose has suggested, young children learn a great deal from the models that are provided for them:

Watch a nursery child put on a pair of high-heeled shoes and a Sloane Ranger hat and toss a giant sized handbag over her shoulder. Listen to the language. Admire the walk. Then, take time to reflect upon the interpretation of her world through her eyes, marvelling that one so young is able to 'read', so meticulously, the adults who people her world . . .

(Pluckrose, 1999)

If we show that we value the new technology and confidently control it, then children will be encouraged to develop the same attitudes. But if we present them with models that are disempowered and helpless in the face of technology, we take the risk of encouraging just the same in them.

Pointers for early years ICT

- Beware of over-using drill and practice software with young children.
- How children access software (QWERTY keyboard; mouse) will change and should not be a central objective of the curriculum.
- Ergonomics are important; consider using touchscreens with the children standing.
- Use software which encourages collaboration.
- Manipulating objects on-screen in a meaningful context provides valuable opportunities for symbolic play.
- Using computers should be part of a wider 'emergent technology curriculum'.
- Children should be provided with opportunities to engage in socio-dramatic play with all kinds of technology.
- Teachers should positive models showing how they use technology.
- Used thoughtfully, technology can empower children with Special Educational Needs and support their inclusion.

References and bibliography

Anning, A. and Edwards, A. (1999) *Promoting Young Children's Learning from Birth to Five*, Buckingham: Open University Press.

Brooker, E. and Siraj-Blatchford, J. (2002) ' "Click on Miaow!" How children of 3 and 4 experience the nursery computer', *Contemporary Issues in Early Childhood*, 3, 2, 251–73; http://www.triangle.co.uk/ciec/

Clements, D.H. (1994). 'The uniqueness of the computer as a learning tool: Insights from research and practice', in J.L. Wright and D.D. Shade (eds) *Young Children: Active Learners in a Technological Age*. Washington: NAEYC, pp. 31–50.

Clements, D.H. and McMillen, S. (1996) 'Rethinking concrete manipulatives', *Teaching Children Mathematics*, Jan., 270–9.

Department for Education and Science (DfEE) (1999) *The National Curriculum Handbook for Primary Teachers in England Key Stages 1 and 2*, London: HMSO.

DeVries, R. (1997) 'Piaget's social theory', *Educational Researcher*, 26, 2, 4–17.

Doise, W. and Mugny, G. (1984) *The Social Development of the Intellect*, Oxford: Pergamon Press.

Dweck, C. (1991) 'Self-theories and goals: Their role in motivation, personality, and development', in R. Dienstbier (ed.) *Perspectives on Motivation: Nebraska Symposium on Motivation*, Omaha, NB: University of Nebraska Press, pp. 199–236.

Dweck, C.S. and Leggett, E. (1988) 'A social-cognitive approach to motivation and personality', *Psychological Review*, 95, 2, 256–73.

Forman, E. (1989) 'The role of peer interaction in the social construction of mathematical knowledge', *International Journal of Educational Research*, 13, 55–69.

Gregory, R. (1997) 'Science through play', in R. Levinson and J. Thomas (eds) *Science Today*, London: Routledge, pp. 192–206.

Hoyles, C. (1985) 'What is the point of group discussion in mathematics?', *Studies in Mathematics*, 16, 205–14.

Katz, L.G. (1992). *What Should Young Children Be Doing?* ERIC Digest. Urbana, IL: ERIC Clearinghouse on Elementary and Early Childhood Education, University of Illinois.

Leontiev, A. (1981) *Problems of the Development of Mind*, Moscow: Moscow University Press.

Light, P. and Butterworth, G. (eds) (1992) *Context and Cognition: Ways of Learning and Knowing*, Hemel Hempstead: Harvester-Wheatsheaf.

NAEYC (National Association for the Education of Young Children) (1996) 'NAEYC position statement: technology and young children – ages three through eight', *Young Children*, September, 11–16.

Negroponte, N. (1995) *Being Digital*, Rydalmere, NSW: Hodder & Stoughton.

Norman, D. (1995) 'Designing the future', *Scientific American*, September, 159.

Oerter, R. (1993) *The Psychology of Play: An Activity Oriented Approach*, Munich: Quintessenz.

Papert, S. (1982) *Mindstorms: Children, Computers, and Powerful Ideas*, Brighton, Sussex: Harvester.

Pluckrose, H. (1999) *The Caring Classroom: Towards a Learning Environment*, Nottingham: Education Now Books.

Sayeed, Z. and Guerin, E. (2000) *Early Years Play: A Happy Medium FOR Assessment AND Intervention*, London: David Fulton Publishers.

Silvern, S. and McCary, J. (1986) 'Computers in the educational lives of children: developmental issues', in J.L. Hoot (ed.) *Computers in Early Childhood Education*, Englewood Cliffs, NJ: Prentice-Hall, pp. 6–21.

Siraj-Blatchford, J. (1996) *Learning Science, Technology and Social Justice: An Integrated Approach for 3- to 13-year-olds*, Nottingham: Education Now.

Siraj-Blatchford, J. (1998) 'Design, technology and the use of computers in the early years', in I. Siraj-Blatchford (ed.) *A Curriculum Development Handbook for Early Childhood Educators*, Nottingham: Trentham Books, pp. 109–20.

Siraj-Blatchford, J. (ed.) (2006) *Developing New Technologies for Young Children*, Nottingham: Trentham Books.

Siraj-Blatchford, J. and MacLeod-Brudenell, I. (1999) *Supporting Science, Design and Technology in the Early Years*, Buckingham: Open University Press.

Siraj-Blatchford, J. and Siraj-Blatchford, I. (2001) *KidSmart: The Phase 1 UK Evaluation: Final Report (2000–2001)*, IBM United Kingdom Ltd, unpublished white paper.

Siraj-Blatchford, I. and Siraj-Blatchford, J. (2006) *A Curriculum Development Guide to ICT in Early Childhood Education*, Nottingham: Trentham Books.

Sylva, K., Melhuish, E., Sammons, P., Siraj-Blatchford, I. and Taggart, B. (2000) 'Effective Provision of Pre-school Education Project: recent findings', Presented at the British Educational Research Conference, Cardiff University, September 2000.

van Oers, B. (1999) 'Teaching opportunities in play', in M. Hedegaard and J. Lompscher (eds) *Learning Activity and Development*, Aarhus: Aarhus University Press.

Vygotsky, L. (1978) *Mind in Society: The Development of Higher Psychological Processes*, Cambridge, MA: Harvard University Press.

Wood, E. and Attfield, J. (1996) *Play, Learning and the Early Childhood Curriculum*, London: Paul Chapman.

Yelland, N. (2002) 'Reconceptualising schooling with technology for the 21st. century: images and reflections', *Contemporary Issues in Early Childhood*, 3, 2; http://www.triangle.co.uk/ciec/

Further information

Further information and guidance on appropriate technology in early childhood is available on the Developmentally Appropriate Technology in early Childhood (DATEC) project website: http://www.ioe.ac.uk/cdl/datec

The CHAT website can be found at: www.ioe.ac.uk/cdl/CHAT

Other useful internet addresses:
Teacher reviews of a wide range of early years software are available at:

http://www.teem.org.uk
http://www.becta.org.uk

http://www.ucc.uconn.edu/~wwwpcse/wcool.html
http://hometown.aol.com/wiseowlsw/index.html

Other sites:

http://www.open.gov.uk/dfee/nursery.htm
http://www.naeyc.org/default.htm
http://www.letsfindout.com
http://www.cyberkids.com
http://www.disney.go.com
http://www.teacherxpress.com
http://www.parentscentre.gov.uk/usingcomputersandtheinternet/

CHAPTER 17

'Mrs Rainbow told us what things were like when she went to school'

HISTORY IN THE EARLY YEARS

Sallie Purkis and Jayne Greenwood

You may think that learning history has no place in early years education. Lively young children, full of energy, seem essentially part of the present, curious to explore the living world around them, nurturing their imagination on stories, particularly those with just a touch of magic and unreality in them. How could the past, which is dead and buried, have any relevance for them?

In this chapter we will consider how we can justify the place of history in teaching and learning in the early years, the skills, knowledge, understanding and attitudes that can be developed through learning history, appropriate resources and activities to promote learning, and how progress can be planned and monitored. We will identify where activities with a historical theme link to the early learning goals for the Foundation Stage and to the programme of study for reception and Years 1 and 2 in the national curriculum as well as addressing the contribution it can make to sound practice and effective teaching and learning.

You may not like the suggestion that 'subjects' should be part of an early years curriculum. Until recently, many practitioners found themselves unable even to use the word 'history', putting forward three main arguments in favour of leaving it aside until the child was much older. Unfortunately these views revealed serious misconceptions about what the subject we call history actually is, but it is worth listing them in order to get them out of the way:

- History is a series of facts and dates that have to be memorised.
- It can only be learned by children who can read history books.

- Young children cannot understand the concept of time, so it is pointless to introduce it in the early years.

In the light of experience, understanding and practice, most modern teachers reject these arguments and recognise the close links between the real discipline of history, which will be examined below, and effective teaching and learning. Exciting classroom displays, learning environments which stimulate further investigation, and resources like oral history, objects and pictures, have enabled teachers to capitalise on the opportunities for developing skills and concepts across the curriculum, including those relating to numeracy and literacy. Many schools, through their history guidelines and policies, have identified what exactly it is they want the children to learn and how they can evaluate, assess and celebrate children's progress and achievement.

What is history?

History is not a body of knowledge about what happened before we were born and not a series of facts that can be learnt by heart. While some events can be dated with a fair degree of accuracy, others cannot. The discipline of history is about analysing the fragments of evidence that people, once alive and with similar human needs and aspirations to our own, left behind. We consider the evidence and have opinions about what it means. From these opinions, history is constructed and the past reconstructed.

Historians, archaeologists and museum professionals reconstruct the past, but so do film makers, novelists and advertisers. Ordinary members of the public have their own way of interpreting the past when they join the Sealed Knot and put on a performance of a civil war battle, dress up to attend an 'Elizabethan banquet' or make bread on a kitchen range in one of the reconstructed communities like the Beamish site in County Durham. Some reconstructions are more accurate than others and debate often rages between heritage purists, conservators, and leisure and tourist interests. Professional historians, revise and reinterpret the work of a previous generation, by looking at new evidence or posing different questions. All these examples highlight the fact that there are no incontrovertible 'right' answers about the past. Questioning and hypothesising lie at the heart of history, and the simple questions are the ones we all want answered whether we are 5 or 50.

Some of these key questions in history are as follows:

- When did these people live?

- What were their lives like?
- How did they feed and clothe themselves?
- What were their homes like?
- What technology did they know about?
- What was the same or different about them and us?
- What happened to them?
- When did things change?
- Why did things change?
- How did things change?
- How do we know?

You will not expect all these questions to be relevant for the youngest children, but each of them can be explored at different levels of understanding. They are a framework around which investigation of the past can be structured. For example, we would expect older children and adults to answer the first question with a date, a century or a period, such as Tudor; in the early years we might be satisfied with the all-pervasive 'in the olden days', but quite soon a more accurate response, such as 'before we were born', 'in the past' or 'twenty years ago' can be applied. The important point to keep in mind is that the methods used by a historian or archaeologist are entirely consistent with the best teaching practice in the early years. The key words are **exploration**, **investigation** and **problem-solving**. Learning objectives should enable the children to both describe and explain the past.

Is history relevant?

When some early years teachers were asked if they would include history in their schemes of work, even if they were not forced to by the national curriculum, the responses received were positive. They gave a number of reasons:

- The importance of subjects concerned with questions like those above.
- The interest value of taking a 'detective' or 'investigator' approach.
- The opportunities for starting with the children's knowledge of themselves, their families and communities, but the potential for extending their horizons, to learn about other people – the product model of the curriculum.
- The links with other areas of the curriculum, through the development of skills, understanding and attitudes – the process model of the curriculum.

They recognised the role of history in the growth of self-esteem, personal identity and social identity. As one early years coordinator commented, 'The sort of history we do is their history and it's a good introduction to a lot of other subjects'.

They further justified it by reference to the children when they first arrive at school. They have enormous energy, but they are usually ego-centric, unpractised in looking beyond themselves and, in some cases, bring anti-social attitudes towards others. Part of the educational objectives of educators in the early years is to help them look beyond themselves, integrate in a group and develop tolerance and social skills. History has a role to play in this programme. The growing awareness that each of us has a past as well as a present and a future extends knowledge of self and is a psychologically healthy sign of developing maturity. Knowledge and understanding of history can help answer the two key questions: 'Who am I?' and 'Where am I?' In the early years, most practitioners think that personal and local history is the most important.

Learning opportunities

History has a language of its own, the language of time, but it is also a vehicle for developing skills and concepts across the curriculum. It helps explain change, similarity and difference, not in a scientific way but in terms of human experience. In the early years, it is the learning process, linked to activities and experiences, which should take priority over any knowledge objectives. Figure 17.1 shows the 'basics' of history as a subject.

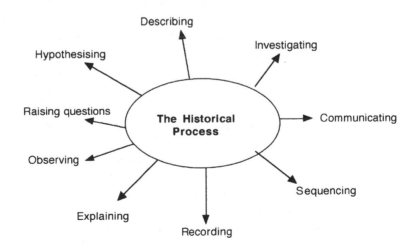

Figure 17.1 *The historical process*

As you look at it, you may like to think about the teaching strategies and resources which would engage 4-, 5- or 6-year-olds in any of the processes and skills listed.

Figure 17.1 is also an affirmation of the central place that talk has in early years classrooms, particularly when teaching about the past. Although the aim is to let the children do most of the talking, it is the teacher who must ensure that there is something interesting to talk about, initiate and sustain the quality of the language, and steer discussion from mere observation and description to investigation and hypothesis. By understanding what history actually is and the uncertainty about conclusions, you will feel comfortable as a teacher when the children raise questions which may not have an immediate answer. Hopefully you will feel able to positively encourage them to pose questions that they would like to know about relating to the topic, object or picture under discussion. As they grow older, they will become familiar with the framework of historical questions, providing there is an agreed policy about their importance in all classes in the school, and will be able to draw up their own historical questions, like those listed above.

You would not, of course, expect all children at every stage to go through the whole range of processes in Figure 17.1, but it is a framework to keep constantly in mind when planning activities in history, so that you will not fall into the trap of thinking that repeating what the teacher says, describing and recording are the only objectives to plan for.

Practical implications of the process model

Let's imagine that an adult, perhaps someone's granny, volunteers to come into the classroom to show the children something old, such as a stoneware hot water bottle. How could even very young children be drawn into the process of learning history? Here are some suggestions for putting the historical process into action. As you read them, think of the opportunities the activity provides for extending the children's vocabulary to include 'historical' language (see below, page 363).

Observing	The hot water bottle would be carefully passed round the group, handled with the help of an adult because of its weight. The children would probably notice the screw top, but might need to have the flat bottom pointed out to them
Describing	Vocabulary would probably include words to describe the colour (brown, grey), the weight (heavy) and the feel (cold). The length and girth could be measured.

Questioning, investigating	The children might ask what it is, where it came from and how it was used. The owner might have a story to tell about how it came into her possession and pointing out the function of the flat bottom, the place where the hot water was poured and how it was secured.
Hypothesising	The children could be asked what they thought it was like to have a hot water bottle like this to warm the bed and why it was necessary. Some children may make guesses about the material from which it is made. Further discussion will develop from those who think it is made of stone or rock. They may also have opinions about why we do not still use them today.
Sequencing	This would only be possible if you had some modern hot water bottles in the classroom (and the children knew what they were). Some may have the cuddly-toy type of warmer which is heated in a microwave oven; others may recognise the traditional rubber bottle.
Explaining	It is an object from the past, when there was no heating in bedrooms. It was last used in the Second World War, more than 50 years ago, when rubber was not available.
Communicating	The children may have more questions or express their opinions about the hot water bottle. All teachers know that it is impossible to predict, with accuracy, just what the children will notice and want to comment on.
Recording	The hot water bottle can be drawn or photographed, with the owner holding it. Four-year-olds will make an impression of the object but 5- and 6-year olds will be able to write some sentences about the bottle and what they have learnt about it. The contributions can be displayed with the object or made up into a book.

You will see how this activity and the framework for learning can be easily adapted to discussion of something like an old toy in Year 1, helping to answer the question posed in the QCA Scheme of Work: 'How are our toys different from those in the past?' (QCA, 1998).

Attitudes

When the teaching and learning is appropriately planned, history has an important contribution to make in the promotion of attitudes to learning and to other people. Figure 17.2 shows some of these.

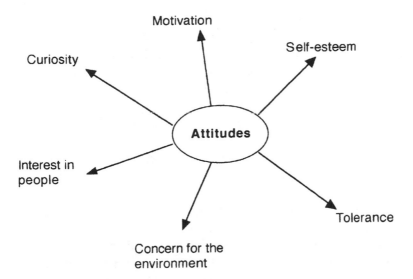

Figure 17.2 *Attitudes promoted by history*

You will not find it difficult to foster interest, enjoyment and curiosity through work in history, providing you provide an active 'hands-on' approach. As a teacher you will find yourself drawn into the excitement of historical detective work, handling objects and listening to reminiscences, and able to pass on this enthusiasm to the children. Some of the other attitudes, however, may have to be deliberately selected and identified in your curriculum planning.

Unfortunately, there is evidence that even small children come to school with values and prejudices towards other people and the environment which are intolerant and anti-social. They include racist attitudes that have been learnt from adults and older siblings at home and in their neighbourhood. They will find that these have no place at school. Of course, education cannot put right the ills in society, but since history is not a subject that deals in fantasy or make-believe but in the lives of people who have actually lived, one can argue that it has a responsibility to put the case for making reasoned and informed judgements, based on evidence.

Historical language

Language empowers, and in order to explain human experiences in the past, with accuracy, the children need to be equipped with vocabulary which encodes meaning. We will begin with the consideration of the language that describes time. There are many ways in which children grow to recognise and understand the passing of time. Talking accurately about *yesterday*, *today* and *tomorrow*, progressing to *last week*, *this week* and *next week*, and then to some understanding of *seasons*, *months*, regular events that happen every year like their *birthdays*, the *summer holidays* and various *festivals*, lay the foundation for describing the past, which is a very big concept indeed for the youngest children. Historical time has its own labels such as *year* and *century*. Where these are a measurement they can be part of the mathematics programme, but unfortunately history also has a series of subject-specific labels, such as *Victorian*. Experience shows, however, that by the age of 7, most children enjoy using the right label and can show that they know what it means, so there is no need to shy away from using the correct terms. It is not in the children's long-term educational interest to persist with labels like *'the olden days'*. They are perfectly able to learn to use *the past* and even the subject label *history*. *Before* and *after* are other concepts that become working components of the young child's vocabulary as they to learn to recognise the sequence of stories and of numbers.

Many teachers introduce historical sequencing by using the photos of the children or their mums when they were babies and discussing how they have changed. A simple timeline can be used to count back in years and language such as 'When I was a baby', 'When I was 2, 3 or 4'. These help explain the passing of time at the young child's level.

The other aspect of historical language which it is appropriate to develop before the age of 7, is the vocabulary to describe old things and age. A brainstorming session with colleagues and friends, or a check in a thesaurus, will reveal a list that can be used to challenge and extend children's language development. Words like *old-fashioned*, *ancient*, *antique*, *decayed*, *worn-out* all have slightly different meanings. They are applied to some things, such as people, but not to others, like buildings. You would not expect everything to be introduced to all children at one time, but knowing what they mean and when they are applied is an essential 'basic' in teaching and learning about the past.

The last group of words are about the key concepts in history – *change and continuity; similarity and difference; cause and consequence*. Of these 'change' and 'difference' most frequently feature in early years history. It is important, however, that you always discuss their binary opposites – 'continuity' and 'similarity' – at the same time. Life in the past may have been different in degree from our own, but what is similar across the barriers of time and culture are human needs for food, clothing, shelter, security and belief. Change does not occur at the same rate in all societies.

It is important not to pass judgement too hastily on other times and cultures, or to use pejorative or evaluative terms like *primitive* or *civilised*. There are still too many people in the world today who do not have access to running water or electric light. Emphasising difference between ourselves and people in the past can be another major pitfall. Care must be taken not to stereotype, but to acknowledge and respect difference. Everyone did not have servants in Victorian times and 'the Tudors' did not all dress like the privileged courtiers whose portraits give us an image of the age.

Continuity is also wide open for discussion. The evidence from the past is all around us. Some of us inhabit houses and schools built a hundred years ago. They have been changed and brought up to date over time, but they remain a living and tangible link with the past. In Britain we frequently celebrate the past, and this includes the popular 'Victorian' school day in primary schools. Even though the concepts of continuity and change are subtle, many young children are able to grasp difficult concepts. What they lack, unless you help provide it, is the language to articulate what they know and understand. It is important to have a framework of language and concepts listed in your school policy document for history, to raise awareness among staff and parents of the stages of knowledge and understanding that will help you support and monitor each child's progress.

Resources

Collecting resources to use in teaching history is not difficult or expensive and we can conveniently classify them under six headings:

- People
- Pictures
- Objects
- Historical sites and museums
- Local environment
- Books

We might also include music, but this needs other resources, such as an old radio or record player, to make it meaningful. Popular songs also have a place under the heading people, particularly when they come as part of an older person's memories.

What follows is a discussion of issues related to the use of these various resources, some of which are illustrated by reference to a delightful local history project carried out by children at Harborne Infant School, Birmingham (Mauser and Reid, 1990).

People

Oral history or reminiscence is one of the approaches most valued by early years educators. Its merit is that it is a contribution to history at school which children and families can make themselves. It is accessible and language-based, and need not come as English, if some groups within the class all have the same mother-tongue. It is easy to organise if you call on the school community and their contacts first. You do not need to restrict yourself to finding someone elderly or retired since everyone has a life story to tell and even 'young' people are old to a 5- or 6-year-old. Oral history is a winner in the classroom and makes an impact because it brings in a perspective on the past that is immediate, personal and alive. The Mrs Rainbow referred to in the title of this chapter was a real person (see Figure 17.3), even though her attractive name could have been a fictional invention.

When the children meet or interview someone, it is not necessary or desirable to draw up a rigid questionnaire, as you want to encourage the visitor to tell their story as a narrative. However, we are assuming that you

Figure 17.3 *'Mrs Rainbow told us what things were like when she was at school'*

will focus the session around a topic, and that you will have discussed this with the interviewee so that you can tell the children before they arrive the purpose behind the interview. Most people can easily talk about their schooldays, their family life, their homes and journeys they have made. The children at Harborne Infant School interviewed past teachers about their memories of the school. The children asked questions reflecting their own interests, such as:

- What time did school start and finish?
- Did you have dinner at school?
- What was your favourite dinner?
- Did you have drinks at school?
- What lessons did you have?
- What games did you play with your friends in the playground?

Having more than one contribution on the same theme can be a positive bonus, since you will have different versions of the past which the children can discuss, describe, compare and explain. For example, everyone had a childhood, but the experiences they talk about will depend how long ago it was, where it was, the size and extent of the family, gender and social class.

The oral history interview becomes more valuable in association with other historical sources such as photographs, objects or places. The history of the school, for example, will make more sense for little children if they can walk round the building, look at old school photographs and hear what it was like 10, 20 or 50 years ago from a former pupil or member of staff.

If you have a particularly good interviewee, one who talks to the point and at the children's level, you may decide to record them. This sounds useful, but you are unlikely to get the same attention from the children listening to a recording, unless they are also part of it, as you will from a real person in the classroom. It is also possible for the children, perhaps working in pairs, to make transcripts of their interviews (see Figure 17.4).

Pictures

Pictures of unfamiliar people and places from the past are also invaluable. They too will make the past accessible, giving something to look at, talk about and compare. The advantages of using old photographs or paintings of familiar situations such as shopping or travelling are obvious and enable the children to work out for themselves what was the same and what was different about then and now. Figure 17.5 shows a good example of this kind of comparison from the Harborne Infant School project.

Most county libraries and local museums collect old photographs and

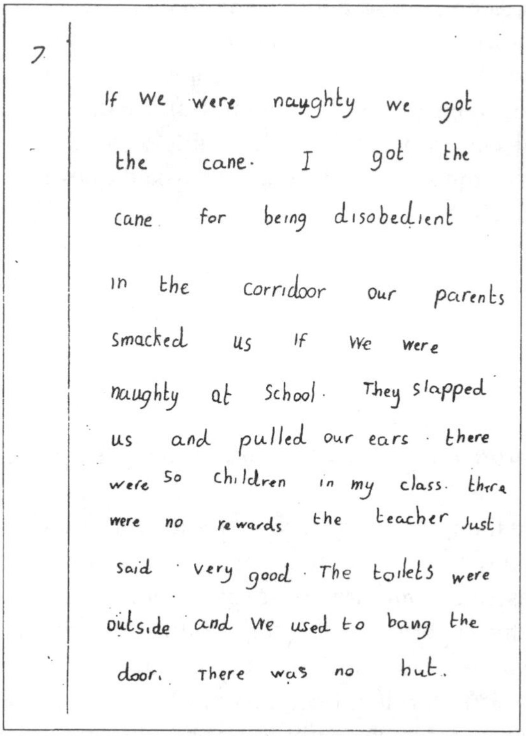

> 7.
>
> If We were naughty we got the cane. I got the cane for being disobedient
>
> In the corridoor our parents smacked us If We were naughty at School. They slapped us and pulled our ears · there were So children in my class. thera were no rewards the teacher Just said · very good · The toilets were outside and We used to bang the door. There was no hut.

Figure 17.4 *Transcript of an interview with an ex-pupil of Harborne Infant School*

can supply prints. You may also find useful material through a web-based image search facility. You will want to select clear images, such as scenes of the milkman with his horse and cart, or the ice-cream vendor on his tricycle, but there are often family groups in collections, which have unfortunately become separated from the families to which they once belonged. These show details of clothes, hair styles, gardens and objects, and have the kind of detail in them that will enable children to pick out features about the past for themselves.

Objects

Objects can be collected as a result of an appeal to parents and friends, as well as from car boot sales and charity shops. Like the invitation to come into school for an oral history interview, parents and friends can be asked to bring in an old object to talk about, as described in the case of the hot water bottle above. Objects collected by you can be touched and handled and presented to the children as mystery objects, in role-play activities similar to the *Antiques Road Show*. They can form valuable contributions to topics

MRs PoRters Room

1923   1989

The desks have changed.
In the old photograph there are
Flowers and there aren't any
Flowers in the new photogrph.
In the new photograph the boys have
different shoes then the
ones in the old photograph.
they both have a radictar.
Mrs porters class room has changed
a lot. the windows are the
same. The old photograph was taken
in 1923 and the new
photogrnaph was taken in 1989

Figure 17.5 *The use of an old photograph of a familiar situation*

like light, food and homes, and can be put on display with their modern equivalents.

Historical sites and museums

You will find good examples of museum visiting with early years pupils in teachers' guides such as those from the Ironbridge Gorge Museum (Forber, undated, 1990). The success of the visits described here was almost certainly because the children were able to enter a reconstructed domestic environment; they could understand the context and make comparisons with their own experiences. A poor museum experience, however, for example where objects are in high glass cases, or where a lot of reading is involved in order to understand the display, is not really worth the effort, with very young children.

It is crucial that you make contact with a curator or education officer and assess the learning outcomes yourself, before booking a visit. The children will need to be well prepared and to have practised the skills – such as close observation of objects, sketching and labeling – that they will need to use in the museum. It is a good idea to go prepared to look closely at one area, painting or object, not the whole museum. Where you do have a suitable museum near your school, consider building visits, activities and areas into your whole-school policy for history, so that the children can consolidate any early years experience as they progress up the school.

Local environment

You may be in an area of old buildings, even at school in one! If your ancient building does not present any hazards, such as road safety, then it may provide an ideal resource for many of the skills discussed earlier in the chapter, for accurate use of historical vocabulary and for drawing up a diagram of historical questions about the building. In terms of schools, the oral history potential is enormous, as can be seen from the work done at Harborne Infant School. However, oral history is of no use in either Ironbridge or in a castle, although both can become suitable places for young children to learn.

Books

Books also have a place in resources for teaching history in the early years. Familiar stories like *Grandpa* by John Burningham, *The Sandal* by Tony Bradman and Philippe Dupasquier, and *Peepo* by Janet and Allan Ahlberg are about history, and other good examples can be found in the Further

Reading section at the end of the chapter. The best bring a past perspective to familiar early years themes and use historical sources like oral history, pictures and objects to bring the past alive.

A variety of resources will contribute to the quality of teaching and learning in the early years, but cannot guarantee it. Resources are only of use when used in a planned scheme of work with a definite purpose in mind.

Activities

Below are listed some suggested activities for young children which can be adapted to particular historical projects.

Activities related to play

- Dressing up can be fun and related to the past by reference to pictures or oral memories.
- Food can be made, for example, favourite dishes parents and older friends ate when they were children.
- Feely boxes can also be used to identify again the old objects like flat irons or candlesticks that have already become familiar from a classroom display.
- Kim's game – old objects on a tray which you have to remember – will require both concentration and memory and again make your resources work for you in different situations.

Nursery songs and stories

- Many nursery songs and rhymes like 'Ride a cock horse', 'Three blind mice' or 'Ring a ring of roses' describe an aspect of life in the past.
- Stories like those mentioned above and others from different cultural traditions are a rich source of cultural and ethnic heritage.

Sorting

- Sort the objects, with modern equivalents, into categories, such as: age or ownership, e.g. *indoors, outdoors; men, women, children; town, country, sea-side*. Relate them to a room where they were used, e.g. *kitchen, classroom, parlour* (discuss the label and how it has changed).
- Sort them according to the material from which they are made, constructing descriptive phrases which can later be incorporated into sentences, e.g. *the felt hat, the leather suitcase, the iron kettle*.
- Sort them into categories for display in the class museum. Write the labels and invite parents and other children to visit the museum.

Detective work

- Make time for the children to speculate about objects, pictures and buildings and for them to pose their own questions such as 'I would like to know . . .'.
- Introduce a collection of objects as a detective exercise by inventing a story about Granny's suitcase and what the contents tell us about her life.
- Use old photographs to 'work out' three things about the people or place in the past. What was *different* about their lives and ours? What has changed?

Time and sequence

- Use buildings around the school – you can take your own photographs of them when you go on a walk – to provide practice with sequencing activities. To begin with you might just use two categories, *now* and *then*, or *past* and *present*, but some children by the age of 7 will be able to sort objects and buildings into centuries.
- Use pictures or postcards to put *homes, clothes* or *transport* into a time order.
- Use strips of paper or washing lines and pegs to arrange the children's drawings or photographs of the locality in a chronological order.

Change

- Use pictures, objects, buildings and oral history to work out not only *what* has changed but *why* and *how*. There is a hierarchy within these questions, moving from what can be seen to analysis and comparison. The questions demand thought and deduction, not just a retelling of information that has been given by the teacher.

Oral history

Information generated in an oral history interview can be used in many ways:

- Make a book with the interviewee and their memories as the subject.
- Discuss why the book is a history book, or non-fiction book. What is the difference between the story of Mrs Rainbow, who actually came into school, and Mairi Hedderwick's fictional story of Morag and the two grandmothers?
- Listen again to the recording of the interview with the visitor. Compare this with the account members of the class wrote about what she said.
- Draw pictures based on what the visitor told them (see example from Harborne Infant School in Figure 17.6).

In the old days the toilets used to be by the Junior gate but now thay are by the hall and not by the gate. This is what might have looked I think it like.

Figure 17.6 *The Harborne Infant School toilets 'in the old days'*

- Round up the book with a special section on change, e.g. the *visitor* then and now, the *area* around the school and *how things were done*. This moves the task on beyond description to explanation and analysis.

The early learning goals

Taking the approach outlined above, historical experiences and activities can be a vehicle for advancing both the underlying principles for early years education and for enriching the areas of learning. The Foundation Stage *Curriculum Guidance* (QCA, 2000) includes a specific recommendation to use the local community and environment as a source for learning. The local community will be the main resource for oral history and discussion of old buildings in the local area will lead to greater understanding of the children's immediate surroundings. Activities suggested in the personal, social and emotional development area of learning include examples of interaction with other people and a growing sense of belonging in a place, a family and a community. The use of questions, vocabulary extension, connecting ideas, understanding, and explaining and solving problems all come within the communication, language and literacy remit. Awareness of the differences in age between different generations becomes an early mathematical concept, and importance is placed on the use of tangible objects in understanding the world in which we live. Things used by previous generations and how they have changed will contribute to knowledge and understanding of the world.

Pointers for teaching history in the early years

- Be aware of the contribution history makes to the growth of personal and social identity.
- Ensure that activities and discussion promote investigation and enquiry.
- Develop language relating to time and open-ended discussion, which helps children explain as well as describe the past.
- Collect and display resources which children can handle (objects), talk about (books and pictures) and listen to (memories of older people, old rhymes and songs).
- Have a policy for history that identifies progression in skills, knowledge and understanding, and which promotes positive attitudes to history.

Acknowledgements

We are grateful to Diane Humphreys, early years coordinator at Arbury Primary School, Cambridge, for talking over many of these findings with us.

References

Forber, D. (ed.) (undated) *Under-Fives and Museums: Guidelines for Teachers*, Telford: Ironbridge Gorge Museum Trust.

Forber, D. (ed.) (1990) *Primary Schools and Museums: Key Stage 1*, Telford: Ironbridge Gorge Museum Trust.

Mauser, M. and Reid, S. (1990) *Harborne Infant School Local History Project*, Birmingham: Education Dept., Birmingham City Council.

QCA (1998) *A Scheme of Work for Key Stages 1 and 2: History*, London: QCA.

QCA (1999) *The National Curriculum*, London: QCA.

QCA (2000) *Curriculum Guidance for the Foundation Stage*, London: QCA.

Further reading

Brodie, A. (2005) *Seaside Holidays in the Past*, Swindon: English Heritage.

Durban, G. (1990) *Learning from Objects*, Swindon: English Heritage.

Fairclough, J. (1994) *History through Role Play*, Swindon: English Heritage.

Purkis, S.(1991, revised 2000) *A Sense of History: Key Stage One Teachers' Book*, Harlow: Pearson Education.

Purkis, S. (2000) *A Sense of History: Key Stage 1 Co-ordinator's Handbook*, Harlow: Pearson Education.

Wright, M. (1992, revised 2004) *The Really Practical Guide to Primary History*, Cheltenham: Stanley Thornes.

CHAPTER 18

'If the world is round, how come the piece I'm standing on is flat?'

EARLY YEARS GEOGRAPHY

Dianne Conway, Pam Pointon and Jayne Greenwood

What is geography? Why teach geography?

One of the aims of the Foundation Stage curriculum is to develop in children an awareness of their place in the world and to help them to make sense of it. This results in geography being central to early learning and apparent in all six areas of learning while being at the heart of 'Knowledge and Understanding of the World'. We use the term 'geography' in this chapter to highlight the experiences and skills that are essentially geographical but often set within the context of other areas of learning and Key Stage 1 curriculum.

That geography is such a wide-ranging subject, which attempts to make connections between the earth sciences and the social sciences, is its strength (which other subject tries to connect the human and natural worlds to the same extent?) – but also its difficulty in common-sense understanding. How many people, if asked to explain what geography is, would refer to trivial pursuits knowledge of countries and their capital cities, naming of capes and bays, listing of major rivers and mountain ranges? Locational knowledge is obviously an important element of geography but if it is merely factual recall then the potential contribution is sadly diminished.

The current, more sophisticated approach includes a much broader view of what geography is about and a more active style of learning which engages children in observation, investigation, analysis and interpretation, and encourages their development as young geographers. At the heart of the subject is its focus on both people and places through active exploration of their immediate environment. Their growing sense of 'their own special places' and curiosity about 'other places' is influenced by a range of experiences – both direct and vicarious through film, television, stories, music, computer games, CD-Roms, etc., as illustrated in the useful model by Goodey (1973).

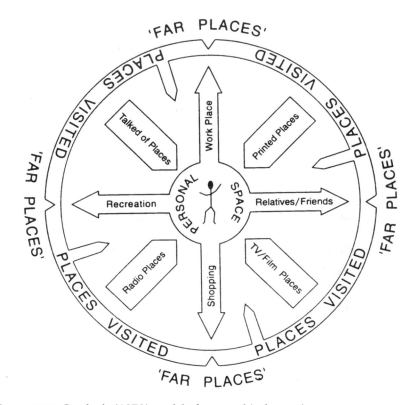

Figure 18.1 *Goodey's (1973) model of geographical experiences*

Developing learning experiences which extend the young child's knowledge and stimulates their curiosity about the wider world is important. The starting point, however, needs to be their perception of their own personal space. This is unique to them and their perceptions may be influenced by a range of variables including age, gender, class, ethnicity, disability. Young children are able to articulate thoughts and feelings about places which have meaning for them and can forcefully express their likes/ dislikes of particular features in their environment, as shown by this conversation between two 6-year-olds on a visit to the city:

I don't think I'd like to live in those flats. I wouldn't have a garden to play in. I think those small houses over there would be better.

Oh no. I'd rather live in the flat. The view would be great and there would be a lift to go in. Those houses are very small and squashed together.

The argument continued along similar lines for quite a while. The group were able to appreciate that everyone has their own point of view and that these views may differ. They were able to see that sometimes there are no right or wrong answers.

Broad aims for geographical education

Geography for Ages 5 to 16 (DES, 1990) set out the following broad aims for geographical education. It should:

- stimulate pupils' interests in their surroundings and in the variety of physical and human conditions on the earth's surface;
- foster their sense of wonder at the beauty of the world around them;
- help them to develop an informed concern about the quality of the environment and the future of the human habitat;
- and thereby enhance their sense of responsibility for care of the earth and its peoples.

These broad aims need to be achieved through a range of teaching objectives which may be subdivided into those concerned with skills, knowledge and understanding, and values and attitudes (see Table 18.1).

Geographical enquiry

Pupils should not be primarily passive recipients of information but should be given adequate opportunities to carry out practical investigations, to explore and express ideas in their own language . . . and to reflect on other peoples' attitudes and values.

(DES, 1986)

Involving young children in effective enquiry helps them to understand geographical concepts, develop geographical skills and explore the importance of values and attitudes in making sense of an increasingly complex and rapidly changing world.

What does enquiry involve?

Table 18.1 Aims for geographical education

Skills	Knowledge and understanding
• *Graphicacy* – the making, using and reading of maps; using globes and atlases; use of photographs, diagrams, graphs	• general locational knowledge
	• specific locational knowledge, e.g. local area, contrasting localities
• *Fieldwork and enquiry skills* – observation, investigation, analysis and interpretation of primary and secondary sources	• understanding key concepts:
	location – where is this place/feature in relation to other places/features?
Values and attitudes	*patterns* – what is this place like? how are its building, parks, shops, etc. organised?
• an interest in other people and places	*relationships* – connections **between different** elements within a place, e.g. where people live and where people shop, etc.
• awareness and appreciation of cultural and ethnic diversity within UK and beyond	*processes* – underlying reasons/causes for patterns and relationships which exist in the environment (local and global scale) and how they change over time
• concern for quality of environments	
• concern to value and conserve resources	*similarity and difference* – how is this place/feature similar/different to other places/features?
• awareness of different perspectives on environmental issues	

- asking questions;
- planning an investigation;
- carrying out the investigation;
- evaluating the conclusions.

Enquiries can be of different lengths (one lesson to a whole term), of different foci (an issue, a place or a theme) and at different scales (local to global). Identifying geographical questions can be a useful initial stage in planning an enquiry. There are seven key geographical questions which provide a framework for enquiry, each question can be a focus for an entire enquiry and further sub-questions developed:

- Where is this place?
- What is this place like?
- Why is this place as it is?
- How is this place connected to other places?
- How is this place changing?
- What is it like to be in this place?
- How is this place similar to or different from another place?

A sample enquiry is shown in Figure 18.2 (Curriculum Council for Wales, 1991).

This next section offers a range of learning activities and useful resources for developing the young geographers' understanding of their world. The case study of 'Teddy's Visit' usefully highlights how an enquiry approach can be used to explore the local area and develop a real 'sense of place'.

Developing map skills through play

All children enter school with some understanding and use of mapping skills. These skills have developed informally, directly from the child's experience. They are the result of activity and movement in and familiarity with the environment. These skills include an ability to:

- remember and find where objects are at home, e.g. their toys;
- remember where features are in the local area and take you or direct you to them, e.g. the swings;
- find their way around their immediate environment, e.g. home, class-room, familiar play area;
- talk about going to places that are some distance away, e.g. the seaside, my gran's, on a train, to London.

	Key questions	Activities
Initial perception	What is it? What do I feel about it?	*Exploring* the beach – a sensory walk *Describing* – is it warm/cold/ exciting/dull?
Description and definition	What is it like?	*Collecting* – pebbles/rocks/sand/ shells Taking photographs, drawing pictures *Observing/counting* – different shops, building
Analysis and exploration	How do people use the beach? Why do they go there?	*Analysing* activities *Analysing* postcards *Explaining* why the seaside is a good place for these activities

This partial enquiry sequence could be followed by:

Collecting artefacts – children bring into school pictures, souvenirs, postcards, photographs of seaside resorts.

Comparing similarities and differences – using artefacts and personal experiences, are all the seaside resorts the same? If not how do they differ?

Questioning/finding out about a contrasting resort – children discuss what they would like to find out about a Spanish holiday resort. In groups they construct four or five questions to ask. Children invite a visitor who has been to a Spanish holiday resort and ask questions: e.g. What is the beach like? What sort of food do you eat? What do people do there? What is the weather like? What sorts of shops are there?

Figure 18.2 *Exploring the seaside: a geographical enquiry (from Curriculum Council for Wales, 1991, p. 42)*

The most successful work will build on each child's spatial awareness and understanding, and will acknowledge their experience in movement and spatial language. Much of it arises spontaneously out of traditional good practice in the early years classroom. It is important to recognise these opportunities to develop mapping skills and to think carefully about how to help children understand more from activities they naturally enjoy. Many of the activities outlined below happen in many early years classrooms as a matter of course.

Developing geographical vocabulary

It is important to emphasise the *where* in talking with children, encouraging them to be precise about direction and location in relation to themselves, others and objects around.

- Reading stories such as *Rosie's Walk* reinforces positional language.
- Encourage children to use locational vocabulary: 'It's behind . . .', 'It's next to . . .', 'It's in front of . . .', rather than 'It's there'.
- Play games such as 'I spy', where children have to name objects where the clue may be: 'It's beside a table in front of the window next to the flowers'.
- When directing children to a resource in the classroom give them directions using direction words; 'Go past the bookshelf, turn left, it is next to the red table'.
- Play games in pairs where the children have to give directions to identify objects or make journeys round the room.
- Encourage the children to give directions. Ask 'Who knows where the . . . is?' If telling is difficult ask children to show others where things are.
- Use pictures, posters, videos, computer images to introduce vocabulary that it is not possible to experience first hand, e.g. mountains, rivers, beaches, etc.

Thinking about distances

Mapping is about how far away things are. The children should be encouraged to think about distances and to make comparisons.

- When giving directions use positional vocabulary: 'It's near the table', 'It's on the other side of the room from . . .'.
- Make comparisons of longer and shorter around the classroom and school.
- Ask 'Is it further to walk to the cloakroom or to the hall?' Ask the children to find out if they are correct.

- When making journeys talk about whether you are 'getting nearer' the destination and 'further away' from the starting point.

  Children can talk about and draw places and things that are:

  Near – you can see it and go over and touch it.
  Quite near – you could walk to it.
  Further away – you need to make a journey by transport to there.
  A long way – you have to go overseas to get to it.
  A very long way – a different area of the world.
  A very, very, long way – space.

Using miniature world play

The activities outlined above can all be transferred to and developed further by using play equipment found in all early years classrooms.

- Wet sand can be transformed into a landscape with model houses and trees for play-people to live in, making a small-world scene that can be viewed from above and from the sides.
- Playmats of road layouts and farm layouts are representations of reality in pictorial form. They allow children to look down on a landscape and make journeys.
- Construction toys on various scales can be used to model environments in which journeys can be made.
- The doll's house provides another miniature environment where positional language can be encouraged.
- Programmable toys such as Pip', 'Roamer' or 'Floor Turtle' can be used to make journeys and create environments.

Using plans and pictures

Photographs taken looking vertically down on objects and places interest young children. Take photographs of objects looking vertically down: the bin, chairs, toys, everyday objects, man-hole covers – anything you see. Can the children match the photograph to the object? Or draw the shapes of the object on card and ask the children to match the shape to the photograph.

- Send the children off to find the object in the photograph.
- Encourage the children to draw their own overhead or bird's eye view of classroom objects.

These activities lead easily into discussions about a bird's-eye view of school or the locality, and the introduction of vertical aerial photographs and plans of the school building.

Using maps

Young children are fascinated by maps of any sort. Many children enter school with experience of a variety of maps:

- the weather map on television;
- pictorial maps from theme parks, holiday resorts, zoos, forest trails, etc.
- maps on postcards;
- the road atlas and maybe a street map.

The early years educator can build on this experience by introducing a wide variety of maps, including the more conventional ones (see the list in Figure 18.3).

A school should have copies of Ordnance Survey (OS) maps of the locality:

street maps	building plans
postcard maps	road maps
maps in adverts	road sign maps
housing estate maps	house plans
tourist area maps	town centre maps
Ordnance Survey maps	trail maps
railway maps	bus route maps
room plans	storybook maps
board game maps	atlas maps
textbook maps	guidebook maps
wall chart maps	teacher drawn maps
maps drawn by children	picture maps
land use maps	'antique' maps
resort maps	sketch maps
playmat maps	newspaper maps
building site plans	globes
teaching pack maps	walkers' maps
aerial photomaps	airline route maps
jigsaw maps	mazes
theme park maps	tea towel maps
underground maps	

Figure 18.3 *Types of maps to show young children*

1 : 50,000 – 2cm on the map represents 1km on the ground.
1 : 25,000 – 4cm on the map represents 1km on the ground.
1 : 10,000 – 1cm on the map represents 100m on the ground.
1 : 2,500 – 1cm on the map represents 25m on the ground.
1 : 1,250 – 1cm on the map represents 12.5m on the ground.

Maps can be included in many activities. The youngest children will need help with orientation. Even if this is difficult, just handling the map is worthwhile.

A school plan can be used for journeys around school, for familiarisation or to carry messages. Groups of children, under the supervision of an adult, can be asked to try to follow a route marked on a school plan as a treasure hunt or an adventure game.

Street plans or Ordnance Survey maps can be used for walks in the local environment or planning the route the postman might take to deliver letters to the children's homes.

Aerial photographs of the local area, both vertical and oblique, can be used alongside local conventional maps. Encourage children to talk about what they see in the picture, and to recognise from where it was taken.

Pictorial maps and theme park maps from holidays and weekend visits are usually attractively presented and give children lots of ideas for creating maps of their own.

The road atlas is often one of the most popular books in the book corner. It gives exciting opportunities for discussion amongst the children. Unfortunately many atlases quickly fall apart. Regular requests to parents for their out-of-date road atlases, particularly the hardback ones, need to be made. The following observations were made while watching a mixed Year 1/Year 2 class working with atlases:

One 7-year-old was observed engrossed in the atlas for quite a long time. When asked what he was doing his reply was: 'I'm planning the route for my holiday in Cornwall'. When asked to show the teacher the route, he proceeded to find Cambridge and work his way through the atlas following the instructions to move to the next page until he arrived at the page showing Cornwall. A discussion followed about the different road colours shown on the map and he was able to pick out the motorways.

Another group of children were to be found poring over the atlas after a coach trip to a small village 15 miles from school. They had identified the correct page and were soon able to find the village. They then spent a while trying to guess which route the coach had taken.

The children discovered for themselves the index and how to use it. They very quickly learned how to look up the name of a place that they knew or had visited and find the correct page in the atlas.

The map of the British Isles is familiar to most young children even if they do not know exactly what it is. It is seen on the weather forecast regularly. A video of several weather forecasts is a useful tool not only when thinking about the weather but also when learning the countries of Great Britain. Most weather forecasters mention and point to the countries as they make their forecast.

The children enjoyed looking at a British Isles wall map and soon learned to spot the nearest large town, the nearest major river and where it reached the coast. They asked about the shading on the map and could think of places where there were hills and mountains.

A globe creates a great deal of discussion and is a source of fascination to young children. Every classroom should have access to one (see Figure 18.4).

Figure 18.4 *'If the world is round, how come the piece I'm standing on is flat?'*

A world map can be used for discussing places children have visited and countries in the news. Giving children opportunities to experience maps of a variety of sizes and scales helps children to understand that maps 'shrink' the real world to fit it onto paper. Large land use atlases are very popular with young children.

All formal maps represent features in plan view, or looking down from directly above. There are many opportunities to give children these experiences through real situations, such as satellite images of Earth from space using Google Earth. Books such as *Owl Babies* provide fictional plans, but nevertheless ones that young children can relate to.

Making maps

Drawing is another way of representing and trying to understand movement, location and distance. Many drawings done by young children show relationships between features, for instance, parts of the body or homes and streets. Map work should involve drawing, painting, making collages and modelling.

- Place objects on the surface of an overhead projector and view the plan view image on the screen.
- Children could draw or paint their route to school. They should be encouraged to remember landmarks and other details (see Figure 18.5).
- Drawings can be made of layouts created with playmats and construction toys such as Lego.
- 'Junk model' representations of the classroom, parts of the school, or the locality can be made. The children can finger walk routes and talk about them or even record them on paper.
- Children could be encouraged to make their own playmats and miniature worlds to use with Playmobile or Lego people and cars.
- Many children are inspired by the idea of making treasure maps
- Creating symbols to label places in the classroom, e.g. computer, book corner, sand tray, etc. helps children to understand that symbols on a map represent a feature.

Using stories

Children's stories often involve journeys and things happening in places, e.g. *Rosie's Walk*, 'Little Red Riding Hood' and many more. Stories need not be confined to story-time! They can be used as a source of geographical information to set alongside fieldwork or mapping activities. They introduce young children to people, places and ideas. They contribute to

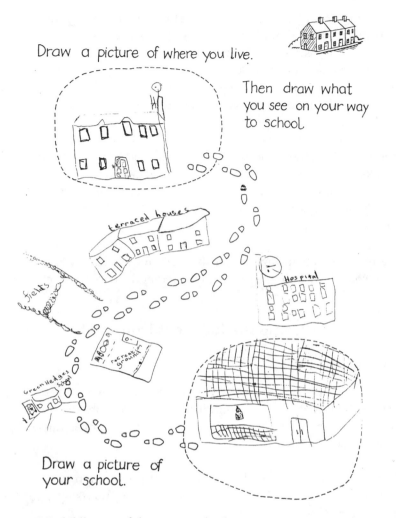

Draw a picture of where you live.

Then draw what you see on your way to school

terraced houses

fields

Hospital

recreation ground

Green Hedges School

Draw a picture of your school.

Figure 18.5 *A child's map of the way to school*

children's understanding of and participation in the world around them. They help to foster children's curiosity about their changing world, e.g. *Where the Forest Meets the Sea*.

- Some stories have maps provided by the author or artist. These can be enlarged so that the route can be followed whist the story is read.
- If there is no map, either you or the children can create one, either small individual ones or a big wall frieze.
- Fairy stories provide rich opportunities for children to create either individual plans or collaborative maps.

- The story could be acted out, creating an imaginary map or using furniture to represent the physical environment.
- Divide a large-scale, child-created plan of a story setting (e.g. 'The Three Bears') into sections (black pen or string) to create a simple grid. Give each section a number or letter and introduce the idea of simple location grids by asking questions using maps such as 'Which square is the park in?'.
- Stories such as 'We're Going on a Bear Hunt' can be acted out and will reinforce the understanding of various physical environments.
- Books such as *Dinosaurs and All That Rubbish* and *Where the Forest Meets the Sea* present environmental issues in an accessible story setting.
- The book 'Window' provides an opportunity to discuss how a local area changes over time.

More ideas for using stories can be found in *Place in Story-time* (Nicholson, 1994). Suitable stories are listed at the end of this chapter.

Using the local environment

Observational walks

Most children, and indeed many adults, are not used to observing their environment closely. It is a good idea to encourage observation when out and about on any visit. Observation skills can be taught as fun activities to the youngest children.

- When out on a walk, look for, count and photograph various items of street furniture, post boxes, telephone boxes, bus stops, road signs, traffic, etc.
- Look at physical features: rivers, hills and farmland or buildings of different types and their use.

Using photographs taken on an observational walk

- Identify the location of photographs taken around the classroom, school grounds or locality.
- Using happy and sad face symbols, ask the children to sort photographs into features they like/do not like. Can they say why?
- Use red counters to place on photographs that the children consider represent dangerous features and green for safe areas.

Choosing a context for a local geographical study

The same principles apply to selecting a geographical theme as to any other area of study.

- Is it relevant and accessible to the children?
- Does it offer the opportunity to work from first-hand experience?
- Does it build on previous experience and knowledge?
- Will it enable the children to ask questions and search for answers?
- Can it be adequately resourced?

Young children should begin their geographical study in their immediate environment around themes such as 'Our School', 'Our Village'. 'Journeys', 'Where I Live', 'Homes', 'A Place to Live' or 'People Who Help Us'. For the older Key Stage 1 children many of these themes can be extended to include localities further afield, for example, the nearest city or a smaller village.

Many of the practical ideas given earlier in this chapter can be used in these themes. A geographical-based theme usually allows study in a cross-curricular way. There are opportunities for work in all areas of the curriculum. Below are two examples of cross-curricular projects that can be included in any locality study.

The picnic

This project involves the children asking questions and considering various possible solutions. It gives opportunities to cover areas of maths and technology as well as geography. There is also some consideration of health issues.

- Where shall we go for our picnic?
- How shall we get there?
- Which route will we take?

A local map is found. The children discuss various local picnic spots. They consider transport and maybe costs. A route is planned.

- Could we go by one route and return a different way?
- Whose route is the quickest or the most interesting?

Then comes the most important set of questions:

- What food shall we eat?

- Which foods are good to eat on a picnic?
- Where can we buy the food we need?

The children plan a walk to the local shop to find the answers. They return with some answers but also with more questions.

- How much of everything do we need to buy?
- Can we bake some cakes and biscuits ourselves?
- What will we put our picnic in?
- Could we design a lunch box?

A list of food is drawn up and each child decides what they would like. The data is gathered and sorted into a shopping list. A request is sent home for the money to cover the cost of the shopping. Recipes are found, ingredients listed, help with cooking is requested. Now there are more questions.

- When shall we go on our picnic?
- When shall we make the cakes?
- When shall we buy the ingredients to make the cakes?
- Can we buy all our food then?
- If not, when do we need to buy the other food for the picnic?

Then it's off to the shop again for the cooking ingredients.

- Perhaps we could find a different route to the shop?
- How long does it take?
- Is it a longer route than last time?

The baking is done. More shopping lists are planned and prepared so that every child can do some of the shopping. It is a good idea to warn the shop that 30 young shoppers will be coming. Try not to choose a busy time of day or delivery day. With 15 lists prepared, 30 children set off to the shop clutching their shopping bags and money.

- What do I do first when I go into the shop?
- How can I find what I want?
- How much does it cost?
- Where do I pay?
- Do I get any change? How much?

On the day of the picnic the bread is buttered, sandwiches and drink are made. Then 30 excited children carrying lunch boxes and maps set off for the picnic spot. If it is a local park or playground there could be a discussion about the play equipment, more observation work, and consideration of the quality of the environment. As a follow-up task the children could be asked to design their own play area and maybe make a model.

By using books like *Sam's Sandwich* and *Sam's Snack* by David Pelham, the children can be encouraged to write and create their own such books.

Teddy's visit

This activity is rather like a story that unfolds and develops as the weeks go by. The ideas for activities have all been tried out by a mixed Year 1/Year 2 class. Some activities can be used by younger children.

The story begins one morning when a small suitcase or bag is found on a chair in the classroom. It has a large label saying:

'Please look after this bear'.

Inside is a small teddy bear. He has a map and a message with him saying that he is lost and needs help to find out which country he is in and to mark his location on the map (see Figure 18.6).

Figure 18.6 *The lost teddy bear*

The map is photocopied and everyone tries to help Teddy out. Teddy spends time with each group as they work.

The next day there is another message from Teddy saying he would like to be shown round the school. So groups of children armed with route maps take him around. On another occasion he asks the children to write about themselves so that he can get to know them. His next request is to be taken on a walk around the neighbourhood. There is another session with the maps and some route planning to make sure Teddy sees all the important parts of the area around school. Teddy is carefully carried in various pockets. He must not get lost again!

He might even request a picnic as a treat, and so we get into planning a picnic as discussed above.

Then one morning Teddy is not in his bag. He has left a note (see Figure 18.7) to say he is hiding and the children are to follow the instructions to find him but they must keep his hiding place a secret.

This game can go on for several days with different hiding places. The children can devise their own instructions to new hiding places. Eventually Teddy grows tired of the classroom and asks the children to take him home to their house to play. But before they can take him they must be able to fill in their address on his label, just in case he gets lost again! While he is visiting them they are asked to do some tasks:

- read Teddy the story book in his bag;
- get a grown-up to read the harder story book to them both;
- write Teddy's diary so he can remember his visit;
- draw a route map of how to get back to school. He might get lost!

Teddy might accompany the children on other trips and visits that the class make. If it is possible he might request a ride on a train or a bus. During his stay, of course, he likes to hear stories about teddy bears, either real books or those stories written by the children. In the end Teddy receives a letter inviting him to visit a relative in another country. So out come the maps. Teddy is helped to plan his journey, his bag is labelled and then one night he disappears.

The class became very involved with Teddy. They were enthusiastic about the tasks he gave them. They were very concerned when he really did get lost! On one walk about he was dropped in a puddle and was left out to dry on a radiator overnight. The caretaker, thinking he had been left by a younger child, put him in the lost property bin. The search the next day was frantic. Teddy was well hugged when he returned.

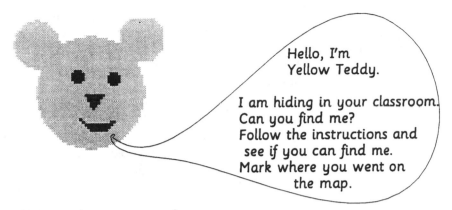

Start at the tape recorder -

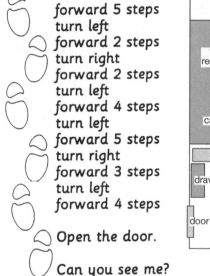

forward 5 steps
turn left
forward 2 steps
turn right
forward 2 steps
turn left
forward 4 steps
turn left
forward 5 steps
turn right
forward 3 steps
turn left
forward 4 steps

Open the door.

Can you see me?

SSHH....Don't tell anyone.

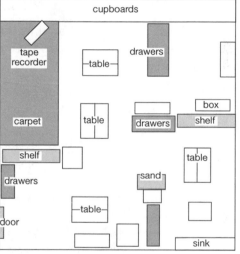

Figure 18.7 *Instructions to find Teddy*

The children were particularly keen to take Teddy home. They learned their addresses quickly. His diary was carefully written. The parents played their part well and shared the children's tasks. Teddy was included in lots of the children's activities: parties, 5 November fireworks in the city, TV, computer games and meals out. There were lots of talking opportunities the next day. Even the shy children had something to say.

So geography is fun. It is happening and probably has been happening in early years classrooms for many years. Young children are fascinated by their surroundings and have the capacity to build upon natural learning experiences. Through topics like those outlined above, young children will learn from first-hand experience that there is a relationship between people and places, and that they themselves can have an influence on the environment. It is important to recognise that many of the things we do have geographical possibilities. A geographical topic gives good opportunities for cross-curricular work in many subjects.

Pointers for early years geography

The following key points are important to recognise and remember when planning for geographical activities in early years classrooms:

- Young children are already active geographers.
- It is important to explore feelings about places as well as developing skills.
- Opportunities should be provided for young children to explore known and unknown worlds through play, stories, maps, photographs, etc.
- Enquiry is central, especially though not exclusively through fieldwork investigations.
- There is a wealth of resources available locally for developing geographical awareness.

Stories involving journeys or places

The Three Bears (1985), Murdock, H., London: Ladybird.
Jack and the Beanstalk (1987), Hunia, F., London: Ladybird.
'Hansel and Gretel', in *Classic Fairy Tales* (1993), Cresswell, H., London: HarperCollins.
Red Riding Hood (1988), Southgate, V., London: Ladybird.
The Three Pigs (1989), Southgate, V., London: Ladybird.
The Gingerbread Man (1966), Southgate, V., London: Ladybird.
Dick Whittington (1986), Southgate, V., London: Ladybird.
Town Mouse and Country Mouse (1982), McKie, A., London: Ladybird.

Three Billy Goats Gruff (1984), Traditional, London: J.M. Dent.
Fantastic Mr Fox (1970), Dahl, R., London: George Allen & Unwin.
Winnie-the-Pooh (1926), Milne, A.A., London: Methuen.
Where The Forest Meets the Sea (1987), Baker, J., London: Julia MacRae Books.
Window (1991), Baker, J., London: Julia MacRae Books.
Don't Forget the Bacon (1978), Hutchins, P., London: Picture Puffin.
Rosie's Walk (1992), Hutchins, P., London: Picture Puffin.
Our Village (1988), Yeoman, J. and Blake, Q., London: Walker Books.
The Little Prince and the Great Dragon Chase (1994), Kavanagh, P., London: Simon & Schuster.
Penguin Small (1992), Inkpen, M., Hodder London: Children's Books.
Finn Family Moomintroll (1950), Janssen, T., London: Ernest Benn.
Enchanted Wood (1991), Hawkesley, G., Shepton Mallet, UK: Tree House Children's Books.
Dinosaurs and All that Rubbish, Foreman, M., London: Penguin.
Owl Babies (1994) Waddell, M., London: Walker Books.
The Jolly Postman (1999) Ahlberg, J., London: Viking Kestrel Picture Books.
We're Going On A Bear Hunt (1993), Rosen, M. and Oxenbury H., London: Walker Books.

References

Curriculum Council for Wales (1991) *Geography in the National Curriculum: Non-Statutory Guidance for Teachers*, CCW.
DES (1986) *Geography from 5 to 16: Curriculum Matters 7*, London: HMSO.
DES (1990) *Geography for Ages 5–16*, London: HMSO.
Geographical Association (1991) *Response to the Draft Orders for the Geography National Curriculum in Wales*, Sheffield: Geographical Association.
Goodey, B. (1973) *Perception of the Environment: An Introduction to the Literature*, Occasional Paper No. 17, Birmingham: University of Birmingham Centre for Urban and Regional Studies.
Nicholson, H.N. (1994) *Place in Story-time*, Sheffield: Geographical Association.
Pelham, D. (1991) *Sam's Sandwich*, New York: Penguin (USA).
Pelham, D. (1994) *Sam's Snack*, New York: Dutton.

Further reading

Catling, S. (2002) *Placing Places*, Sheffield: Geographical Association.
Geographical Association (2003) *Finding Time for Things that Matter: Geography in the Primary Schools*, Sheffield: Geographical Association.

Geographical Association, *Primary Geographer* (quarterly magazine published specifically for non-specialist primary teachers, available from Geographical Association, 343 Fulwood Rd, Sheffield, S10 3BP).

Hulme, B., James, F. and Kerr, A. (1995) *A Sense of Place*, Twickenham: Belair.

May, S. and Richardson, P. (2006) *Fieldwork File for the Primary Years*, Sheffield: Geographical Association.

Scoffham, S. (2004) *Primary Geography Handbook*, Sheffield: Geographical Association.

PART D

The way
forward

CHAPTER 19

Whatever next?

FUTURE TRENDS IN EARLY YEARS EDUCATION

Mary-Jane Drummond

In this chapter I explore the proposition that the ways in which we think and talk about young children can and do affect the ways in which we provide for their learning and support their development. To put it another way, what we know about children, or think we know, shapes what we do for them in the name of education. I examine some ways of thinking about children, and children's learning, taken from recent accounts of early years classrooms (and other settings) and try to show how we might take steps to reorganise and re-shape our thoughts, our assumptions and our expectations. Future developments in early years education will, I believe, spring from the efforts of educators who prioritise the serious work of thinking for themselves about children's learning, and thereby achieve an enhanced understanding of children and childhood.

Teachers teaching and children learning

One of the most challenging and entertaining books I have ever read about children's learning is *GNYS AT WRK: A Child Learns to Write and Read* (Bissex, 1980). It is a detailed, vivid, first-hand narrative account of how 5-year-old Paul became an accomplished writer and reader; what makes it unique is not just its puzzling title (taken from a notice Paul pinned over his workbench-desk at the age of 5 years 6 months) but its insider's viewpoint: the author, Glenda L. Bissex, is Paul's mother. She was also, when the story began, a teacher studying for her master's degree in education. One afternoon, when she was trying to read, Paul wanted to play with her. Frustrated in his attempts to make her put down her book, Paul disappeared for a few minutes, returning with a piece of paper, on which he had printed, with rubber stamps from his printing set, the letters RUDF (Are you deaf?). His mother was dumbstruck and, in her own words, 'Of course I put down my book.'

The bulk of the book comprises Bissex's regular observations of her son's acts of writing and reading, illustrated with copious extracts from the written material that Paul produced over the six years of the study: there are excerpts from stories, lists, notices, books of jokes, report cards for his pets (including marks for PEING) and, in due course, when he starts school (at 5 years 10 months) his first written texts from the classroom, sadly stilted, after the richness of his earlier output. For example, at 6 years 10 months, at school, he writes: 'This is my reading book', whereas three months earlier, in just one day at home, he had written four newspapers, complete with cartoons, news, advertising and weather (THE SAFTERNEWN IT'S GOING TO RAIN).

Bissex's commentary and conclusions are based on her privileged position as both mother and teacher. With a kind of binocular vision, she sees some disconcerting truths about how educators intervene in children's learning. In one memorable passage she writes:

> We speak of starting with a child 'where he is', which in one sense is not to assert an educational desideratum but an inescapable fact; there is no other place the child can start from. There are only other places the educator can start from.
>
> (Bissex, 1980, p. 111)

I hope I am not alone in finding this insight an uncomfortable one. Bissex seems to me to be suggesting, all too credibly, that educators do (sometimes? often?) start in 'other places', and that the consequences for children's learning are frequently undesirable. Furthermore, this suggestion seems to be an alternative version of the proposition with which I began: that how we think and talk about children – or 'the child' – is of crucial importance in how we educate them – or him, or her. And this proposition, however we phrase it, raises questions worth worrying about. If early years educators do not, as Bissex suggests, start 'where the child is', with a coherent and principled understanding of the child's learning, then where do they start? And why? Can we learn to move closer to a more desirable starting point? What would it look like? What do we really mean by this 'educational desideratum', or a principled understanding of children?

My conviction that Bissex is telling us something important about teaching and learning is based on two distinct sources of evidence: first, my own experiences as a educator and observer in early years classrooms and other settings for young children, and, second, written accounts and research studies of what early years educators actually do, and how they conceptualise the relationship between teaching and learning.

My own first-hand experience tells me that, all too often, my carefully prepared activities, my lovingly drawn-up topic webs, my finely adjusted schemes of work, have failed to connect with children's pressing intellectual and social concerns, or with their energetic and enquiring minds. My observations in other classrooms have, over the years, confirmed my awareness of what I think of as 'the curriculum gap', the distance – sometimes a hair's breadth, sometimes a yawning chasm – that stands between what educators teach and what children learn.

If there is such a gap, and I am certain that there is, at least some of the time, in every setting for young children, I am equally certain that it cannot be attributed to malice or apathy in the hearts and minds of early years educators. Nor do published studies of children's early experiences at school (Brooker, 2002; Hughes, 1989; Wells, 1987, for example) resort to the language of blame to account for what they see in classrooms. These authors do not mince words in identifying the mismatch between the educators' benevolent and educational intentions and the children's learning. But nor do they suggest that educators deliberately disable learners, or consciously create dysfunctional learning environments. So what is going wrong? And what can we do to put it right?

Some of the evidence suggests that part of the problem lies in the weakness of the language in which we describe and justify our work. In an early study of infant teachers' thinking (or, rather, a study of what infant teachers are prepared to say about their work to investigative sociologists), Sharp and Green (1975) report an interview with 'Mrs Carpenter', a teacher of a vertically grouped class of rising-fives to rising-sevens. The discussion turned to the need for structure in teaching.

The interview proceeded as follows:

Interviewer: How do you mean?

Teacher: I mean we all, well, I have a little plan but I don't really . . . I just sort of, mmm, try and work out what stage each child is at and take it from there.

Interviewer: How do you do this? How does one notice what stage a child is at?

Teacher: Oh, we don't really know, you can only say the stage he isn't at really, because you know when a child doesn't know but you don't really know when he knows. Do you see what I mean? You can usually tell when they don't know [long pause]. [There was a distraction in the interview at this point.] What was I talking about?

Interviewer:	Certain stages, knowing when they know –
Teacher:	– and when they don't know. But even so, you still don't know, when they really don't [pause] you can't really say they don't know, can you? . . . That's why really that plan they wanted wouldn't have worked. I wouldn't have been able to stick to it, because you just don't . . . you know when they don't know, you don't know when they know.
Interviewer:	How do you know when they don't know?
Teacher:	How do I know when they don't know? [pause] Well, no, it's not so much that you don't know. I know when they're not ready to know, perhaps that's a better way of putting it.

(Sharp and Green, 1975, p. 168)

The disarming candour of these statements should not blind us to the poverty of the understanding they express. This teacher, for all her good intentions, which I am willing to take for granted, is unlikely to be able to start 'where the child is'. She does not, on the evidence of this interview, have a way of explaining, even to herself, what it is that the educator knows when she or he knows where a child is, or what it is that the educator must then do with that knowledge.

Sharp and Green's work has been succeeded by other enquiries, less ideologically driven, but reaching similarly worrying conclusions. For example, Bennett *et al.* (1984) investigated the match between tasks and pupils, and identified a chronic weakness in educators' skills of diagnosis. In this carefully planned and cautiously quantified study of 'the quality of pupil learning experiences', the researchers found that more than half the observed tasks were badly matched to the child's level of understanding and achievement. High attainers were regularly under-estimated and low attainers over-estimated (1984, p. 65).

The diagnostic skills of a group of 17 experienced infant teachers were studied in detail. As part of an in-service course, they were asked to examine transcriptions of some of the mismatched tasks recorded in the early part of the study. They were invited to discuss what seemed to be going on, to hypothesise about the children's understanding, and to explore any questions raised by the observations. The authors report that the teachers were extremely unwilling to respond to the classroom material in this way. 'They saw all problems as self evident . . . [they] made no use of the notion of hunch or hypothesis . . . all problems were to be solved by direct teaching' (1984, p. 197). It seems as though these teachers' prime concern was with the quality of teaching, and that they had correspondingly little interest in learning.

Evidence from studies such as these suggests that there is indeed a serious problem. The professional language of the early years educator does not seem to be robust enough to frame adequate or effective descriptions of children and their learning. It is, I believe, not just the looseness and vagueness of the words we use that let us down, but a more fundamental issue. Starting 'where the child is', for all its familiarity as a slogan, as an 'educational desideratum', is simply not the best place to start; it is not an effective way of conceptualising the enterprise of early years education.

'To have' and 'to be'

I am influenced in this argument by the work of Erich Fromm, sociologist and psychoanalyst, who suggested in *To Have or To Be* (1976) that the human condition in general is suffering from the dominance of Western society's desire 'to have', at the expense of our understanding of what it is 'to be'. Applying this distinction to early years education, to its curriculum, its pedagogy and its most idealistic aspirations, suggests to me that there is a need to re-emphasise our understanding of what children are, rather than where they are, or what we want them to have. Since, as Fromm says, 'there is no being that is not, at the same time, becoming and changing', it follows that, if we know what we want children to be, in the first four or five years of their educational lives, then we are likely to be effective in helping them to become the well-educated 7- or 8-year-olds who will move into the next stage of their education. We will be well placed too, during their years of early education, to support to the utmost their present 'powers to be', another of Fromm's memorable phrases (in *Man for Himself*, 1949).

Since reading and re-reading Fromm, I have been drawing on his concept of children's 'powers to be' in my thinking and writing, and I am slowly becoming convinced of the strength of this starting point in thinking about the future of early years education. This vital phase of education has, until recently, straddled the statutory/pre-statutory divide. Now the years from birth to 5 have been retitled the Early Years Foundation Stage, and educators are being encouraged to think of this period as a distinct phase of education. By the time they enter Key Stage 1, 'Foundation Stage children' will have been living and learning for five solid years, in their homes and in a bewildering variety of other settings. But both before and after the children's fifth birthdays, we, their educators, are still at liberty to think about them in ways that match our philosophy and our principles. In Key Stage 1, and in terms of teaching, coverage and content, we will, for the foreseeable future, be working with the core and foundation subjects and religious education. In the early years, we will be working within the terms of the *Early Years Foundation Stage* (DfES 2007). But, in terms of children's learning, we are still at liberty to think for ourselves, using the categories and concepts of the DfES documents as a support, not a substitute, for our own thinking work. And my argument is that we cannot do better than to think in terms of what we know for certain about children's powers – their powers to do, to think, to feel, to know and understand, to represent and express. There is no requirement for us to think of children in the early years as students of numeracy, literacy and so on. If children's learning is our priority, there are more effective ways to be their educators than by surrendering our own powers to think to the volumes of guidance we have so generously been offered.

By way of encouragement, we would be wise to turn to the early years curriculum document in use in New Zealand (Ministry of Education, 1996), which sets out guidelines for the education of children from birth to six (the age of starting school). The Maori title of this bilingual document, *Te Whariki*, refers to a traditional hand-made mat, which can be woven in an infinite variety of patterns; it represents the idea that the planned curriculum, based on commonly agreed goals and principles, can have a different pattern for every kind of early years service, in every individual early years centre. This in itself is a stimulating approach from the perspective of this country, but even more challenging is the set of ideas embodied in the five goals that constitute the heart of the guidelines.

These goals are:

- well-being
  (the health and well-being of the child are protected and nurtured);
- belonging
  (children and their families feel a sense of belonging);
- contribution
  (opportunities for learning are equitable and each child's contribution is valued);
- communication
  (the languages and symbols of their own and other cultures are promoted and protected);
- exploration
  (the child learns through active exploration of the environment).

Early years educators in New Zealand, in whatever kind of setting, are invited to commit themselves to these goals for children; some of them may seem to go almost without saying, but others are well worth thinking about more carefully. The goal of well-being fits securely within the English tradition; we are still proudly conscious of our legacy from the great pioneers of early education – Rachel and Margaret McMillan, for example, working in the back streets of Bradford and Deptford to bring health and hygiene into the lives of young children (Steedman, 1990). The goal of communication is equally likely to receive general assent from early years educators here, though it may be some years yet before our Department for Education publishes its curriculum guidelines in two languages. But the goals of belonging and contributing are radical departures from our familiar ways of thinking.

In these goals, it seems to me, the New Zealand educators are boldly articulating their aspirations for children's 'powers to be'; they are explicitly prioritising the principle that children can, and should, be members of a harmonious community, in which they have a place, to which they can make a contribution. This is a way of thinking about young children and the education they deserve that, I believe, we might enthusiastically try for ourselves.

The New Zealand representation of children's powers set out in *Te Whariki* reads easily enough across onto a model of children's learning that is proposed in a series of questions set out in *Making Assessment Work: Values and Principles in Assessing Children's Learning* (Drummond *et al.*, 1992). In this discussion pack, the authors argue that effective assessment is predicated on the educator's principled understanding of the purposes of early years education. Practitioners are invited to ask themselves about their aspirations for children. What do we want our young children:

- to do?
- to feel?
- to think?
- to know and understand?
- to represent and express?

Answering these questions, is, I believe, part of the way forward for early years education in this country. And there are, fortunately for us, many sources to which we can turn to support us in our thinking. In this volume too, other authors have written of their personal experiences of children's powers, and the versatility and enthusiasm of children's learning in appropriately structured environments. There is a healthy emphasis, throughout this collection, on the range of children's powers, and an accompanying emphasis on the context – children's play – in which so many of these powers are exercised.

Play and imagination

This emphasis on play is an important element in the argument to be made for a distinctive approach to early years education. But it is also a particularly challenging part of the task that lies ahead. Every early years educator, it is safe to assume, has at some time been made painfully aware that the importance of play in educational settings is not universally acknowledged. Although numbers of recent publications have taken up the challenge and defended the educational value and outcomes of play, perhaps we have put too much professional energy into defending the contentious verb 'to play', which in some quarters is used as the polar opposite of the verb 'to learn'. Perhaps we would do better to emphasise 'play' in its noun form, and to construct our arguments around a full description of what, in the context of play, children think, feel, do, understand and express. What kinds of important thinking and feeling characterise play? Should we not be making a case for these, for imagination, for empathy, for experiment and exploration? (Just some of the acts of mind and will that can readily be seen whenever children play.)

In making such a case as an in-service educator, working with practitioners from settings across the Early Years Foundation Stage, I have found it salutary to see the confidence and the zeal with which other educationalists, outside the early years community, argue a position that I find thoroughly convincing. Mary Warnock, for example, moral philosopher as well as educational reformer, argues in *Schools of Thought* that the imagination is good in itself. Being more imaginative, like being more healthy, needs no further justification (Warnock, 1977, p. 153). In *Imagination*, Warnock makes even bolder claims:

> I have come very strongly to believe that it is the cultivation of imagination which should be the chief aim of education, and in which our present systems of education most conspicuously fail, where they do fail. . . . In education we have a duty to educate the imagination above all else.
>
> (1976, p. 9)

She characterises imagination as the human power 'to go beyond what is immediately in front of [their] noses', and, in a telling phrase she has borrowed from Wordsworth's *Tintern Abbey*, as the capacity to 'see into the life of things'. It is a power which is not only intellectual: 'its impetus comes from the emotions as much as from the head'. Imagination is both necessary and universal; as part of human intelligence, it needs educating, and this will entail 'an education not only of the intelligence but, going along with it, of the feelings' (1976, p. 202).

The need for high expectations

Warnock's aspirations for the human condition, even in this briefest of summaries, seem to me to illuminate some exciting possibilities for children's early learning. If we can recognise, as I believe we can, the young child's powers to think and to feel, we can see clearly the weight of our responsibility to educate, to exercise and strengthen those powers.

In recent years, there has been considerable interest in an approach to early years education practised in the Emilia-Romagna district of Northern Italy. A touring exhibition of their work, *The Hundred Languages of Children*, which has visited the UK three times in recent years, testifies to the extraordinary richness of their early educational provisions. 'The cornerstone of our experience', says Carla Rinaldi, former Director of Services to Young Children in the region, is an understanding of children as 'rich, strong and powerful'. She spells out what this means:

> they have . . . plasticity, the desire to grow, curiosity, the ability to be amazed, and the desire to relate to other people and communicate. . . . Children are eager to express themselves in a plurality of symbolic languages . . . [they] are open to exchanges and reciprocity as deeds and acts of love which they not only want to receive but also want to offer.
>
> (Edwards *et al.*, 1993, pp. 101–2)

There are interesting parallels here, I think, with the New Zealand educators' categories of belonging and contributing. But the Italian educators are not exclusively interested in the social dimension of learning; a central feature of their provision is the atelier, a creative workshop, rich in materials and tools, in which children from birth to 6 years old become masters of the 'plurality of symbolic languages' (such as painting, drawing, dancing and working in clay). In the atelier, 'children invent autonomous vehicles of expressive freedom, cognitive freedom, symbolic freedom and paths to communication' (1993, p. 120). In the atelier, surely, they are exercising the powers that Warnock describes: 'to see into the life of things' – and not just to see, but to represent and express what they see.

The Reggio Emilia approach to early childhood provision has, I am arguing, much to teach us in this country. I am not suggesting that we should follow their prescriptions to the letter, or that we should swallow, wholesale, their priorities and perceptions. But I am convinced that their way of seeing children, from birth, as strong to do and feel, skilled in learning, powerful in communicating, has profound effects upon the curriculum they provide, a curriculum that is sensitively and challengingly matched to the children's developing 'powers to be'. Their expectations of what children can do, and think and feel, are, to English eyes and ears, extraordinarily high. But the children in their settings rise to these expectations, as they explore both the world that is opening out in front of them, and their own interior worlds of feeling and imagination. As one reads the detailed accounts of their cross-curricular projects, given in Edwards *et al.*'s book, and in a growing number of other publications (for example, Comune di Sant'Ilario d'Enza, 2001; Vecchi, 2002), one wonders what these Italian educators would make of some of the experiences provided in early years settings in this country.

My own observations of 4-year-olds in their first terms in primary school in several local authorities suggest that, in some classrooms, children's powers are seriously undervalued. The demands made on the children – to follow instructions, to complete worksheets, to cut and stick and colour in, as required by their educators, do not do justice to the children's energetic and enthusiastic minds. In one classroom, as part of a local authority evaluation programme (Drummond, 1995), a child was observed using a template to draw a shape representing a T-shirt on a square piece of wallpaper. The T-shirt was one of 20 similar cut-outs, destined for a frieze of teddy bears, who were being changed from their winter outfits to their summer clothes as part of the classroom topic on 'The Summer'. The child followed his teacher's directions as best he could, but the scissors were far from sharp and the wallpaper prone to tear. After some frustrating minutes had passed, the child looked up at the teacher who was leading this activity and said 'I can sew, you know.' I take this child's comment seriously, as a gentle – even forgiving – admonition to his educators. It is as if he were telling them to think again, to question their motives in asking him to perform this meaningless and unrewarding task. It is as if he were pointing out, most politely, that his powers to think, and do and feel, were not being nourished or exercised by a curricular diet of templates and teddy bear friezes.

Bennett *et al.* (1984), we have already noted, found evidence that teachers both over-estimated and under-estimated children's abilities to complete language and number tasks. One particularly interesting finding from this study is that the problem of under-estimation, when the task set was too easy for a child, seemed to be 'invisible to teachers in classrooms' (1984, p. 49). The teachers in the study did not identify any tasks as beneath the child's current level of achievement, or not challenging enough, or as a waste of a child's time. Bennett *et al.* explain this finding by reference to the emphasis placed on procedure, rather than product, in literacy and numeracy tasks. When teachers saw children correctly following these procedures (using full stops in their writing, for example, or carrying a 10 in an addition task), they 'did not compare the child's product with his actual level of understanding' (1984, p. 63). They appeared to be satisfied with the children's compliance with the procedures they had been taught. This explanation seems reasonable enough, but it may only be half of the story. If one piece of the puzzle is excessive concern for procedures as defined by the educator, then another, equally important, element in the picture is a serious lack of concern for what children can do for themselves. It appears that the teachers in this study were not interested in the possibility that the children could do more than was required of them. They seemed to be blind to children's inventiveness, their individual ways of seeing, their personal explorations into the unknown.

By contrast, in another classroom in the evaluation study cited above (Drummond, 1995) a group of young children spent 25 minutes absorbed in water play. The nursery nurse had, at their request, added some blue dye to the water, and the children were intrigued by the different shades of blue they could see: paler at the shallow margin, and darker at the deepest, central part of the water-tray. One child was even more interested in another, related phenomenon. He spent nearly 10 minutes of this period of water play observing his own shoes and how their colour appeared to change when he looked at them through the water and the transparent water tray. The child seemed to be fascinated by what happened when he placed his feet in different positions; he leaned intently over the tray to see what colour his shoes appeared to be at each stage. He did not use the words 'experiment' or 'observation', but that was what he was engaged in, nonetheless. After each trial, he withdrew his feet into the natural light of day, as if to check that they retained their proper colour. Had the dye stayed in the water, where he had seen it put? Or had some of it seeped out, into his shoes?

At the end of the morning session, the teacher and nursery nurse announced that it was time to tidy up. The children worked together to empty the water tray of the sieves, funnels and beakers they had been using. They took out the jugs, the teaspoons and the ladles, emptied them, and put them away. When they had nearly finished, the boy stopped and asked aloud, of no-one in particular, 'How do we get the blue out?'

I think this is a remarkable question, showing as it does, this young scientist's mind at work. Only further conversation with him would reveal his present understanding of the concepts of light, colour and reversibility; but his question is incontrovertible evidence of his urgent desire to find out how the world works, how its regularities and unpredictabilities can be accounted for. It is evidence too of his already firmly established knowledge that, as an active member of the world, he can experiment with it, act on it, question it and reflect on it, on the way to understanding it.

This powerful child's question offers his educators exciting opportunities for development, but only if they respond to what he can do, and is doing. If they focus on what he does not know, or does not fully understand, they will miss the chance to feed and exercise his growing powers to hypothesise and experiment. The way they conceptualise this child's question – as genuine enquiry, or unthinking ignorance – will directly affect the experiences they go on to provide for him.

Conclusion

I have been arguing that the way forward for early years education is in a re-examination of some of our taken-for-granted assumptions and expectations. If educators, without any ill-will, choose to think of young children as immature, incapable, illiterate or ignorant pupils, then the experiences and activities they provide will not give children opportunities to prove themselves to be what they really are – rich, strong and powerful, as Rinaldi argues: accomplished learners, passionate enquirers, loving companions. The primary classroom and its pre-defined tasks, the early years setting and its learning goals, will simply not be spacious enough for the exercise of children's powers to be: to be scientists, artists, citizens, dramatists, moralists, constructing and reconstructing the world.

But if early years educators can free themselves from any notion that, because the children they work with are the youngest children in the system, not yet ready for the academic demands of Key Stage 1, they are therefore the least capable and least competent, then the future looks bright. There is then a real possibility that we can provide experiences, time and space, food and exercise, for learners who are already, long before they start school, capable, competent, imaginative and eloquent.

The co-founder and, for many years, Director of the Reggio Emilia programme is the late and much revered Loris Malaguzzi. In a long interview about the principles underpinning their developing pedagogy he describes how, in Italy too, pressure from later stages of education threatens to distort and deform early years practices.

> If the school for young children has to be preparatory, and provide continuity with the elementary school, then we as educators are already prisoners of a model that ends up as a funnel. I think, moreover, that the funnel is a detestable object, and it is not much appreciated by children either. Its purpose is to narrow down what is big into what is small. This choking device is against nature.
>
> (Malaguzzi, in Edwards *et al.*, 1993, p. 86)

But Malaguzzi is optimistic, visionary even, in his determination that early years education will not choke or be choked. His fundamental position is a succinct summary of the argument I have proposed here: 'Suffice it to say that the school for young children has to respond to the children.' I have suggested that, for settings for young children to do this, our starting point must be a thorough understanding of what children are, in order that we can support their being and becoming. And if we can achieve such an understanding, we will be well placed to share in the glory of Malaguzzi's vision of the future. 'The continuing motivation for our work', he claims, is:

> 'to liberate hopes for a new human culture of childhood. It is a motive that finds its origin in a powerful nostalgia for the future and for humankind'
>
> (in Edwards *et al.*, 1993, p. 88).

References

Bennett, N., Desforges, C., Cockburn A. and Wilkinson B. (1984) *The Quality of Pupil Learning Experiences*, London: Lawrence Erlbaum Associates.

Bissex, G.L. (1980) *GNYS AT WRK: A Child Learns to Write and Read*, Cambridge, MA: Harvard University Press.

Brooker, L. (2002) *Starting School: Young Children Learning Cultures*, Buckingham: Open University Press.

Comune di Sant'Ilario d'Enza (2001) *The Future is a Lovely Day*, Reggio Emilia: Reggio Children.

DfES (2007) *The Early Years Foundation Stage*, Nottingham: DfES.

Drummond, M.J. (1995) *In School at Four*, Hampshire's earlier admissions programme final evaluation report, spring, Hampshire County Council.

Drummond, M.J., Rouse, D. and Pugh, G. (1992) *Making Assessment Work: Values and Principles in Assessing Young Children's Learning*, Nottingham: NES Arnold/National Children's Bureau.

Edwards, C., Gandini, L. and Forman, G. (1993) *The Hundred Languages of Children: The Reggio Emilia Approach to Early Childhood Education*, Norwood, NJ: Ablex Publishing.

Fromm, E. (1949) *Man for Himself*, London: Routledge & Kegan Paul.

Fromm, E. (1976) *To Have or To Be?*, London: Jonathan Cape.

Hughes, M. (1989) 'The child as learner: the contrasting views of developmental psychology and early education', in C. Desforges (ed.) *Early*

Childhood Education, British Journal of Educational Psychology Monograph Series No. 4 pp. 144–57.

Ministry of Education (1996) *Te Whariki: Early Childhood and Curriculum*, Wellington, New Zealand: Learning Media.

Sharp, R. and Green, A. (1975) *Education and Social Control: A Study in Progressive Primary Education*, London: Routledge & Kegan Paul.

Steedman, C. (1990) *Childhood, Culture and Class in Britain: Margaret McMillan, 1860–1931*, London: Virago.

Vecchi, V. (ed.) (2002) *Theatre Curtain: The Ring of Transformations*, Reggio Emilia: Reggio Children.

Warnock, M. (1976) *Imagination*, London: Faber & Faber.

Warnock, M. (1977) *Schools of Thought*, London: Faber & Faber.

Wells, G. (1987) *The Meaning Makers*, London: Hodder & Stoughton.

INDEX